English For Careers

FIFTH EDITION

English For Careers

BUSINESS, PROFESSIONAL, AND TECHNICAL

LEILA R. SMITH

Los Angeles Harbor College

Prentice Hall, Englewood Cliffs, New Jersey 07632

Library of Congress Cataloging-in-Publication Data

Smith, Leila R.
    English for careers: business, professional, and technical/
Leila R. Smith.—5th ed.
      p.   cm.
    Includes index.
    ISBN 0-13-276460-1
      1. English language—Business English-Problems, exercises, etc.
2. English language—Technical English—Problems, exercises, etc.
1. Title.
PE1115.S62 1992   91-22365
428.2′02465—dc20   CIP

Editorial / production supervision: Janet M. DiBlasi
Development editor: Joyce F. Perkins
Interior design: Suzanne Behnke
Cover design: Sheree Goodman
Cover art: Frances Wells
Section opening art: Kathleen Keifer
Manufacturing buyer: Ed O'Dougherty
Prepress buyer: Ilene Levy
Acquisition editor: Maureen P. Hull
Marketing manager: Robert B. Kern
Supplements editor: Lisamarie Brassini
Editorial assistant: Marianne J. Bernotsky

© 1992 by Prentice Hall, Inc.
A Simon and Schuster Company
Englewood Cliffs, New Jersey 07632

Printed in the United States of America

10 9 8 7 6 5 4 3 2 1

ISBN 0-13-276460-1

ISBN 0-13-276643-4

Prentice-Hall International (UK) Limited, *London*
Prentice-Hall of Australia Pty. Limited, *Sydney*
Prentice-Hall Canada Inc., *Toronto*
Prentice-Hall Hispanoamericana S.A., *Mexico*
Prentice-Hall of India Private Limited, *New Delhi*
Prentice-Hall of Japan, Inc., *Tokyo*
Simon & Schuster Asia Pte. Ltd., *Singapore*
Editora Prentice-Hall do Brasil, Ltda., *Rio de Janeiro*

To Seymour, Eric, Karen, Roberta, Udaya, Sean,
Sarala Rose, Sheela Danielle, Nina Beth

A word fitly spoken is like
apples of gold in settings of silver.

the Bible

Contents

Section 3

AIN'T IS IN THE DICTIONARY
(Dictionary Use)

Section 4

APPLES, TIGERS, AND SWAHILI
(Plural, Compound, and Proper Nouns)

Section 5
BE KIND TO THE SUBSTITUTE WEEK
(Pronouns)

Section 6
LOOKING FOR THE ACTION? THEN STUDY VERBS!

Section 7

LOVE LINES
(Adjectives and Adverbs)

Section 8

THE TAMING OF THE APOSTROPHE

Section 9

THE PAUSE THAT REFRESHES
(Commas)

Section 10

PUNCTUATION POTPOURRI
(. ? ! ; : " - ' —)

Section 11

A BUSINESS DICTIONARY

Section 12

WORD POWER
(Homonyms, Prepositions, Pronunciation)

Section 13

SENTENCE POWER

(Fragments, Comma Splices, Run-Ons, Danglers, Misplaced Parts,
Parallel Construction, Active/Passive Voice, Vague Pronouns,
"Choppy" style, Gobbledygook)

Section 14

SINCERELY YOURS

(Introduction to Business Letters)

APPENDICES

Preface

Dear Instructor and Training Director

Textbooks come alive through creative and caring teachers. I am, therefore, proud to present you with the fifth edition of the book that has helped many of you inspire students to develop good English for their careers. I hope you and your students will enjoy the new content, layout, and color features. My editors at Prentice Hall and I are excited about the enhanced teachability and learnability of this new edition.

We as well as our students understand that while technology is in the process of making many job skills obsolete, basic communication skills will remain essential. But what are basic communication skills in the "real world?" What is the real world? A graduate took a job with a company producing synthetic fuels, artificial colors and flavors, and artificial sweeteners. On the graduate's first day at work, the boss's greeting was "Welcome to the real world."

In 1975 I began the first edition of this book because most business English instruction was based, not on "real world" usage, but on grammar rules ignored by many of America's most effective and articulate communicators. More recently, during the 1988–89 academic year, I taught English to the English at a London college. I discovered that even the most proper British don't follow certain archaic rules that many American business English students are burdened with.

For example, H. W. Fowler defends ending a sentence with a preposition (see *with* at the end of the preceding paragraph) as "a valuable idiomatic resource." He describes the rule about never ending sentences with prepositions as a "cherished superstition." Shakespeare, Keats, John Kennedy, and James Thurber have all used *like* as a synonym for *as*. According to *Webster's Ninth New Collegiate Dictionary,* "after 450 years of use, *like* is firmly established as a conjunction. . . ." Linguist Theodore Bernstein says of *loan/lend* usage that the distinction is not necessary and that most authorities accept *loan* as a verb. I've never seen a red circle around the comparative form of the absolute adjective in the opening lines of the U. S. Constitution, "In order to form a *more perfect* union. . . ."

English for Careers still focuses on the premise that our students need "real world" language skills, as defined by America's eminent linguists, not as restricted by *all* the pet rules you and I learned at school. The content is based on how today's qualified users of American English actually speak and write.

English for Careers' organization, writing style, format, and layout are based on brain and mind research. The studies reveal we function better in learning situations that are relaxed yet structured, lighthearted rather than formal, personal instead of impersonal.

An extensive supplements package supports the text. For a description of these supplements and full ordering information, see the preview pages in the front of this book.

My editors and I, along with the help of many of you, have aimed for content that's "real world" and a textbook plan conducive to high-quality learning. I sincerely appreciate the ideas many of you have contributed through the years—during a phone conversation or a brief chat at a business education or business communication conference or in a letter to me or a publisher-solicited review.

At this time I am especially grateful for your help in creating a realistic, practical approach to teaching English for careers: Ellen D. Alderman, Moultrie Technical Vocational School; Louise Brooks, Champlain College; Susan R. Dennis, Bay De Noc Community College; Dolores Denova, Los Angeles Harbor College; Betty M. Dooley, Clark Technical College; Loretta J. Drummond, Strayer Business College; Yolanda V. Foley, American Business Institute; Lucie Givins, Heald College; H. Grace Heringer, Skyline College; John Holmstedt, Clatsop Community College; Edna V. Jellesed, Lane Community College; Sheila L. Long, Miami-Dade Community College; Joelene L. Mack, Golden West College; Quilvie G. Mills, Miami-Dade Community College; Joanne Murcar, Spokane Falls Community College; Carol Ann Pitz, Kensington Business Institute; Dorothy Prevatt, Miami-Dade Community College; Mary Rowe, Miami-Dade Community College; Ruth Sanford, Spokane Community College; Joy D. Schuhmann, International Business College; Joan Sterns, Southeast Community College; Jo Ann Sumner, Sierra College; Margaret Helen Taylor, Coastline Community College; Joan Teufel, Rio Hondo Community College; Norma R. Vara, Laredo Jr. College; Nita Wade, Louisiana Business College; Scott Frazier, North Park College; Candyce H. Miller, Ricks College; Judith Prescott, MCI; Cindy Welch, Kelsey Jenney Business College; Kathleen Mennen, ITT Tech; Alex Baxter, LES-BAX Enterprise, Inc.; Rose Wrolstad, Inver Hill Community College; Susan Carol Mitchell, Detroit College of Business; Rennie Hicks, ITT Tech; Linda Moen, Webster Career College; Daneen Jones, National Education Center; and Mary Schlegel. I sincerely appreciate your comments and suggestions.

I always enjoy hearing from business English or communication teachers—so please write or call with your questions or comments. I'm at Los Angeles Harbor College, 1111 Figueroa Place, Wilmington, California 90744, 310-518-1000.

Dear Student

This book is different. You don't browse through it. You don't read it like other books. What you do is *learn* your way through it!

Each of the 14 sections has a starting page or two followed by unique *learning units* called *read* and *replay.* In each Read unit, you read information arranged step by step in short portions. Then you apply the newly learned skill immediately in a Replay unit. Many of the Read units include *Recaps,* in which you answer a question or two summarizing what you've just learned. When you get to the Replay, you have already "recapitulated"— or reviewed—several key items in the Read. As soon as you complete a Recap or a Replay, you check your answers in the back of the book.

Not only does the Read and Replay system enable you to learn and to remember, but you also enjoy the process. Students are extremely enthusiastic about this way to learn.

Because doing the Replays is interesting and challenging, however, some students are tempted to pretest their English knowledge by doing the

Replay exercises without reading the material in the Read unit. Please resist doing this because:

- The formula—first, read; second, respond; and third, check your answers—has been proven effective through research and testing. If you shortcut the process, you learn less and are not as well prepared to take the quizzes.
- You miss the personal satisfaction that comes from making correct responses.
- When you make more mistakes, you lose rather than save time.

So, please play the game according to the rules: Read before you Recap and before you Replay.

Why is Read and Replay a good learning system?

- By quickly making active responses, you immediately apply what you learn; therefore, you understand it better and retain it longer.
- Small learning units are more efficient than longer ones.
- Read and Replay units hold your attention, and your powers of concentration improve.
- The Read and Replay system motivates you to continue beyond normal attention spans.

Other special features of the Read and Replay system are the learning goals at the beginning of each section. Read these starting pages carefully. They enable you to find out exactly what skills and knowledge you'll master by the time you complete each section. The Read and Replay units come next. Finally, Checkpoint (which usually summarizes what you've just learned), Special Assignment, Proofreading for Careers, and Practice Quiz end each section.

While studying *English for Careers*, you not only learn more about the world of business, but you also increase or develop a success-oriented attitude. This side-by-side learning happens because many of the sentences illustrating English points deal with business matters or with personal development. The *English for Careers* learning strategy helps form a success habit that carries over to on-the-job activities.

Enjoy the Read and Replay system. Give it a chance, and you'll find that your command of English will be a lifelong asset to your career.

Leila R. Smith

Write the letter of the correct answer in the blank or on an answer sheet.

_____ 1. I think the carton of books and papers (a) were (b) was (c) are lost.

_____ 2. Etymology is the study of (a) insects (b) synonyms and antonyms (c) ancient history (d) the derivation of words.

_____ 3. If the first line of the inside address of a business letter is "Mr. Samuel E. Smith," the preferred salutation would be (a) Ladies and Gentlemen: (b) Dear Sir: (c) Dear Sirs: (d) Dear Mr. Smith: (e) Dear Mr. Samuel E. Smith.

_____ 4. *Per diem* means (a) by the person (b) by the day (c) for the year (d) for God and country (e) punched card is needed.

_____ 5. This (a) phenomena (b) phenomenae (c) phenomenon (d) phenomeni (e) phenomenae has never before occurred.

_____ 6. The (a) General Manager (b) general manager (c) General manager (d) general Manager of the

_____ 7. new (a) Company (b) company is a wealthy woman.

_____ 8. After three (a) year's (b) years' (c) years work in

_____ 9. the (a) children's (b) childrens' (c) childrens department, she resigned.

_____ 10. Please give the reports to Bonnie Albert and (a) I (b) me (c) myself.

_____ 11. Ms. Denova is the one (a) who (b) whom we believe will be offered the job.

_____ 12. If you had (a) drive (b) drove (c) driven to work this morning, you would have seen the accident.

_____ 13. Which would be (a) easyer (b) easiest (c) easier (d) easyest for you to prepare, a letter or a short report?

_____ 14. We hope to receive (a) a (b) an 18 percent discount.

_____ 15. **After working in the store all day, his feet were tired.** The sentence in boldface type is an example of a (a) comma splice (b) sentence that lacks parallel construction (c) sentence with a misplaced part (d) sentence with a dangler (e) correctly written sentence.

For items 16–20, write *a* in the blank if all the punctuation is correct. If there is any kind of punctuation error, write *b* in the blank.

_____ 16. "The new office furniture," he said, "is too expensive".

_____ 17. Money, beauty, intelligence, and charm—she has all of them.

_____ 18. Mr. Crane is not here, however, I can help you.

_____ **19.** We've mailed you a copy of the new book and hope it will reach you before the end of the month.

_____ **20.** Will you please send us your check for our Invoice No. 4268 within ten days.

After you find out how many you answered correctly, check below for your fortune.

Number Right _____

18–20 You have a good command of English for your career. This course will serve as a brushup, and you'll easily achieve expertise.

15–17 Your business English skill is fair. After the practice provided in this course along with the review of some rules you've forgotten, you'll be an expert in the English required for your career.

12–14 Your English for your career needs improvement. Because your basic language skill is good, you'll enjoy studying and mastering the skills that will make you an expert.

0–11 You came to the right place! Taking this course is a wise decision. You'll find the instruction extremely informative. Because you are now motivated to learn English for your career, you'll capture those principles that escaped you in the past. **Your participation in this course + enthusiasm = success.**

The Fresh Start

After completing this introduction, you will:

- Know what is meant by "English for careers."
- Understand why this course is the realistic and businesslike way to improve English skill for your career.
- Be confident about succeeding in *English for Careers.*

In the year 1414, Sigismund, Emperor of the Holy Roman Empire, said to an important church official who had objected to His Majesty's grammar: "Ego sum rex Romanus et supra grammaticam." (I am the Roman king and am above grammar.)

If *you* are a Roman king, you don't need to read on. For the rest of us, the language we use, both spoken and written, can significantly affect our success at earning a living and advancing in a career.

The Language of Careers

What language does a business, professional, or technical career require? "Career English" is not a special or separate language. It is the language style you hear spoken by network television newscasters and is sometimes called **standard English.** It includes the English principles you may have learned in the past and forgotten or wish you had learned.

Other Types of Language

We all use several different language styles to help us communicate successfully with different people in different situations. To see this, imagine yourself talking with a group of other adults at a party and then warning a young child away from a hot stove.

Some of us use nonstandard English—possibly slang, regional dialect, or ethnic dialect—in everyday conversation with certain friends and family. Then we may switch to standard English with other friends or business and professional acquaintances. Like the other language styles you use, the standard English you'll improve in *English for Careers* is right for communicating in particular situations.

Upon successful completion of the *English for Careers* program— you'll communicate confidently in the style of English that leads to success in a business, professional, or technical career.

The English for Careers System

English for Careers is a realistic and businesslike system to help you master standard English for your career. It is not based on long lists of grammar rules found in traditional grammar books. You'll learn only the grammar terms and usage principles necessary to enable you to use standard English with confidence:

- Many grammar terms have been simplified and others left out because they don't contribute to English improvement. You focus on correcting the errors often made by those without this training. Most adults need instruction in standard English for careers to be sure of being "right."
- Out-of-date grammar rules are omitted. You focus on principles that reflect today's speaking and writing style of well-educated and well-informed people.
- Read and Replay units give information in an interesting and amusing way and make learning efficient. Your success on the quiz at the end of each section provides assurance that you're achieving your goals.

Challenge for the Expert

Some of you have previously mastered grammar terminology as well as many of the traditional grammar rules and now want to strive for perfection in standard English usage. In the "Grammar Supplement for the Expert" in the back of the book, you can review traditional grammar. This supplement can also serve as a reference if you want to check the grammatical facts about a particular usage.

Remember—the Grammar Supplement will **not** make the work in the Read and Replay sections easier to complete. Instead, it can be an additional challenge for some students. Follow your instructor's suggestions regarding its use.

What's In It for You?

After successfully completing *English for Careers*, you will enjoy feeling confident not only in speech but also in the business letters, reports, and other documents you are responsible for in your career. You'll also be confident that your business letters and memos are effective and up-to-date in appearance and writing style.

Good communication skills, more than any other factor, determine who gets the good job, who does the job well, and who gets the promotion.

What's in *English for Careers* for you? It's the sure route toward those all-important communication skills—and you'll have some fun along the way.

Replay the Fresh Start

Fill in the blank for question 1, and answer *T* (true) or *F* (false) for the rest of the questions. If you're unsure of any answers, reread pages xviii–xiv.

1. The language style appropriate for most business and professional careers is known as _____

_____ 2. It's wrong to use slang when writing a letter to a friend.

_____ 3. You should be sure to use the same style of language in all your communications.

_____ 4. Standard English is always superior to other types of English.

_____ 5. To use standard English, you must memorize a long list of grammar rules and strictly obey them.

_____ 6. In this course you'll learn an effective and up-to-date format and writing style for business letters and memos.

_____ 7. The single most important ability required to get a good job or a promotion is good communication.

_____ 8. If you want to pass this course, you must refer frequently to the Grammar Supplement.

_____ 9. By carefully completing this book, you will achieve thorough mastery of traditional grammar terminology and rules.

_____ 10. By carefully completing this book, you will gain confidence in your ability to speak and write English in the style that leads to success in business, professional, and technical careers. You'll also have some fun along the way.

Check your answers in Appendix H.

Tools of the Trade

1

*C*arpenters can name and use the tools of their trade. They do not, however, need to know everything about the construction and manufacture of those tools.

To learn touch typing, students first learn a few basic typewriter or computer "tools"—the return key, the paper release, the space bar, and so on. Learners must know where the space bar is before they can respond to "Press the space bar with your right thumb." Although some people might want to understand *how* a typewriter works, this knowledge is not necessary for becoming an expert typist.

If you decide to be a linguistics expert or an English teacher, you'll study English grammar in depth. To master English for most other careers, however, you need only identify and use correctly the basic tools of the English "trade." These tools are called the **parts of speech**.

The parts of speech reveal the system for placing words into these categories: nouns, pronouns, verbs, adjectives, adverbs, prepositions, conjunctions, interjections. Every word in English can be grouped into those categories.

The ability to identify parts of speech in certain sentences enables you to understand the English principles explained in later sections. That's why a minimal grammar vocabulary—the tools of the trade—is needed. If you've learned the parts of speech in the past, this section will be a pleasant review. (Additional information on parts of speech are in Sections Four, Five, Six, and Seven and in the Grammar Supplement.)

Uh oh. I just heard somebody say, "Oh, no, not that; I never *could* understand those things." Well, the English for Careers method is different! Try it with an open mind: You'll discover an enjoyable and efficient way to acquire language style that helps your career.

Read Unit

NOUNS AND VERBS

Nouns

Nouns name persons, animals, things, ideas, places, times, activities; they tell "who" or "what."

Proper nouns name specific persons, animals, things, ideas, places, times, and activities—and begin with capital letters: for example, *Oregon, Dr. Hom, Lake Champlain, Boris*. Nouns beginning with lower-case letters are **common nouns**. Here are some common nouns related to the proper nouns you just read: *state, physician, water, neighbor*.

Here are examples of various kinds of nouns as individual words and in sentences:

PERSONS instructor   accountant   woman
Lee   members   father

> **Lee** is studying to be an **accountant**.
>
> The **instructor** and her **father** are **graduates** of the same school.

ANIMALS goldfish   Fido   eagle
dog   cockroach   dinosaur

> **Fido** has **fleas**.
>
> **Dinosaurs** were prehistoric **animals**.

THINGS desk   merchandise   New York Times
pencil   machines   telephone

> Two **machines** process the **merchandise**.
>
> He put the **pencil**, the **telephone**, and the *New York Times* on the **desk**.

IDEAS honesty   Buddhism   kindness
beauty   democracy   modesty

> My **beauty** is exceeded only by my **modesty**.
>
> His **honesty** cannot be questioned, but he lacks **kindness**.

PLACES home   moon   city
Illinois   kitchen   factory

> My **home** in **Illinois** has a modern **kitchen**.
>
> We plan to build a **factory** in this **city**.

Recognizing Nouns

Most nouns have two forms: **singular** (to name one) and **plural** (to name more than one).

SINGULAR	PLURAL
one **boy**	two **boys**
one **salesperson**	a few **salespeople**
a **book**	several **books**

A few nouns do not have plural forms: *honesty, merchandise, running,* for example.

TIMES   birthday   Christmas   yesterday
             Saturday   month   21st century

My **birthday** will be on the first **Saturday** of next **month**.
Christmas was **yesterday**.

ACTIVITIES   drinking   running   sleeping
                  driving   playing   thinking

Drinking and **driving** do not mix.
The child spent the day mostly **running** and **playing**.

Recap   Two of the example sentences in Read Unit 1 contain nouns that are not printed in bold type. Find these nouns and write them in the blanks.

1. _____   2. _____   3. _____

4. Circle the nouns in the following sentence:

   People who interview jobseekers look for intelligence, integrity, and

   adaptability. (5 nouns)

5. Write a proper noun that names the city or town where you would

   like to live. _____

6. Look around and write five common nouns "naming" what you see:

   _____   _____   _____

   _____   _____

7. An example of a proper noun for a person is *Josephine.* Some common nouns that apply to a person I know named Josephine are *friend, sister, realtor, teacher.* Write one proper noun and four common nouns that "name" someone you love:

   _____   _____   _____   _____

Check your answers in Appendix H.
Your score: Great _____ Good _____ Fair _____ Ugh _____

Verbs

Verbs show or suggest action (doing) or existence (being).

Every sentence includes at least one verb. The verb may be an action word or an existence word. Or a sentence may use an action or existence verb together with one or more helping verbs.

Action Verbs

Most verbs are action words. Here are some representative action verbs, listed individually and used in sentences:

type	worry	buy
read	dance	sit
have	go	do
think	relax	accumulate

She **typed** the letter of application.

The personnel manager **read** the application carefully.

I **think** that I **have** a job for you.

The salespeople **go** to San Francisco often.

He **danced** all night with the princess.

I **do** needlework when I **relax**.

Existence, or State-of-Being, Verbs

Existence, or state of being, verbs (also known as *linking verbs*) include the verb *be*, and a few other verbs like *appear* and *remain*, and verbs of the senses:

EXISTENCE VERBS be* (am, is, are, was, were, be, been, being) appear

become seem remain

SENSE VERBS feel sound taste smell look

She **is** capable and efficient.

I **am** glad the program **sounds** interesting to you.

All the employees **were** on vacation last week.

It **seemed** as though he **was** at the beach all summer.

The accounts payable manager **appears** efficient.

Helping Verbs

Helping verbs join with an action or existence verb to help show time and sometimes emphasis or possibility. (When a verb shows "possibility," you understand "maybe" about what it is telling you.)

A few of the verbs you just saw as existence verbs can also function as helping verbs:

be (am, is, are, was, were, been, being)

have (has, had)

do (did, does)

The following words are always helping verbs:

can	might	shall
could	must	would
may	will	should

* In career-related writing and speaking, do not use the dialect style *be*—as in "We be going." Further details on *be* are in Read and Replay Unit 34. In the meantime, ask a friend or an instructor whether you use *be* in this way.

Helping verbs together with main verbs can show time—now, before, later. They can also show duration—something continuing for a while.

is reading [now]

has danced [before]

will have worked [time continuing into the future]

Helping verbs together with main verbs can show possibility or emphasis as well as time:

does wonder [emphasis + now]

could invest [possibility, or "maybe" + later]

might have eaten [possibility + before]

The following sentences show helping verbs working together with main verbs:

He **is reading** the application form. [*is* = helping verb; *reading* = main verb; together they show reading "right now"]

She **was typing** until 11:00. [*was* = helping verb; *typing* = main verb; together they show typing "before"]

In June you **will have worked** for them for 25 years. [*will* and *have* = helping verbs; *worked* = main verb; together they show working continuing to some time in the future]

He **could have danced** with the princess all night. [*could have* = helping verbs; *danced* = main verb; together they show possibility about dancing in some time that's over]

She **does sign** all the letters herself. [*does* = helping verb; *sign* = main verb; together they show emphasis about signing]

Verbs: Showing Time

- Main verbs can change form or pronunciation to show time:

You **type** now.   I **typed** yesterday.

I **read** now.   You **read** yesterday.

- Main verbs also join with helping verbs to show time:

Professor Dowd **has gone** to the office at Mission College. [helping verb = *has*]

Linda Walsh **was reading** that letter. [helping verb = *was*]

Joan McCullough **will be** early for work. [helping verb = *will*]

Recognizing Verbs and "It Looks Like a Verb but It's Not!" Words

-ING WORDS*

■ Nearly all verbs can add *-ing: see—seeing, have—having, eat—eating, cooperate—cooperating, be—being,* and so on. When these *-ing* words express action or existence, they are verbs and are **always** preceded by a helping verb:

He **was typing** the applications.

■ When an *-ing* word names an activity, however, it's a noun and is *not* preceded by a helping verb:

Typing is not difficult. [*Typing* is a noun that names an activity; the verb is *is.*]

TO EXPRESSIONS

■ When *to* comes before a verb form, the expression may be a noun naming an activity or may be functioning in some other way—but it's never a verb:
to eat, to play, to dance, to work.

To know me is **to love** me. [*To know* and *to love* name activities; therefore, *to know* and *to love* are nouns. The verb is *is.*]

* Words that look like verbs but aren't are discussed further in Appendix G, "Grammar Supplement for the Expert."

Replay Unit

1

A. Fill in the blanks with verbs.

EXAMPLE

A word to the wise _____is_____ enough.   LAURENCE STERNE*

1. Many office workers _____ additional training, but they

   don't _____ time for regular college classes.

2. Four out of five companies _____ money on training their employees.

3. I am _____ for your help.

4. He _____ the letter yesterday, but it _____ too many errors.

5. I'll _____ the letter after you _____ the corrections.

* Laurence Sterne was an 18th-century British cleric and novelist.

B. First, underline the verbs in the following sentences. When a main verb is combined with a helping verb, underline both. See *could help* in the example.

Second, circle the 54 nouns in these sentences. Use just one circle for names. See *Ms. Adams* in the example.

EXAMPLE

(Paul) could help (Ms. Adams) with her (work.)

	NO. OF NOUNS IN SENTENCE
1. Competent secretaries type accurately and rapidly.	1
2. Students frequently think about careers.	2
3. The manager and the accountant already have many reports on that subject.	4
4. Fred is the president of the company.	3
5. Sheela Danielle was the winner of the scholarship.	3
6. The clerks were typing the answers in the blanks.	3
7. The salesperson will have completed the work before Tuesday.	3
8. Martha should go to the conference in Milford.	3
9. The wife of the manager had arrived in Nebraska.	3
10. Joan Sterns will ask for the letter.	2
11. These instructions have been sent to Southeast Community College.	2
12. Nina knows a lawyer in that building.	3
13. Reuben Singer, the actor, will present a special concert.	3
14. Joe should mail the tickets.	2
15. The paper is in the box near the window.	3
16. Our bookkeeper will mail the invoice.	2
17. The Aldrich Company received the check.	2
18. Their auditor checked the books for accuracy.	3
19. Frankenstein built a factory in a city on the moon.	4
20. In this office the managers have new terminals.	3

Check your answers in Appendix H.

Read Unit

2

PRONOUNS

Pronouns substitute for nouns.

For example, the pronoun *she* could substitute for any of these nouns: *Mary, girl, lady, typist, baby, president, woman, Ms. Parks.* We substitute pronouns for nouns to avoid repeating the nouns.

NOUNS   **Ms. Applebaum** has finished **Ms. Applebaum's work**.

PRONOUNS   Ms. Applebaum has finished **her** work.

She has finished **her** work.

She has finished **it**.

NOUNS   **Dick Tracy** won the **prize**.

PRONOUNS   **He** won **it**.

Who won **it**?

Somebody won **it**.

Did **anyone** win **this**?

All you need do in this section is recognize a pronoun when you see one. (In Section Five, you'll find answers to questions about specific forms of pronouns such as *who* and *whom, me* and *I,* and so on.)

Pronouns that substitute for the names of specific kinds of people, animals, or things are grouped according to whom or what they substitute for:

- First-person pronouns refer to the person(s) speaking or writing.
- Second-person pronouns refer to the person(s) spoken or written to.
- Third-person pronouns refer to the person(s) spoken or written about.

FIRST PERSON SINGULAR

I, me, my, mine,* myself

FIRST PERSON PLURAL

we, us, our, ours, ourselves

SECOND PERSON

you, your, yours [singular or plural]

yourself [singular]

yourselves [plural]

THIRD PERSON

he, him, his, himself [singular, masculine]

she, her, hers, herself [singular, feminine]

it, its, itself [singular]

they, them, their, theirs, themselves [plural]

Here are some pronouns that are less specific or definite about whom or what they substitute for:

---

* Adding an *-s* to *mine* is dialect and should not be used when standard English is required:

NO   That book is **mines**.

YES   That book is **mine**.

who	whose	those	everyone	everybody
whoever	this	someone	somebody	something
whom	that	anyone	anybody	anything
whomever	these	no one	nobody	everything
				nothing

Pronouns substitute not only for nouns but also for other pronouns; for example—

Everyone in the men's locker room is responsible for keeping **his** own locker secure. [Pronoun *his* substitutes for pronoun *everyone*.]

Replay Unit

2

A. Substitute pronouns for the words in square brackets.

EXAMPLE

[My brother and my father] _____They_____ found [a strange item] _____something_____ in [the person I'm writing to] _____your_____ house.

1. [The weather] _____ is raining today.

2. Almost [all persons] _____ would prefer sunshine today.

3. [Which person] _____ will be the next president?

4. [Eleanor] _____ didn't lightly dismiss the opinions of [Eleanor's] _____ friends.

5. [These friends] _____ urged [Eleanor] _____ to marry [Franklin] _____.

B. The directions are short and simple. Please read them carefully. List the *pronouns* that refer to—

1. The person speaking or writing (first-person singular)

   _____   _____   _____

   _____   _____

Recognizing Pronouns

- A pronoun takes the place of a noun previously mentioned. One way to recognize pronouns, then, is to look for the noun being replaced by a word you think is a pronoun.
- A pronoun can also replace a noun that hasn't been previously mentioned. For example, "**It** is hot today" really means "**The air** is hot today." We understand *air* to be what the pronoun *it* refers to.

2. You and me together (first-person plural)

——————— ——————— ———————

——————— ———————

3. The person you are speaking or writing to. (2nd person singular and plural)

——————— ——————— ———————

——————— ———————

4. Anita (3rd person singular, feminine)

——————— ——————— ——————— ———————

5. Lionel (3rd person singular, masculine)

——————— ——————— ——————— ———————

6. The car (3rd person singular, neutral)

——————— ——————— ———————

7. Donna, Dion, and the dog, Daisy (3rd person plural)

——————— ——————— ———————

——————— ———————

C. Circle the 20 pronouns in the following sentences:

EXAMPLE

(My) luck improves—(anyone's) does—whenever(I) work at (it.)

1. Do you know whose report is better?
2. He used better judgment in preparing it than she did when she prepared hers.
3. I myself caught these in the river and cooked them.
4. They said, "Anyone who is anybody was at your party."
5. We were paid nothing for our work, but we learned almost everything about the job.

After verifying your answers in Appendix H, check one of these blanks.
How did you do? Wonderful ——— So so ——— I'd rather not say ———

Read Unit

3

ADJECTIVES

Adjectives describe or explain nouns or pronouns. They add information about which, what kind, or how many.

We'll cover four types of adjectives below: articles, pointing, limiting, and descriptive, starting with the easiest to recognize.

Articles

Articles tell "which one," and there are only three of them: *a, an, the.* (A review of when to use *a* or *an* is in Section 7.)

An apple **a** day keeps **the** doctor away.

Pointing Adjectives

Four words "point" at nouns—just as you might do with an outstretched finger. When *this, that, these,* and *those* "point" at nouns following them, they are adjectives that tell "which one."

this book	**these** books
that machine	**those** machines

I just heard an alert student protest, "Hold on a minute, Ms. Smith. In Unit 2 you told us *this, that, these,* and *those* are pronouns. Now you're telling us they're adjectives!" *This, that, these,* and *those* are adjectives when used before a noun:

    adj   n
This book is the one I want to read.

This, that, these, and *those* are pronouns when the noun is left out or when one of these words and the noun are separated by a verb:

    pron v
This is the one I want to read.

    pron v   n
This is the book I want to read.

Limiting Adjectives

Words that "limit" nouns in the sense of quantity are also adjectives. They tell "how many." Limiting adjectives include words such as these:

more	enough	most
several	few	any
many	some	22
fifty	no	

         n
Several cabinets were purchased last month. [The adjective *several* limits the noun *cabinets*.]

             n
There aren't **enough** workers to do the job properly. [The adjective *enough* limits the noun *workers*.]

           n
He submitted **22** ideas for the project. [The adjective *22* limits the noun *ideas*.]

Descriptive Adjectives

Descriptive adjectives tell "what kind," adding details about a noun or pronoun. They help a reader or listener picture the noun or pronoun. Without adjectives we couldn't describe anything. To communicate effectively about the noun *house*, you might choose some descriptive words: *yellow*, *brick*, *contemporary*, *shabby*, *two-story*, *luxurious*, and so on. By careful selection of descriptive adjectives, you create a picture with words for the reader or listener.

The **blue** car is **old** but **clean**. [Adjectives *blue*, *old*, and *clean* all describe the noun *car.*)

Did you see the **miniature** typewriter on the shelf? [Adjective *miniature* describes the noun *typewriter.*]

Gourmet food is served in that restaurant. [Adjective *gourmet* describes the noun *food.*]

That man is **honest** and **reliable**. [*Honest* and *reliable* both describe the noun *man.*]

He is **honest** and **reliable**. [*Honest* and *reliable* both describe the pronoun *he.*]

Recognizing Adjectives

A word that describes, explains, or restricts a noun or a pronoun is an **adjective**.

- Adjectives usually precede nouns:

  rock music   **red** dresses   **hot** potatoes
  an idea   **those** pens

- Adjectives often follow existence verbs:

  You are **efficient**.
  Ms. Murcar is **rich**.
  Judi Parks seems **happy**.

- Even though a word looks like a verb, if it describes a noun or a pronoun, it's functioning as an adjective in that sentence:

  He folded **typing** paper to make a **flowering** blossom, a **flying** bird, and a **bent** tree.

Replay Unit

3

A. Circle all nouns and underline each of the five limiting and three pointing adjectives.

EXAMPLE

Please pay <u>this</u>(bill) within <u>five</u>(days)

1. These offices don't have any carpeting.
2. They have many windows, however.
3. This office is mine; that is yours.
4. Some floors have five departments.
5. Several managers have quit this year.

B. The paragraph below, about resort communities, is from a sales letter meant to bring business to a resort hotel. In it you can find 11 nouns in bold type. Adjectives accompany these nouns: descriptive, pointing, or articles. Write in the blanks the adjectives that belong with the given nouns. The numbers in parentheses tell you how many adjectives to look for. As you can see in the example, just one adjective, *a*, describes or explains the noun *person*. For item 1, write in the three adjectives that describe the noun *community*. Continue until you have completed all 10 items.

Surveys show you are a **person** who would be interested in visiting an exclusive resort **community**, located on the beautiful **Pacific**, where the crystal blue **waters** meet the white sandy **beaches**. You will enjoy exquisite guest **rooms** in Spanish **decor**, gourmet **dining**, and a heated **pool**. The **view** is serene, smogless, and sunny. You will want to stay in this **paradise** forever.

EXAMPLE

_____ a _____ person (1)

1. _____ community (3)

2. _____ Pacific (2)

3. _____ waters (3)

4. _____ beaches (3)

5. _____ rooms (2)

6. _____ decor (1)

7. _____ dining (1)

8. _____ pool (2)

9. _____ view (4)

10. _____ paradise (1)

C. On the lines below write six adjectives that could be used to describe the noun *office*.

1. _____   3. _____   5. _____

2. _____   4. _____   6. _____

D. Write five different sentences. In each sentence, use an article, a limiting adjective, a pointing adjective, and a describing adjective. Circle each adjective.

EXAMPLE

(The) girl bought (two)(red) apples (this) morning.

1. _____
   _____

2. _____
   _____

3. _____
   _____

4. _____

5. _____
   _____

Check answers in Appendix H.
Now turn to Appendix A and take the **POP QUIZ** on Units 1–3.

Read Unit 4 — ADVERBS

Like adjectives, adverbs describe or explain. Adverbs, however, describe or explain verbs, adjectives, or other adverbs.

Adverbs add information about when, where, how, how much.

> Barbara will arrive **soon**. [when]
> Michael walked **away**. [where]
> Robert is working **quickly**. [how]
> Jon's fees seem **very** high. [how much]

ADVERBS DESCRIBING VERBS

v
Always type invoices **carefully**. [The adverb *always* tells when and the adverb *carefully* tells how about the verb *type*.]

v
He printed the list **fast** and **accurately**. [The adverbs *fast* and *accurately* tell how about the verb *printed*.]

ADVERBS DESCRIBING ADJECTIVES

adj
The book is **extremely** expensive. [The adverb *extremely* tells how about the adjective expensive; *expensive* describes the noun *book*.]

adj
The **most** difficult courses are given in the morning. [The adverb *most* describes the adjective *difficult; difficult* describes the noun *courses*.]

Marjorie is **too** intelligent to have said that.

ADVERBS DESCRIBING OTHER ADVERBS

They are working **exceptionally hard**. [The adverb *hard* describes the verb *are working;* the adverb *exceptionally* describes the adverb *hard*.]

Recap   Look at the example sentence above, about Marjorie.

1. What is the adverb? _____
2. What is the adjective? _____
3. What is the noun? _____
4. What word does *too* describe? _____
5. What word does *intelligent* describe? _____

Check answers in Appendix H.

Recognizing Adverbs

- Any word that describes or explains a verb, an adjective, or an adverb is an adverb.
- Many adverbs—but not all—are formed by adding *-ly* to an adjective.

Adjective   + *-ly* = *Adverb*

peaceful	peacefully
quiet	quietly
exceptional	exceptionally
intelligent	intelligently
attractive	attractively
final	finally
real	really

- Some words often used as adverbs don't end in *-ly:*

almost	more	never	so	very
even	much	not	too	well

James McFarlan works **so efficiently** that he **almost never** makes a mistake. [The adverb *so* describes the adverb *efficiently; efficiently* describes the verb *works;* the adverb *almost* describes adverb *never; never* describes the verb *makes.*]

Mervin's company manufactures tools **very cheaply**.

Recap Look at the example sentence about Mervin's company.

1. What word does the adverb *cheaply* describe?

   _____

2. What word does the adverb *very* describe?

   _____

Check answers in Appendix H.

Replay Unit

A. In each blank, insert an adverb to describe or explain the word in bold type. The adverb you select will tell when, why, where, how, or how much. To be sure you select an adverb, refer to the Recognizing Adverbs box in Read Unit 4. Use only one word for each blank.

EXAMPLE

Dorothy Neeley **speaks** _____ clearly _____ .

1. He **was discharged** _____ .

2. The children in that class **read** _____ .

3. Do you think that I **drive** _____?

4. You **did** not **add** the figures _____ .

5. They **should** _____ **use** good quality paper for that job.

6. When you **go** _____ , you will find the front door open.

7. A new calculator **would cost** _____ than a used one.

8. We _____ **gave** the old duplicator away.

9. We didn't believe Delilah when she said she **had** _____ **cut** Samson's hair.

10. Ms. Burchfield _____ **attends** Memphis meetings.

11. Mr. Robbio is a/an _____ **creative** person.

12. Those are _____ **expensive** books.

13. Nutrition is one of the _____ **impor-tant** parts of this program.

14. This _____ **designed** home was de-scribed in *Architectural Digest*.

15. Good database software is _____ **ex-pensive**, but it results in long-range economies for the business.

16. The story is _____ **true**.

17. That machine works _____ **well**.

18. They are working _____ **hard**.

19. I can't keep up with him because he runs

    _____ **fast** for me.

20. I think Clark Gable was _____ **more** attractive than your boyfriend.

B. Circle the right word from each pair in parentheses.

1. In sentences 1–10 of part A, the adverbs I added all described (verbs/other adverbs).

2. In sentences 11–16 of part A, the adverbs I added all described (verbs/adjectives).

3. In sentences 17–20 of part A, the adverbs I added all described (verbs/other adverbs).

See possible answers in Appendix H.

Read Unit

5

LITTLE WORDS

Conjunctions

Conjunctions join two words or two groups of words.

∨   Coordinate Conjunctions

Some conjunctions join equals—such as two sentences or two nouns, adjectives, verbs, and so on. Conjunctions that join equals are called **coordinate conjunctions**:

and	or	for	yet
but	nor	so	

Mildred Sweet is a car salesperson in New York, **and** Melanie is a pediatrician in Texas.

Kathy Allen works as a receptionist, **but** she has considerable artistic talent.

By the end of the century, computers might be worn on the wrist, **or** they might be sewn into clothing.

I've decided not to become a movie star, **for** the money and fame might go to my head.

Not many jobs are available for movie stars, **yet** I know you'll find a good one.

After the storm the roads were extremely slippery, **so** I decided not to go to work.

Coordinate conjunctions are used in other ways as well. In the following examples, they join words or groups of words, but not sentences.

We will ship the merchandise today **or** tomorrow.

Ms. Jackson seems to work hard **but** doesn't accomplish much.

The Beatles **and** the Beach Boys were two famous rock groups of the 1960s.

✓ Dependent Conjunctions

Other conjunctions, called **dependent** or **subordinate conjunctions**, precede a noun or pronoun followed by a verb.

if	since	unless	while
as	although	after	so that
when	before	though	whenever
because	until	even though	than

The new Bond's branch will be successful **if** Mickey manages it. [*If* is a dependent conjunction preceding the noun *Mickey* and the verb *manages.*]

Often the normal order of a sentence is reversed; then the conjunction might be the *first* word of the sentence.

If Mickey manages the new Bond's branch, it will be successful.

Unless it is repaired this week, our Apple cannot be used for preparing the report. [*Unless* is the dependent conjunction with the pronoun *it* and the verb *is repaired.*]

Recognizing Conjunctions

Conjunctions join—or connect—words, groups of words, or complete sentences.

In Unit 12, you'll discover more about dependent conjunctions. For now, just identify the words listed above as conjunctions when they are before a noun or pronoun followed by a verb.

Recap   Circle the conjunctions in the following sentences.

1. What would you do if you could do anything?
2. Some people don't get what they want because they don't let themselves think about it, or they forget to keep their goals in mind.
3. "Many employers complain about the English errors of their employees, so it's important to do well in this course," said Ms. Taylor.
4. Since employers want employees who don't make English errors, it's important to do well in this course.
5. Thinking about your goals is extremely important, but it is not enough.

See Appendix H for answers. How many right? ____

∨   **Prepositions**

A preposition is a word that comes before as noun or pronoun to form a prepositional phrase—a word group that does not contain a verb.

Here are some words often used as prepositions:

about	behind	from	over
above	below	in	since
across	beneath	inside	through
after	beside	into	to
against	between	like	toward
along	by	near	under
among	during	of	up
around	except	off	upon
at	for*	on	with

A preposition cannot operate by itself. It is meaningless unless a noun or a pronoun comes right after it or soon after it. This noun or pronoun is the **object of the preposition**. The preposition and its object plus any words between them are a **prepositional phrase**.

* *For* is a conjunction when it means "because." Otherwise, it's a preposition.

You should see that movie, **for** you like Tom Hanks. [*for* = conjunction]
Send Mickey out **for** ice cream. [*for* = preposition]

A prepositional phrase is a group of related words that begins with a preposition and ends with the noun or pronoun that is its object.

Only the preposition and its object are essential for making a prepositional phrase. (In these examples, the objects in the left column are all pronouns, and those in the right column are nouns.)

to me	by Mary
of him	near London
with you	except caterpillars

Sometimes other words separate the preposition from the object. The preposition, however, is always first and the noun or pronoun last. In these examples the preposition and its object are in bold type.

under the antique **table**	**below** the newly painted **roof**
with my adorable little **sister**	**through** the **air**
in the decrepit **plane**	**across** the **street**
from Mary's **window**	**in** the leather **briefcase**

Notice that the preposition shows some kind of relationship between the object of the preposition and the rest of the sentence.

In the following examples, the prepositional phrases are underlined and the prepositions are in bold type.

I hid **under** the antique table **with** my adorable little sister.

I will go **with** you **in** the decrepit plane **to** a village **near** London.

The burglars, who were quite clever, hid the diamonds **in** the leather briefcase.

I saw the newly painted roof **from** Mary's window.

Recap   How can you tell that "hid the diamonds" and "newly painted roof" in the preceding sentences are not prepositional phrases?

_____

_____

See Appendix H for the answer.

Although prepositions are usually small words, they are extremely important for determining the exact meaning of a sentence:

The pen is **on** the desk.

The pen is **in** the desk.

The pen is **under** the desk.

The pen is **near** the desk.

The pen is **beside** the desk.

Recognizing Prepositions

A preposition is the first word of a prepositional phrase. A prepositional phrase consists of the preposition and the object of the preposition. Say the preposition aloud and then ask "whom" or "what" to get the object. A prepositional phrase never contains a verb.

Replay Unit

5

A. Insert a suitable conjunction in the blank.

EXAMPLE

People who stand still may avoid stubbing their toes, _____but_____ they won't make much progress.

1. Neither Susan _____ Jeffrey wants to return to the New York area.

2. Ivy has been a commercial artist for an advertising agency,

   _____ she prefers to be a landscape artist.

3. I was there to meet Sue and Steve _____ they arrived.

4. Earl Hines was raised in Pittsburgh, _____ that's where he started his jazz career.

5. "_____ I used my formal piano training as a foundation, I've always tried to be original," said Hines.

6. Management consultant Peter Drucker said "The better a man is,

   the more mistakes he will make _____ the more new things he will try."

7. Who can tell for sure whether a new idea will work _____ it is tried?

8. "_____ you want the rainbow, you must put up with the rain," said Dolly Parton.

9. He arrived on time every day _____ he would have a reputation for promptness.

10. Do you prefer Seattle _____ Tacoma?

B. Almost any word that makes sense filling in the blank in the sentence below is being used as a preposition. The prepositions you write in the blanks will show the relationship between the verb *walked* and the noun *mountain*. Notice how the choice of preposition controls the meaning of the sentence.

Read Unit 6 / Versatile Tools

EXAMPLE

They walked _____around_____ the mountain.

1. _____   5. _____
2. _____   6. _____
3. _____   7. _____
4. _____   8. _____

C. Underline the prepositional phrases, and circle the prepositions.

EXAMPLE

She looked (at) the return address and threw the envelope (in) the trash.

1. He will be in touch with you during the first part of next week. (4 phrases)
2. Advertising has a substantial influence on the behavior of people and on their lifestyles. (3 phrases)
3. Do you know the difference between a wish and a goal? (1 phrase)
4. Media for advertising are rated in several ways. (2 phrases)
5. Radio advertisers are experts at producing spot announcements for their customers. (2 phrases)

Check your answers in Appendix H, and write down how many you did correctly in each part.

Read Unit 6

VERSATILE TOOLS

Some tools are quite versatile because they're used for more than one kind of job. So it is with words. That is, most words may be used as more than one part of speech. You can't really be sure of the part of speech of a word until you see it in a particular sentence. Although that sounds confusing, the idea is simple. Here's what you need to remember.

> The part of speech is determined by the way that a word functions in a sentence.

Consider the word *dancing.* It looks like a verb, doesn't it? After all, it represents *action.* It sounds like a verb too—because it ends in *-ing.* As a matter of fact, it is a verb . . . *sometimes:*

He is **dancing** with a princess. [The complete verb here is made up of the helping verb *is* and the main verb *dancing.*]

Dancing is enjoyable. [*Dancing* is a noun because it's naming an activity. *Is* is the verb. A helping verb doesn't precede the *-ing* word.]

adj
The child attends **dancing** school. [*Dancing* is an adjective because it describes the school. A helping verb does not precede the *-ing* word. *Attends* is the verb.]

The **-ing** form is a verb only when a helping verb precedes it. When there's no helping verb, the *-ing* word is a noun or an adjective.

Words that look like verbs but are functioning as adjectives or nouns are often called **verbals**.

How about the word *brown*? What part of speech is it? Since it's a color, it must be a describing word—an adjective. That's right . . . *sometimes.*

adj
Brown carpet was installed in the treasurer's office. [*Brown* is an adjective describing the noun *carpet.*]

n
Mr. **Brown** is the new treasurer. [*Brown* is a noun because it names a person.]

n
Brown is my favorite color. [*Brown* is a noun because it's being used to name a color.]

v
First, I **brown** the onions. [*Brown* is the action word of the sentence, a verb.]

Replay Unit

6

A. The word *fish* may be a noun, an adjective, or a verb. What part of speech is *fish* in each of these sentences?

EXAMPLE

Let's go to the fish market.   adjective

1. He will fish while he is on vacation.   _____

2. We'll eat a fish dinner.   _____

3. Fish is my favorite food.   _____

B. The word *trade* may also be a noun, an adjective, or a verb. What part of speech is *trade* in each of these sentences?

EXAMPLE

A career in international trade can be exciting.   noun

1. That was not a fair trade.   _____

2. I will not trade that stock.   _____

3. He reads several trade papers.   _____

C. *Typing* is another word that readily changes its part of speech. Write a sentence using *typing* as each part listed.

EXAMPLE

[adjective] _____He is a typing teacher._____

1. [verb] _____
2. [noun] _____
3. [adjective] _____

D. Write two sentences using *plant*, first as a verb and then as a noun.

1. [verb] _____
2. [noun] _____

E. Please answer the following questions.

1. The words *city* and *country* are what part of speech in the following sentence? The researcher plans to compare **city** schools with **country** schools. _____

2. Write a sentence in which *city* and *country* are nouns.

   _____

   _____

The answers to this Replay are in Appendix H.
For **POP QUIZ,** turn to Appendix A.

Read Unit

7

INTRODUCING THE BUSINESS LETTER

On page 27 you will see a business letter. This **courteous complaint letter** illustrates standard English for business. The sentence structure, grammar, punctuation, and spelling are correct; the word choices are suitable; and the content is effectively arranged. This letter and others in this book are examples of good business communication.

Notice that various parts of this personal business letter have been labeled. The writer's **home address** is typed above the **date**, and the **writer's name** is typed below the **signature**. The other parts of a personal business letter are the **inside address**, **salutation**, **body**, **complimentary close**, and in this case, a **copy notation** indicating that a copy was sent to someone other than the addressee.

Replay Unit

7

All the parts of speech reviewed in Section One are included in Read Unit 7's business letter: nouns, verbs, pronouns, adjectives, adverbs, prepositions, conjunctions. Refer to the letter to answer the questions.

A. What part of speech are these words, which are from the first paragraph of the letter?

1. I _____

2. van _____

3. purchased _____

4. on _____

5. prompt _____

6. also _____

7. appreciate _____

B. What are the two verbs in the first line of the second paragraph?

1. _____   2. _____

C. What are the pronouns in the second paragraph?

1. _____   2. _____   3. _____   4. _____   5. _____

D. What is the prepositional phrase in the first line of the third paragraph? _____

E. What parts of speech are these words from the last paragraph?

1. some _____

2. error _____

3. misunderstanding _____

4. has occurred _____

5. your _____

6. or _____

7. dealer _____

8. for _____

Answers are in Appendix H.

Checkpoint

This section presented a brief review of the "tools of the trade": seven of the eight parts of speech. The eighth is the **interjection**, an exclamatory word or phrase—such as No! Wow! That's great! Perhaps you have special ones for when you've made a mistake or are angry.

You should now be able to recognize parts of speech sufficiently so that you can master the principles of this course. Learning the tools of the English trade makes the work that follows much easier. That's why after you complete this section carefully, you can progress smoothly through the rest of the course.

Write a check in the blank after you know the definition.

_____ **Noun**—names something or somebody.

Beauty is in the **eye** of the **beholder**.

Sports are an important **part** of physical **education**.

<pre>
                                    30711 Fairplay
      Writer's Address   Wilmington, DE 19809
                                   July 1, 19_ _   Date
</pre>

<pre>
Owner Relations Department
Chevrolet Central Office   Inside Address
Chevrolet Motor Division
Detroit, MI 42842

Ladies and Gentlemen: Salutation
</pre>

My husband and I are pleased with the new Chevrolet van we purchased
June 21. The dealer, Morris Owens Chevrolet, has given us courteous and
prompt service, which we also appreciate.

We believe this dealer and General Motors conduct business fairly and
honestly. Yesterday, however, we paid $42.20 to repair a defect that
existed when we bought the van. At the time of purchase, although
unknown to us, the wheels needed balancing.

We note the exclusion provisions of the warranty, which read, "Normal
Maintenance services (such as . . . wheel balancing)" are not covered by
the warranty. A condition existing at the time of purchase cannot be
considered "Normal Maintenance."

We assume, therefore, some error or misunderstanding has occurred.
Would you please send us your check (or instruct your dealer to do so)
for $42.20.

<pre>
      Complimentary Close   Sincerely yours,

      Writer's Signature   Leila R. Smith
Copy
Notation   Leila R. Smith   Writer's Name

C: Morris Owens Chevrolet Service Department
</pre>

_____ **Pronoun**—substitutes for a noun. To decide whether a word is a pronoun, see if it can substitute for a noun.

Give **that** to **me**. = Give the **tape** to **Ms. Smith**.

It injured **its** paw in **our** yard. = The **squirrel** injured the **squirrel's** paw in **Jenny** and **Sam's** yard.

_____ **Verb**—expresses action or existence (state of being). To decide whether a word is a verb, see if it sounds right with a noun before it.

Accountants **have** many responsibilities.

Technicians **were paid** more.

_____ **Adjective**—tells something about nouns: describes (what kind), points to (which one), or limits (how many). _A, an,_ and _the_ are the three adjectives known as articles.

This clever accountant has **a good** job with **many** responsibilities.

_____ **Adverb**—tells when, how, or where about a verb, an adjective, or another adverb. Adverbs often (but not always) end with _-ly._

Yesterday I **gladly** went **home**.

_____ **Conjunction**—joins two words or groups of words.

Coordinate conjunctions are _and, but, or, nor, for, yet, so._ Dependent conjunctions precede either a noun + verb or a pronoun + verb combination. Examples are _when, as, if, since, because, although._

Although he loves both Lois **and** Louise, he will have to choose one **or** the other.

_____ **Preposition**—introduces a prepositional phrase. A prepositional phrase does not contain a verb. Its first word is a preposition, and its last word is a noun or a pronoun, known as the object of the preposition. The prepositional phrases below are underlined, and the prepositions are in boldface type.

During the last month he took each woman **to** dinner **at** his parents' home.

Additional details regarding the parts of speech are in Appendix G.

Special Assignment

A. Compose sentences using each of these words as an adjective, a verb, and a noun: _running, program,_ and _radio._

B. Compose sentences using _after_ as a preposition and as a conjunction.

C. The ability to present a clear explanation or description is vital to successful business, professional, and technical communication. Read the following paragraph and compose a clear description using complete sentences. (Your instructor will give you the name of the object you are to describe.)

You and your partner on a TV game show have a chance to win a new Mercedes and a trip to Paris. All you have to do is describe the object (without naming it) given to you by the master of ceremonies. Your partner must name the object, which cannot be seen. Your description should be so vivid that your partner gets it right on the first try. You'll want to tell your partner facts such as size, weight, shape, texture, color, and whatever else will help. The rules require complete sentences and a maximum of 50 words.

Assignments to be turned in by _____ (date).

Memo from the Wordsmith

WEBSTER'S DICTIONARY

Several good dictionaries carry the name of Webster as part of the title; however, the name Webster does not in any way ensure the quality of a dictionary. "Webster" cannot be copyrighted; anyone can compile a reference book and give it that name. (Noah Webster was a 19th-century lexicographer who compiled THE AMERICAN DICTIONARY, an outstanding language reference book of its time.)

Part-of-speech information is just one of the things you can find out about a word from its dictionary entry. If you need a new dictionary, see page 61 for a list of recommended dictionaries. Be sure to get the latest edition.

Proofreading for Careers

Everyone makes mistakes; even I have made one or two in my lifetime. But for success on the job, why advertise mistakes! Instead proofread, *proofread*, **proofread**.*

- Proofreading tests alertness and knowledge
- Proofreading is done more slowly than other types of reading
- Proofreading calls for reading what you've written more than once

Proofreading is much more than checking for spelling and typographical errors. Don't let anything get by your desk that doesn't make sense to you.

This classified advertisement appeared in the *Kingsport* (Tennessee) *News.* Show the necessary correction:

Telephone receptionist for doctors' office. Duties are to relay massages between patients and doctors.

Proofread and correct the following disclaimer, which appeared below a supermarket advertisement in a Los Angeles newspaper:

NOT RESPONSIBLE FOR TYPORGRAPHICAL ERRORS

From this answer on a science student's test, biology history was made. Proofread it for meaning and make the correction:

An example of animal breeding is the farmer who mated a bull that gave a great deal of milk with a bull with good meat.

Verify the corrections with your instructor. What's your score in proofreading?
A = Alert, M = mediocre, or U = Ugh _____

* Special symbols are often used to mark errors found by proofreading. Typists interpret these symbols and make corrections accordingly. These symbols are shown under the heading "Proofreaders' Marks" in college dictionaries, typing books, and reference manuals—as well as inside the back cover of this book.

Practice Quiz

Take the Practice Quiz as though it were a real test; Don't look back through Section One while you take this Practice Quiz. After the quiz is corrected, refer to the appropriate Read Units, shown in parentheses, for explanations of any item you may have missed.

A. Fill in the blank with the name of a part of speech.

1. To name a person or a thing, use a/an _____. **(Unit 1)**
2. To describe a noun or a pronoun, use a/an _____. **(Unit 3)**
3. To describe a verb, an adjective, or an adverb, use a/an _____. **(Unit 4)**
4. To substitute for a noun, use a/an _____. **(Unit 2)**
5. To join two words or groups of words, use a/an _____. **(Unit 5)**
6. To begin a prepositional phrase, use a/an _____. **(Unit 5)**
7. To express action or existence, use a/an _____. **(Unit 1)**

B. After reading the sentence about Sarala, fill in the part of speech of each word.

> While Sarala dined leisurely, she thought about skiing with Sean in the lofty mountains of Vermont and New Hampshire.

8. While _____ **(Unit 5)**
9. Sarala _____ **(Unit 1)**
10. dined _____ **(Unit 1)**
11. leisurely _____ **(Unit 4)**
12. she _____ **(Unit 2)**
13. thought _____ **(Unit 1)**
14. about _____ **(Unit 5)**
15. skiing _____ **(Unit 1)**
16. with _____ **(Unit 5)**
17. Sean _____ **(Unit 1)**
18. in _____ **(Unit 5)**
19. the _____ **(Unit 3)**
20. lofty _____ **(Unit 3)**
21. mountains _____ **(Unit 1)**
22. of _____ **(Unit 5)**
23. Vermont _____ **(Unit 1)**
24. and _____ **(Unit 5)**
25. New Hampshire _____ **(Unit 1)**

Practice Quiz Grade _____

Secret Life of a Sentence Revealed

2

Run-On

Complete Sentence!

Comma-Splice

Fragment

✔ Identify and correct a sentence fragment, a run-on sentence, and comma splice.

✔ Construct complete sentences and end them at the appropriate place.

*W*e've all learned to understand certain combinations of letters. For example, when we combine the following letters in the order shown, we can pronounce a word and understand it:

S–P–E–L–L

We can't, however, be sure of whether *spell* refers to magic or to the arrangement of letters to form a word. (Perhaps the latter is also magic.)

Thus, to increase our understanding of words, we arrange them into groups.

Here is one group of words:

A when not word spell how to you sure are.

Even though this group of words begins with a capital letter and ends with a period, you know it isn't a sentence. You don't receive a sensible message from this word arrangement.

Here's another word group:

When you are not sure how to spell a word.

Now you receive a sensible message, but you probably have a feeling of incompleteness: you sense something is missing. Even though you can interpret the group of words, you are waiting for completion of the thought.

Now read this group of words:

When you are not sure how to spell a word, look it up in the dictionary.

At last, the familiar signals—capital letter and period—enclose a *complete* thought that *can* be understood.

Expressing ideas and information clearly is essential to successful business writing, and complete sentences are the first step toward that goal. Incomplete sentences are called **fragments**.

FRAGMENT   When you are not sure of how to spell a word.

The opposite of a fragment is the run-on. **Run-ons** occur when writers forget to stop. They go on and on and don't insert a period until the end of two or even several complete thoughts:

RUN-ON   The location of vending machines is important they must be placed in areas with a large amount of foot traffic.

Some writers remember to stop between two complete thoughts, but not firmly enough. They are guilty of the **comma splice**—a run-on with a comma between the complete thoughts.

COMMA SPLICE   The location of vending machines is important, they must be placed in areas with a large amount of foot traffic.

Fragments, run-ons, or comma splices in business writing may make the message unclear. These sentence faults keep the reader from understanding the important message in the letter or report.

You'll be confident of your ability to avoid fragments, run-ons, and comma splices when you've completed Section Two.

Read Unit

PSYCHOLOGY AND SENTENCE CONSTRUCTION

Just as you and I have basic needs, a sentence also has basic needs. When our needs are not met, we feel a lack of completeness; we are frustrated. When the needs of a sentence are not met, it is "incomplete"; it is a fragment. A "complete" sentence reveals three characteristics:

- Identity
- Action
- Independence

Identity

A sentence includes at least one word that identifies who or what the sentence is about. This part of the sentence is called the **subject** and is always a noun or a pronoun.

(Various kinds of nouns are listed in Unit 1, and pronouns are shown in Unit 2.)

In the following examples, the words in bold type are subjects. They are subjects because they're the nouns or pronouns that identify who or what the sentence is about.

Ms. Ramirez is an expert secretary. [who]

The new **treasurer** stole our money. [who]

My **coat** is hanging in the closet. [what]

It is torn but can be repaired. [what]

She takes dictation at 120 words a minute. [who]

Is the **location** of vending machines important? [what]

The **windows** and **doors** had been left open. [what]

The **building** in Plantation is in very good condition. [what]

The **manager** ordered a new typewriter for Ms. Carmona. [who]

The **desk** is just the right size. [what]

Understood Subjects

Sometimes, a subject is a "missing person." Look at these examples:

Leave the file on my desk.

Have lunch in the cafeteria today.

The "understood" subject in these sentences is *you:*

> [you] Leave the file on my desk.
> [you] Have lunch in the cafeteria today.

In commands—that is, sentences that tell somebody what to do—*you* is understood to be the subject even though the word isn't used. Often, commands can be expressed more courteously with the addition of "please"; however, the subject is still *you:*

> [you] Please introduce all the new employees to their supervisors.

Action

A sentence includes at least *one* word that tells what the subject does or is or has. This part of the sentence is the verb.

(Various kinds of verbs are shown in Unit 1.)

The verbs in the following sentences are in bold type. They tell what the subject **does**, **is**, or **has**.

> Ms. Ramirez **types** a letter efficiently.
> She also **knows** about various filing systems.
> My horse **ate** the hay.
> Then he **trotted** around the race course.
> The treasurer and the president **will** both **speak** at the stock holders' meeting.
> He **flew** to South America.
> Embezzlement **is** a serious crime.
> **Was** your coat in the closet?
> The horse **seemed** sad and lonely.
> I **worked** at the computer all day.
> Your money and jewelry **are** under your mattress.
> Please **turn** the air conditioner on.

Recap   Here are the verbs from the preceding examples. In the blanks, write the *subject(s)* from each example sentence that goes with the given verb.

1. _____ types
2. _____ knows
3. _____ ate
4. _____ trotted
5. _____ will speak
6. _____ flew

7. _____ is
8. _____ Was
9. _____ seemed
10. _____ worked
11. _____ are
12. _____ turn on

Check answers in Appendix H.

Word to the Wise

Just because a word is a noun or a pronoun doesn't mean it's the subject. For example, the object of a preposition is always a noun or a pronoun but is never a subject. (To review prepositional phrases, see Unit 5.)

To be sure a noun or pronoun is the subject, find the verb. If the noun (or pronoun) *does, is,* or *has* whatever the verb states, it is the subject.

Replay Unit

8

A. There are seven prepositional phrases in the example sentences under the ACTION heading. You can see the first one in the example below. Find the six others, and write them in the blanks.

EXAMPLE

about various filing systems

1. _____

2. _____

3. _____

4. _____

5. _____

6. _____

B. The subject tells who or what does, is, or has something; it tells who or what the sentence is about. The verb tells what the subject does or is or has. For each sentence, write the subject in the left blank and the verb in the right blank. One sentence has the understood subject *you.*

EXAMPLE

	SUBJECT	VERB
The new secretary is in the office now.	secretary	is
1. Joanna Warner was the president.	_____	_____
2. You introduced her to the staff yesterday.	_____	_____
3. The winner sees an answer for every problem.	_____	_____
4. The loser sees a problem in every answer.	_____	_____

5. The books were on the shelf.　————————　————————

6. He wanted the report.　————————　————————

7. The new members of the team have uniforms now.　————————　————————

8. Three visitors arrived at the same time.　————————　————————

9. Please give me the ledger.　————————　————————

10. The supervisor found five errors.　————————　————————

C. The ten sentences in part B are incomplete sentences—fragments. They're fragments because either the subject or the verb is missing. Write *S* in the blank if the subject is missing or *V* if the verb is missing.

EXAMPLE

MISSING

Our new secretary, Ms. Ramirez.　　_V_

1. The former treasurer of this company.　————

2. Runs for exercise every day.　————

3. Usually eats hay every morning.　————

4. Costs a great deal of money.　————

5. The big black race horse in my stable.　————

6. Was caught stealing the sugar.　————

7. A new factory equipped with the latest in robotics.　————

8. Is a very good typist.　————

9. The little old lady in tennis shoes.　————

10. The experienced and competent accountant.　————

D. Using the ten fragments in part B, compose five complete sentences. Combine them in any way you wish as long as each combination includes both subject and verb.

1. ————————————————————

————————————————————

Word to the Wise

Did you notice that "of the team" in item 7 of Part B is a prepositional phrase? The object of this phrase is *team;* the object of a preposition cannot be the subject.

2. _____
_____

3. _____
_____

4. _____
_____

5. _____
_____

The answers are in Appendix H.

Read Unit

9

THE CLINGING VINE

Riddle: What do a clinging vine and a complete sentence have in common?
Answer: Nothing!

Independence

The third (and final) requirement of the complete sentence is its independence.

> A sentence needs to be able to stand alone—that is, it must be independent to be *complete.*

When a word group cannot stand alone, it is **dependent**. It is like a clinging vine, needing something to support it. It must lean on another word group to form a complete sentence. A word group may have both subject and verb but still not express a complete thought. Such a word group is a **dependent clause*** and starts with a dependent conjunction (see Unit 5). If a dependent clause begins with a capital letter and ends with a period, it's a **fragment**; it isn't a sentence.

INDEPENDENT (SENTENCES)	**DEPENDENT (FRAGMENTS)**
PCs are relatively cheap.	If PCs are relatively cheap.
Prices will continue to fall.	Because prices will continue to fall.
The competition intensifies.	Since the competition intensifies.
The software is becoming easier to use.	As the software is becoming easier to use.

Although the entries in both columns include subjects and verbs, only the ones on the left—the independents—are sentences.

The four *dependents* on the right are fragments. The first word—a

---

* A **clause** is a group of words with both a subject and a verb. Clauses are either dependent—clinging vines—or independent—able to stand alone.

Recognizing Dependent Clauses

A dependent clause begins with a word that makes it dependent, followed by a subject and a verb. Here are some words that make a clause dependent. You saw some of them—the dependent conjunctions—in Read Unit 5. Some other words are new to the list.

after	before	since	until	which
although	even though	so that	when	while
as	if	that	where	who/m
because	provided	unless	whether	why

dependent conjunction—makes the group of words dependent. When a dependent doesn't have anything to lean on or to "depend on," it lacks completeness. It is not a sentence even though it has a subject and a verb.

A dependent (or fragment) can be completed by attaching it to an independent clause—that is, a word group that can stand alone as a sentence. In the following examples, the independent clauses are in bold type, and the dependent clauses are underlined.

Since PCs are relatively cheap, **the business software market will continue to grow.**

The competition will intensify because the prices will continue to fall.

Although the software is becoming easier to use, **well-trained people still command high salaries.**

Please join me at the company cafeteria, where the beans taste like caviar.

Each group of words printed in bold type has identity (subject), action (verb), and independence—the three requirements of a sentence. That's why each group can stand alone as a complete sentence. Each underlined word group is dependent and would be a fragment if it were not attached to an independent clause.

Replay Unit

A. The word groups in items 1–10 include both fragments and sentences. Notice how the fragments leave you with a feeling of incompleteness. You sense that a complete thought has not been expressed; something is missing. Write F in the blanks next to the fragments and C next to the sentences.

EXAMPLES

___F___ Whether it can be done.
___C___ We do not know.

_____ 1. If you do a good job on the Mendocino project.

_____ 2. You will get a raise after the first of the month.

_____ 3. Although most corporations use the services of an auditor to examine the books.

_____ 4. Some errors may never be found.

_____ 5. She will start to work for the new treasurer.

_____ 6. So that it would have enough cash to keep its shelves stocked through the holiday season.

_____ 7. Because this policy is illegal and immoral.

_____ 8. Caye resigned.

_____ 9. The company stopped paying its bills.

_____ 10. Now that Ms. Berg has completed the training.

B. Use the ten items in part A to compose five sentences. Combine each dependent clause with one of the independent clauses.

EXAMPLE

   We do not know whether it can be done   .

1. _____
   _____

2. _____
   _____

3. _____
   _____

4. _____
   _____

5. _____
   _____

Possible answers are in Appendix H.

Read Unit

10

FRAGMENTS, ANYONE?

Here's another type of fragment to guard against. The following samples are also dependents, but their construction differs from those of Unit 9.

FRAGMENT   Mr. Henry, while jogging around the block.

To feel you have read a complete sentence, you want to know what Mr. Henry did. Here are two ways the fragment can be made into a complete sentence:

CORRECT   Mr. Henry was jogging around the block.

By changing "while" to "was," you construct a complete sentence.

CORRECT   Mr. Henry, while jogging around the block, sprained his ankle.

Here, the new information, "sprained his ankle," tells what Mr. Henry did. Both correct versions satisfy your sense that a sentence must be complete.
Try another:

FRAGMENT   Mr. Lopez, who is the president of the company.

For a feeling of completion, you want to know something else about Mr. Lopez. Here is one way to correct the fragment:

CORRECT   Mr. Lopez is the president of the company.

By omitting the word "who," you construct a complete sentence.

CORRECT   Mr. Lopez, who is the president of the company, saw Mr. Henry fall.

Adding other information, about Mr. Henry's fall, also satisfies your need for a feeling of completion.
Here's another example:

FRAGMENT   Mr. Henry's office, which is closed today because of his fall.

To have a complete sentence, you need to know something more about Mr. Henry's office. The fragment can be corrected in several ways:

CORRECT   Mr. Henry's office is closed today because of his fall.

CORRECT   Mr. Henry's office, which is closed today because of his fall, will be open all next week.

Replay Unit

10

A. Write *F* for fragment or *S* for sentence in the blanks below.

EXAMPLE

___F___ A stock certificate, which is a valuable document.

_____ **1.** The man whom we met yesterday in Fullerton.

_____ **2.** The personnel department, which is on the third floor.

_____ **3.** Mr. Shade, feeling that he was right.

_____ 4. David Shade felt that he was right.

_____ 5. Mr. Shade, feeling that he was right, continued to argue the point.

_____ 6. The staff, having been on vacation last week.

_____ 7. The staff was on vacation last week.

_____ 8. The team that won all the games last year.

_____ 9. That team won all the games in Philadelphia last year.

_____ 10. The Bridgeport team that won all the games last year is losing today.

B. Part A has five fragments. You can see the first one in the example below. Find the four others, and write the item number for each fragment in the blank. Then correct each fragment so that it becomes a sentence. Make up any necessary information to complete the sentence.

EXAMPLE

___1___   The man whom we met yesterday in Fullerton is the

treasurer of the Cambridge Corporation.

_____   _____

_____

_____   _____

_____

_____   _____

_____

_____

Please check your answers in Appendix H.
Then review Units 8–10 before taking the **POP QUIZ** in Appendix A.

Read Unit

11

CAPITAL PUNISHMENT

Riddle: What kind of sentence requires capital punishment? Do you want a hint? Here's a sentence that needs capital punishment:

Make a list of all the things you want to achieve in your life, be creative and adventuresome.

Now here's what happens after capital punishment:

Make a list of all the things you want to achieve in your life. **B**e creative and adventuresome.

Answer to riddle: A comma splice.

A **comma splice** is the incorrect joining with a comma of two or more independent clauses. If the independent clauses just run together, with no conjunction or punctuation, the error is a **run-on**.

> To avoid run-ons and comma splices, just remember to separate the independent clauses with a period and a capital letter.

Study the examples of run-ons and comma splices. Observe how they are corrected by separating the two complete sentences with a period and a capital letter. (Three other ways to correct run-ons and comma splices are shown in Units 12 and 13.)

RUN-ON	Don't limit your options just be specific.
COMMA SPLICE	Don't limit your options, just be specific.
CORRECT	Don't limit your options. Just be specific.
RUN-ON	Business is the factory you see from the freeway it is the bank downtown.
COMMA SPLICE	Business is the factory you see from the freeway, it is the bank downtown.
CORRECT	Business is the factory you see from the freeway. It is the bank downtown.
RUN-ON	Business is part of our society there is no escape.
COMMA SPLICE	Business is part of our society, there is no escape.
CORRECT	Business is part of our society. There is no escape.
RUN-ON	American Telephone and Telegraph Company has equipment worth billions of dollars it is one of the giants of American business.
COMMA SPLICE	American Telephone and Telegraph Company has equipment worth billions of dollars, it is one of the giants of American business.
CORRECT	American Telephone and Telegraph Company has equipment worth billions of dollars. It is one of the giants of American business.

Word to the Wise

A run-on and a comma splice have the same construction. The comma splice, however, has a comma between the independent clauses and the run-on does not.

RUN-ON The recession is over salaries and prices are rising.

COMMA SPLICE The recession is over, salaries and prices are rising.

CORRECT The recession is over. Salaries and prices are rising.

Replay Unit

11

Determine your ability to spot and correct run-ons and comma splices. Write *C* in the blank for a correct sentence. Otherwise, insert a period and a capital letter to make the correction. Be sure you don't place a period after a dependent clause; if you do, you will create a fragment.

EXAMPLES

_____ Sticks and stones will break my bones. W / words will never harm me.

__C__ Sticks and stones will break my bones. Words will never harm me.

__C__ Although sticks and stones will break my bones, words will never harm me.

_____ 1. The winner always has a program the loser always has an excuse.

_____ 2. Since the new equipment is being shipped to you at once, you should receive it by the end of the week.

_____ 3. These statistics deal only with symptoms, they do not reveal the fundamental economic problems.

_____ 4. Geriatrics, the study of dealing with problems of the aged, is a relatively new science.

_____ 5. Geriatrics is the study of dealing with problems of the aged, it is a relatively new science.

_____ 6. The tax return is inaccurate he should ask the accountant to prepare a new one.

_____ 7. As the tax return is inaccurate, he should ask the accountant to prepare a new one.

_____ 8. Many students are attracted to a business career, they like the challenge it offers.

_____ 9. Because of the challenge it offers, many students are attracted to a business career.

_____ 10. Each year *Fortune* magazine publishes a list of the top five hundred American corporations.

_____ 11. Although there have been many small automobile manufacturers in the United States, only General Motors, Ford, Chrysler, and American Motors have survived and grown big.

_____ **12.** Many of today's corporations started in colonial times. They became far bigger than anyone expected.

_____ **13.** Most large corporations have become multinational. In other words, they have gone international. They do business in many foreign countries.

_____ **14.** A good example of such a corporation is IBM, it has an office in almost every major city in the world.

_____ **15.** A good example of such a corporation is IBM, which has an office in almost every major city in the world.

_____ **16.** The in-service training at this company includes instruction in Lotus 1, 2, 3 and in desktop publishing.

_____ **17.** The job requires someone who can operate folding machines, drills, and stitchers.

_____ **18.** Entry-level positions in the manufacturing technology field often require a knowledge of die making and tool design.

_____ **19.** After you have made your list of goals, prioritize them in order of importance to you.

_____ **20.** Set a realistic, but ambitious, timetable for each of your goals.

See answers in Appendix H.

Read Unit

12

JOINING INDEPENDENTS

In Read Unit 11 you _separated_ the independent clauses (or complete sentences) of run-ons and comma splices. When two independents are closely related, however, _joining_ them may be preferable to separating them. Here are three correct ways to join independent clauses:

> To join independent clauses, use a semicolon (;).

Get organized**;** handle each piece of paper only once.

> To join independent clauses, use a comma followed by a coordinate conjunction: _and, but, yet, or, nor,_ or _for._*

You cannot control what anyone else does**, but** you can take charge of your own life.

> If the independent clauses together make a sentence no longer than nine or ten words, you can join them with _and_ or _or_ without using a comma.

Get organized and handle each piece of paper only once.

* _For_ is a coordinate conjunction (a joining word) when it means "because."

Here are some of the same run-ons and comma splices as in Unit 11. This time I'll *join* them correctly, instead of *separating* them as in Unit 11.

RUN-ON   American Telephone and Telegraph has equipment worth billions of dollars it is one of the giants of American business.

COMMA SPLICE   American Telephone and Telegraph has equipment worth billions of dollars, it is one of the giants of American business.

CORRECT   American Telephone and Telegraph has equipment worth billions of dollars; it is one of the giants of American business.

American Telephone and Telegraph has equipment worth billions of dollars, and it is one of the giants of American business.

RUN-ON   Greet your clients by name welcome them with a friendly smile and a handshake.

COMMA SPLICE   Greet your clients by name, welcome them with a friendly smile and a handshake.

CORRECT   Greet your clients by name; welcome them with a friendly smile and a handshake.

Greet your clients by name, and welcome them with a friendly smile and a handshake.

Greet your clients by name and make them feel welcome.

RUN-ON   Business is part of our society there is no escape.

COMMA SPLICE   Business is part of our society, there is no escape.

CORRECT   Business is part of our society; there is no escape.

Business is part of society and there is no escape.

Business is an essential part of society in all nations, and there is no escape from it.

Recap

RUN-ON   Don't fill a letter with very long sentences or with words of many syllables it doesn't impress anyone.

COMMA SPLICE   Don't fill a letter with very long sentences or with words of many syllables, it doesn't impress anyone.

Correct the run-on and comma splice—

    1. with a comma and a coordinate conjunction. _____

    _____

    2. with a semicolon. _____

    _____

    3. so that it becomes two sentences. _____

    _____

Check your answers in Appendix H.

The Transition Trap

Transitions are words or expressions that skillful writers use to help the reader cross over from one idea to the next closely related idea. Here are some common transition words:

also	hence	moreover	then
consequently	however	nevertheless	therefore
for example	in addition	otherwise	thus
furthermore	in fact	that is	yet

When a transition is between **independent** clauses, insert a semicolon. *Don't* place a comma *before* the transition word. The result would be a comma splice.

The *Correct* examples show how to fix the comma splices by either separating, as explained in Unit 11, or correctly joining as shown here in Unit 12. The transition words are in bold type.

COMMA SPLICE   About 50 percent of our employees are engaged in the distribution of goods and services, **however**, about 40 percent are in production.

CORRECT   About 50 percent of our employees are engaged in the distribution of goods and services; **however**, about 40 percent are in production.

About 50 percent of our employees are engaged in the distribution of goods and services. **However**, about 40 percent are in production.

COMMA SPLICE   Please order the new equipment first, **then** you can inquire about the training program.

CORRECT   Please order the new equipment first; **then** you can inquire about the training program.

Please order the new equipment first. **Then** you can inquire about the training program.

Please order the new equipment first, and **then** you can inquire about the training program.

The word *yet* is an exception; use either a comma or a semicolon when *yet* precedes an independent clause. A period separating the two sentences is also correct:

CORRECT   Average business letter cost is increasing, **yet** the percentage of increase in declining.

Average business letter cost is increasing; **yet** the percentage of increase is declining.

Average business letter cost is increasing. **Yet** the percentage of increase is declining.

If the sentence totals more than about 15 words, the period or the semicolon is better than the comma, but all three methods are correct.

Commas and Transitions

The comma *after* a transition expression is unrelated to the comma splice or run-on question. Use a comma *after* a transition word of more than one syllable. Do not use a comma after *also* and one-syllable transitions, such as *yet, thus, then,* and *hence.*

Details of correct punctuation are presented in Sections 9 and 10. For now, just remember this:

> Use a semicolon or period directly *before* a transition expression that joins two independent clauses.

Replay Unit

12

A. Write *C* in the blank for the two correct sentences you'll find in items 1–7. For the others, insert semicolons (;) to correct the two run-ons and the three comma splices. Write *R* in the blank for the run-ons and *CS* for the comma splices.

EXAMPLE

__CS__ A stock does not have a fixed worth; it's only as valuable as people think it is.

_____ 1. Consumers have the last word, that is, if they accept and buy a fashion, retailers profit.

_____ 2. Teenagers are very fashion-conscious, however, they closely follow the dictates of their crowd.

_____ 3. These statistics deal only with symptoms, therefore, they do not reveal the fundamental economic problems.

_____ 4. Some people buy because they want to be distinctive they want to be recognized as leaders.

_____ 5. Businesspeople avoid wearing outdated clothes because they don't want to make a poor impression on their colleagues and clients.

_____ 6. This equipment is easy to use, yet you'll need to practice with it.

_____ 7. Be sure to include all the steps necessary to complete the job also list them in the correct order.

B. In the next 8 items, write *C* for correct, *R* for run-on, and *CS* for comma splice. Then correct the run-ons or comma splices by using a comma and one of the six coordinating conjunctions. Choose the word that makes sense in the sentence.

EXAMPLE

__R__ You can vote in person by attending a corporation's annual meeting, or you can vote by using an absentee ballot.

_____ 1. Mr. Evans was able to repair the motor quickly, for he is an expert mechanic with many years of experience.

_____ **2.** He didn't notice any of the errors, nor would he have known how to correct them if he had.

_____ **3.** The Personnel Department is on the third floor the interviewers are out to lunch now.

_____ **4.** The new equipment is being shipped to you at once, you should receive it by the end of the week.

_____ **5.** Possibly Joyce Tarr can attend the conference maybe her partner can go in her place.

_____ **6.** Sticks and stones will break my bones, words will never harm me.

_____ **7.** Goods are delivered either to the receiving area of a department store or to the central warehouse of a chain.

_____ **8.** Experience is an expensive school, but fools will learn in no other.   BENJAMIN FRANKLIN

C. Answer the following questions.

1. List six common transitions:

_____ _____ _____

_____ _____ _____

2. When a transition joins independent clauses totaling more than 10 words, it's correct to insert a comma plus _and, but, yet, or, nor,_ or _for_ before the transition.   True _____   False _____

3. When a transition joins independent clauses, it's correct to place a period after the first independent, and capitalize the first letter of the transition.   True _____   False _____

4. When a transition is between independents, the independents may be joined by a semicolon before the transition.
True _____   False _____

5. In the following sentence, it would be correct to replace the comma with a semicolon before "however."   True _____   False _____
He will not, however, take the blueprints with him.

6. Item 5 is (true/false) because _however_ is not used between clauses but merely separates the helping verb from the main verb.

7. Two ways to escape from the Transition Trap are to insert a _____ or a _____ before the transition.

8. If a comma is used between the independent clauses of a run-on, the result is a comma splice.   True _____   False _____

9. If the comma is removed from between the independent clauses of a comma splice, the result is a run-on.   True _____   False _____

10. Before calling a word group a run-on or a comma splice, be sure a period could be inserted between the clauses.
True _____   False _____

Please check your answers in Appendix H.

LEANING

> When a dependent clause "leans" on an independent clause, the result is a complete sentence.

Therefore, another way to correct a run-on or a comma splice is to change one of the independents into a dependent. A dependent conjunction before an independent clause makes that clause dependent. Take a moment now to review the dependent conjunctions listed on page 19.

Usually, a dependent conjunction changes the emphasis of the original sentence. The choice of whether to use two independent word groups or one independent and one dependent is based on how you want to express a particular idea.

When *and, but, yet, or, nor, for,* or *so* joins two independents, both parts of the sentence remain independent and of equal importance. When a dependent conjunction precedes a subject/verb, that clause becomes dependent and may appear less important. The examples that follow correct run-ons and comma splices by making one of the clauses dependent—the dependent can lean on the independent:

RUN-ON The sales target of $3 million dollars was extremely demanding this target was exceeded by 26 percent.

COMMA SPLICE The sales target of $3 million dollars was extremely demanding, this target was exceeded by 26 percent.

CORRECT Even though the sales target of $3 million dollars was extremely demanding, this target was exceeded by 26 percent. [dependent leans on independent]

RUN-ON The tax return is inaccurate Ms. Keogh should ask the accountant to prepare a new one.

COMMA SPLICE The tax return is inaccurate, Ms. Keogh should ask the accountant to prepare a new one.

CORRECT Because the tax return is inaccurate, Ms. Keogh should ask the accountant to prepare a new one. [dependent leans on independent]

RUN-ON First you should discuss the plan with Mr. Cacciotti of Salinas then you might give the instructions to Ms. Seilo of Irvine.

COMMA SPLICE First you should discuss the plan with Mr. Cacciotti of Salinas, then you might give the instructions to Ms. Seilo of Irvine.

CORRECT You should discuss the plan with Mr. Cacciotti of Salinas before you give the instructions to Ms. Seilo of Irvine. [dependent leans on independent]

Writing for Your Career

When writing for business, you are the one to decide whether to join correctly or to separate closely related ideas. Writing practice, reading well-written business communications, and your own good judgment enable you to make these decisions quickly.

Skillful business writers use dependent clauses to deemphasize ideas they don't want the reader to focus on; independent clauses *emphasize* information or ideas. Use the independent clause for the point you want to give extra importance:

┌──── DEPENDENT CLAUSE ──────────────┐ ┌─ INDEPENDENT ──────
Although we don't give refunds on earrings, we'll be happy to
┌ CLAUSE ──────────────────────────────────┐
exchange them for any other jewelry in the store.

This writing technique enables you to emphasize the positive idea and make the negative (Although we don't give refunds on earrings) seem less important.

RUN-ON	The manager finished the report her husband was busy making a fruit cake.
COMMA SPLICE	Eleanor finished the report, Mike was making a fruit cake.
CORRECT	Eleanor finished the report while Mike was making a fruit cake. [dependent leans on independent]

Replay Unit
13

A. Write *R* for run-on, *CS* for comma splice, *C* for correct sentence. Underline the six dependent clauses.

EXAMPLE

__C__ When you buy more shares of stock, you increase your voting power at the corporation's annual meeting.

_____ **1.** Ms. Hicks buys a new car every year, she saves money by doing that.

_____ **2.** Because Ms. Hicks buys a new car every year, she saves money.

_____ **3.** You have broken one of our important rules the warden has promised to give you another chance.

_____ **4.** You have broken one of our important rules, but the warden has promised to give you another chance.

_____ 5. Even though you have broken one of our important rules, the warden has promised to give you another chance.

_____ 6. Susan Dennis at last succeeded in closing the difficult sale she decided to make no more calls that day.

_____ 7. After Susan Dennis succeeded in closing the difficult sale, she decided to make no more calls that day.

_____ 8. Always part from employers on good terms, for you may need another reference some day.

_____ 9. During an interview, don't forget to ask _your_ questions also remember to thank the interviewer for the appointment.

_____ 10. Listen attentively during an interview, make eye contact with the interviewer.

_____ 11. Interviewers are skilled at asking questions that cannot be answered by a simple "yes" or "no."

_____ 12. The winters are long and cold in Indianapolis, but this gives IVY Tech students more time to study.

_____ 13. Since he was a native of the place, Thoreau knew the neighborhood of Concord thoroughly.

_____ 14. Thoreau knew the neighborhood of Concord thoroughly because he was a native of the place.

_____ 15. A rolling stone gathers no moss; yet it does get a certain smoothness from its rolling.

B. Change the run-ons that follow into correct sentences by making one of the clauses dependent. Use one of the following dependent conjunctions in each sentence: _when, because, even though, although_. If you make the first clause dependent, separate the clauses with a comma.

EXAMPLE

because
A company may initiate a stock split͜its high stock price seems to be discouraging new investors.

1. I exceeded last year's sales by 150 percent I was extremely proud of myself.
2. Ari Optical companies place big orders with us the manager gives them a special discount.
3. The plant was operating on a 24-hour basis top management refused to adopt a three-shift schedule.
4. Professor Sumner explained that studying English is fun the new student wouldn't believe it.
5. The method of shipment was not vital we gave it careful consideration.

Check your answers in Appendix H.
Now take the **POP QUIZ** in Appendix A.

THE MISSING KEY

As you read the letter on the opposite page and the other examples of well-written business letters throughout this book, observe the simple and easy-to-read style of good business writers.

But . . . there are some problems with this letter. The typewriter had one key missing and a shift key that didn't always work. That's why the typist used commas not only where they belong, but also wherever the missing key was needed. Use a pen to repair the damage without changing or adding any words.

Then study the appearance of the letter. Notice the various parts of the letter and their placement on the page:

> letterhead
>
> date
>
> inside address (outside address is on the envelope)
>
> salutation
>
> body
>
> complimentary close
>
> writer's name
>
> title
>
> typist's initials (use when the signer of the letter is not the one who typed it)
>
> postscript (use only for emphasis or a personal note)

Checkpoint

Place a check next to each item below when you're sure you understand it.

_____ A **phrase** is a word group without a subject and verb.

> having a great deal of money
>
> during the past year

_____ A **clause** is a word group containing a subject-verb combination:

> s   v
> we enjoyed the show

> s   v
> because the acoustics were perfect

P R E N T I C E   H A L L   Letterhead

December 9, 19_ _   Date

Professor Joanna M. Head
Indiana Vocational Technical College
P.O. Box 1763   Inside Address
Indianapolis, Indiana 46206-1763

Dear Professor Head: Salutation

Thank you for the time and courtesy you extended to our
representative, Debbie Morgan, when she was at your
school last month, she enjoyed her visit with you,

At Ms. Morgan's request we have sent you the new edition   Body
of MATHEMATICS OF BUSINESS, this was sent to you several
weeks ago, and you should have it by now, we do hope you have
an opportunity to look it over carefully,

Your name has also been placed on our mailing list to receive
an examination copy of BUSINESS MATH: PRACTICAL APPLICATIONS,
a new edition of this book by Cleaves, Hobbs, and Dudenhef
will be in stock sometime next month,

Your copy will be sent to you just as soon as it is available, if there is any way we can be of service to you,
Professor Head, please let us know, best wishes for a
happy holiday season,

Complimentary Close   Cordially,

Maureen Hull

Writer's Name   Maureen Hull
Title   Vice President

lrs   Initials

PS Don't write comma splices, they are hard to read.

See Appendix H to check your responses.

_____ An independent clause may be used as a sentence:

> We enjoyed the show.
>
> The acoustics were perfect.

_____ A semicolon is one correct method of joining two independents:

> We enjoyed the show; the acoustics were perfect.

_____ Another way to join independents correctly for business writing is to insert a comma followed by one of these conjunctions: *and, but, yet, or, nor, for:*

> We enjoyed the show, **for** the acoustics were perfect.

_____ A dependent conjunction may be used for correct joining of clauses.

> We enjoyed the show **because** the acoustics were perfect.
>
> **Because** the acoustics were perfect, we enjoyed the show.

_____ A **fragment** is a word group that expresses an incomplete or dependent idea; it masquerades as a sentence because it begins with a capital letter and ends with a period.

> Because the acoustics were perfect.

_____ A **run-on** is a sentence fault caused by combining of two or more independent clauses into one sentence without punctuation or a conjunction where they join.

> We enjoyed the show the acoustics were perfect.

_____ A **comma splice** is a sentence fault caused by using a comma without a conjunction to join independent clauses.

> We enjoyed the program, the acoustics were perfect.

_____ Identification as fragments, run-ons, and comma splices is not based on length, but on structure.

> Birds sing they also fly. [run-on]
>
> Birds sing, they also fly. [comma splice]
>
> Although most large and colorful birds not only sing but also fly. [fragment]

_____ Run-ons and comma splices are unacceptable in business writing.

_____ Fragments are unacceptable in most business writing.

Writing for Your Career

 Experienced writers who clearly understand sentence structure occasionally use fragments to create certain effects, particularly in advertising material. After you're recognized as a business writing expert, you may intentionally use a fragment. Until then, keep fragments out of your writing.

Have you used the answer section in the back of the book to verify your answers to Replay Units 7–13?

In conversation, fragments are frequently used and are acceptable. Imagine this conversation:

INSTRUCTOR What did you study in Units 7 through 9 of this section?

STUDENT The difference between sentences and fragments.

If you were to *write* your reply, you would insert a subject and a verb. This would change the *acceptable conversational fragment* to an *acceptable written sentence*. Write the acceptable written reply in the blank below.

Proofreading for Careers

When *you* are typing, proofread each page before removing it from the typewriter or before printing from the computer. It is insufficient to rely on "sensing" when you've made a typographical error. Additional errors can be made—errors not immediately "felt" while typing.

When someone is typing for you, submit, sign, or okay the document only after you've proofread it. Don't rely on anyone else's accuracy or skill when a document is your responsibility.

Everyone makes errors, but successful people find and correct their own before anyone else finds them. After you've proofread a document slowly and carefully, reread it **starting with the last word** and continuing until you've reread the first word.

Make the necessary corrections in this short article. Use a dictionary. Look for spelling, typographical, grammar, and sentence errors. Change punctuation only if you find a run-on, comma splice, or fragment.

CORPORATE ORGANIZATION: A VIEW FORM THE TOP

The owners of a corporation are called stockholders or shareholders, each stock holder have one vote for each share of stock he or she owns. At the annual meeting the stock holders elect a board of directors. The board represents the stockholders and elects the high-ranking corporate officers, or at least the president. The officers are responsible for the day-by-day operation the of corporation, boreds of directors usually have between 7 and 17 members.

The board of directors, the officers, and the stockholders are require by law to meet at least once eacy year. The corperate secretary notifies the stockholders of the meeting by male. It is common practice to enclosre a proxy form. With the notice of the meeting, use of such a form allows the stockholder to submit his vote in lieu of attending the meeting in person.

Total Errors = 15. Your score is (circle one) Excellent, Good, Fair, Ugh

Practice Quiz

Take the Practice Quiz as though it were a real test. Don't look back through Section Two while you take this Practice Quiz. After the quiz is corrected, refer to the appropriate Read Units, shown in parentheses, for explanations of any item you may have missed.

Write A in the blank next to each correct sentence, B next to each fragment, C next to each run-on, and D next to each comma splice.

_____ 1. The need for an improved worldwide food reserve policy. **(Unit 8)**

_____ 2. Janet Lowe is the new accountant in our office she is not a CPA. **(Unit 11)**

_____ 3. The law authorizing this activity. **(Unit 8)**

_____ 4. Although Ms. Allen is an accountant, she is not a CPA. **(Unit 13)**

_____ 5. To show the exact number of hours before school is out. **(Unit 9)**

_____ 6. The carpenter is working very hard, nevertheless, we don't think he can finish today. **(Unit 12)**

_____ 7. While the carpenter is working hard. **(Unit 9)**

_____ 8. While the carpenter is working hard, we don't think he can finish the job on time. **(Unit 13)**

_____ 9. Although his writing is better than mine. **(Unit 9)**

_____ 10. His writing is better than mine, but I speak better than he does. **(Unit 12)**

_____ 11. It is the weak who are cruel, gentleness can be expected only from the strong. **(Unit 11)**

_____ 12. Leaders have different styles, they all need, however, to be skilled in handling people. **(Unit 11)**

_____ 13. Meetings must proceed according to rules business must be conducted fairly. **(Unit 11)**

_____ 14. Because many informal meetings occur. **(Unit 9)**

_____ 15. That capable and intelligent market research analyst from your office. **(Unit 10)**

_____ 16. That market research analyst from your office is both capable and intelligent. **(Unit 8)**

_____ 17. Is going to take a trip to Europe. **(Unit 8)**

_____ 18. She flew to Spain last year, then she took a Mediterranean cruise. **(Unit 12)**

_____ 19. Naomi Simon is capable and intelligent, we need more market research analysts like her. **(Unit 11)**

_____ 20. Mrs. Powell, carrying the coffee in one hand and the keys in the other. **(Unit 10)**

_____ 21. Carolinda and Eric are our most talented writers, in fact, they have won several awards. **(Unit 12)**

_____ 22. Do you want to go? **(Unit 8)**

_____ 23. Even though you want to go. **(Unit 9)**

_____ 24. About an hour later the students arrived. **(Unit 8)**

_____ 25. When you can do all the common things of life in an uncommon way, you will command the attention of the world. George Washington Carver **(Unit 13)**

Special Assignment

A. Select the fragments from the Practice Quiz. In the blank at the left, write the Practice Quiz item number of the fragment. Then write a complete sentence to correct the fragment.

EXAMPLE

    3   The law authorizing this activity was passed in 1985.

B. Now select the run-ons and comma splices from the Practice Quiz. In the blank at the left, insert the item number. Then create a correct sentence by either separating or correctly joining the independent parts.

EXAMPLE

    2   Janet Lowe is the new accountant in our office, but she is not a CPA.

_____   _____

          _____

_____   _____

          _____

_____   _____

          _____

Submit this assignment to your instructor on _____. (date)

Ain't Is in the Dictionary

3

After Completing Section Three, You Will

Locate the various kinds of information included in your dictionary.

Interpret the symbols, abbreviations, and special terms used in your dictionary.

Choose English usage based on information in your dictionary.

✓ Spell more accurately than you did before.

✓ Refer to your dictionary as a valuable resource.

ain't

*H*ow do words get into the dictionary to start with? Who makes the decisions? When Moses received the Ten Commandments, did he also receive a list of spelling rules? Then why can't I spell *enough* with just four letters—*enuf*?

Lexicographers (dictionary writers) review tremendous numbers of words spoken and written throughout the country and then report how all kinds of people use the language, both formally and informally. They observe language patterns in various parts of the country and in different types of work—from armed robbery to zoology.

The lexicographers find new words, old words used in new ways, new spellings or pronunciations of words, and even slight changes of meaning for old words. Each word of interest is recorded, along with information on how the word was used, by whom, and the date. Thousands of entries, called citations, may be added to the computerized file daily. These files are so valuable that they may be insured for over a million dollars. When it's time to print the new edition of a dictionary, the entries are sorted to determine what should be added, deleted, or changed based on usage.

Thus your dictionary provides a *description* of how Americans use English. Slang, street language, and other non-Standard expressions such as "ain't" are used, whether we like the words or not. Therefore, contrary to the slogan you may have heard in your childhood ("*Ain't* ain't in the dictionary"), *ain't is* in the modern dictionary that *describes* rather than *prescribes*.

This modern dictionary doesn't prescribe—or inform you of exactly what to do—as the doctor does when giving you medicine for an illness. You, not your dictionary, make the decision about how to spell, pronounce, or use a word.

Then what good does it do to look up a word in the dictionary? The dictionary can, however, tell you a good deal about the word's meanings and the way—in general—it is used. You should make a dictionary your first resource for discovering what words mean. Also, when you interpret the various symbols and abbreviations, you can use your dictionary to make intelligent choices about choosing and using words. For example, if you look up the pronunciation of *hospitable*, you'll find two pronunciations. You decide which to use, keeping in mind that the first one might be used more frequently by good speakers of American English.

Knowing the information in the dictionary about *ain't*, a job applicant will not use it when applying for a job. However, this same person might write "He ain't here" as part of the dialogue in a story.

Types of Dictionaries

Various types of dictionaries are available, from the comprehensive kind describing American English to specialized ones: medical, shorthand, slang, synonyms and antonyms, foreign language, children's, and so on.

In addition, spelling dictionaries, which list spelling and syllables only, provide quick reference for the most commonly used words. If you keep one of these mini-dictionaries on your desk alongside the comprehensive desk dictionary, you'll save time when checking spelling or syllables.

A thesaurus is another useful reference book for people interested in words. (*Thesaurus* is pronounced the · SOR · us, with the *th* pronounced as it is in *th*ink, not as in *th*is.) Have you ever been writing something and just couldn't think of the right word? If you keep a thesaurus on your desk, you immediately reach for it at such times. Here's a sample entry from *The Random House Thesaurus:*

---

beautiful *adj.* **1** *His sister is a beautiful woman. The music is beautiful:* pretty, handsome, good-looking, fine-looking, lovely, gorgeous, attractive, exquisite, ravishing, comely, fair, bonny, seemly, beauteous, radiant, pulchritudinous, resplendent; pleasing, enjoyable, captivating, alluring. **2** *You did a beautiful job of cleaning up the kitchen:* very good, excellent, first-rate, superb, wonderful, fine, splendid, admirable, great, stupendous, commendable, estimable, worthy.
Ant. 1 ugly, unattractive, bad-looking, hideous, grotesque; unpleasant, bad, awful, disgusting, repulsive, repugnant, revolting. **2** bad, awful, terrible, lousy, second-rate.

Reprinted by permission from *The Random House Thesaurus*, College Edition, Copyright © 1985, 1991 Printing by Random House, Inc.

If you don't own a thesaurus, look at a few the next time you're in the library or a bookstore. They're available in hardcover and paperback. Two other widely available thesauruses are *Roget's International Thesaurus,* and *Roget's Thesaurus II* (*Roget* is pronounced ro · ZHA). Dictionaries of synonyms and antonyms are also available.

Section Three deals with comprehensive English-language dictionaries. In our rapidly changing society, language is alive and changing also. It's important, therefore, to use a recent dictionary. To determine how up-to-date your dictionary is, check the copyright date.

Here are the names of some good comprehensive dictionaries for personal and career use:

American Heritage Dictionary of the English Language, 2nd College Edition (or latest)*

Funk & Wagnalls Standard College Dictionary (latest)

Random House Webster's College Dictionary (latest)

Webster's Ninth New Collegiate Dictionary (or latest)

Webster's New World Dictionary of the American Language, 3rd College Edition (or latest)

Read Unit

GETTING TO KNOW YOU

Do you remember the song "Getting to Know You" from the musical *The King and I?* Because the dictionary is the single most valuable reference

---

* The editions given here are the latest ones in March 1991. Always ask for the most recent edition when you buy a dictionary.

Word to the Wise

English is a lively language that has kept pace with the rapid changes of 20th century life. That's why it's essential to check the copyright date before buying a new dictionary. The newest college dictionary, *Random House Webster's College Dictionary*, has hundreds of new words and meanings that are not in any other dictionary. *Webster's New World Dictionary*, 2nd College Ed., added 20,000 new words and meanings and the Third Edition added 5,000 more. AHD* added 25,000 to the latest college edition. Of the 25,000 additions, 10,000 are business-related, office automation, and technical terms.

See if your dictionary passes this open-book test. Are these words included in your dictionary: *palimony, paralegal, biodegradable, feminist, telecommunications, sushi, fax?* If not, it may be time to buy a new edition.

When shopping for a dictionary, check the copyright date before buying so that you'll be sure to get the latest edition.

* American Heritage Dictionary

tool, think of it as a friend you wish to get to know better. In this unit you'll get to know more about comprehensive dictionaries. They come in three general sizes:

- pocket dictionaries
- desk or college dictionaries
- unabridged dictionaries

A **pocket dictionary** is usually a paperback with around 60,000 entries along with limited explanations of each word. A small amount of introductory material and possibly a brief appendix are included. Because a pocket dictionary is convenient to carry, you should own one.

A **college dictionary** is usually a hardcover book with at least 150,000 entries. The explanations about each word are fairly complete. Lengthy front matter (introductory materials) and appendixes (back matter) are parts of a good college dictionary. Everyone interested in using English effectively should have one at home and at work. A student should own a college dictionary as well as a pocket dictionary.

An **unabridged dictionary** may contain between 350,000 and 450,000 entry words—or all the words lexicographers feel belong in an unabridged dictionary. You can tell from this number of words that pocket and college dictionaries are condensed—or abridged.

The explanatory material for each entry is extensive in an unabridged dictionary, as are the front matter and appendixes. Unabridged dictionaries are found in libraries, schools, newspaper offices, and similar places. Unless you have a professional or a strong personal interest in words, there is no need to own an unabridged dictionary.

No dictionary is a complete listing of all the words in the language. *Webster's Third New International Dictionary* (the most prestigious American dictionary) has about 450,000 entries. However, several million insects, at least a million different kinds of other animals, and about half a million varieties of plants have been named. Dictionaries for general use simply have no room for all these words.

Information and Aids in the Dictionary

To use your dictionary effectively and receive maximum benefit from it, you should know exactly what kinds of information and aids are included.

Front Matter and Appendixes

Front matter is everything before the first *a* entry. Appendixes follow the last *z* entry. In the front matter you will find details about how to interpret the information given about each entry. A variety of other information is presented in both the front matter and in the appendix. Exactly what you will find and where you'll find it vary from dictionary to dictionary. Here are some possibilities:

> history of the English language
> grammar, spelling, and punctuation rules
> notes about language usage
> dialects
> colleges and universities
> geographic names with brief explanations
> foreign expressions
> abbreviations
> biographical names
> first names and their meanings

Entries

These are the alphabetically arranged words (or word parts, such as prefixes and suffixes), together with the information supplied for each:

- Every entry includes spelling, syllables, pronunciation, definitions, and parts of speech.

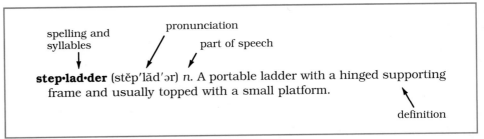

Copyright © 1985 by Houghton Mifflin Company. Reprinted by permission from *The American Heritage Dictionary, Second College Edition.*

- Some entries have one or more of these: etymology—history of the word; usage label—how the word is usually used, spelled, or pronounced; illustrations; synonyms; run-ins—not run-*on* sentences, but words derived from the entry word, such as *accidentally* near the end of the listing for *accidental;* plurals; capitalization; and other helpful notes.

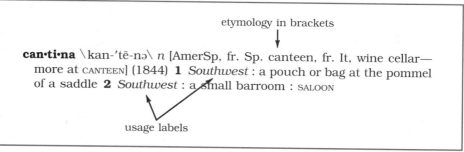

etymology in brackets

can·ti·na \kan-'tē-nə\ *n* [AmerSp, fr. Sp. canteen, fr. It, wine cellar— more at CANTEEN] (1844) **1** *Southwest* : a pouch or bag at the pommel of a saddle **2** *Southwest* : a small barroom : SALOON

usage labels

By permission. From *Webster's Ninth New Collegiate Dictionary* © 1991 by Merriam-Webster, Inc., publisher of the Merriam-Webster ® dictionaries.

Aids for Efficient Use of Dictionary

Guide words at the top of each page show the alphabetic range of that page. The guide words enable you to locate words. The word on the left is the first entry word of that page, and the guide word on the right is the last entry.

Guide Words

1163   Roentgen / roller coaster

the quantity of radiation that will produce, in 0.001293 grams (1 cubic centimeter) of dry air at NTP, ions carrying one electrostatic unit of electricity of either sign

Roent·gen (rent'gən; *Ger* rënt'gən), **Wil·helm Kon·rad** (vil'helm'kōn'rät') 1845–1923; Ger. physicist: discoverer of X-rays

roent·gen·ize (rent'gə nīz', ren'chə-) *vt.* **-ized'**, **-iz'ing** [Obs.] to subject to the action of X-rays

yarn **11** to turn in a circular motion or move back and forth [with eyes *rolling*] **12** to rock from side to side [the ship pitched and *rolled*] **13** to walk by swaying **14** to become flattened or spread under a roller **15** to make progress; advance [start *rolling*] **16** to take part in a bowling game **17** [Colloq.] to have plenty; abound (*in*) [*rolling* in wealth] ☆**18** *Football* to move laterally: said of the

roll (rōl) *vi.* [ME *rollen* < OFr *roller* < VL **rotulare* < L *rotula*: see the *n.*] **1** *a)* to move by turning on an axis or over and over *b)* to rotate about its axis lengthwise, as a spacecraft in flight **2** *a)* to move or be moved on wheels *b)* to travel in a wheeled vehicle **3** to travel about; wander **4** to pass; elapse [the years *rolled* by] **5** *a)* to flow, as water, in a full swelling or sweeping motion [the waves *rolling* against the boat] *b)* to be carried in a flow **6** to extend in gentle swells or undulations **7** to make a loud, continuous rising and falling sound [thunder *rolls*] **8** to rise and fall in a full, mellow cadence, as sound, speech, etc. **9** to trill or warble

rolls, or trills, its notes —**adj.** of or having to do with roller skating [roller disco] —**SYN.** WAVE

☆**roller bearing** a bearing in which the shaft turns with rollers, generally of steel, arranged in a ring-like track: used to reduce friction

☆**roller coaster** an amusement ride in which small, open cars move on tracks that dip sharply

at, āte, cär; ten, ēve; is, īce; gō, hôrn, look, tool; oil, out; up, fur; ə *for unstressed vowels, as* a *in* ago, u *in* focus; ' *as in* Latin (lat''n); chin; she; zh *as in* azure (azh'ər); thin, *the;* ŋ *as in* ring (riŋ) *In etymologies:* * = unattested; < = derived from; > = from which ☆ = Americanism

Pronunciation Key

From the book, *Webster's New World Dictionary*, Third College Edition © 1988. Used by permission of the publisher, New World Dictionaries/A division of Simon & Schuster, New York, NY.

A **pronunciation key** is at the bottom of every page or on alternate pages. A complete pronunciation key is also found in the front matter. This key explains and gives examples of a dictionary's system for showing how to pronounce its entries.

Please fill in the blanks.

EXAMPLE

Name any one of the dictionaries mentioned in this unit.

_____ Webster's Ninth New Collegiate Dictionary _____

1. What is the name of your desk dictionary? _____

   What is its most recent copyright date? _____

2. What is the name of your pocket dictionary? _____

3. What is the term for the words at the top of each page?

   _____

4. Open your dictionary to any page. Then look at the page on the left and write the guide words in these blanks.

   _____   _____

5. What is the purpose of the guide words? _____

   _____

6. What information can you find out about every entry word?

   _____   _____   _____

   _____   _____

7. What other types of information are included with some entry words?

   _____   _____   _____   _____

   _____   _____   _____

8. A comprehensive dictionary containing at least 350,000 entries is

   known as a/an _____ dictionary.

9. The other two types of comprehensive dictionaries are known as

   _____ and _____.

10. If you're interested in using English effectively, you should have a

    _____ dictionary at home and at work.

11. If you are a student or for some other reason need to carry a dictionary with you often, you should have a _____
    dictionary.

12. What do you usually find at the bottom of every page or every other

    page of a good dictionary? _____

13. Open the dictionary to a randomly selected page, see if you find what you named in item 12, and check one of these blanks:

    Yes, it's there. _____   No, it isn't. _____

14. Details about how to interpret the information given about each

    entry word can be found in the _____.

15. Look at the appendix items listed in the table of contents of your desk dictionary. Then thumb through the appendix. What are the main titles of each section in the appendix of your desk dictionary?

_____

_____

_____

The answers to this Replay are in Appendix H.

Read Unit

16

CRACKING THE CODE

To save space, dictionaries use a code—made up of symbols, special words, and abbreviations. Cracking this code is essential for intelligent use of the dictionary. (In fact, few skills are more valuable than knowing how and where to find information.)

The code varies somewhat from one dictionary to another. Here are some explanations of the codes as given in the front matter of the *American Heritage Dictionary* and *Webster's Ninth New Collegiate Dictionary*. The abbreviations AHD and WNCD refer to these two dictionaries. For details that may differ in *your* dictionary, see its front matter.

Spelling and Variations

The entry word is the correct spelling of the word. The dots in the entry word indicate syllables to be used for word division. If there's a second correct spelling, it follows a comma or the word *or*.

Although both spellings are correct, if one form is seen in print more often than the other, that form often appears first. The first spelling is sometimes called the **preferred** form. Choose this first form for business and professional writing. Etymology in brackets **precedes** definitions in WNCD.

two spellings   usage label for
                                                 pronunciation

¹the·ater *or* the·atre \'thē-ət-ər, 'thi-ət-, *oftenest in Southern* 'thē-,āt-
also thē-'āt-\ *n* [ME *theatre,* fr. MF, fr. L *theatrum,* fr. Gk *theatron,* fr.
theasthai to view, fr. *thea* act of seeing; akin to Gk *thauma* miracle]
(bef. 12c) **1 a :** an outdoor structure for dramatic performances or
spectacles in ancient Greece and Rome **b :** a building for dramatic performances **c :** a building or area for showing motion pictures **2 :** a
place of enactment of significant events or action ⟨the ~ of public life⟩
3 a : a place rising by steps or gradations ⟨a woody ~ of stateliest view
—John Milton⟩ **b :** a room often with rising tiers of seats for assem-
blies (as for lectures or surgical demonstrations) **4 a :** dramatic literature : PLAYS **b :** dramatic representation as an art or profession :
DRAMA **5 :** dramatic or theatrical quality or effectiveness

By permission. From *Webster's Ninth New Collegiate Dictionary* © 1988 by Merriam-Webster, Inc., publisher of the Merriam-Webster ® dictionaries.

Etymology in brackets **follows** definitions in AHD.

---

prep·pie or **prep·py** (prĕp′ē) *n., pl.* **-pies.** *Informal.* **1.** A student in a preparatory school. **2.** A student or young adult whose manner and dress are traditional and conservative. [Shortening and alteration of PREPARATORY SCHOOL.] **—prep′pie, prep′py** *adj.*

Copyright © 1985 by Houghton Mifflin Company. Reprinted by permission from *The American Heritage Dictionary, Second College Edition.*

When the word *also* separates the two spellings, the second one is less acceptable than a spelling preceded by a comma or *or*.

lovable *also* loveable

Some words are spelled differently in British English. This variation is shown by a label, such as *chiefly British.*

color *also chiefly British* colour

Sometimes the second spelling is a separate entry word. You can tell this is not the preferred form because there's no definition. Instead, the preferred spelling is given. To find the definition, look up the word under the preferred spelling.

---

usage label

↓

al·right (ôl-rīt′) *adv. Nonstandard.* All right.

Copyright © 1985 by Houghton Mifflin Company. Reprinted by permission from *The American Heritage Dictionary, Second College Edition.*

---

al·right \(′)ol-′rīt, ′ol-,\ *adv or adj* [ME, fr. OE *ealriht*] (14c): ALL RIGHT **usage** In now obsolete senses *all right* or *alright* was formed in Old English as *ealriht*. Variation in early scribal and printing practices and in spoken stress patterns has given us this and similar pairs in *all ready, already* and *all together, altogether*. Since the 19th century some have insisted that *alright* is wrong, but, though it is less frequent than *all right*, it remains in common use and appears in the work of reputable writers ⟨the first two years of medical school were *alright* —Gertrude Stein⟩ ⟨it is doing a bit of *alright* —P. H. Dougherty, *N.Y. Times*⟩

→ usage only; no definition given as this is not the "preferred" spelling.

By permission. From *Webster's Ninth New Collegiate Dictionary* © 1988 by Merriam-Webster, Inc., publisher of the Merriam-Webster ® dictionaries.

Compound expressions consist of two or more words combined to express one concept:

fire department

nationwide

hand-me-down

A compound expression might also consist of a prefix and a root word, such as *de-escalate.*

Please look up *fire department* and notice the space betwen *fire* and *department.* If you don't find an entry for a compound expression in a college dictionary, assume it's two separate words, such as *apple tree.* Now look up *nationwide.* The dot or accent mark between the syllables is how you know it's spelled as one solid word. When you look up *de-escalate* and *hand-me-down,* you see hyphens between the parts. Spell such words with hyphens, just as shown in your dictionary. Please look up *fire department, nationwide,* and *de-escalate* now, and notice the space, dot, and hyphen.

Plurals of nouns are also shown in the dictionary. If no plural is shown, form the plural by adding *-s* or *-es.*

Pronunciation

The pronunciation follows the entry word and is often found in italics—*slanted letters*—or enclosed in parentheses ( ) or diagonal lines \ \.

---

fu·ror (fyoo′rôr′, fyoor′ôr′; *also* fyoor′ər) *n.* [ME *furour* < OFr *fureur* < L *furor*, rage, madness < *furere:* see FURY] **1** fury; range; fenzy **2** *a)* a great, widespread outburst of admiration or enthusiasm; craze; rage *b)* a state of excitement or confusion; commotion or uproar. Also [Chiefly Brit.] **fu·ro|re** (fyoo̅ rō′rē, fyoo rôr′ē; fyoo′rôr′)

From the book, *Webster's New World Dictionary,* Third College Edition © 1988. Used by permission of the publisher, New World Dictionaries/A division of Simon & Schuster, New York, NY.

Special symbols called **diacritical marks** show how to pronounce the letters:

—   ··   ˘   ˆ

These symbols are interpreted in the pronunciation key at the bottom of each page or every other page of the dictionary.

---

at, āte, cär; ten, ēve; is, ice; gō, hôrn, look, to̅o̅l; oil, out; up, fur; ə *for unstressed vowels, as* a *in* ago, u *in* focus; ′ *as in* Latin (lat′'n); chin; she; zh *as in* azure (azh′ər); thin, *the;* ŋ *as in* ring (riŋ) *In etymologies:* * = unattested; < = derived from; > = from which ☆ = Americanism
        See inside front and back covers

From the book, *Webster's New World Dictionary,* Third College Edition © 1988. Used by permission of the publisher, New World Dictionaries/A division of Simon & Schuster, New York, NY.

Sometimes more than one pronunciation is given. This may mean the first is more common than the others. For business and professional communication, use the first, which is sometimes referred to as the preferred pronunciation.

Please open your dictionary now and use the **pronunciation key** at the bottom of the page to interpret the diacritical marks for pronouncing *apricot*.

---

apri•cot \'ap-rə-,kät, 'ā-prə-\ *n, often attrib* [alter. of earlier *abrecock*, deriv. of Ar *al-briqūq* the apricot] (1551) **1 a :** the oval orange-colored fruit of a temperate-zone tree (*Prunus armeniaca*) resembling the related peach and plum in flavor **b :** a tree that bears apricots **2 :** a variable color averaging a moderate orange

---

By permission. From *Webster's Ninth New Collegiate Dictionary* © 1988 by Merriam-Webster, Inc., publisher of the Merriam-Webster ® dictionaries.

---

a•pri•cot (ăp′rĭ-kŏt′, ā′prĭ-) *n.* **1.** a tree, *Prunus ameniaca*, native to western Asia and Africa, widely cultivated for its edible fruit. **2.** The juicy, yellow-orange peachlike fruit of the apricot. **3.** A moderate, light, or strong orange to strong orange yellow. [Alteration of earlier *abrecock* < Port. *albricoque* < Ar. *al-birqūq*, the apricot : *al*, the + LGk. *praikokion* < Lat. *praecoqquus*, ripe early (*prae-*, before + *coquere*, to ripen).]

Copyright © 1985 by Houghton Mifflin Company. Reprinted by permission from THE AMERICAN HERITAGE DICTIONARY, SECOND COLLEGE EDITION.

Accent marks also help you to know how to pronounce words. The relative degree of loudness with which syllables are spoken is shown by accent marks ('). The three degrees of loudness (or stress) are:

Weak—no accent mark

Strong—primary accent mark

Medium—secondary accent mark

A word with two or more syllables always has one *primary* accent, or stress, mark and may have one or more *secondary* accent marks. Please look up *chauvinism* in your dictionary.

Memo from the Wordsmith

The symbol ə (called a *schwa*) usually occurs in an unaccented syllable. Regardless of whether the vowel is actually *a, e, i, o,* or *u,* the schwa means that the vowel is pronounced something like "uh," as in the underlined vowels in these words: <u>a</u>go, c<u>o</u>mply.

primary and secondary
accent marks

chau·vin·ism (shō′və-nĭz′əm) *n.* **1.** Militant devotion to and glorifica-
tion of one's country; fanatical patriotism. **2.** Prejudiced belief in the
superiority of one's own group: *male chauvinism.* [Fr. *chauvinisme,*
after Nicholas *Chauvin,* a legendary French soldier.] **—chau′vin·ist** *n.*
—chau′vin·is′tic (-nĭs′tĭk) *adj.* **—chau′vin·is′ti·cal·ly** *adv.*

Copyright © 1985 by Houghton Mifflin Company. Reprinted by permission from *The American Heritage
Dictionary, Second College Edition.*

In the AHD, the darker accent mark indicates primary stress, and the
lighter one, secondary. Both appear *after* the syllable to be stressed.

chau·vin·ism \′shō-və-ˌniz-əm\ *n.* [F *chauvinisme,* fr. Nicolas *Chauvin,*
character noted for his excessive patriotism and devotion to Napoleon
in Théodore and Hippolyte Cogniard's play *La cocarde tricolore* (1831)]
(1870) **1 :** excessive or blind patriotism—compare JINGOISM

2 : undue partiality or attachment to a group or place to which one
belongs or has belonged **3 :** an attitude of superiority toward members of the opposite sex; *also :* behavior expressive of such an attitude
—chau·vin·ist \-və-nəst\ *n or adj* **—chau·vin·is·tic** \ˌshō-və-′nis-tik\
adj **—chau·vin·is·ti·cal·ly** \-ti-k(ə-)lē\ *adv*

By permission. From *Webster's Ninth New Collegiate Dictionary* © 1988 by Merriam-Webster, Inc., publisher
of the Merriam-Webster ® dictionaries.

In the WNCD, the raised accent mark shows primary stress and
the lowered one, secondary. They both appear *before* the syllable to be
stressed.

If you're using some other dictionary, interpret the code for showing
the syllables to be accented, or stressed. You'll find the explanation in the
front matter.

Recap   1. Look up the pronunciation of the following words and, with the help of
the pronunciation key at the bottom of the dictionary page, say them
aloud.

hors d'oeuvre   decadence   sadism   irreparable   nausea   coerce

2. Underline the schwa sounds in these words.

banana   collect   easily   gallop   circus

Match your answers for No. 2 in Appendix H.

Definitions

Both WNCD and *Webster's New World Dictionary of the American Language*
list the earliest definition of a word first and continue in more or less chron-

ological order. AHD and *Funk & Wagnall's* give the central meaning first. Look at these definitions for the verb *quiz:*

AHD   1. To question closely . . . 3. *Chiefly British.* To poke fun at; mock.

WNCD   1. to make fun of: mock . . . 3. to question closely.

As you can see, it's important to know the order of definitions in your dictionary. You'll find this information in the front matter.

Etymology

In WNCD the etymology (origin or historical development of the word) is in square brackets *before* the definitions. In the AHD the etymology appears *after* the definitions, also in square brackets: [   ]. Find the WNCD and AHD etymologies in the entries for **theater** and **preppie** on pages 66 and 67. Now look up *sandwich* in your dictionary. Notice *where* the etymology appears, and read the etymology of this interesting word.

The etymology may give the languages a word was derived from, such as Middle English, French, Latin, and so on; or it may tell how the word originated or came into use—as in the case of the word *sandwich*. When the languages of origin are given, they are abbreviated; for example, *OE* (Old English), *ME* (Middle English), *L* (Latin), and *F* or *Fr* (French). The abbreviation *f.* or the symbol > may be used to mean "from" or "derived from."

Replay Unit
16

Answer the following questions with the help of your dictionary. Use your own dictionary so that you'll become accustomed to its code.

EXAMPLE

Use your dictionary to look up the word *smog*. Write the etymology in the blank. ꜱᴍ(oke) + (f)ᴏɢ (This etymology is from *Webster's New World*. The form of the etymology in your dictionary may be slightly different but it will mean the same.)

Please look up the word *leotard* in your dictionary and answer these questions.

Word to the Wise

When looking up a meaning, be alert to the etymology so that you don't mistake it for a definition.

1. How many syllables does it have? _____

2. Which syllable has the primary accent? _____ (1st, 2nd, 3rd)

3. Which syllable has the secondary accent? _____ (1st, 2nd, 3rd)

4. Which syllable has no accent? _____ (1st, 2nd, 3rd)

5. What is the etymology of this word? _____

   _____

6. Which syllable has the secondary accent in *biographical?* _____
   (1st, 2nd, 3rd, 4th, 5th)

7. According to the pronunciation key at the bottom of the page in
   your dictionary, the first *e* in *wrecker* is pronounced the same as

   the *e* in what word? _____

8. *Disinterested* and *uninterested* mean the same.

   True _____ False _____ Maybe _____

9. Circle the correct form for t-i-c-k-e-r-t-a-p-e.
   tickertape   ticker-tape   ticker tape   any of these
   none of these

10. Which spelling would you choose for business and professional

    writing, *cooperate* or *co-operate?* _____

11. Does *catalog* have more than one correct spelling? _____

12. Circle the correct spelling of *antitrust.* antitrust   anti trust
    anti-trust   any of these   none of these

13. When using the preferred pronunciation, which syllable should

    have the primary stress in *affluent?* _____ (1st, 2nd, 3rd)

14. How do you say *entrepreneur* and what does it mean? _____

    _____

15. What words in the pronunciation key of your dictionary illustrate

    the sound of the schwa (ə)? _____ _____

    _____ _____ _____ _____

Please check your answers in Appendix H.

Read Unit

17   ***THE TRANSLATION***

In Unit 16 you decoded dictionary information. Continue to use the dictionary as you study this unit. Look up each entry word that is given as an example; translate the symbols and abbreviations into information meaningful to you.

Syllables

To determine the syllables, look at the centered dots or hyphens in the entry word. Some dictionaries use accent marks instead of dots.

Syllable marks show where a hyphen belongs if a word is to be completed on the next line in books, newspapers, and other printed matter. However, word-division custom for typing or keyboarding business communications is based not only on the entry-word syllables but also on the rules in Unit 63 and the "Word Division" section in Appendix F. Sometimes the syllables shown in the pronunciation differ from the syllables appearing in the entry word, but the entry word is the guide for word division.

Please look up *multiplication* and observe the system for showing syllables in your dictionary. Now look up *full-fashioned;* notice that the hyphen divides the first and second syllables and the centered dot divides the second and third. While you're in the *F* section, turn to *furious;* the entry word syllables differ from the pronunciation syllables in most dictionaries.

Parts of Speech

Abbreviations show the usual parts of speech for a word. The names of the parts of speech studied in Section One are used, except that verbs are shown in two categories—transitive and intransitive. These are abbreviated in several ways, depending on the dictionary; for example *vi* and *vt* or *tr.v* and *int.v.*

When a word is used as more than one part of speech, separate definitions are given for each. Study the entry for *brown* in your dictionary. Look it up right now and notice the abbreviations your dictionary uses for the parts of speech. Observe that *brown* is defined as a noun, an adjective, and a verb (both transitive and intransitive) and that other words using *brown* as a root (the central meaning of a word) are shown also.

Usage or Style Labels

A usage or style label is a notation of a special way a word is used. Words, definitions, and spellings are labeled in a number of ways; the system varies with the dictionary. Most words, however, do not have labels because they are standard English and have no particular special usages.

A word labeled *archaic* (or *arch.*) is used only in special contexts, although it was appropriate for general use in the past. Picture a store named Ye Olde Sweete Shoppe. This name consists of the archaic word "ye" and three archaic spellings.

A word labeled *obsolete* (or *obs.*) is no longer used except historically, and a word labeled *rare* is rarely used. Other examples are subject labels such as *chemistry, biology, medicine;* regional labels such as *British, Scottish, Southwest, Canadian;* and style labels such as *slang, colloquial, substandard, nonstandard, illiterate, dialect, obscene, offensive, vulgar, poetic, informal.* The labels are usually abbreviated.

In AHD the system is explained in the front matter under the heading "Labels" in the section called "Guide to the Dictionary." In WNCD, explanations about labeling are under the heading "Usage" in the front matter section called "Explanatory Notes." In *Webster's New World Dictionary,* the explanation is in the section called "Usage Labels and Notes" in "Guide to the Dictionary."

Recap

1. Look up *ain't* in three different dictionaries. What labels do you find? _____

Although the labeling systems and usage explanations differ, *ain't* is inappropriate in business situations unless the purpose is clearly to emphasize something jokingly.

2. Look up the verb *yak*. What usage label does it have? _____

Check your answers in Appendix H.

Other Information

Read the table of contents and scan the front matter and appendix to see the other categories of information available. Then look for the following in your dictionary:

Symbols used in various sciences and math are in the appendix section called "Signs and Symbols" in WNCD and in *Webster's New World Dictionary*. However, in AHD, symbols are in the regular alphabetic listing under the word *symbols*.

Abbreviations such as *i.e.*, *lb*, and *hr.* are in the regular alphabetic listing of *Webster's New World Dictionary* and AHD. However, they are in a special appendix section of WNCD. Explanations of abbreviations that are part of the dictionary code are usually in the front matter.

Miscellaneous information such as Morse Code, money (or currency) equivalents for various countries, proofreaders' marks, Roman numerals, weights and measures, the metric system, chemical elements, musical notes, and punctuation and grammar rules are other features you might find either within the alphabetic listing or in the appendix.

Geographical Names and **Biographical Dictionary** are in the back of WNCD and AHD. They are, however, in the regular alphabetic listing of *Webster's New World*.

Synonyms sometimes follow definitions. Synonyms are words with similar meanings. Sometimes synonyms are inaccurately defined as words that mean the same; no two words have exactly the same meaning. When synonyms are provided, they help in understanding the definitions and in finding a word with the exact shade of meaning desired. When there is no special synonym listing, you can often locate a synonym by reading the definition.

Writing for Your Career

Use a thesaurus for additional synonyms and for other related words. **Antonyms** are words with opposite meanings—such as *huge/tiny*—and are also easy to locate in a thesaurus.

Foreign words and phrases used in American communication are in the general alphabetic list. The appendix of WNCD, however, has a supplementary list of foreign expressions not often used in American English.

Here's an opportunity to reinforce the dictionary habit. Use your dictionary to answer these questions. What is important on this page is not the information but your ability to find it. Even if you already know the answer, look it up anyway.

EXAMPLE

Is *s m a l l p o x* written with a hyphen between *small* and *pox*, a space between these parts, or as one solid word? ___one solid word___

1. Give a synonym and the part of speech for each word:

   talkative _____

   evident _____

   vacillate _____

2. Divide these words into pronunciation syllables and mark them for stress; use the accent-mark system of your own dictionary.

   subtlety _____ rationale _____

   thundershower _____ wilderness _____

3. The word *January* is derived from the name of the ancient Roman god of gates and doorways. What was his name?

   _____

4. What does *faux pas* mean? How is it pronounced? _____

   _____

5. Where is Victoria College? _____

6. What do these proofreaders' marks mean? # _____

   tr _____ stet _____

Word to the Wise

Inside the front cover of AHD is a key to locating the special reference materials. In WNCD an index on the last page is a useful guide to finding the various sections. Both dictionaries have a table of contents as well. Look for a table of contents and/or an index in your dictionary.

7. What is the capital of Kentucky? _____

8. What page in your dictionary provides information for writing the number 137 in Roman numerals? _____ Write 137 in Roman numerals. _____

9. How old was Mozart at his death? _____

10. What is the basic unit of money (or currency) in Kenya?

    _____

11. What does the abbreviation OPEC stand for? _____

12. Show the preferred pronunciation for _hospitable._ _____

13. Illiterate expressions, vulgarities, and slang are not found in the better dictionaries. True _____ False _____

14. What usage label, if any, does your dictionary show for these words: irregardless _____ nerd _____

    anyways _____ critter _____

15. What does _colloquial_ mean? _____

    _____

Check answers in Appendix H.

Read Unit

_18_ MISSPELLERS ANONYMOUS

If you've ever wished to be a member of Misspellers Anonymous, here's your chance to improve your spelling and remain anonymous; no one has to know about that "spelleton" in your closet.

Believe you can spell well.

Good spelling takes no special talent. _Most important_ is to want to be a good speller and to believe you can. _What you can believe, you can achieve._

Don't put all your faith in a spelling checker.

An electronic spelling checker is helpful to poor spellers, but it doesn't re-place the computer between your ears for checking spelling and proofread-ing. For example, if you substitute _lead_ for _led, sing_ for _sign,_ or _wired_ for _weird,_ the mistake must be highlighted by your brain, not by your Apple or IBM.

Notice words in books and newspapers.

For overall spelling improvement, consciously look at words you're reading for about five minutes a day. That is, instead of reading quickly for content,

Memo from the Wordsmith

The ancient Greeks considered a certain type of purple stone to be a remedy for drunkenness. They called the stone *amethystos* (*a* = "not" and *methyein* = "to be drunk"). We call this stone the *amythyst*.

The word for the bluish-green mineral *turquoise* literally means "Turkish" in French and has this name because it was first found in Turkey.

spend just five minutes of your reading time looking at the appearance of words in the newspaper or whatever book or magazine you're reading. That's all it takes to store a tremendous number of words in the magnificent personal computer between your ears.

Relax and trust your first impulse.

To retrieve a word from your "computer," relax and write what you think of first. If spelling has been a problem for you, you probably remember a spelling test when you erased and replaced the correctly spelled word with an error. In other words, your first hunch is usually right.

When in doubt and you can use a dictionary, do.

If you often use your dictionary for spelling, it probably means you're a good speller; remember, no one knows your secret. The reader just sees the page with correctly spelled words.

Use memory devices for your personal hard-to-spell words.

If a particular word has been troublesome, try to develop a memory device. Here are 15 commonly misspelled words, each with a memory device to correct the part that gives the trouble. Just stare at the word and the memory device; then say the word and the memory device aloud three or four times; you'll know the correct spelling for life.

accommodate   2 *c*'s, 2 *m*'s; a *co*at *c*loset in a *mo*dern *mo*tel

recommend   *re* + *commend*

privilege   has a *leg* in it

bachelor   has an *ache* because he's sad not to be married

superintendent   he fixed the *dent*

conscience   *science* is in it

pursue   *pur*sue the *purse* snatcher

pronunciation   a Catholic word because it has a *nun*

persistent   your *sister* has a *tent*

congratulate   *rat* is in the middle

dilemma   *Emma* has a dil*emma*

embarrassed   railroad (RR) and steamship (SS)

Word to the Wise

A positive attitude toward spelling and frequent use of a dictionary are the two most important ways to improve spelling.

> **villain**   the villain lives in a *villa*
> **separate**   *Pa* is in the middle
> **weird**   *we* are *we*ird

The sillier the memory device, the more effective it will be.

"Blow up" hard-to-remember words.

If you don't readily think of a memory device for a particular word you want to remember, here's another way to master the spelling of it for life. On a sheet of notebook paper, print the word across the page in normal size, but "blow up" the troublesome letter or letters—that is, print them in huge letters. Then stare at the word for about 15 seconds. Repeat the staring procedure each day for three days, and you'll never again forget that word.

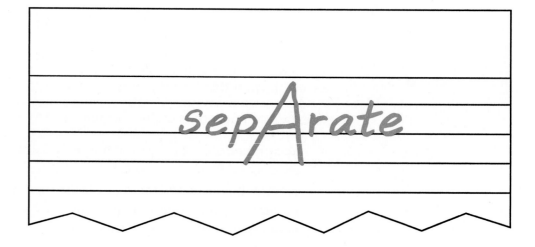

Get a spelling dictionary.

Keep handy one of the spelling dictionaries I told you about on page 60.
    Although spelling ability is not related to intelligence, most people tend to view the inaccurate speller as uneducated, careless, or generally incompetent. Therefore, accurate spelling (and proofreading) are extremely important to success in most careers.

Writing for Your Career

What can you do if you can't find a word in the dictionary because you have no idea of how to spell it?

1. Try several possible letters that may fit in the questionable part of the word; look through a couple of pages of your dictionary trying to find it.

2. If you're using WNCD, see pages 37–39 for "English Spelling and Sound Correspondences." The equivalent section of AHD, "Sound-Spelling Correspondences," is on pages 44–46. The appendix of *Webster's New World Dictionary*, Compact School and Office Edition, has a section called "Spellings of English Sounds: Finding a word you don't know how to spell."

3. Look the word up in the *Misspeller's Dictionary* published by Random House. If that doesn't work, go to step 4.

4. Telephone a friend and ask for help. If your friend isn't in, then . . .

5. Think of another word to use instead and get back to work.

To increase the number of commonly used business words you spell confidently, use the 3, 2, 1 Plan explained in "Spelling for Careers" in Appendix B. Your spelling and dictionary usage will also improve as you complete the rest of this course.

Replay Unit 18

A. Write *T* or *F* in the blank.

EXAMPLE

___T___ "Privilege has a leg in it" is an example of a spelling memory device.

_____ 1. To be a good speller requires a special talent.

_____ 2. Almost anyone who wants to be a good speller can be a good speller.

_____ 3. Poor spellers are always looking up words in the dictionary.

_____ 4. One can improve spelling while reading.

_____ 5. Most people tend to assume that an inaccurate speller is uneducated and incompetent.

_____ 6. A highly intelligent person will just naturally be a good speller.

_____ **7.** A list of words frequently seen in business writing is in Appendix B of this book and may be used for spelling improvement.

_____ **8.** A spelling dictionary doesn't include definitions.

_____ **9.** One way to memorize the spelling of a word is to print it and exaggerate the size of the problem letter(s).

_____**10.** Another way is to use a silly memory device.

B. Please fill in the missing letters. Then rewrite the word twice in the blank if it is a problem word for you. Use large printing for the troublesome letters.

1. sep__rate _____

2. w____rd _____

3. re_____end _____

4. ac_____date _____

5. priv_____ _____

6. bach____or _____

7. superintend__nt _____

8. persist__nt _____

9. dil_____a _____

10. vil_____n _____

11. con_____s _____

12. p__rsue _____

13. congra__ulate _____

14. pron__nciation _____

15. emba_____ed _____

C. Here are common misspellings for additional words frequently used in business. Write the correct spelling in the blank at least once. Use the dictionary when in doubt.

1. WRONG: accidently   RIGHT: _____

2. WRONG: existance   RIGHT: _____

3. WRONG: deductable   RIGHT: _____

4. WRONG: fullfilled   RIGHT: _____

5. WRONG: heighth   RIGHT: _____

6. WRONG: irrevelant   RIGHT: _____

7. WRONG: occassion   RIGHT: _____

8. WRONG: occured   RIGHT: _____

9. WRONG: personel (staff) RIGHT: _____

10. WRONG: rediculous   RIGHT: _____

See Appendix H for correct answers.
Now take the **POP QUIZ** in Appendix A.

Memo from the Wordsmith

Curfew was derived from an old French word *covrefeu,* which meant "cover fire," the fixed hour when the peasants of the Middle Ages were required to extinguish their fires.

Sadist is the word derived from the name of an 18th-century French nobleman, the Marquis de Sade. He delighted in describing to his friends cruel treatment of women.

Checkpoint

In this section you've been familiarizing yourself with the *many* kinds of information available in a comprehensive desk or college dictionary. By exploring the front matter and appendixes of the particular dictionary you use, you've become aware of what a versatile reference book you have right on your desk; it can often save you a trip to the library. By studying the explanatory notes, you can decipher dictionary code and interpret the information provided in the entries.

Just because a word is heard on television or is used in print in a particular way doesn't mean it's correct. In fact, just because a word is in a dictionary doesn't mean that the writers of that dictionary approve of the word. Dictionaries describe how people are using the language. Language style books and textbooks such as this provide further information on what is considered good English usage.

Our changing society causes not only the rapid accumulation of new words but also the loss of outmoded words. All this happens so fast that our dictionaries cannot really keep up to date. Although *automobile* is still used, *car* is now the word in general use. What used to be called a "gear shift" is now a "stick shift." Jack Smith, a columnist for the *Los Angeles Times,* wrote, "[Old words] hang in the dictionary like dead leaves on a tree; nobody bothers to blow them away. In time they simply fall, unheard, unseen, unmourned."

Place a check in the blank when you are confident you can interpret the symbols or abbreviations in your own dictionary for the following:

_____ Spelling and variations

_____ Pronunciation

_____ Syllables

_____ Parts of speech

_____ Labels: subject, style, regional

_____ Etymology

Write a check in the blank—

_____ When you know the order in which definitions are listed in your own dictionary.

_____ After you read the table of contents and scan the front matter and appendixes of your own dictionary.

Special Assignment

To the Student of Apothegms:

What? You don't know who, why, or where apothegms are? Neither did I until I looked in my dictionary for a synonym for the common word *proverb.* Short, witty, and instructive sayings are remembered much better than long-winded ones. Use your dictionary and your childhood memories to fill in the blanks with the simple words you remember. If you get stuck, ask your family and friends to join you in some fun with words.

EXAMPLE

Repetition of an erroneous act will not constitute that which is morally good, equitable, and fitting.

   Two wrongs don't make a right

1. Precipitance effectuates thoughtless, careless expenditure.

2. A beheld vessel never exceeds 100 C.

3. Pulchritude does not penetrate below the dermal plane.

4. A plenitude of gourmand-satiating scullions tend to obviate, obstruct, undermine, decompose, and otherwise boggle the mulligatawny.

5. From deliberative investigation it has come to our attention that the anticipatory aviatorial member of the phylum Chordata will invariably apprehend the member of the slender soft-bodied bilateral invertebrates.

6. It is fruitless to become lacrymous because of scattered lacteal fluid.

7. The inner surface of every visible mass of vapor in the upper atmosphere is covered with a precious metallic chemical element that is very ductile and malleable.

8. Using any other appellation to refer to a specimen from the floriferous shrub of the family *Rosaceae* would not render the perception of it by means of the olfactory nerves to be any less saccharine.

9. Precipitately abandon the celibate condition and experience remorse and self-reproach during the period of freedom provided by the cessation of activities.

Proofreading for Careers

The letter that follows was a response to a complaint letter. Please proofread it carefully because I planted 16 spelling errors; they were not in the original. Read one word at a time. Circle the errors first; then write corrections in the blanks below. Use your dictionary,

---

Dear Ms. Kaye:

Your July 1 letter was recieved, and we appreciate your bringing this experence to our attension. I've asked our Marketing Department to look into the matter.

We are grately conserned about the customer relasions of our dealers. Even through they are independant owners who operate stations least from us, they are, in many instanses, Barko's only contact with the public.

We certinly expect our dealars to respond apropriately to any compliant. As soon as we've reveiwed all the facts in this situation, we'll be in touch with you again.

Very truely yours,

Write the correct spellings below.

Paragraph 1

_____ _____ _____

Paragraph 2

_____ _____ _____

_____ _____ _____

_____

Paragraph 3 and complimentary close

_____ _____ _____

_____ _____ _____

Proofreading score is: Excellent_____ Good_____ Fair_____ Ugh_____

Practice Quiz

Take the Practice Quiz as though it were a real test. Don't look back through Section Three while you take this Practice Quiz. After the quiz is corrected, refer to the appropriate Read Units, shown in parentheses, for explanations of any item you may have missed.

A. Use your dictionary to answer these questions. Read all possible answers for each item. Then write the letter of the best choice in the blank.

_____ 1. The verb *record* should be pronounced with the stress on the: **(Units 16 and 17)**
    a. 1st syllable   **d.** secondary accent
    b. 2nd syllable   **e.** primary accent
    c. 1st or 2nd syllable

_____ 2. Which spelling (or spellings) is preferred?   **(Unit 16)**
    a. *lovable*   **c.** neither *lovable* nor *loveable*
    b. *loveable*   **d.** both *lovable* and *loveable*

_____ 3. *Wall* is what part of speech?   **(Unit 17)**
    a. noun   **d.** noun and verb
    b. verb, adverb   **e.** noun, verb, and adverb
    c. adjective

_____ 4. Martin Van Buren died in: **(Unit 17)**
    a. 1782   **d.** 1841
    b. 1862   **e.** the arms of his paramour
    c. 1837

_____ 5. The word *thee* is: **(Unit 17)**
    a. archaic   **d.** colloquial
    b. obsolete   **e.** slang
    c. British

_____ 6. The astronomy symbol (●) stands for: **(Unit 17)**
    a. sun   **d.** new moon
    b. star   **e.** asterisk
    c. Mars

_____ 7. The Roman numeral XC is the same as which Arabic numeral?   **(Unit 17)**
    a. 100   **d.** 90
    b. 110   **e.** none of these
    c. 60

_____ 8. We may describe a book not having a hard cover as: **(Unit 16)**
    a. soft bound   **c.** softbound
    b. soft-bound   **d.** all three are correct

_____ 9. What does the French phrase *raison d'etre* mean?   **(Unit 17)**
    a. increase in wages   **c.** raisin pudding
    b. the same as the Latin *racemus*   **d.** reason or justification for existing

_____ 10. Guide words appear: **(Unit 15)**
    a. at the bottom of every page   **d.** only in unabridged dictionaries
    b. at the bottom of every page or alternate pages   **e.** in the front matter or appendix
    c. at the top of every page

_____ 11. A short horizontal line (-) over a vowel is a: **(Unit 16)**
    a. secondary stress mark   **d.** short-sounded vowel
    b. primary accent mark   **e.** diacritical mark
    c. syllable indicator

_____ 12. *Etymology* means a word's: **(Unit 15)**
    a. part of speech   **d.** secondary stress
    b. history   **e.** usage label
    c. synonyms and antonyms

_____ 13. You look up a word in a college dictionary and don't find a usage **(Unit 17)**
    label. Therefore:
    a. You're using an   **d.** The word is standard English;
        inadequate dictionary.   there's no special restriction
    b. The word is colloquial.   for its use.
    c. You should look it up in   **e.** You should refer to the front
        an unabridged dictionary.   matter to be sure you're
                                   interpreting the code correctly.

_____ 14. *Twinkling* is correctly divided into syllables (for word division) in which **(Unit 17)**
    of the following ways?
    a. *twin kling*   **d.** *twi nkling*
    b. *twink ling*   **e.** *twi nkl ing*
    c. *twinkl ing*

_____ 15. *Miniature* and *huge* are: **(Unit 17)**
    a. synonyms   **d.** colloquials
    b. homonyms   **e.** antonyms
    c. diacriticals

_____ 16. What is the capital of Sweden? **(Unit 17)**
    a. Swedenborg   **d.** Scandinavia
    b. Stocklohm   **e.** Oslo
    c. Stockholm

_____ 17. Which word is incorrectly spelled? **(Unit 18)**
    a. occured   **d.** recommend
    b. accommodate   **e.** dilemma
    c. weird

B. Write *T* or *F* in the blank.

_____ 18. Biographical entries are found in the appendix of all good dictionaries. **(Unit 17)**

_____ 19. A dictionary containing 350,000 or more entries is an unabridged dictionary. **(Unit 15)**

_____ 20. Just as the dollar is the unit of exchange in the United States, **(Unit 17)**
    the pound is the Israeli unit of exchange.

_____ 21. *Superintendant* is correctly spelled. **(Unit 18)**

_____ 22. The word in the preceding item has five syllables. **(Unit 17)**

_____ 23. You would avoid using the adjective *wight* in a business letter because **(Unit 17)**
    it is slang.

_____ 24. The usual sign of a poor speller is frequent use of the dictionary. **(Unit 18)**

_____ 25. The abbreviation GOP means "Grand Old Party." **(Unit 17)**

NOTES

Apples, Tigers, and Swahili

4

✔ Apply standard English principles to
  —forming plurals of regular and irregular nouns
  —writing compound nouns
  —capitalizing nouns
✔ Know the meaning of the words presented in this section and spell them correctly.
✔ Avoid using biased nouns.

Woman ○○○ Women
Man ○○○ Men
Horse ○○○ Horses

*N*ouns name people, animals, places, things, ideas, and actions. When you think about exotic faraway places or your hometown . . . movie stars, kings, and the person next door . . . life, health, peace, success . . . Monopoly®, jogging, and homework . . . apples, Apples, Swahili, or a tiger—you are thinking **nouns.** Look around and you'll see nouns.

Reading, listening, and general experience enable you to use a great many nouns correctly. The study of a few simple rules plus intelligent use of the dictionary means you can be sure **all** nouns in your business communications are correct.

Sometimes a noun error is simply using the wrong word because of inadequate vocabulary, carelessness, or poor spelling—such as the real noun bloopers that follow:

Starlings ate the farmer's grain and spoiled his corpse.

The ship was bound for Nausea in the Bahamas.

My sister writes in her dairy every night.

When we went to Canada, we had to pass through costumes.

Other types of noun errors occur because English has so many irregular forms—or exceptions. These exceptions are especially confusing to people learning English—young children and those who speak some other native language.

THE MOTHER TONGUE

English, they say is the language most used,
Most spoken, most written, most cruelly abused.
The plural of box we all know is boxes,
Yet the plural of ox is oxen, not oxes.*
A goose is a goose, but two are called geese,
But why isn't more than one mouse quoted meese?
A mouse and his family are mentioned as mice,
But the plural of house is houses, not hice.
The plural of brother is brothers or brethren,
And yet we say mothers, but never say methren.
You can readily double a foot and have feet,
But try as you might, you can't make root reet.
If the singular's this and the plural, these,
Should the plural of kiss ever be keese?

Some exceptions, however, are not so obvious, even to people who have used English all their lives; those difficult-to-spot irregularities are the ones we'll review in this section. You'll develop two important abilities as you work through Section Four:

- Spotting troublesome irregular nouns.
- Interpreting dictionary symbols that enable you to use those nouns correctly.

* Now acceptable—but not preferred.

You'll remember much of what you look up in the dictionary. Without even trying, you will automatically learn correct forms of troublesome irregulars and improve your spelling and vocabulary.

Read Unit

19

SAFETY IN NUMBERS

A singular noun means just one of whatever person, place, or thing the noun names; a plural noun means more than one. Spelling most plural nouns is easy. We usually just add *-s* to the singular noun to make it plural; for example, *one check* but *three check**s***. When the singular noun ends with *s, z, x, ch,* or *sh,* we add *-es* to spell the plural; for example, *one box* but *three box**es**.**

As you know, however, nearly all English rules have exceptions. Therefore, to be safe when spelling plurals, develop the knack of recognizing nouns that might be exceptions. This unit includes three types of irregular nouns to spot when writing, so that you can verify the plural spelling:

- nouns ending in *y*
- nouns ending in *o*
- nouns ending in *f*

Nouns Ending in *Y:* Is It *-YS* or *-IES?*

When a vowel (*a, e, i, o, u*) comes before the *y,* simply add *s* to form the plural.

vall**ey**, vall**eys**   attorn**ey**, attorn**eys**   turk**ey**, turk**eys**

When a consonant (all letters other than vowels) precedes the *y,* change the *y* to *i* and add *-es*:

indust**ry**, indust**ries**   compan**y**, compan**ies**   hobb**y**, hobb**ies**

Remember, plurals of nouns ending in *y* are often misspelled. Then, if you forget the preceding rules, you will remember to refer to your dictionary.

Nouns Ending in *O:* Is It *-OS* or *-OES?*

For nouns ending in *o* relating to music, add just an *-s* to form the plural.

banjo, banjo**s**   solo, solo**s**

* All proper nouns form the plural by adding *-s* or *-es*—no exceptions. (Proper nouns are nouns that start with a capital letter even when they're not the first word in a sentence.)

Word to the Wise

When looking in the dictionary for the plural of a noun ending with *o*, you'll sometimes find two spellings. This means both are correct, but it's better to use the one appearing first.

For nouns ending in *o* preceded by a vowel, add just an *-s* to form the plural.

    stud**io**, stud**ios**   rod**eo**, rod**eos**   rad**io**, rad**ios**

If a noun that ends in *o* does not relate to music and is preceded by a consonant, look it up to find out whether to add *-s* or *-es* for the plural or whether it's correct both ways.

    silo, silo**s**   tomato, tomato**es**

    domino, domino**s**, domino**es** [both plurals are correct]

Nouns Ending in the Sound of *F*: Is It *-FS*, *-FES*, or *-VES*?

No useful rules determine whether to spell the plural of nouns ending in the sound of *f*. Some simply add *-s*:

    chief, chief**s**   rebuff, rebuff**s**   giraffe, giraffe**s**

Others change the *-f* to *v* and add *-es*:

    wife, wi**ves**   wolf, wol**ves**   leaf, lea**ves**

Just remember to use the dictionary when in doubt about the plural of a noun ending in *f* or *fe*.

Apostrophes? No!

In general, apostrophes do not make a noun plural.

The occasional exceptions are in Read Unit 48 of Section 8, which is all about apostrophes. Most nouns become plural by adding *-s*, not by adding *'s*.

Recap   Fix any errors in plurals in the following paragraph by crossing out what is incorrect and writing the correct version above the error. Use your dictionary to look up any plurals you're not sure about.

A recent change in the American diet pleases nutritionist's, but not turkies. Carving knifes used to threaten turkey's only two daies a year: Thanksgiving and Christmas. In recent years', however, cheves across America have served roast turkey and mashed potato's every day. In countless kitchens', cooks have turned ground turkey into meat loafs and turkey burgeres.

See answers in Appendix H.

Replay Unit

19

Place your dictionary beside you right now! This is not a spelling test. It is a test of your alertness to words that sometimes present spelling problems and of your ability to use the dictionary efficiently. If in doubt about the spelling of any of these words, **use your dictionary.**

A. Spell the plurals of these nouns.

EXAMPLE

attorney _____ attorneys _____

1. ally _____

2. alley _____

3. itinerary _____

4. proxy _____

5. facility _____

6. copy _____

7. journey _____

8. authority _____

9. accessory _____

10. survey _____

B. Spell the plurals of these nouns. If there are two correct ways to spell the word, write both in the blank.

EXAMPLE

domino _____ dominoes, dominos _____

1. soprano _____

2. dynamo _____

3. embargo _____

4. piano _____

5. hero _____

6. ego _____

7. potato _____

8. cargo _____

9. portfolio _____

10. memento _____

C. Spell the plurals of these nouns.

EXAMPLE

rebuff _____ rebuffs _____

1. thief _____

6. half _____

    2. handkerchief _____   **7.** safe _____

    3. knife _____   **8.** wolf _____

    4. tariff _____   **9.** plaintiff _____

    5. calf _____   **10.** self _____

D. Correct the plural errors in this paragraph.

EXAMPLE

Globetrotter✂s

    The Globetrotter's are organized into a National and an International team. During a recent tour of the United State's and Canada, they played before more than 1,400,000 fan's in 263 game's. They continue to amuse and delight audience's with a combination of incredible ballhandling, seemingly impossible shooting, and classic comedy routine's. METRO-MEDIA, INC.

Answers to part D are in Appendix H. To find out how well you did on parts A–C, check your spelling of each plural with the dictionary.

Read Unit

20 PLURALS OUT OF UNIFORM

Plurals that don't require adding -s are a little like soldiers out of uniform: you can't recognize their occupation by their appearance, although their behavior might reveal military training. When a noun doesn't need an -s to make it plural, it seems to be out of uniform; but its "behavior" in the sentence reveals its plural status.

    Sometimes you recognize a plural without an -s uniform because you're familiar with the word. To form the plural of the following nouns, the spelling is changed; but since they are commonly used, you recognize them instantly:

Word to the Wise

A few dictionaries give the plural spelling for every noun that has a plural form. In most dictionaries, however, the plural spelling is not given if all that's needed is an -s—or -es for nouns ending in s, z, x, ch, and sh. This means if you don't find the plural spelling, the noun is spelled in the regular way; it is not an exception. In some cases, however, the plural is shown even when only an -s is called for—if the lexicographer believes a question might arise, such as for nouns ending with o.

SINGULAR	PLURAL
man	men
woman	women
mouse	mice
tooth	teeth
child	children
foot	feet

Other plurals that don't add *-s* may be more of a challenge because they are not seen as often as the words listed above. The nouns that follow, though taken from other languages, are now firmly a part of English. The plurals, however, conform to the spelling rules of the language of origin. Sometimes an English spelling has been adopted as well; then the writer or speaker has two plurals to choose from. In some cases, the English and original-language plurals have different usages.

Singular	Original-Language Plural	English Form	Usage Alerts
formula	formulae	formulas	*formulae* is used in scientific and technical writing
vertebra	vertebrae	vertebras	—
alumnus	alumni	—	—
stimulus	stimuli	—	—
analysis	analyses	—	—
diagnosis	diagnoses	—	—
criterion	criteria	criterions	(1) *criteria* is the preferred plural in English usage (2) a very common mistake is using *criteria* as the singular form—remember, one *criterion*, two *criteria*
medium	media	mediums	(1) *mediums* is always used when the meaning is "people who communicate with spirits" (2) *media* is the plural used for most other meanings of *medium.* (3) *media* is often used as both singular and plural for radio, TV, newspapers, etc., as means of communication
curriculum	curricula	curriculums	—
datum	data	—	*data* is acceptable as as both singular and plural
memorandum	memoranda	memorandums	—
addendum	addenda	—	—

Word to the Wise

Remember, when a plural is regular—formed by adding -s or -es—it will probably not be shown in your dictionary. (If you're not sure what your dictionary does about regular plurals, open it up right now to find out. Look in the section of the front matter that describes and explains entries.) Why is this so important? If you look up *crisis* and find next to it "*pl.* **-ses**," should you spell the plural *crisises* or *crises*? If your dictionary doesn't show regular -s and -es plurals, you can feel confident that "*pl.* **-ses**" means the plural is *crises*. (If your dictionary shows regular plurals, it will spell out *crises* for the plural of *crisis*.)

Careful communicators recognize nouns that might require some change other than adding -s to become plural. Many of these nouns end in *us, um, a,* or *is.* Yet some words that look as though their plurals might be irregular just add -s or -es; for example, the plural of *sinus* is *sinuses,* not *sini.* Develop an "instinct" for noticing words like those listed in this unit and refer to the dictionary when using them.

Replay Unit
20

A. With the help of your dictionary, spell the plurals of these words. If two plurals are correct, write them both in the blank.

EXAMPLE

memorandum _____ memoranda, memorandums _____

1. formula _____
2. addendum _____
3. alumnus _____
4. appendix _____
5. basis _____
6. bureau _____
7. census _____
8. criterion _____
9. datum _____
10. index _____
11. medium _____
12. goose _____
13. ox _____
14. parenthesis _____
15. diagnosis _____

Memo from the Wordsmith

- The word *school* was derived from the Greek word *skhole*, which means "leisure" or "spare time," since only the leisure classes could afford an education.
- The study of the origin of words is called etymology.

B. Write *S* or *P* in the blank to indicate whether these nouns are singular or plural.

EXAMPLE

nucleus _____ S _____

1. focus _____
2. stimulus _____
3. hypotheses _____
4. vertebra _____
5. oxen _____

6. alumna _____
7. criteria _____
8. crises _____
9. addenda _____
10. basis _____

C. After reading each sentence carefully, circle the correct form.

EXAMPLE

The (campi/campuses) are empty from Friday night to Monday morning.

1. TV, radio, and newspapers are the (media/mediums) we prefer for our advertisements.
2. She broke several (vertebra/vertebrae/vertebraes) in the accident.
3. How many (criterion/criterias/criteria) did they consider?
4. To type the closing (parentheses/parenthesis), shift on the zero.
5. Several (alumnus/alumni/alumna) attended the opening game.

Answers are in Appendix H.

Read Unit

21

THE ECCENTRIC S

An eccentric person or thing is odd or strange and doesn't follow an expected pattern. This unit deals with additional eccentricities of English plurals. Using them correctly will be easy when you've finished this unit.

In Unit 20 you reviewed words that are spelled differently in the plural form—such as *foot, feet.*

Here is a list of words spelled exactly the same whether they are singular or plural.

SINGULAR	PLURAL
deer	deer
sheep	sheep
series	series
statistics	statistics
aircraft	aircraft
salmon	salmon
fish	fish
corps	corps [See the dictionary for pronunciation]
Chinese	Chinese
British	British
Dutch	Dutch

Since you cannot tell by the *s* at the end of the word whether or not it is plural, you rely on other clues when you are reading.

Check some of the listed words in your dictionary; you'll find each word respelled following the abbreviation "pl." When a plural spelling is the same as the singular, the dictionary makes this clear. For some words in the list, the dictionary shows two correct plurals—either without an *-s* or with it: for example, *deer, deers.* In these cases, the first word is much more commonly seen and heard.

Some nouns that end in *s* are usually used in a singular sense. The verb form that goes with a singular noun is needed.

Here are some examples:

civics	economics	measles
ethics	news	mumps

Civics was [not *were*] studied by all the freshmen.

The **news is** [not *are*] all bad today.

Measles is [not *are*] a contagious disease.

Economics has [not *have*] been taught here since 1922.

Writing for Your Career

Provide clues for the reader. For example, the words *a, one, few,* or *several* might be used as clues before a noun spelled the same whether singular or plural.

A deer stopped at the pond. [*Deer* is singular.]

Several deer lunched on our yellow roses. [*Deer* is plural.]

A pointing word before the noun is a clue as to whether a noun is singular or plural. For these nouns that are always singular, pointing words must be singular too.

YES   I like **this news.**

NO   I like **these news.**

(Section Six gives a further explanation about verbs.)

> Some nouns that end in *s* are usually used in a plural sense. This means the verb form that agrees with a plural noun is used.

trousers
scissors
clothes
goods
proceeds
premises

NO   The **scissors was** lost.

YES   The **scissors were** lost.

NO   The **goods has** not yet been shipped.

YES   The **goods have** not yet been shipped.

> Plurals of proper nouns (ones beginning with capital letters) follow the rules for **regular** nouns.

That means to add -*s* to all proper nouns except those that end in *s, z, x, ch,* and *sh,* to which you add -*es.*

The spelling of a name should not be changed to form a plural even though it may end in *y, o,* or *f.* For example, if you were to apply the rule given in Unit 17 for plurals of nouns ending in *y* to the proper noun *Mary,* you would end up—incorrectly—with *Maries.* To form the plural of *wolf* you change the *f* to *v* and add -*es*—*wolves.* However, if you're referring to Mr. and Mrs. Wolf, you don't say "The Wolves are coming for dinner," but rather "The Wolfs. . . . "

> To make a proper noun plural, just add -*s* or -*es*; do not add an apostrophe.

When I sign my family name to a greeting card, it reads *The Smiths,* not *The Smith's.*

Here are some sentences with plural proper nouns. Notice that they do not have apostrophes:

> The **Wolfs** have a son who manages the San Diego plant. [Don't change *f* to *v.*]

There are two **Marys** in the Houston office. [Don't change *y* to *ie.*]

There are many **Smiths** in the telephone book.

The **Lopezes** are coming for dinner. [Because **Lopez** ends with *z,* add -*es* for the plural.]

Replay Unit

21

A. Write the plurals in the blanks. Use your dictionary when in doubt about the common nouns (those that don't begin with capital letters).

EXAMPLE

Perkins _____Perkinses_____

1. corps _____
2. politics _____
3. deer _____
4. Mary _____
5. series _____
6. Japanese _____

7. Fife _____
8. aircraft _____
9. fish _____
10. DeSoto _____
11. statistics _____
12. Ramirez _____

B. Write *S* or *P* in the blank to show whether the noun is usually used in a singular or plural sense. Use your dictionary.

EXAMPLE

premises _____P_____

1. trousers _____
2. economics _____
3. measles _____

4. clothes _____
5. news _____

C. The verb form in the left column is used with singular nouns; the verb form on the right, with plurals. Circle the appropriate verb in the sentence. The subject is in bold type. Use your dictionary as well as word clues to decide whether each noun subject (shown in bold type) requires a singular or a plural verb.

SINGULAR	PLURAL
is	are
was	were
has	have

EXAMPLE

The new **pants** (was/were) shortened.

1. The **trousers** (have/has) pockets.
2. **Statistics** (is/are) my favorite course.
3. These **statistics** (is/are) accurate.

4. The **goods** (was/were) shipped yesterday.
5. All **proceeds** from this show (are/is) being given to charity.
6. **Clothes** (is/are) all over the floor.
7. **Measles** (is/are) preventable.
8. Each day's **news** (was/were) carefully edited.
9. A new lecture **series** (have/has) been completed.
10. Several **series** (was/were) offered in a variety of fields.

Please check your answers in Appendix H.
Review Units 19–21 before taking the **POP QUIZ** in Appendix A.

Read Unit
22   *COMPOUNDS AND PROPERS*

Together, Split, or Separated?

A noun made up of more than one word is a **compound noun**—such as *high school*. Compound nouns are written in three ways: as one word, split with hyphens, or separate words:

ONE WORD	letterhead	checkbook
SPLIT WITH HYPHENS	tie-in	follow-up
SEPARATE WORDS	price tag	stock car

To be sure of writing a compound correctly, refer to the dictionary.

Develop the ability to recognize an expression that might be a compound noun. When you suspect that two or three words might be a compound, look at the entry word in the dictionary. Some compound expressions may be used as a noun, an adjective, or a verb. Be sure to look at the form for the part of speech required in your sentence.

If a dot or an accent mark appears between the parts, write the expression as one word. The dot or accent mark indicates syllables, not separation of words.

brick•layer [dictionary version]
bricklayer [write as one word]

If a space appears between the parts or if the expression cannot be found in a good desk dictionary, write each part as a separate word.

brick cheese

Use a hyphen only if the hyphen appears between the parts of the entry word.

bric-a-brac

(Other uses for hyphens are discussed in Section 10.)

Plurals of Compound Nouns

Plurals of compound nouns are written in several ways.

A compound noun written as one solid word usually adds *s* or *es* to the end of the word to form the plural.

bookshelves   spoonfuls   headlines

A compound noun spelled with a hyphen or with a space between the words usually makes the more (or most) important word of the compound plural.

brothers-in-law   write-offs   letters of credit

Since it's not easy to be sure which is the more important noun, I recommend consulting a dictionary.

If the dictionary shows two ways to form the plural, choose the first for business writing:

notaries public, notary publics [use *notaries public*]

A Guided Tour of the Capital

A noun that begins with a capital letter is called a proper noun. (Nouns that do not begin with capitals are common nouns.) A complete guide to capitalization is in the "Reference Manual" in Appendix F. In this unit you review only noun capitalization principles most often questioned by business writers.

Capitalize official titles only when used directly before the person's name.

Memo from the Wordsmith

COMPOUND SPORTS
When basketball, baseball, and football were first invented, they were written as separate words: basket ball, foot ball, and base ball. As each game became more popular, it became a hyphenated word: basket-ball, foot-ball, base-ball. Eventually all become the one-word compounds they are today. Many compound words that stay in general use or become more widely used do that in time—they progress from separate words to hyphenated compounds to one-word forms.

I think **P**resident Humphrey Bogart called the meeting to order.

Give the award to **C**olonel Alfred Adler.

A letter of recommendation was received from **S**ister Phyllis Taufeen.

BUT

Humphrey Bogart is the **p**resident of the company.

The **c**olonel, Alfred Adler, is a graduate of West Point. [No capital for colonel because a comma separates it from the name.]

Rachel Rothstein, a **p**rofessor of business, sent the letter.

Exceptions

Always capitalize titles of high-ranking government or church officials when the titles refer to a specific person and not just anyone of that rank.

The **P**ope is going to visit the United States this month.

Harry S. Truman was **P**resident at that time.

BUT

A **p**resident of the United States is also commander in chief of the armed forces.

Capitalize titles in addresses and signatures even when they appear after the name.

In address Mr. Ira Simon, **G**eneral **M**anager

In signature Carol Zaidow, **G**eneral **M**anager*

Words such as *company, college,* and *association* are usually capitalized only when used with the name of the organization.

Tully Plumbing **C**ompany is on Fifth Street.

BUT

The **c**ompany is on Fifth Street.

Capitalize the name of a department or a committee only when you are a member of the organization.

Make out a requisition and send it to **P**urchasing.

Make out a requisition and send it to the **P**urchasing **D**epartment.

BUT

He works in the **p**urchasing **d**epartment of our major competitor.

Capitalize the words *town, city, state, county,* and so on only when they follow the name.

New York **S**tate   New York **C**ity   Kansas **C**ity

* Avoid "honorifics"—*Mr., Ms., Dr., Mrs., Professor,* and the like—in signatures.

BUT

the **s**tate of California and the **c**ity of Portland

Capitalize definite geographic regions that have compass point names. Do not capitalize directions or general locations.

He lives in the **E**ast, but he talks like a **W**esterner.
Disneyland is **e**ast of Los Angeles and **n**orth of the **S**outh Pole.
The people are very friendly in **s**outhern Ohio.
Is mint julep still a popular drink in the **S**outh?
Migratory birds fly **s**outh every winter.

Usually use lower case letters for the names of seasons.*

The office will close for a one-week vacation this summer.

Always capitalize names of languages; do not capitalize the name of a course unless it is a language *or* the full official name of the course.

(Official course names are usually followed by a number.)

English	**S**panish	**S**wahili
French	**H**indi	**R**ussian

He is studying **b**usiness **E**nglish, **m**anagement, **a**ccounting, and **G**reek at Gonzaga University.
Next year he will take **B**usiness **L**aw 230.

Replay Unit
22

A. Refer to your dictionary for spelling these compound nouns. Show whether the expression is one solid word, a hyphenated word, or two or three separate words. Some dictionaries give more than one spelling for some of the plurals; if so, include both.

Example	SINGULAR	PLURAL
notary public	notary public	notaries public, notary publics

1. spoonful   _____   _____

2. textbook   _____   _____

3. postcard   _____   _____

4. editorinchief   _____   _____

5. stockholders   _____   _____

6. passerby   _____   _____

* Exceptions in Appendix F.

  7. businesswoman   _____   _____

  8. brotherinlaw   _____   _____

  9. outoftowner   _____   _____

10. billoflading   _____   _____

B. Read "Read About Capitalization" and do the Replay Exercise in the Reference Manual.

C. Write _C_ in the blanks below if the capitalization is correct. Otherwise make the necessary corrections.

EXAMPLE

If their $\overset{s}{\cancel{S}}$ales $\overset{m}{M}$anager calls, let me talk to her.

_____   **1.** Wade Boggs is the General Manager of Coronet Manufacturing Company.

_____   **2.** It's our policy to hire former professional athletes to work in the Sporting Goods Department.

_____   **3.** Who is the Manager of their Shipping Department?

_____   **4.** The association relies on its members to distribute the information.

_____   **5.** The secretary of state has just entered the White House.

_____   **6.** Do you think the Cardinal discussed the problem with the bishops and other catholic leaders?

_____   **7.** The typed signature at the end of the letter should appear like this: Dorothy Prevatt, office manager.

_____   **8.** I headed North last Spring, calling on every appliance dealer between here and Carson city.

_____   **9.** The City of Azusa, which is in the State of California, is named after everything from _A_ to _Z_ in the USA.

_____   **10.** The clerks in our Credit Department speak english and spanish.

_____   **11.** My Uncle has taught Business english at several Colleges.

_____   **12.** Until the 1950s there had been no Black or Jewish managers in that Company, and black and white factory workers used separate lunchrooms.

_____   **13.** We bought Hewlett-Packard computers for all our offices west of the Mississippi River.

_____   **14.** Governor Shawn A. Taylor joined his famous sisters, Christa and Ashley, at the Inauguration Ball.

_____   **15.** Christa Taylor won the academy award for her performance in _The Iron Magnolia_ and Ashley Taylor was awarded the nobel prize for her efforts on behalf of world peace.

The answers are in Appendix H.

Read Unit

23

BANISHING BIAS FROM BUSINESS ENGLISH

Business people know—or should know—that offending customers or clients is bad business. So is offending co-workers, for people don't work well together when they're angry. This unit will give you some simple advice about using language that will banish bias and bolster businesslike behavior.

> Don't talk about people's race, religion, nationality, age, physical characteristics, or disabilities unless you have a business reason for doing so. Don't identify people by such characteristics—use names or other neutral characteristics.

This rule doesn't really require much discussion. What you talk about outside business hours is—your own business. During business hours, however, if you don't talk about the topics listed above except for business reasons, you'll lower the risk of offending other people about things many of us take personally.

NO A black girl and a Puerto Rican boy earned 95 percent on the test, and the rest of the students scored below 80.

YES Two students earned 95 percent on the test, but all the others scored below 80.

NO You will like working with Harley. Despite being confined to a wheelchair, he is one of our most caring and capable counselors.

YES You will like working with Harley. He is one of our most caring and capable counselors.

> Prefer words that identify people by what they do.

Many words we all use without thinking define people by sex as well as by role. The following list points out some of the problem words and suggests alternatives for you to use:

AVOID	USE
authoress	author, writer
poetess	poet
directress	director
businessmen [as a general term]	business people, executives, managers, entrepreneurs
cameraman	photographer
stewardess	flight attendant

career girl, career woman	*Name the occupation; have you ever heard of a career boy?*
male nurse	nurse
male secretary	secretary
woman manager	manager
lady lawyer, woman doctor, *etc.*	lawyer, doctor
man and wife	man and woman *or* husband and wife
men and girls	men and women *or* boys and girls
managers and their wives	managers and their spouses
clergymen	clergy
mailman	mail carrier
fireman	firefighter
policeman	police officer
manmade	synthetic, artificial, manufactured
manpower, workmen	workers, work force, human resources, staff, crew, laborers
woman, man	person [unless gender matters]

Waitress and *actress* have been in use for a long time and still seem to be generally acceptable, although some restaurants use the terms *server* or *waitperson. Chairman* is also acceptable, but *head, chair, leader, moderator,* and *chairperson* are riskfree alternatives.

Use *woman/women* and *man/men* to refer to adults.

NO The gals [or girls or ladies] in my office work faster than the men.

YES The women in my office work faster than the men.

Memo from the Wordsmith

Detail man is a term created in the 1920s for a salesperson who introduces new products to pharmacists and doctors. Today either a man or a woman may have this job and is now called a *detailer.*
Etymology: The Old French word *detaillier* meant "to cut in pieces," related to the modern word *tailor;* the tailor's cuttings were "details."

Replay Unit

23

Make changes in the following sentences to banish any bias.

EXAMPLE

>   average person
> The (common man) wants peace.

1. The girls in my office go to lunch at 12.
2. He promised to send his girl over with the contracts.
3. Considering he's a senior citizen, Harry does the job well.
4. The president invited the managers and their wives to a dinner at his club.
5. Our hotel offers special rates for businessmen.
6. We have several lady policemen guarding against intruders.
7. He's studying to be a male nurse.
8. A Jewish programmer is installing the new software, and a girl from Data Processing is helping him.
9. The authoress of the book you ordered is going on a book tour next month.
10. The directress of the organization is doing a man-sized job.

See Appendix H for answers.

Read Unit

24

VOCABULARY AND SPELLING

A large vocabulary is vital to obtaining and holding a good job in business. Vocabulary building involves learning new words and adding meanings to words previously acquired. Here are the steps usually involved, although we are often not aware of them as they take place:

1. We **recognize** a written word; that is, it looks familiar to us.
2. Eventually we understand the meaning of that word when we **read** it because we've seen it a few times within sentences.
3. Later we understand the meaning when we **hear** the word.
4. After that, we are ready to use the word in our own **writing.**
5. Finally, we're able to use the word correctly in **conversation;** this means the word has been mastered.

The process just described continues as long as we read a wide assortment of materials, watch movies and TV alertly, and communicate with a variety of people. The result is a gradual increase in vocabulary over a period of years. Although this natural process is slow, we can speed up vocabulary growth by consciously working on it. This section may include some words you're not sure of. Now is the right time to increase your vocabulary by learning them.

An extensive vocabulary and the ability to spell are a big boost to a successful career. While studying the vocabulary in this unit, **look** carefully at the words. You'll find you can spell most of them by the time you've finished the unit. Even any you're not sure of will look "funny" if misspelled, prompting you to refer to a dictionary. (That's an important cue to respond to—if a word looks "funny," look it up!)

When studying any subject, you can improve spelling and vocabulary by learning words from the textbook, the lectures, or the discussions. This unit provides the opportunity to be sure of words appearing in this section of the text. Here are sentences in which words from Units 19–22 are used. Each word for you to note for spelling, definition, or both is in bold type. Review both singular and plural spellings as well as definitions. Use the dictionary for pronunciation and/or meaning.

1. My **allies** left the **cargo** in the **alley**.
2. Please put the **bill of lading** in the **portfolio**, for it will be a good **tie-in** with the evidence.
3. She was given a copy of the **itinerary** as a **memento**.
4. Never before in this school's history has an **alumna** broken her **vertebrae** by lifting a **chassis**.
5. What **criteria** are you using to determine the amount of the **tariff**?
6. There is an **embargo** on **dynamos** from Pandora.
7. The **plaintiff** insists that the **proceeds** from the sale of the factory be distributed equally to the partners.
8. Several new **hypotheses** are included in the **addendum**.
9. The **survey** of the **out-of-towners** was completed last week.
10. **Proxies** from 1,000 **stockholders** were received at this facility.
11. Some Native American tribes used shells and blankets as **mediums** of exchange.
12. When the committee's proposal was **rebuffed**, I accused the bureau chief of **bias**.
13. The new **curriculums** were widely advertised in the local **media**.

Memo from the Wordsmith

- The word *gymnasium* entered the English language through the Greek word *gymnos*, which means "naked." The ancient Greek athletes trained naked.
- The word *curriculum* originally meant "race course" in Latin—and there are still some today who believe that a curriculum is a runaround.

14. Two **businesswomen** in the sales contest each received a marketing **textbook**.

15. The accountant recommended using the loss as a tax **write-off** instead of treating it as a **crisis**.

Replay Unit

24

Check your spelling and vocabulary prowess.* The first letter of each word is given.

EXAMPLE

My sister's husband: **b**rother-in-law_____

1. My husband's sisters: **s**_____
2. Several male graduates or male and female graduates (it's a word with a foreign plural): **a**_____
3. One who starts a legal action: **p**_____
4. Standard on which a decision can be based:

   c_____
5. Plural of answer to item 5: **c**_____
6. A compound noun meaning programs for use in a computer:

   s_____
7. People working together for a cause: **a**_____
8. Narrow road behind buildings: **a**_____
9. Freight carried by a vehicle, especially a ship:

   c_____
10. Receipt from a shipping company: **b**_____
11. Carrying case for holding papers or a list of investments:

    p_____
12. Elimination of an item from an account (it's a compound noun):

    w_____
13. A plural noun that means "profits from a commercial or other venture"; when the same word is a verb, the accent is on the second syllable: **p**_____
14. Travel plan, including transportation, times, dates, hotels, and so on: **i**_____
15. Object that is a reminder of the past, such as a souvenir (this word is frequently misspelled): **m**_____
16. Frame for a vehicle (this word ends with a silent *s*):

    c_____
17. Plural of answer to item 16: **c**_____

* Did you expect to find the definition down here? Please look it up.

18. Written authorization to act for another:

     p_____

19. Belief that is stated for purpose of experimenting, arguing, reasoning, or coming to tentative conclusions:

     h_____

20. Government order prohibiting trade with a particular country or of

     a product: **e**_____

Check your answers in Appendix H.
Now take the **POP QUIZ** in Appendix A.

Checkpoint

A regular noun becomes plural by adding -*s*—or by adding -*es* for those ending in *s, x, z, sh,* or *ch*. Many nouns, however, don't follow the preceding rule; that is, they are irregular. You've reviewed in this section irregular plural spellings and pronunciations as well as the dictionary code for plural forms.

In addition to irregular plurals, business writers should be experts in compound nouns, capitalization, and using bias-free language.

While reviewing Section 4, you also increase your vocabulary and spelling ability, as emphasized in Unit 24.

Game from the Wordsmith

The words represented by the following brief definitions rhyme with *bird*. Fill in the blanks.

EXAMPLE

Slang for a person regarded as clumsy and dull _____nerd_____

1. Listened _____

2. Next after second _____

3. You should put one in each blank _____

4. A group of large animals _____

5. Unreasonable and ridiculous _____

6. The thick part of sour milk _____

7. Went astray or made a mistake _____

8. Postponed _____

9. Came together to discuss _____

10. Agreed; were of the same opinion _____

If you want hints, here's the first letter of each:

1. *h*	6. *c*
2. *t*	7. *e*
3. *w*	8. *d*
4. *h*	9. *c*
5. *a*	10. *c*

Special Assignment

A. Use the proofreader's mark (≡) to show which words should be capitalized, or number a page from 1–10 and write the words to be capitalized beside each number. Capitalization rules are in Appendix F.

EXAMPLE

karen is an occupational therapist in a washington hospital.

1. joseph flew via united airlines to uganda on veteran's day.

2. world war II interrupted the era known as the fabulous forties.

3. our english professor met reverend perez in this city last fall.

4. the senator from new jersey made an embarrassing mistake when she visited our main office on the west coast.

5. drive east along mohegan and clinton avenues.

6. we bought a bag of yum yum popcorn and koka kola drinks while we watched "the city slickers."

7. my uncle jack is an auditor for the state.

8. if you speak spanish and take international trade classes, you're likely to qualify for a good job.

9. although she has bs and ma degrees, she does not have a doctorate.

10. a salutation of a business letter could be "dear credit manager," and the complimentary close might be "very truly yours."

B. In the Special Assignment for Section One, you were encouraged to write *clearly*. The ability to write *concisely* is also vital to successful business communication.

> Concise writing means using as few words as possible while writing clearly, correctly, and interestingly.

The subject is big enough for a long essay in an English composition class. Only 100 to 120 words, however, will be acceptable for this assignment.

Write about any job you have held or about a job you wish you had. You might include some or all of the following information in **paragraph** form:

- kind of work you did or do
- name of company
- type of business
- name and/or title of supervisor
- approximate dates of employment
- whether the work was part time or full time

- what you liked or didn't like
- something you learned

Have your dictionary close by as you work. Use standard English—no slang. You will have several opportunities to apply rules for correct capitalization.

Here are some sample opening sentences:

1. Selling tires at Sears last summer was a valuable experience for me.
2. I was a part-time typist for the Fitrite Shoe Company during my senior year in high school.
3. During the past two years, I've been assembling lamps for Aurora Lighting Company.
4. Working under the supervision of Ms. Bush was an experience I would never want to have again.
5. My first job after completing college was that of computer programmer for a small electronics firm.

Sometimes I receive assignments from students who stretch their writing as though it were a piece of taffy. When that happens, the ideas that should be combined into one concise sentence appear in several rambling sentences with many unnecessary words. Compare this wordy paragraph, full of choppy sentences, to concise sample sentence 1:

I am going to tell you about my job. The work I did on my job was selling. I was a tire salesman. I sold tires at Sears. I did this work during the summer. It was last summer. The experience I had was valuable to me.

After composing the opening sentence, write several more sentences giving some details about the work. If you sold tires at Sears, you might tell about how difficult it is to deal with the public and some techniques you used to handle customers effectively.

Write the closing sentence as a summary or conclusion. Do not introduce new information in the closing sentence.

If possible, type this assignment and use double spacing.

This report is due _____ (date).

Proofreading for Careers

Proofreading is a challenge because it requires concentration on several subjects at the same time:

spelling	sentence construction
word division	capitalization
punctuation	word choice
grammar	number accuracy
format	number usage
typographical errors	meaning

With your dictionary beside you, hold your pen upside down or closed and slowly draw it along under each line of type. This "underlining" changes to pointing when you catch a possible error. This underlining-pointing process focuses your attention on proofreading.

Correct the noun errors studied in Section Four, as well as other errors, in the letter to Ms. Gonzalez; or use proofreader's marks (see Appendix D or back inside cover) to show the needed corrections:

Dear Ms. Zonzalez:

We can help your Sales Staff by providing you firm with a new demension of client service——an interior design tiein with the sale of office space.

clients' looking for office space often ask about desks, filling cabinets, chairs, and carpeting. They are interested the in prices and availability of these items, this is were we can come in to help close the sale for you.

At not charge toyou, we will furnish a complete plan that will be designed to fit any size office area that you offer. This will be an important sales aid to you that will pay off in faster and increased sales.

Alert Realty Firm's like yours are always looking for new and creative consepts in selling. The next time you have a cleint with an office furnishing need. Give us a call or reffer your client to us, we will proof that this service will work for you.

May get to gether with you or one of your key sales representative's soon so that we can discuss presise arrangemts we can make with you.

Yours Very Truely,

Manny Errata

What's your score? Excellent? Good? Fair? Or?? _____
Have you completed and reviewed the Reference Manual section on capitalization (Appendix F)?

Practice Quiz

Take the Practice Quiz as though it were a real test. Don't look back through Section Four while you take this Practice Quiz. After the quiz is corrected, refer to the appropriate Read Units, shown in parentheses, for explanations of any item you may have missed.

Read each sentence carefully to decide which form makes sense and is spelled correctly. It's all right to use your dictionary; however, know the material well enough so that you can easily finish within 20 minutes.

_____ 1. These (a) phenomena (b) phenomenas (c) phenomenae (d) phenomenon **(Unit 20)**
were discovered

_____ 2. through the marketing (a) survey's (b) survies (c) surveys. **(Unit 19)**

_____ 3. The (a) stock-holders (b) stocks holder (c) stockholders (d) stock holders **(Unit 22)**

_____ 4. will mail in their (a) proxys (b) proxi (c) proxyes (d) proxies. **(Unit 19)**

_____ 5. Several (a) beneficiary's (b) beneficiarys (c) beneficiaries are **(Unit 19)**

_____ 6. (a) allies (b) allys (c) alleys (d) alloys in this controversy. **(Unit 19)**

_____ 7. His (a) brother-in-laws (b) brother in laws (c) brothers-in-law **(Unit 22)**
(d) brothers-in laws manage the office.

_____ 8. The manager wants all employees to learn the (a) cargos (b) criteria **(Unit 24)**
(c) proceeds (d) mementos for requesting printouts.

_____ 9. To import from the French company, we need two (a) letters of credit **(Unit 22)**
(b) letter of credits (c) letters of credits (d) letter of credit

_____ 10. The ranchers told (a) Congress man (b) congressman (c) Congressman **(Unit 22)**
(d) Congress-man Lane of their problems with their

_____ 11. (a) sheeps and oxes (b) sheep and oxen (c) sheeps and oxen **(Units 20 and 21)**
(d) sheep and oxes.

_____ 12. The nouns (a) *cargo* and *embargo* (b) *vertebra* and *chassis* (c) *addenda* **(Unit 24)**
and *appendix* (d) *tariff* and *bill of lading* have almost the same meaning.

_____ 13. Both (a) attornies (b) attorneys (c) attornys (d) attorney's seemed **(Unit 19)**
confident as they awaited the verdict.

_____ 14. The inventory indicates that we have only three (a) celloes (b) cello **(Unit 19)**
(c) cellos in our Music Department.

_____ 15. Although James McCarthy is the president, three other (a) McCarthy's **(Unit 21)**
(b) McCarthies (c) McCarthys (d) McCarthys' hold managerial positions

_____ 16. with this (a) company (b) Company. **(Unit 22)**

_____ 17. The medical students submitted accurate (a) diagnosis (b) diagnosises **(Unit 20)**
(c) diagnoses (d) diagnosi.

_____ 18. The (a) Jones's (b) Joneses (c) Jones (d) Jones' invited the entire staff **(Unit 21)**
to dinner.

_____ 19. Our (a) Marketing department (b) Marketing Department (c) marketing **(Unit 22)**
department (d) marketing Department

_____ 20. is headed by the (a) merchandise manager, (b) Merchandise manager, **(Unit 22)**
(c) Merchandise Manager, (d) merchandise Manager, Mr. Frank Perez.

_____ **21.** We will be closed for two weeks during the (a) summer (b) Summer.   **(Unit 22)**

_____ **22.** A (a) congresswoman and a waitress (b) female congressman and lady   **(Unit 23)**
waiter (c) congressperson and a waitress (d) congressman and waitperson
were both trying on the same style dress at Marshall Field's.

_____ **23.** The (a) senator (b) Senator from Oregon voted for a million dollar grant   **(Unit 22)**
to Clatsop Community College.

_____ **24.** (a) The men will take their girls with them to take the notes. (b) The   **(Unit 23)**
men will take the ladies with them to take notes. (c) The gentlemen will take their
secretaries with them to take notes. (d) The managers will take their secretaries
with them to take notes. (e) The girls will go along to take notes for the men.

_____ **25.** Anne Campbell is a (a) female policeman (b) female police officer (c) lady   **(Unit 23)**
policeman (d) woman policeman (e) police officer.

Be Kind to the Substitute Week

5

Just between **you** and **me** **this** is **my** basket!

✔ Use pronouns according to the principles of standard English.

*S*ome people like to tell about junior high school experiences with substitute teachers. The appearance of a substitute was the signal for class clowns to go into action; even usually well-behaved students would sometimes join in the fun. When the substitute lost control of the class, the students knew they had achieved the ultimate in success. As adults, you probably feel a bit remorseful now when you recall how mean your classmates (not you, of course) were.

This section is a chance to be kind to substitutes—noun substitutes, that is—by using them correctly.

A word that substitutes for a noun is a pronoun. A pronoun refers to a person or thing previously named by a noun.

For example, after naming a thing as a *pencil*, you may later use the pronoun *it*; the reader or listener will understand that *it* means "pencil." To substitute for the plural noun *pencils*, the pronoun *them* might be used:

Give the **pencils** to me. I need **them** now.

Several pronoun rules that used to be essential to standard English are now no longer followed in speaking. For example, according to English-language traditionalists, this is what the dialogue should be when you knock on someone's door:

"Who's there?"
"It is I."

The use of *I* in the preceding conversation is technically correct, and many well-educated people do follow the traditional pronoun rules. However, a number of today's English-language authorities endorse the spoken reply "It's me." (Better yet, they suggest avoiding the issue by giving your name: "It's Algernon.") The rule in question is in transition, and that is why the authorities don't agree.

That's also why the rule, which arose in the 18th century, about which pronouns to use after existence verbs will not be emphasized in this section. You will instead find a simple trick to apply this rule in **writing**. In fact, the only place you'll find information about the grammatical foundations of the simple trick is in the "Grammar Supplement for Experts" in the back of the book.

Another problem area is distinguishing between *who* and *whom*. Have you ever heard someone doing this?

"Who . . . ah . . . whom . . . ah . . . who . . . ah . . . is the treasurer of the company?"

Who/whom cowards mumble when the mystery word is needed and hope the listener won't notice. Modern language authorities have simplified the dilemma, as you will read later in this section.

Just apply the basic and easy principles given here for appropriate pronoun usage in modern business communication.

Read Unit
25

JUST BETWEEN YOU AND ME

Or should it be "Just Between You and I"? Are you sure? Well, let's settle it by saying "Just Between Us." There's no question about that; it couldn't be "Just Between We."

As soon as you replaced the two pronouns with one, the wrong answer "sounds" wrong. However, with **two** pronouns—*you* and *me* or *you* and *I*—it's harder to tell which one belongs. Which is right?

> You and I   You and me   he and her
>
> him and her   he and she

Only one of these combinations is wrong— *he and her.* You can't tell about the others until they are in sentences.

Omit it

Most pronoun errors occur when two or more are used together or when a noun is used with a pronoun. You will usually make the right choice if you imagine omitting one of the two words and then decide whether the sentence "sounds right."

Here's an example:

John and me went to the meeting.

Leave John home, and you immediately know that "**Me** went to the meeting" sounds **terrible**! You therefore change the sentence to

YES   John and **I** went to the meeting.

Try another:

Give the papers to John and I before noon.

Omit *John,* and you immediately know that "Give the papers to **I** before noon" doesn't sound right. So . . .

YES   Give the papers to John and **me** before noon.

How does the system work with two pronouns? Just fine, if you take them one at a time. Look at this example:

Mr. Adamczyk wants to talk to **he and I.**

NO   Mr. Adamczyk wants to talk to **he.**

YES   Mr. Adamczyk wants to talk to **him.**

NO   Mr. Adamczyk wants to talk to **I**.

YES   Mr. Adamczyk wants to talk to **me**.

YES   Mr. Adamczyk wants to talk to **him and me**.

Sometimes the noun and pronoun have no conjunction between them. This happens when a noun and pronoun that mean the same thing are used together for emphasis or clearness. Which is right?

we secretaries   **us** secretaries

we boys   **us** boys

These combinations are all standard English. You can't tell which form to use until you see the rest of the sentence. You will usually make the right choice if you imagine omitting the **noun** to decide whether the sentence sounds right. Here's an example:

Us secretaries need a longer lunch break.

Omit the noun *secretaries* and you immediately know that "**Us** need a longer lunch break" isn't right. You change the sentence to

YES   **We** secretaries need a longer lunch break.

Try another:

Please give **we** secretaries a longer lunch break.

Omit the noun *secretaries* and you immediately know that "Please give **we** a longer lunch break" can't be right, so using *us* must be right:

YES   Please give **us** secretaries a longer lunch break.

Reverse It

Reverse the part of the sentence that has a *be* verb (*am, are, is, was, were,* and with helping verbs, *be* and *been*) to determine the pronoun.

It **is** (him/he), not Jerry, who should get the promotion.

REVERSE IT

NO   **Him** is it.

YES   **He** is it.

It is **he**, not Jerry, who should get the promotion.

Notice that *he* renames the subject *it*.
The same principle works with a contraction:

It's he, not Jerry who should get the promotion.

Sometimes, you'll have to combine the reverse-it and omit-it tricks:

> The winners might have been (her/she) and Raul.

> **REVERSE IT**

> (Her/She) and Raul might have been the winners.

OMIT IT

NO   **Her** might have been the winner.

YES   **She** might have been the winner.

Then, you can put the sentence together again with the right pronoun:

> The winners might have been **she** and Raul.

In Love

Applying the omit-it and reverse-it tricks can be complicated in a particular sentence. At those times, try another trick. Memorize these two sentences. (It's easy to remember them because they're about a subject that interests everyone: love.

SENTENCE 1   I love you.

SENTENCE 2   I am in love with you.

Any pronoun that fits at the beginning of these sentences is a **subject pronoun**. If it fits at the end, it is an **object pronoun**. Here are pronouns grouped as subjects or objects:

	Subject Pronouns	Object Pronouns
1st person	I, we	me, us
2nd person	you[a]	you[a]
3rd person	he, she, it, they	her, him, it, them

[a] You can't go wrong with *you*; this one word serves as the second-person pronoun for subject *and* object, both singular (one) *and* plural (more than one). Also notice *it* as third person subject and object.

Any subject pronoun (from the left column) can begin the *love* sentences. Any object pronoun (from the right column) can end either of the *love* sentences:

> **You** love **them**.
> **He** loves* **you**.
> **We** love **it**.

> **I** am in love with **him**.
> **You** are* in love with **them**.
> **She** is* in love with **us**.

* Change *love* to *loves* with *he, she,* and *it.* Also, the verb *be* changes with several pronouns: I *am,* you (they) *are,* he (she, it) *is.*

The love sentences give you an easy way to tell subject pronouns from object pronouns. When you can do *that*, you can confidently substitute any pronoun from the appropriate group. For example, you can now answer the question in the opening paragraph of this unit. Since "Just between us" sound right, an object pronoun is required; therefore, "Just between **you** and **me**" is correct. Remember from Section One that a preposition is always followed by a noun or pronoun object. Since *between* is a preposition, you use the object pronoun *me*.

Replay Unit
25

Use the simple methods described in this unit to determine the correct pronoun; then circle it.

EXAMPLE

My brother and (I/me) attend Bradford Business School in Houston.

1. If you assign the report to Keith and (I/me), it will never be completed.
2. Please tell Anna and (I/me) when Laurel is ready to leave.
3. Chelsey and (he/him) are working on the project.
4. Please give more homework to (we/us) students.
5. Kasey and (I/me) should work together frequently.
6. (We/Us) shipping clerks want to affiliate with the union.
7. Mr. Roth telephoned Marvin and (I/me).
8. Myrna is pleased she assigned the work to Laurel, Davon, and (him/he).
9. Do (we/us) parents get a chance to vote?
10. Michael and (her/she) could take the trip together.
11. Linda gave Jeffrey and (I/me) the blueprints.
12. Christopher asked both you and (we/us) to visit her.
13. (They/Them), as well as Terry, will serve on the committee.
14. Everyone except Dr. Marshall and (he/him) will be at the San Francisco session.*
15. (Him and me/He and I) have an advantage in this situation.
16. The money should be divided between Harold and (I/me).
17. Mr. Heffron saw you and (she/her) arrive late to class.
18. (We/Us) accountants can no longer work under these conditions.
19. Please authorize Ms. Papachristos and (I/me) to attend the conference in London.
20. All the responsibility was given to the auditor and (I/me).
21. The personnel director told Sean and (I/me) about the job requirements.
22. Were you and (he/him) using the Dictaphone that day?

* *Hint: except* is a preposition.

23. Mr. Hicks invited you as well as (he/him).
24. The production manager doesn't want Barry and (I/me) to work together.
25. You and (them/they) should devise a new production schedule.
26. Our best district managers are Mr. Chandra and (him/he).
27. Next to be promoted are Sue Johnson and (she/her).
28. The guests of honor were Dr. Gluckson and (me/I).
29. I think it was (they/them) who requested the report.
30. The first one to return from the meeting was (me/I).

Check answers in Appendix H.

Read Unit

26

ME, MYSELF, AND I

As a child, you probably asked your parents questions like "Can Johnny and me go to the movies?" Your mom or dad may have replied "Johnny and I" and wouldn't give you the money until you changed that evil word "me" to "I." Although they were right in that instance, a number of incidents like that through your growing up years may have made you a firm disbeliever in the word "me." It really is quite a respectable word and does not deserve an X rating. Oddly enough, it's people who try their best to be correct who use *I* where *ME* belongs.

Complete It

When the omit-it and reverse-it methods of Unit 25 don't apply, decide whether some "understood" words could complete the thought. By "understood" words, here, I mean verbs or subject-verb combinations that complete comparisons. Because understood words repeat words that have already been used in a sentence, they are left out to avoid wordiness. Here are two examples:

> Harry sold more tickets than Carl. ["than Carl *sold*" or "than Carl *did*" is understood]
> Monica is as tall as Mrs. Banks. ["as Mrs. Banks *is*" is understood]

The words *than* and *as* are a clue to sentences that may have "understood" words omitted from them.

> If you're not sure whether to use subject or object pronouns when understood words are missing, all you have to do is imagine the missing words back in.

If an understood comparison is giving you a pronoun problem, just complete it.

> No one wants to please you more than the manager and [me *or* I].

If you try out each pronoun followed by the understood words "want to please you," you'll find it easy to make the right choice:

NO No one wants to please you more than the manager and me [want to please you].

YES No one wants to please you more than the manager and I [want to please you].

Try another:

Do you like him better than [I *or* me]?

Again, if you add the understood words "like him" (or just "do") after each pronoun in turn, you easily choose *I* instead of *me*:

NO Do you like him better than me [do]?

YES Do you like him better than I [do]?

BUT

In some sentences, either a subject pronoun or an object pronoun is appropriate, and you can make the choice depending on what you intend the sentence to mean. Let's take another look at our example sentence:

Do you like him better than [I *or* me]?

If you add the understood words "you like" *before* the pronoun in question, then the sentence has a different meaning—and you need a different pronoun:

NO Do you like him better than [you like] I?

YES Do you like him better than [you like] me?

To be absolutely certain you choose the right pronoun, complete in your imagination any sentence that omits understood words in a comparison. Make sure to supply the words that deliver the meaning you intend in sentences with more than one possible meaning.

Recap Circle the number of the statement that is grounds for divorce. In the blanks, write the understood words you supplied for each sentence.

1. My husband likes golf better than I. _____
2. My husband likes golf better than me. _____

Check answers in Appendix H.

Self, Selves

When *-self* or *-selves* is added to a pronoun, the resulting word is a compound pronoun. Here are the standard English compound personal pronouns. Any other spellings of these words are unacceptable:

myself	itself
yourself, yourselves	oneself
himself	ourselves
herself	themselves [*never* theirselves]

Use compound pronouns only when no other pronoun with the same meaning makes sense in the sentence. Use the *-self* pronouns either for emphasis or for clearness.

We ourselves are to blame. [emphasis]

He corrected **himself** immediately. [clearness]

The most common *-self* error is using *myself* when *I* or *me* would fit.

NO   The manager and **myself** will attend the meeting. [Using *myself* is an error because *I* makes sense.]

YES   The manager and I will attend the meeting.

(How do you know to use *I* instead of *me*? Imagine omitting "the manager," as explained in Unit 25. You'll know that "*me* will attend the meeting" would be incorrect.)
    Here are some examples of *-self* words used correctly:

YES   He placed **himself** at great risk. [No other pronoun makes sense after *placed.*]

YES   She does the easy work by **herself**. [No other pronoun makes sense after *by.*]

YES   She **herself** does the easy work. [No other pronoun makes sense after *she,* so *herself* is correct.]

Replay Unit

26

A. Make the necessary pronoun corrections. Write *C* in the blank if a sentence is already correct.

EXAMPLE

_____ Just between you and ~~I~~, (me) I think we should prepare a new proposal.

_____ **1.** The president himself will attend the meeting.

_____ **2.** The twins learned how to dress theirselves at an early age.

_____ **3.** She can do the work faster than him.

_____ **4.** When it comes to his work, he is more confident than she.

_____ **5.** Give the papers to Linda West and myself.

Word to the Wise

Here's the test for compound pronouns. Can you insert another pronoun at the exact place where the *-self* or *-selves* word appears? If so, use the other pronoun. If not, keep the compound pronoun right where it is, but be sure that it is correctly spelled.

_____   6. His younger brother is just as tall as him.

_____   7. The other workers always leave as soon as myself.

_____   8. Mr. Adams does not work as efficiently as she.

_____   9. Since he is a physician, he gave hisself the injection.

_____   10. No one wants to please you more than Ms. Valdivia and myself.

_____   11. The lawyer and myself listened to the case with great interest.

_____   12. We may find ourself looking for a new manager.

_____   13. We ourselves are excluded from the contract.

_____   14. The members of the cast felt like themselves again after the crisis had passed.

_____   15. She injured herself while in Oshkosh.

_____   16. We voted ourself a pay increase at De Anza.

_____   17. They also voted theirself a pay increase at Los Angeles Trade Tech.

_____   18. He gave hisself a raise.

_____   19. I gave myself a permanent.

_____   20. It was himself who should have known better than to buy 100 shares of GYPCO in a bear market; don't blame yourself.

B. Show by the complete-it method why all these sentences are correct. In each blank write the understood word or words.

1. He loves his wife more than she [_____].

2. He loves his wife more than [_____] her.

3. I know the vice president better than he [_____].

4. I know the vice president better than [_____] him.

5. Ms. Mosson can operate the device as well as he [_____].

Check your answers in Appendix H.

THE LIZARD'S TAIL

If, as a child, you never tried to pull a lizard, tail first, out of a crevice in a rock, you've missed the shock of a lifetime—that of discovering that although its tail was in your hand, the rest of it didn't come along. (This is not as horrible as it seems, for the lizard manages to grow a new one.)

If you had wanted to tell your buddy, you might have said in amazement, "The lizard lost its tail!" Although you wouldn't have known it as a child, that sentence skillfully uses a possessive pronoun to substitute for a possessive noun.* Without that substitution, the sentence would be "The lizard lost the lizards's tail," using a possessive noun and sounding rather silly.

The following sentences illustrate how possessive pronouns substitute for possessive nouns:

That is *my* book.   That book is *mine.*

That is *his* book.   That book is *his.*

That is *her* book.   That book is *hers.*

That is *our* book.   That book is *ours.*

That is *your* book.   That book is *yours.*

That is *their* book.   That book is *theirs.*

The lizard lost *its* tail.   *Whose* tail is that?

The possessive pronouns in the preceding sentences are **never** used with apostrophes.

Some **possessive pronouns** and **contractions** sound alike but are spelled differently. As shown below, **the contractions require apostrophes.** The apostrophe replaces the space and letter omitted when forming the contraction.

Do *not* use an apostrophe with a possessive pronoun—except with *-one* and *-body* pronouns.

POSSESSIVE PRONOUNS	CONTRACTIONS
your **Your** job is interesting.	**you're** (you are) **You're** a good programmer.
its **Its** wing was injured.	**it's** (it is) **It's** a cockatoo.
whose **Whose** book is on the desk?	**who's** (who is) **Who's** reading the book?
their **Their** problem is serious.	**they're** (they are)—**They're** in trouble.

Here are the *-one* and *-body* pronouns referred to in Section One. To form possessives, add **'s**:

* Possessive nouns are explained in Section Eight.

PRONOUNS	POSSESSIVE PRONOUNS
anybody	That could be **anybody's** calliope.
somebody	It must be **somebody's** saxophone.
everybody	That is **everybody's** banjo.
anyone	That isn't **anyone's** music.
someone	**Someone's** harp was left behind.
everyone	**Everyone's** music books are on the table.
one	One should mind **one's** own business.

The -*body* and -*one*, as well as -*thing* words, are used not only as possessives but also as part of contractions:

Everything is	**Everything's** fine.
Everyone is	**Everyone's** going to the concert.
Somebody is	**Somebody's** in the kitchen with Dinah.

Replay Unit

27

Correct the pronoun and contraction errors in the following sentences. Write *C* to the left of the sentence if it is already correct.

EXAMPLE

They can help ~~their~~selves to the supplies. *(them)*

_____ 1. Are you the one whose going to attend the sales meeting in Minneapolis?

_____ 2. Whose work do you prefer?

_____ 3. Reserve the apostrophe for it's proper use, and omit it when its not needed.

_____ 4. Its color has faded.

_____ 5. The carpeted office is our's.

_____ 6. Your's is on the 18th floor of the New Otani.

_____ 7. I think the one on the right is hers.

_____ 8. The disks are mine; the books are their's.

_____ 9. Your to use your own books today.

_____ 10. I don't believe your's is here.

_____ 11. Their all going with us.

_____ 12. No ones work was checked yet.

_____ 13. Whether or not we'll get that account is anybody's guess.

_____ 14. Whose going to do the graphics?

_____ 15. Almost anyones work would have been better than their's.

_____ **16.** Its a beautiful day.

_____ **17.** Its a new sweater.

_____ **18.** I like its warmth.

_____ **19.** Somethings better than nothing.

_____ **20.** Anythings better than that.

Answers to this Replay are in Appendix H.
Review Units 25–27; then turn to **POP QUIZ** in Appendix A.

Read Unit

28

TWO'S COMPANY; THREE'S A CROWD

That's what the girl whose boyfriend was visiting used to tell her little brother. The boyfriend would toss a quarter to the brother, encouraging him to go to the movies. That's the way it was in the good old days.

A crowd, however, still means a collection of people; and "crowd" is a **collective noun**.

> **Collective nouns** are words that represent a group of people or animals.

Notice that each collective noun below is singular, even though it represents a group of people or animals:

class	jury	team	group	committee
company	herd	staff	family	

Organizations such as companies, unions, stores, educational institutions, governments, and government agencies always act as one.

Pronouns frequently substitute for collective nouns. Otherwise we'd have awkward repetition of the nouns.

Memo from the Wordsmith

Student is a word derived from the Latin _studium_, meaning "zeal" or "eagerness."

Sophomore literally means "wise fool." It is an invented word combining two Greek words: _sophos_ (wise) and _moros_ (foolish).

Pedagogue, which now means "teacher," originally meant "a slave in charge of children"—from the Greek _paidagogos_. The Romans, who respected the learning of the Greeks, assigned Greek slaves to train their children.

Singular pronouns such as it, its, or itself substitute for collective nouns when the members of the group act as a unit—or as one.

Even though the college referred to above has many students and employees, the sentence is about one organization. Therefore, it's necessary to choose a singular pronoun. You can also omit the pronoun:

NO   Bay de Noc College opens Bay de Noc College offices at 8 a.m.

YES   Bay de Noc College opens **its** offices at 8 a.m.

Bay de Noc College offices open at 8 a.m.

BUT **don't** write the incorrect form:

NO   Bay de Noc College opens **their** offices at 8 a.m.

Occasionally, a sentence is about the members of a group who are acting as separate individuals or disagreeing. Then use a plural pronoun: they, their, them, themselves.

YES   The jury ate **their** lunch at noon.

NO   The jury ate **its** lunch at noon.

The plural *their* is used with the collective noun *jury* because the individual members of the jury are eating separate lunches and are not acting as a unit. You can also revise the sentence to omit the pronoun:

YES   The jury ate lunch at noon.

BUT

NO   The jury announced **their** verdict.

When a jury arrives at a verdict, it acts as one, or as a unit. Therefore the singular pronoun *its* substitutes for the collective noun *jury*.

YES   The jury announced **its** verdict. [one verdict]

Or replace the pronoun with an article:

The jury announced **the** verdict.

When a collective noun is plural (juries, companies, colleges, classes, teams, etc.), a plural pronoun is always used as the noun substitute.

The **juries** announced **their** verdicts simultaneously in New York and in Chicago.

Recognizing collective nouns enables you to avoid choosing an incorrect pronoun to substitute for them. Understanding collective nouns also helps in Section Six, when you'll need to check that both the subject and the verb in each sentence "agree" in showing one or more than one.

Writing for Your Career

Often, rephrasing to omit the pronoun, as in some of the examples above, results in more concise and smoother wording.

Replay Unit

28

A. List collective nouns in the six blanks below. See how many you can think of without referring to the preceding pages.

1. _____   4. _____

2. _____   5. _____

3. _____   6. _____

B. Circle the correct answer in the following sentences.

1. A pronoun that substitutes for a collective noun is usually
   (a) singular (b) plural.

2. When the members of the group named by a collective noun are acting separately, the pronoun is (a) singular (b) plural.

3. When the group named by a collective noun acts as a unit, a pronoun substituting for it is (a) singular (b) plural.

4. Aerojet Corp. has (its/their) offices in Escanaba, Michigan.

5. The Accounting Department is on the third floor; (they/it) will be open until five o'clock.

6. Dennis, Kaufman, Inc., insists on having (its/their) bills paid promptly.

7. The Internal Revenue Service revised (its/their) forms again.

8. Her family are taking (its/their) vacations at different times this year.

9. Her family is taking (its/their) vacation in August this year.

10. The Board of Directors will hold (its/it's/their) annual meeting at Pacific Institute in Guam.

11. The city should regulate (its/it's/their) hiring policies more carefully.

12. The committee will review the new data at (its/it's/their) next meeting.

13. This firm is old, but (its/it's/their) management team is progressive.

14. If the unions lowered (its/their) dues, (their/its) membership would grow.

See if your answers match those in Appendix H.

Read Unit

29

A WHODUNIT

Most of us are familiar with movie and TV whodunits. If you're a mystery fan, you've probably read many of them. The best known English-language whodunit is the Mystery of Who and Whom. (Although it qualifies as a mystery, it's not exactly a thriller.) Often those who try to use *whom* correctly in speech use it where *who* belongs, and others mumble so that listeners will be unsure whether they heard *who* or *whom.*

Many well-educated people still use *who* and *whom* traditionally, but the pendulum is swinging toward **who**. Some language authorities suggest that we stop trying to solve the Mystery of Who and Whom by eliminating *whom* entirely. A larger number of experts suggest eliminating *whom* just from speech. For writing, however, the experts recommend making the traditional distinction between who and whom.

Since a middle-of-the-road approach is desirable for business communication, you should take a few seconds when writing to determine whether *who* or *whom* should be used. In that way, you'll be more confident about the correctness of your writing. In speech, avoid *whom* unless you're certain it's the correct choice.

You can be right nearly all the time when deciding between *who* and *whom* if you use either of the clues described here.

Clue 1: *Who* Subject/*Whom* Object

Use **who** as a subject. Use **whom** as the object of a verb or of a preposition. The subject tells who or what *did* the action referred to in the verb. The object of the verb tells who or what *received* the action. The object of a preposition completes a prepositional phrase.

Who gave me the portfolio? [*Who* is the subject of the verb *gave.*]

He is the man **who** gave me the portfolio. [*Who* is still the subject of the verb *gave,* even though the sentence is longer.]

He is the man **who** I think gave me the portfolio. [*Who* is still the subject of the verb *gave* even though the two-word clause *I think* interrupts the subject and verb.]

To **whom** did he give the portfolio? [*Whom* is the object of the preposition *to.*]

He is the man **whom** you should marry. [*You* is the subject of the verb *should marry*—"you" tells who is doing the action; *whom* is receiving the action of the verb *should marry,* the object of the verb.]

Word to the Wise

To determine whether to use *who* or *whom*:

1. Find the verbs.
2. See whether each verb has a subject.
3. If a verb doesn't have a subject, choose *who*.
4. If each verb has a subject, choose *whom*. It will be the object—of either a verb or of a preposition.

Clue 2: *He* or *Him*

Change the order of the words so that you can replace the *who* or *whom* in question with *he* or *him* (regardless of whether the person is male or female). If *he* sounds right, use *who*; if *him* sounds right, use *whom*. If you're not sure of how to rearrange the clauses or phrases, follow the steps outlined in the Word to the Wise message you just read.

He is the man (who/whom) gave me the portfolio. [**He** *gave me the portfolio*—not **him** *gave me the portfolio;* therefore, choose *who*.]

Dan Foster, (who/whom) we understand visited your office yesterday, is a Database expert. [*Dan Foster is a Database expert;* we understand **he** *visited your office yesterday*—not **him** *visited;* therefore, choose *who*.]

Rebecca Renee, (who/whom) Prudential hopes to hire, was trained at Harbor College. [*Rebecca Renee was trained at Harbor; Prudential hopes to hire* **him**—not *hire* **he**; therefore, choose *whom*.]

I'll assign the report to (whoever/whomever) I wish. [*I'll assign the report to* **him**; therefore, choose *whom*.]

He is the one (who/whom) should do the work. [**He** *should do the work;* therefore, choose *who*.]

Extra Clues

Use whichever method seems easier, or combine them. By the time you finish the Replay, you'll feel like an expert. No matter which method you apply, the following clues are also essential:

If the who/whom (whoever/whomever) sentence is a question, imagine it as a statement before making the who/whom choice.

(Who/Whom) are you going with?

Change to a statement—You are going with (who-he/whom-him). *Him*, not *he*, sounds right. Or, because *with* is a preposition, the **object** *whom* must be used.

When either *he* or *him* fits in the same place, choose *who* or *whoever*.

You should go with (whoever/whomever) is ready first.

Him sounds right after *with*; *whom* would be the object of the preposition.

BUT

He sounds right before *is*; *who* is needed as the subject of the verb *is*.

THEREFORE

Use *who*:

You should go with **whoever** is ready first. [*he is ready first*]

Always allow the subject to take priority over the object.

I want (whoever/whomever) can do the job best.

Him fits after *want* but *he* fits before *can*:

THEREFORE

I want **whoever** can do the job best. [*he can do the job best*]

Use *whoever* as the subject of *can do*, not *whomever* as the object of *want*.

Recap   Circle the correct word.

1. Give the money to (whoever/whomever) will take it.
2. (Whom/Who) do you think won the contest?

Check answers in Appendix H.

Replay Unit

29

Insert *who* or *whom* in the blanks. To benefit from this Replay, apply Read Unit 29 clues to choose *who* or *whom*. *Practice*, not guessing, makes perfect.

First, show where *he* or *him* would be inserted; then write the correct answer in the blank.

EXAMPLE

We referred a programmer to you _____whom_____ we believe you will like.
                                                                                    him
                                                                                    ∧

1. The man _____ I met at your office is an engineer.

2. _____ do you prefer for the job?

3. _____ would you like to accompany me?

4. Give the scholarship to the one _____ needs it most.

5. They are the ones _____ are needed for the job.

6. He is the boy _____ I took to be your brother.

7. Each candidate should support _____ ever the convention chooses.

8. I don't know _____ will do the work.

9. _____ ever is willing to do the work will be given the responsibility.

10. He is a professor _____ we are confident you will want at Gonzaga University.

11. I am the one _____ must make the decisions.

12. Give it to _____ ever gets there first.

13. My secretary is the one _____ I believe was chosen.

14. Give the scholarship to _____ ever needs it most.

15. The secretary _____ you sent for is a very nervous man.

16. Ms. Cates is the accountant _____ I feel would be best able to devise a new system.

17. Mrs. Siegel, _____ we met for the first time last week, is a talented artist.

18. Eric Smith is the one _____ helped me most.

19. Mr. Schaefer, _____ I told you about last week, will speak on the subject of business schools in Buffalo.

20. We selected Ken Geary, _____ we know has been active in many organizations in Independence.

21. _____ do you suppose will get the position?

22. _____ do you think we should get to make the investigation?

23. The question of _____ should handle the advertising will be discussed.

24. Give the package to _____ ever can identify it.

25. He _____ has courage and faith will never perish in misery. ANNE FRANK

See if your answers match those in Appendix H.

Read Unit

30

EVERYBODY NEEDS MILK

This title was a radio and TV commercial a few years ago. Was it *every body* or *everybody*? That's just one type of question occurring with the use of indefinite pronouns—pronouns that don't refer to a definite person or thing:

INDEFINITE PRONOUNS

each	anybody	somebody	nobody	few
everyone	anyone	something	all	many
everybody	anything	none	any	others
everything	someone	no one	both	several

One Word or Two

Except for *no one,* the compound pronouns listed above are one word. In some sentences, however, these expressions are not pronouns at all; instead, the first part is an adjective and the second a noun. Then two words are used. Fortunately it isn't necessary to analyze the grammar to determine whether to use one word or two. Just apply these two easy word tricks:

Any one and *every one* are two words when the word *of* follows.

Any one of you may attend the conference.
Every one of you may attend the conference.

BUT

Everyone may attend the conference.

Any of the compound expressions listed above are two words when your own good judgment indicates a special meaning.

Dr. Cutup took the medical students to the morgue and told them to examine **any body**.
The man I met at Muscle Beach has **some body**.
Phyllis Diller said, "(Every body/Everybody) needs milk."

In the last example, both are correct since *every body* stresses the needs of the body for milk, and *everybody* stresses that all people need milk. The double meaning is probably why the sentence was selected by the dairy industry for use in its commercial.

The Singles Scene

Although the following words are frequently indefinite pronouns, when the first four are used just before a noun, they are adjectives. Fortunately again, it isn't necessary to identify the part of speech—just remember that they are all **singular**.

each	everyone	everybody
every	someone	nobody
either	anyone	somebody
neither	one	anybody
	no one	

Although *everyone* might include five hundred people, it is still singular because it refers to each one acting individually. Therefore:

When another pronoun substitutes for one of the words listed above, that pronoun must be singular.

Since *everybody, every,* and *each* are singular, use the singular pronouns *his, hers,* or *its* instead of the plural *their.* (In informal speech this rule is frequently violated, but it is still considered important in writing.)

USE   **Everybody** went to **his** seat.
AVOID   **Everybody** went to **their** seat.

USE   **Every** worker should use **his** own tools.
AVOID   **Every** worker should use **their** own tools.

USE   **Each** room has **its** own heating unit.
USE   **Each** of the rooms has **its** own heating unit. [See the following Writing for Your Career.]
AVOID   **Each** of the rooms has **their** own heating unit.
AVOID   **Each** room has **their** own heating unit.

Since *everybody, every,* and *each* are singular, choose the singular pronouns *his, hers,* or *its* instead of the plural *their.*

Gender in Modern Business Communication

Gender refers to male, female, and neutral words. You may have noticed that in two sample sentences above, *his* is used even though there may have been some females who went to their seats or who had tools. The English language, rich as it is, makes no provision for a neutral gender third person singular pronoun (except for *it*).

When both a masculine and a feminine pronoun would be logical, choose from these alternatives:

Use *his, he,* or *him* to represent both sexes.

Masculine pronouns have long been accepted as carrying both meanings; that is, male only, as well as male and female.

Each person did **his** work quietly.

Although this example is technically correct, knowledgeable business communicators avoid the masculine pronoun to mean both male and female when a better alternative is available.

Writing for Your Career

The careful, trained business writer omits the unnecessary *of the* from sentences like the one above. While "Each of the rooms has its own heating unit" is correct, "Each room has its own heating unit" is better. When you eliminate words that contribute nothing to clearness, smooth flow, or desired emphasis, you improve the writing. Adding unnecessary words is a "skill" developed by some students when they are asked to submit a 1,000-word report and don't know enough about the subject to do so.

Use his or her, he or she, or *him or her* to represent both sexes.

Using both pronouns is grammatically correct but often awkward.

> **Each** person did **his or her** work quietly.

A good solution is to reword the sentence so that a pronoun isn't needed—provided you don't change the meaning or tone intended.

> Each person did the work quietly.
> Each person worked quietly.
> Everyone worked quietly.

Another good solution is to reword the sentence so that the plural may be used correctly.

> The people went about **their** work quietly. [Since *people* is plural, the plural pronoun *their* is acceptable.]

BUT

Don't compromise by using the nonstandard form.

NO   **Each** person did **their** work quietly.

NO   **Everyone** did **their** work quietly.

AND

To avoid the risk of offending a client, customer, or co-worker, develop sensitivity to sexism in language.

Replay Unit

30

A. Revise this sentence:

> Every student should use singular pronouns with singular nouns in their writing.

_____

_____

_____

B. Circle the correct form in the following sentences.

EXAMPLE

(No body/Nobody) was found where the fatal accident occurred.

   1. (No one/Noone/No-one) but the owner knows the combination to the safe.

2. Please distribute the flyers to (any one/anyone) who wants them.

3. (Every body/Everybody) should learn how to keyboard.

4. He asked that (some one/someone) from this office visit his store.

5. (Any one/Anyone) of you is qualified to prepare the report.

6. Although it was assumed the pilot was killed, (no body/nobody) could be found in or near the wreckage.

7. Each person did (his/their) work quietly.

8. Everyone should complete (his/their) assignment before Friday.

9. Every woman in this office needs (their/her) own phone.

10. If (some one/someone) needs more paper, (he/they) should fill out Form 26.

11. Whenever (some body/somebody) loses (his/their) keys, (he/they) should come in through my private office.

12. (Every one/Everyone) of the members must vote.

13. (Every one/Everyone) should write (their/his or her) name in the upper right corner.

14. Each senator must use (his/their) own funds for this project.

15. (Every body/Everybody) must make (his or her/their) own decision.

C. In the blank on the left, write the letter of the form most suitable for modern business communication. In the next blank, write the letter of the only form that is incorrect.

Best	Wrong	
_____	_____	1. (a) A person can usually improve if he really tries. (b) A person can usually improve if they really try. (c) People can usually improve if they really try. (d) A person can usually improve if he or she really tries.
_____	_____	2. (a) When customers express their dissatisfaction, listen courteously. (b) When a customer expresses his dissatisfaction, listen courteously. (c) When a customer expresses his or her dissatisfaction, listen courteously. (d) When a customer expresses their dissatisfaction, listen courteously.
_____	_____	3. (a) Every one of the contractors submitted his or her bid today. (b) Every one of the contractors submitted their bids today. (c) The contractors all submitted their bids today.
_____	_____	4. (a) Did anyone here lose his notebook? (b) Did any one of you lose your notebook? (c) Did anyone here lose their notebook?

———   ———   5. (a) Everyone should write his name on the
form immediately.
(b) Everyone should write their name on the
form immediately.
(c) Everyone should write his or her name on
the form immediately.

Check answers in Appendix H.
The **POP QUIZ** for Units 28–30 is in Appendix A.

Checkpoint

Along with our rapidly changing technologies and lifestyles, language styles also change. As with all changes, there are those who resist and use their energies defending the old; others are at the head of the parade. When selecting language style for business or profession, being in the middle is advisable. "Being in the middle" means readers and listeners concentrate on the message instead of becoming distracted by something unusual about the language.

When preparing a report for the president of your company or a letter to an important customer, you should not have to ponder over whether to use *I* or *me*, *who* or *whom*, and so on. You should **know** how to decide. When with your business and professional colleagues, you should not have to be self-conscious about your grammar. You should be **confident** that your grammar is correct.

Pronouns are often a trouble spot for people who are comfortable with standard English as well as for those who grew up using a dialect or another language. Section Five principles provide the standard pronoun usage acceptable for business, professional, and technical careers.

Place a check in the blank when you understand the principle.

_____ 1. Use subject pronouns as the subject of a verb and object pronouns as the object of a verb or a preposition. Several "trick" devices make it easy to apply this principle. (Units 25, 26, 29)

_____ 2. Use a *-self* or *-selves* pronoun only when another pronoun will not make sense in that position in the sentence. **Never** use *hisself, theirselves,* or *theirself.* (Unit 26)

HANDY PRONOUN DISPLAY

	Singular			Plural		
Person	Subject	Object	Possessive	Subject	Object	Possessive
1st	I	me	my, mine	we	us	our, ours
2nd	you	you	your, yours	you	you	your, yours
3rd	he, she, it	him her, it	his, hers, its	they	them	their, theirs
Indefinite	who whoever	whom whomever	whose	who whoever	whom whomever	whose

-self/-selves:
1st   myself, ourselves
2nd   yourself, yourselves
3rd   himself, herself, itself, themselves

_____ **3.** Possessive pronouns that refer to specific people or animals never have apostrophes. Possessive pronouns that do not refer to specific people (those ending in *one* or *body*) do have apostrophes. Distinguish between possessive pronouns and contractions. Some of them sound alike but are spelled differently. (Unit 27)

_____ **4.** Pronouns should agree in number (singular or plural) and in gender (masculine, feminine, or neutral) with the noun or other pronoun for which they're substituting. (Units 28, 30)

_____ **5.** Except for *no one*, compound indefinite pronouns are written as one word. Simple methods enable you to determine when the expression is not a pronoun and requires two words instead of one. (Unit 30)

More detailed pronoun explanations appear in the Grammar Supplement in Appendix G.

Special Assignment

A British steamship company operating vacation cruises wrote to the British Admiralty asking permission for its officers, like British naval officers, to wear swords. The Admiralty did not like the idea but didn't want to refuse permission. The ambiguous reply from the Admiral's office granted permission, adding, "provided the swords are worn on the right side." The cruise company dropped the idea, feeling foolish about writing again for clarification of the expression "the right side." This was probably an intentional lack of clearness, since the Admiral's office achieved its purpose.

Perhaps this reminds you of when you were a child and an elderly relative asked, "Honey, do you know you put your left shoe on your right foot?" After you looked at your feet in confusion, the double meaning of "right foot" was explained and everyone guffawed.

These little stories are to remind you of the importance of clearness in writing—especially business writing. Concentrate on writing clearly as well as correctly when completing this brief report.

Choose a type of work that interests you: fashion merchandising, secretarial work, business management, computer technology, law, teaching, auto mechanics, or whatever. Interview a worker in the chosen field. Prepare questions in advance, such as these:

What does the work consist of?

What is a typical daily routine?

What about salary?

Advancement possibilities?

What are the advantages and disadvantages to this kind of work?

What kind of training do you need to qualify?

Include only the ideas that interest you. What do *you* want to know about this kind of work? Summarize the information you obtain and prepare a typewritten report of 175 to 200 words.

Start with a topic sentence that tells the reader in an interesting way what the report is about. Here are sample topic sentences:

TOPIC SENTENCE 1

"Accounting is an excellent career for women," states my friend, Maria Lopez, who works in the controller's office of Hughes Aircraft Company.

TOPIC SENTENCE 2

I learned a great deal about the work of an accountant by interviewing Maria Lopez, who works at Hughes Aircraft Corporation.

TOPIC SENTENCE 3

Like other careers, teaching has many advantages as well as disadvantages.

Follow through with what you promised in your topic sentence. For example, the rest of the report for topic sentence 1 would give reasons why accounting is a good career for women. With the second opening, the writer would describe the work of an accountant. The report beginning with topic sentence 3 should inform the reader of the advantages and disadvantages of being a teacher.

Stay on the track right to the end. Here are sample closing sentences. The closing should be a conclusion or summary of what went before.

CLOSING SENTENCE 1

Business management sounds like an exciting career filled with challenges and rewards.

CLOSING SENTENCE 2

Because of the long hours and the problems of dealing with difficult customers, I've decided to change my career goal: I no longer want to become a retail store manager.

CLOSING SENTENCE 3

Now that I've learned about the training for the profession of neurosurgery, I realize that I do not have the tremendous drive, ambition, and ability required to prepare for this career.

This report is due on _____ (date)

American Graffiti
(in a Washington phone booth)

Who should I call first?

An English teacher!

Proofreading for Careers

A memo, also called an interoffice memorandum, is usually a message to one or more members of the same organization.

Most organizations have specially printed forms for memorandums. On page 141 is a memo typed on a typical interoffice memorandum form. Please show the necessary corrections of the grammar, spelling, sentence construction, capitalization, and typing. When you get to the third paragraph, refer to "Read About Numbers," in Appendix F, and learn the preferred way to express the time.

NEW AGE COMPUTER CORPORATION

DATE: June 30, 199-

TO: New Employees

FROM: Ruth Warren, Personnel Director

SUBJECT: New Age Employment Policies

Welcome to the New Age Computer corporation. We hope you will find your employment here enjoyable and personaly rewarding. These policies will help you understand our operation, and it will help you to realize the importance of you're job.

■ **Security**   Each new employee should promptly obtain their permanent identification card from the personnel department. A Guard is on duty around the clock. Every one who enters the building is required to show their identification card.

■ **Absenteeism**   Employees are expected to be in their assigned departments and ready to begin work at 8:30 am. If you are unable to come to work, please call my Administrative Assistant, Mr. Harrison, at Ext. 711, or myself. Him or I will inform the department Manager to who you have been asigned.

■ **Loyalty**   Loyalty is expected from all employees, information about new products or financial matters should not be disclosed to the publick. Any one who passes on such information is subject to immediate dismissal.

■ **Smoking**   Because most New Age people do not smoke, smoking is not permitted in the cafeteria, employees may, however, smoke on the terace outside the cafeteria.

If you have any questions about these policies, please see Mr. Harrison or myself.

What's your proofreading score?
Excellent_____ Good_____ Fair_____ Undistinguished_____

Practice Quiz

Take the Practice Quiz as though it were a real test. Don't look back through Section Five while you take this Practice Quiz. After the quiz is corrected, refer to the appropriate Read Units, shown in parentheses, for explanations of any item you may have missed.

Circle the correct pronoun.

1. Her family is taking (its/it's/their) vacation in August this year. **(Unit 28)**

2. Her family are taking (it/it's/their) vacations at different times this year. **(Unit 28)**

3. The Internal Revenue Service revised (its/it's/their) forms again this year. **(Unit 28)**

4. The Data Processing Department is on the third floor; (it is/they are) open every weekday. **(Unit 28)**

5. (No one/Noone) regrets this incident more than (I/me/myself). **(Units 26 and 30)**

6. Is Fran Smith better qualified than (her/she)? **(Unit 26)**

7. Sam and Jenny completed more of the programming than (I/me). **(Unit 26)**

8. No group is better liked than (they/them). **(Unit 26)**

9. The property on Adams Avenue was recently purchased by Goldman, Martinez, and (me/I/myself). **(Unit 25)**

10. Neither Mr. O'Connor nor (I/me/myself) will visit the Akron plant this year. **(Units 25 and 26)**

11. (Some one/Someone) from your office left (his or her/their) keys at the reception desk. **(Unit 30)**

12. (Every body/Everybody) in this office is being asked to do (his/their/they're) own thinking. **(Unit 30)**

13. The new copier on the counter is not (hers/her's/hers'). **(Unit 27)**

14. (Who/Whom) did you say will handle the new account? **(Unit 29)**

15. The new member was seated between Johnson and (me/I/myself). **(Units 25 and 26)**

16. (Who/Whom) was he talking to when he disclosed our plans? **(Unit 29)**

17. (Him/He) and Stranix will discuss it with (whoever/whomever) you suggest at Yuba. **(Unit 29)**

18. The guests of honor were Carol Potter and (I/me/myself). **(Unit 25)**

19. If (anyone/any one) of the boys would like a ticket, (he/they) may have one. **(Unit 30)**

20. He (hisself/himself) thinks (it's/its) too late. **(Unit 26)**

22. That young man is one upon (who/whom) you can rely. **(Unit 29)**

23. We sent letters to all (who/whom) we thought might visit our showroom. **(Unit 29)**

24. It is (I/me) who should take the risk. **(Unit 25)**

25. The one who complains the loudest is generally (him/he) (who/whom) contributes the least. **(Units 25 and 29)**

6

Run

Jump

Splash!

After Completing Section Six, You Will

- ✔ Use verbs so that the time (or tense) is expressed correctly.
- ✔ Use subjects and verbs that agree in number and person.

*E*very sentence has at least one verb. The verb tells either:

- what the subject **does** or **has** (action verb)
- what the subject **is** (existence, or state of being, verb)

Some verbs consist of one word, as in these sentences:

The personnel manager **interviewed** two applicants. [action verb]

The personnel manager **was** in the office. [existence verb, also known as state-of-being verb or linking verb]

Other verbs consist of two or more words—a main verb and one or more helping verbs—as in these sentences:

The personnel manager **has been interviewing** those applicants all day. [Action verb *interviewing* is the main verb; *has* and *been* are helping verbs.]

The personnel manager **should have been** in the office today. [Existence verb *been* is main verb; *should* and *have* are helping verbs.]

To use verbs correctly, please learn these principles:

Principle 1: Every verb has a basic form called the infinitive. The infinitive consists of *to* plus the verb spelled the way it is as a main entry in the dictionary.

Examples of infinitives are *to eat, to dance, to have, to be, to love, to work, to type.* The basic verb form that follows the word *to* is what to look for in the dictionary in order to find other forms of that verb.

Principle 2: The verb form depends on:

- **Time:** When does the action or existence take place?
  before (past)
  now (present)
  later (future)
- **Number:** Is the subject of the verb singular or plural?
  singular (one)
  plural (more than one)
- **Person:** Is the subject of the verb first, second, or third person?

1st person	*I* or *we*
2nd person	*you*
3rd person	*he, she, it,* or *they*; other pronouns such as *who, everybody,* or *which* (see Read Unit 30 for others); any noun, such as *story, supervisor,* or *pens*

Only the important rules governing verb forms are in this section. You may find that some of these rules don't require your study if you automatically choose the correct form.

BUT

If you grew up in—

- a non-English-speaking country
- a community where English is a "second language" for many of the residents
- a community where regional or ethnic English is usually used—

THEN

Getting the habit of applying these rules could mean the difference between success and failure in your career. Most of the nonstandard verb forms brought to your attention are the ones that are very noticeable in a business or professional environment. Therefore, it's helpful to apply the rules in this chapter to your everyday speech so that you'll automatically choose the standard forms.

Read Unit

31

TIMELY TIPS

Action or existence may occur in three principal time periods: past, present, and future. (Time periods are called *tense* in traditional grammar books.)

But time is not so simple as just before, now, or later. Some action or existence includes more than one period of time. For example, something may start in the past and continue into the present. Other action might start in the present and continue into the future. Using a combination of endings (or other form changes for "irregular" verbs) and helping verbs, our language expresses a complex range of time. Here are just a few of the kinds

Memo from the Wordsmith

"For there be women, fair as she,
Whose verbs and nouns do more agree."
                                        BRET HARTE

of time periods we can express. (The *time* of the action is interpreted after each sentence.)

> I **have been working** on this for days. [I started working in the past and am still working now in the present.]
>
> I **worked** on this for days. [I started in the past but am no longer working on it.]
>
> I'**ll work** on this for days. [I will continue to do the work in the future.]

Most grammar **rules** about verbs expressing time aren't included in this section; adults usually select the appropriate verb form without thinking about it. You're asked to learn, therefore, only those principles that will eliminate the kinds of errors that do occur in the language of intelligent adults.

TIME FOR REGULAR VERBS

BEFORE—past (With or without a helping verb)	NOW—present (No helping verb)	IN PROGRESS—*-ing* form (Helping verb required)	LATER—Future (Helping verb required)
talked	talk	is talking	will talk
has talked	talks	was talking	shall talk
have talked		am talking	would talk
had talked		are talking	should talk
		were talking	
		has been talking	
		have been talking	
		had been talking	
		will be talking	
		will have been talking	
		would have been talking	
		should have been talking	

Regular and Irregular Verb Forms

A verb is *regular* if it adds *-s, -ed* or *-ing* to the basic (infinitive*) form in the usual way.

Regular Verb Form Changes

Basic form	*walk*	They **walk** home every day.
Add *-s*	*walk**s***	He **walks** home every day.
Add *-ed*	*walk**ed***	We **walked** home today.
Add *-ing*	*walk**ing***	You are **walking** home today.

It is important to understand the code for verbs in your own dictionary. Look up the verb *walk* right now. Be sure to look at the **verb** *walk*, not the noun.

In some dictionaries, *walked, walking, walks* are right next to the entry word. This means all the forms of **regular** verbs are included in the dictionary.

---

* See Principle 1 on page 144.

In other dictionaries, you won't find the three other forms of *walk*. This means the changed forms of regular verbs are not included. When you don't find the other forms of a verb next to the entry word, it means the verb is regular and adds *-s*, *-ed*, or *-ing* as shown above.

An *irregular* verb does not follow any set pattern. Look, for example, at the irregular verb *begin*:

Basic form	*begin*	When I **begin** a new book, I hate to be interrupted.
Add *-s*	*begins*	Mari **begins** school today.

But from then on, *begin* doesn't obey the rules. It doesn't add *-ed;* instead, it changes to *began* or *begun*:

Nina **began** the project yesterday. Even though she had **begun** it, Claudio took it over.

Also, *begin* doubles its last letter before adding *-ing: beginning.*

The manager is **beginning** her speech now.

For irregular verbs, use a good dictionary to find the various forms.

Please look up *begin* in your dictionary now.

-S for Regular and Irregular Verbs

Add *-s* to the present time of a verb if the subject is a singular noun.

Ms. Henneman listen**s** carefully.

Add *-s* to the present time of a verb if the subject is a singular pronoun except *you* or *I*.

He (She *or* It) listen**s** carefully.
This (*or* That) feel**s** good.
Everybody (*or* Everyone, Anyone, Someone) listen**s** carefully.
Everything seem**s** fine at American Business Institute.

If the subject is a plural noun or pronoun or you or I, do not add s to the verb.

Pilots listen carefully. [plural noun *Pilots*]
They listen carefully. [plural pronoun *They*]
I listen carefully. [pronoun *I*]
You listen carefully. [pronoun *You*]
We listen carefully. [plural pronoun *We*]
These (*or* Those) seem useful. [plural pronoun *These* or *Those*]

Word to the Wise

If English is your second language, be especially alert to adding *-ed* to regular verbs:

- if the action is in the past
- if the main verb follows have, has, or had

Sentences with Two or More Verbs

When a sentence has two or more verbs, we generally express them in the same time (or tense).

PRESENT   She **thinks** that I **am** a millionaire.

PAST   Mr. Ivener **wrote** me a note in which he **implied** that I **passed** the accounting test.

In the preceding sentences, the same **time** is used for verbs in the same sentence. However, to express a general truth or something still happening now, use the **present**, even if the verb elsewhere in the sentence is in the **past**.

RIGHT   Ms. Zwolenski told us that Tokyo **is** larger than New York City.

WRONG   Ms. Zwolenski told us that Tokyo **was** larger than New York City. [Even though she told us in the past, Tokyo is still larger.]

RIGHT   The sales manager had demonstrated several times that our equipment **performs** better than any other on the market.

WRONG   The sales manager had demonstrated several times that our equipment **had performed** better than any other on the market. [If our equipment is still performing better now, in the present, then *had performed* is wrong.]

RIGHT   What **are** the titles of the books you borrowed from the library?

WRONG   What **were** the titles of the books you borrowed from the library? [Although you borrowed the books in the past, the titles are still the same.]

Recap   Change the incorrect verb.

1. I write the letter and Gloria mailed it.
2. Bernice tells Harry that I went to the party after all.
3. I said that you are wonderful in the play yesterday.

Check answers in Appendix H.

Replay Unit

31

A. Write in the blank a correct form of the verb in parentheses. Notice the **time** of the action stated in brackets at the end of the sentence. Add a helping verb when necessary.

EXAMPLE

They (talk) _____talked_____ every day on the telephone last week. [past]

1. He (type) _____ very accurately. [present]

2. The vice president (need) _____ to make a decision at once. [present]

3. The merchandise (arrive) _____ yesterday. [past]

4. They (sail) _____ to Catalina this week. [-*ing* form]

5. The floor is slippery because the custodian (wax) _____ it today. [past]

6. Mr. Martinez (paint) _____ beautiful landscapes. [present]

7. The world (look) _____ brighter from behind a smile. [present]

8. The foreman (climb) _____ up the ladder in order to reach the carton. [past]

9. We (gain) _____ some insight into why the problems exist. [past]

10. They (want) _____ something they cannot have. [present]

11. She (want) _____ something she cannot have. [present]

12. He (want) _____ something he could not have. [past]

13. She (want) _____ something she cannot have. [future]

14. They (offer) _____ the employees a raise. [past]

15. He believes he (select) _____ a business career. [future]

16. Daniel (look) _____ handsome today. [present]

17. Dara (look) _____ beautiful. [past]

18. The manager (consider) _____ that problem tomorrow. [future]

19. Michael (consider) _____ that problem now. [-*ing* form]

20. You (want) _____ those items yesterday. [past]

21. I (stay) _____ at that hotel every July. [present]

22. They (stay) _____ there now. [-*ing* form]

23. We (watch) _____ television all day. [past]

24. You (need) _____ these items in order to build the
stereo. [present]

25. Marketing people (talk) _____ about local, regional, and
national markets. [past]

B. Each of the following sentences has a verb error. Cross out the incorrect verb and write the correct form in the blank.

EXAMPLE

_____has_____ We discovered that Disneyland h̸a̸d a parade every night.

_____ **1.** The officer said that obeying traffic laws was necessary for accident prevention.

_____ **2.** Seth knew that New York was the biggest city in the
United States.

_____ **3.** All the students agree that the new courses were
more difficult than the old ones.

_____ **4.** What were the names of the authors of the books on
last week's bestseller list?

_____ **5.** Robert Stern said the Hewlett-Packard 150 was still
being used in his office.

_____ **6.** The group meeting in the conference room were
former employees of General Motors.

_____ **7.** He taught us that rivers flowed into oceans.

_____ **8.** We learned that no scientist knew with certainty
how the universe originated.

_____ **9.** Ms. Anderson assured us that there were many fine
people in Suisun City.

_____ **10.** Although the thief has been caught, tried, and con-
victed, no one has yet discovered where the $5 mil-
lion was.

Check your answers in Appendix H.

Read Unit

32 *DELINQUENT VERBS*

Delinquents—verbs that won't behave as they should—are introduced in
this unit.

> The best way to deal with these irregular verbs is (1) to recognize
> they are irregular, and (2) look them up in the dictionary when
> uncertain of form or spelling.

IRREGULAR VERBS

Column 1		Column 2	Column 3
		Simple Past (no helping verb)	Past Participle (use helping verb)
A	B		
begin	begins	began	begun
break	breaks	broke	broken
choose	chooses	chose	chosen
do	does	did	done
drink	drinks	drank	drunk
eat	eats	ate	eaten
fly	flies	flew	flown
give	gives	gave	given
go	goes	went	gone
hang (to suspend)	hangs	hung	hung[a]
ring	rings	rang	rung
rise	rises	rose	risen
run	runs	ran	run
see	sees	saw	seen
speak	speaks	spoke	spoken
stand	stands	stood[b]	stood[b]
swing	swings	swung	swung
take	takes	took	taken
wear	wears	wore	worn

[a] *Hang* referring to a method of putting to death is regular: *hang, hangs, hanged, hanged.*
[b] Using *stood* for *stayed* is a serious error in both writing and in speech. *Stayed* is the simple past and past participle of *stay.*

For information about irregular verbs, look up the "basic" form—the one shown in column 1, side *A* for the "delinquents" listed here.*

About Column 1

Side A

The words under *A* are the basic forms. Use them with the helping verbs *will, shall, would, should, do, did, does, might, may, can,* and *could* no matter what the subject is.

> He **did begin**.
> I **should begin**.
> She **will begin**.

Also use *A* words without helping verbs when the subject is *I, you,* a plural pronoun, or a plural noun.

> I **speak** the truth. [*I*]
> Please **join** us. [*you* understood]
> Those **break** easily. [plural pronoun]
> The two little boys **break** everything. [plural noun]

* For *lie/lay* information, see "Grammar Supplement," Section 12 and a college dictionary.

Side B

Use the *B* words (which end in *s*) with any singular subject except *I* or *you.*

Everybody **begins** at the same time.
She **begins** at 9 a.m.
Jamie Lynn **begins** later.

About Column 2

Use these verbs with any subject to express the past without a helping verb—**but never with helping verbs**.

She **began** the work.
The glass **broke**.
The bells **rang**.

About Column 3

Use these forms **with a helping verb,** such as *have, has, had, been, was, were.*

I **have begun** the work.
The glass **was broken**.
The bells **will have been rung** by that time.

Replay Unit

32

Refer to the Irregular Verbs table on page 151 when necessary in order to write the correct verb form in the blank. Change only the incorrect verbs. Do not make a change just because you feel another word would sound better. If all the verbs in a sentence are correct, write *C* in the blank.

EXAMPLE

_____hung_____   I ~~hanged~~ up all my clothes.

_____   **1.** I thought it was broke, but it had just worn out.

_____   **2.** He had just began work when the bell rang.

_____   **3.** He choose the best one for himself. [present]

_____   **4.** He had chose the best one for himself yesterday.

_____   **5.** She do all the complaining. [present]

_____ 6. He has drunk all the tea.

_____ 7. Everyone in this office eat donuts. [present]

_____ 8. Smith done a good job in figuring those prices. [past]

_____ 9. They flies to New York every year. [present]

_____ 10. He give his secretary an increase in salary. [past]

_____ 11. They had went to the convention before they saw him.

_____ 12. We have rose up together to fight the enemy.

_____ 13. The treasurer has ran away again.

_____ 14. She had wore the new suit to the office again.

_____ 15. He should have stood in bed today.

_____ 16. I seen him when he was reading the letter.

_____ 17. I have taken it with me.

_____ 18. The men always wears suits to the office.

_____ 19. She had saw that file before.

_____ 20. I spoke to him on the telephone yesterday.

_____ 21. If a man don't know what port he's steering for, no wind is favorable.   SENECA, Roman philosopher

_____ 22. The maid rung the dinner bell 15 minutes ago.

_____ 23. The maid has already rung the dinner bell three times.

_____ 24. The puppy ran away again.

_____ 25. They always gives the assembler three days to complete that kind of job.

Please check your answers in Appendix H.

Word to the Wise

The irregular verbs in the table on page 151 are among the most commonly misused verbs. Since other irregular verbs are used incorrectly also, careful writers refer to the dictionary to make sure of the standard form.

Read Unit

33 DICTIONARY DATA

The verbs that don't behave as they should—the delinquents—included in Unit 32 are just some of over 100 verbs that change forms in irregular ways. By using English over a period of years, you've automatically mastered most of the irregularities. If, however, you're like most people, a few still cause you to hesitate. You may also use a few incorrectly without being aware of it.

Since there are more irregular verbs than is practical to study, it's important to know how to interpret verb information in the dictionary. When looking up a verb, you can find its "principal parts." The **principal parts** of any verb are:

- Basic form (*break, see, walk,* and so on)
- Simple past form *(broke, saw, walked)*
- Past participle form *(broken, seen, walked)*
- Present participle form *(breaking, seeing, walking)*

The explanations below will enable you to use the dictionary intelligently.

Basic Form

The basic form (infinitive without "to") is easily recognized because it is the dictionary entry word for that verb. Samples are in column 1, side *A* of the Irregular Verbs table in Read Unit 32.

Present Participle

The present participle is easy to recognize because it always ends with *-ing.* Be aware, however, of spelling variations.

- Usually the *-ing* is simply added to the unchanged infinitive form: *see, seeing.*
- Sometimes a final *e* is omitted before adding *-ing: love, loving.*
- Sometimes a final letter is doubled before adding *-ing: win, winning.*

Simple Past and Past Participle
Regular Verbs

For regular verbs, the simple past and the past participle are the same: just add *-ed—talk**ed*** is both simple past and past participle. Therefore, we use *talked* or the *-ed* form of any regular verb either with or without a helping verb. Both *I talked* and *I have talked* are correct, depending on which idea you intend to express.

Irregular Verbs

The explanation that follows **requires the use of your dictionary.**

1. All the column 2 verb forms in Unit 32 are simple past, which means they are used **without** a helping verb. In the dictionary, the form following the entry word (sometimes after the -ing form) is the simple past. This means it belongs in Column 2 and may not be used **with** a helping verb. Look up *begin* as an example and see where *began* appears in your dictionary.

2. The form in the dictionary **after** the simple past is the past participle and could be listed in column 3 of the table. Therefore, a helping verb **is required.** Notice how *begun* follows *began* in your dictionary.

3. If only one *past* form appears, that form is both the simple past *and* the past participle. In that case, use that verb form **with or without** a helping verb. Look up *bring*. Notice that only one past form appears: *brought.*

4. Sometimes the dictionary entry has *or* or *also* between two forms of the verb. This means either word can be used with or without a helping verb. *Also*, however, means the second word is less acceptable. Look up *broadcast*. Notice that the simple past is either *broadcast* or *broadcasted*. Since no other form follows, the same two words are also suitable for the past participle, as explained in item 3 above.

5. Now look up *show*. Notice that the first form after the entry (or after the -ing word) is *showed*, which means it's the simple past—the one to use with no helping verb. Following *showed* is "*shown or showed*." Therefore, either one can be used with a helping verb. With that particular word, if you use *showed*, you can't go wrong; but it you use *shown* without a helping verb, you're in trouble.

6. Finally, look up *occur*. Notice that the *r* is doubled before adding -*ed* or -*ing*. When in the slightest doubt about whether to double the last letter before adding -*ed* or -*ing* or whether to drop a final *e* before adding -*ing*, **look it up!**

Memo to the Conscientious but Restless Student

Did you take the necessary few minutes to look up each word suggested in the preceding six dictionary-use hints? Did you also refer to columns 2 and 3 in the table in Unit 32? If you did, you now know how to use your dictionary intelligently to obtain information about verbs. It's not necessary to memorize hundreds or thousands of forms; just know how to look them up.

Replay Unit

33

A. Fill in the blanks with the principal parts of these irregular verbs. Please use your dictionary whenever you have the slightest doubt about the correct form.

INFINITIVE	PRESENT PARTICIPLE (*ing* ending)	SIMPLE PAST (no helping verb)	PAST PARTICIPLE (use helping verb)
EXAMPLE			
beat	beating	beat	beaten or beat
1. be*			
2. bite			
3. blow			
4. come			
5. cost			
6. draw			
7. fall			
8. forecast			
9. forget			
10. freeze			
11. grind			
12. hide			
13. lead			
14. pay			
15. shake			
16. sink			
17. sing			
18. throw			
19. win			
20. write			

B. Each sentence below has an incorrectly used irregular verb. Write the correct form in the blank. Use your dictionary to be sure of the correct spelling.

EXAMPLE

    frozen   My toes were ~~froze~~.

* Other parts are *am, are, is.*

_____ **1.** Roberta Simon has beat all previous sales records.

_____ **2.** Ms. Jaffe done the job right.

_____ **3.** Because Sam has broke one of the rules, the boiler burst.

_____ **4.** Laurie hanged the picture, but it fell.

_____ **5.** I should have stood at that job for another month.

Please check your answers in Appendix H.
Then take the **POP QUIZ** in Appendix A.

Read Unit
34

TO BE, OR NOT TO BE

"To be, or not to be: that is the question" is one of the most often quoted Shakespearean lines. The infinitive _to be_ has yet another claim to fame: It is the infinitive of the most irregular verb in the English language—and probably the most commonly used. If you grew up where a community dialect is frequently spoken, give careful attention to the forms below. They are extremely important for your business career.

The forms of the verb _be_ are _am, is, are, was, were, be, being,_ and _been._

Always precede _been_ by _have, had,_ or _has._

We **have been** healthy all year.

Always precede _be_ by _could, would, should, will, shall, can, may, might,_ or _must_ or by _to._

He **may be** an expert.

Always precede the infinitive _to be_ with a verb.

I **want to be** successful.

IF THE SUBJECT IS _I_

Use	As in These Sentences	Avoid	As in These Sentences
I am	**I am** busy now.	I be	× **I be** busy now.
I was	**I was** busy then.	I is	× **I is** busy now.
I will (shall) be	**I will** (shall) **be** busy tomorrow.		
I have been	**I have been** busy for days.	I been	× **I been** busy for days.
I will (shall) have been	**I will** (shall) **have been** busy long before he arrives.	I been	× **I been** busy long before he arrives.

IF THE SUBJECT IS *YOU*

Use	As in These Sentences	Avoid	As in These Sentences
you are	**Are you** busy now?	you be	✕ **You be** busy now?
you were	**You were** my best friend.	you is	✕ **You is** my best friend.
you will be	**You will be** busy tomorrow.	you was	✕ **You was** busy yesterday.
you have been	**You have been** busy for 15 minutes.	you been	✕ **You been** busy for 15 minutes.
you will have been	**You will have been** to see him before I get there.	you been	✕ **You been** to see him before I get there.

IF THE SUBJECT IS A SINGULAR NOUN OR SINGULAR PRONOUN EXCEPT *YOU* OR *I*

Use	As in These Sentences	Avoid	As in These Sentences
he is	**He is** home now.	he be	✕ **He be** home now.
she was	**She was** home yesterday.	she be	✕ **She be** coming over soon.
it will be	**It will be** there for a week.	it been	✕ **It been** there for a week.
he has been	**He has been** busy for a week.	he were	✕ **He were** here.
he had been	**He had been** busy all week.		
everybody is	**Everybody is** here.		✕ **Everybody be** here. [except as a command]
everyone was	**Everyone was** busy.		✕ **Everyone were** going.
anyone was	**Was anyone** busy?		✕ **Were anyone** going?
Jorge is	**Jorge is** the new accountant.		✕ **Jorge be** the new accountant.
the book had been	**The book had been** lost.		✕ **The book been** on the table.
the train was	**The train was** late.		✕ **The train were** late.

IF THE SUBJECT IS A PLURAL NOUN OR PRONOUN

Use	As in These Sentences	Avoid	As in These Sentences
we (they) are	**We** (They) **are** busy.	we (they) be	✕ **We** (They) **be** busy.
we (they) were	**We** (They) **were** busy.	we (they) is	✕ **We** (They) **is** busy.
we (they) will be	**We** (They) **will be** here today.	we (they) was	✕ **We** (They) **was** busy.
we (they) have been	**We** (They) **have been** busy all day.	we (they) been	✕ **We** (They) **been** busy all day.
we (they) had been	**We** (They) **had been** busy all week.		
we (they) will have been	**We** (They) **will have been** here for a year when the new building opens.		
the boys have been	**The boys have been** late every day.		✕ **The boys has been** late every day.
the accountants are	**The accountants are** early.		✕ **The accountants is** early.
the disks were	**The disks were** ready.		✕ **The disks was** ready.

Memo from the Wordsmith

ARITHMETIC PROBLEM

2 plus 2 *is* 4, but 2 and 2 *are* 4, and 2 times 2 *is* 4.

I don't know why; that's just the way it is . . . are?

Contractions of many expressions in this unit are appropriate for speech and for nearly all business writing:

CORRECT   **We're** shipping your order today.

CORRECT   **We are** shipping your order today.

CORRECT   **She's** the new accountant.

CORRECT   **She is** the new accountant.

Replay Unit

34

If the form of the verb *be* is correct, write *C* in the blank. Otherwise, make the necessary correction.

EXAMPLE

_____were_____ They ~~was~~ at work yesterday.

_____ 1. We was going to meet them in Miami for the meeting.

_____ 2. They be going to Miami for the meeting also.

_____ 3. How long you planning to be gone?

_____ 4. We been gone for a year and no one misses us.

_____ 5. We is pleased to announce a new policy.

_____ 6. We hope this new service be helpful to you.

_____ 7. We be enclosing your new catalog.

_____ 8. We're hoping to visit your new showroom soon.

_____ 9. I'll be happy to ship the toasters today.

_____ 10. You is required to pay for them within thirty days.

_____ 11. Was you present when the officers of the company entered the room?

_____ 12. Taylor were happy to receive the new terminal for his office.

Writing for Your Career

Modern business communicators know the value of a natural and conversational writing style. One technique that contributes to a natural tone is to use contractions. Do not, however, contract *would* (*I'd, you'd, we'd,* etc.), although this contraction is fine for conversation. Also avoid contractions such as *sec'y* (for *secretary*) and *ass'n* (for *association*). Read Unit 48 has a list of contractions appropriate for business writing.

_____ 13. Everyone in our office are planning to take the night flight to Dallas.

_____ 14. Do you think everybody is going?

_____ 15. The account books was misplaced because the clerk misfiled them.

_____ 16. The shipping clerks was late every day this week.

_____ 17. However, the salespeople is always on time.

_____ 18. The new saleswoman been meeting her quota every week.

_____ 19. I have been away from my office all day and missed your calls.

_____ 20. Was you away from your office yesterday also?

_____ 21. The women was waiting in the lobby.

_____ 22. Mark Allen be directing the film.

_____ 23. Mark is a graduate of Columbia University.

_____ 24. Dr. Melanie Sweet be in Philadelphia today.

_____ 25. The toe be the part of the foot used to find furniture in the dark.

Answers are in Appendix H.

Read Unit

35

THE SUBJECT-VERB COMBO

Every sentence has at least one subject-verb combination. The verb is the action or existence word, and the subject names who or what is acting or existing. Every subject is either a noun or a pronoun. A word group that lacks a subject-verb combination is neither a sentence nor a clause; it is a phrase.

Recognizing the Subject-Verb Combination

■ Find the verb—the action or existence word.

Carmen dances in the show. [*dances* = word telling an action]

■ Ask "Who or what is doing the action?"

Carmen dances in the show. [*Carmen* = word telling who does the action—dancing]

Carmen is the subject of the verb *dances*.

To apply the principles of English usage reviewed in Units 36 and 37, you need to identify subject-verb combinations.

The subject is usually at the beginning of a clause—a word group containing a subject and a verb.

The student studies. [Subject = *student*—tells who is doing the action; verb = *studies*—the action.]

If a sentence has more than one clause, each clause has its own subject and verb.

Some students study and others daydream. [Subjects = *students, others;* verbs = *study, daydream*.]

In questions, a helping verb usually precedes the subject, and a main verb usually follows the subject. The helping verb plus the main verb make up the complete verb.

Do students study? [Subject = *students;* verb = *do study*.]

Sometimes an introductory expression precedes the subject.

In Schenectady, students do study. [Subject = *students;* verb = *do study*.]

Describing words sometimes precede the subject.

Ambitious and diligent students study. [Subject = *students;* verb = *study*.]

Sometimes a prepositional phrase separates the subject from the verb. The subject is never within a prepositional phrase.

Karen, along with several other occupational therapists, is due for a salary increase. [Subject = *Karen;* verb = *is;* prepositional phrase = along with several other occupational therapists.]

Word to the Wise

A prepositional phrase is a word group beginning with a preposition and ending with a noun or pronoun called an object. A prepositional phrase never has a subject-verb combination within it. A few common prepositions are *in, to, with, by,* and *for.* Examples of two- or three-word prepositions are *along with, in addition to,* and *as well as.* You can review prepositions and prepositional phrases in Unit 5.

In a sentence with more than one clause, one of the clauses may "interrupt" another; that is, one clause separates the subject from the verb of another clause.

⌐———— interrupting clause ————⌐
A person who has many skills and talents is fortunate. [Subject and verb of independent clause = *person* and *is;* subject and verb of interrupting dependent clause = *who* and *has.*]

Some subjects have two or more parts. These are called *compound subjects.*

Laziness and irresponsibility hinder success. [Compound subjects = *Laziness* and *irresponsibility;* verb = *hinder.*]

A subject may have two or more verbs. These are called *compound verbs.*

Robin sings and dances. [Subject = *Robin;* compound verbs = *sings* and *dances.*]

Although the subject normally is before the verb, sometimes the order is reversed. The order is almost always reversed in questions.

In the supply cabinet will be found six typewriter ribbons and four floppy disks. [Compound subject = *ribbons* and *disks;* verb = *will be found.*]

Are six ribbons enough? [Subject = *ribbons;* verb = *are.*]

Recap   Circle the subjects and underline the verbs in the following sentences.

1. A bird in the hand is worth two in the bush.
2. Everyone except your brothers Anthony and Mark was laid off.
3. Lewis and Martin told jokes and sang.

Check your answers in Appendix H.

Although the subject is always a noun or a pronoun, it may look like a verb when it names an activity.

Remember that a subject names who or what does the action or exists. A word that names who or what acts or exists is automatically a subject and therefore a noun or a pronoun.

Studying is my favorite pastime. [Subject = *studying;* verb = *is.*]
To run would be foolish. [Subject = *To run;* verb = *would be.*]

Sometimes the subject is invisible; that is, it is understood but not expressed. The "understood" subject is always *you* and introduces a sentence that gives a command or a polite request.

Put a new ribbon in the printer. [Subject = *You* understood; verb = *put.*]
Please call before Friday. [Subject = *You* understood; verb = *call.*]

Replay Unit

35

Underline the verb and circle the subject. When a verb is preceded by a helping verb, underline the two or three words making up the *verb phrase*. Remember that a sentence may have more than one subject-verb combination, which means it has two or more clauses.

EXAMPLE

A (company) may issue preferred stock after common (stock) has been issued.

1. I enjoy the sunset.
2. The salespeople are doing their jobs well.
3. Do you read many magazines?
4. He did such a fine job that I could not find a mistake.
5. We voted for him and he was elected.
6. Under the circumstances we won't issue a statement now.
7. For the position of receptionist, a pleasant manner is important.
8. Advancement comes to workers who do their work well.
9. Hard, steady work turns daydreaming into reality.
10. Playing Monopoly is fun.
11. During the past year our sales have risen dramatically.
12. Success-oriented students study several hours a day.
13. Brian is the one who presented the more accurate analysis.
14. Two old memory typewriters are in the rear of the word processing center.
15. Rachel will probably receive the promotion because of her mathematics ability.
16. Everyone in the shop is working on the blueprints.
17. Xerox manufactures copiers and computers.

18. My assistant, who is on vacation this week, will gladly help you next week.

19. Would you like my secretary's help next week?

20. Considerable turnover of personnel is one of the problems prevalent in the fast-food business.

21. Both poverty and riches are a state of mind as well as of pocketbook.

22. The English Shoe Company distributes its shoes through over two thousand shoe stores all around the United States.

23. We are returning your money order and hope that you will take it to your local English Shoe Store at 30711 Ganado Drive.

24. The fabulous Mr. J. C. Penney, who started with a small store in 1902, built a multibillion-dollar business empire.

25. The mind, like a parachute, functions only when open.

Read Unit

36

SUBJECT-VERB HARMONY: STEP 1

A subject and its verb should be in harmony. This means they must get along with each other—or *agree*. To make a subject and verb agree, the first step is to locate the subject and decide whether it's singular or plural.

Singular Subjects

A singular subject is one person, place, thing, idea.

lady	it	glass
book	he	this
computer	honesty	that

A singular subject may be a collective noun acting as "one."

club	jury	staff
class	herd	committee

A collective noun is like a single package that contains several items. If you refer to the entire "package," the collective noun is singular. (See Unit 38.)

A singular subject results when a singular noun follows *or* or *nor*.

president or general manager	the boy or the girl
Mary nor he	noun or pronoun

A singular subject results when *each, every,* or *many a* precedes it.

each accountant   every secretary   many a child

A singular subject may be an indefinite singular pronoun.

In addition to the following examples, indefinite singular pronouns include any pronoun ending with *one*, *body*, or *thing*—such as *anyone*, *somebody*, *everything*.

each	one	either
another	neither	

Recap   Circle the correct verb of each pair in parentheses.

   1. Every one of the students (work/works) efficiently.

   2. Either the treasurer or the controller (were/was) at the meeting.

   3. Many a person (are/is) in need of food and shelter.

   4. The staff always (vote/votes) for him.

Check your answers in Appendix H.

Plural Subjects

A plural subject means more than one person, place, thing, idea.

ladies	glasses	they
books	these	all
computers	those	committees

A collective noun is a plural subject when the members act as separate individuals.

club	herd	faculty
class	staff	committee
jury	family	management

The **faculty disagree** about the new grading policy. [not *disagrees*]

If reference is made to *parts* of the "package" (or collective noun), the package is broken. Then consider all the separate items in the package and make the collective noun plural. (Review Unit 28 now.)

A subject is plural if it has two or more words joined by *and*.

man and woman	John and she	IBMs and Apples

However, if *each*, *every*, or *many a* precedes the parts of a subject joined by *and*, the subject is singular:

Each boy and girl is ready to learn. [singular subject]

A plural subject results when a plural noun or pronoun follows *or* or *nor*.

one boy or three girls	Mary nor they
vice president or general managers	nouns or pronouns

Both, *many*, *several*, and *few* are plural.

Recap   Circle the correct verb of each pair in parentheses.

1. Either one boy or two girls from this class (has/have) parts in the play.
2. The jury (are/is) arguing among themselves about the physical evidence.
3. Each man and woman (go/goes) in different directions.
4. The ladies in waiting (serve/serves) Princess Diana.

Check your answers in Appendix H.

Singular or Plural Subjects

The subject must agree in number (singular or plural) with the verb. The subjects *all, none, any, more, most, some,* or a fraction such as *half* are, however, **singular or plural** depending on the word they refer to.

Some of it **is** on the table. [Subject *Some* refers to singular *it;* verb, *is,* must then be singular.]

Most of them **are** on the table. [Subject *Most* refers to plural *them;* verb, *are,* must then be plural.]

If the item referred to in the prepositional phrase can be counted, use a plural verb.

Half of the apples **are** on the floor.

If the item cannot be counted because it is in bulk or is not in separable condition, use a singular verb.

All of the applesauce is on the floor.

The word following *of* or *of the* in each example sentence above cannot be the subject because this word is the object of the prepositional phrase.

Writing for Your Career

For more concise writing, you can omit the preposition *of* with certain words:

Half [omit *of*] the apples are on the floor.
All [omit *of*] the applesauce is on the floor.

If *of* is omitted, *all, half, none, any, more, most, some,* or *a fraction* becomes an adjective and the word described is the subject. It isn't important, in this case, to analyze the grammar. Just try to express ideas concisely; sometimes this will mean avoiding prepositional phrases that use *of.*

Replay Unit

36

In these sentences, the subjects and verbs are in harmony; that is, they agree in number (singular or plural). First underline the verb, which may be one or two words. Then circle the subject, which also might be more than one word. In the blank, write *S* or *P* to show whether the subject is singular or plural.

Either a (government) or a (corporation) <u>issues</u> bonds.   _S_

1. Several groups were invited to the meeting.   _____
2. For years the Penney stores were called The Golden Rule Stores.   _____
3. My family took separate vacations this year.   _____
4. My family piled into the truck and left the old homestead.   _____
5. Wong & Lopez, Inc., has an office in the new building.   _____
6. Everyone was waiting in line quietly.   _____
7. Neither of your responses seems satisfactory.   _____
8. The report and the letter were on my desk.   _____
9. Either the report or the letter was on my desk.   _____
10. Neither the engineer nor the drafters are here now.   _____
11. Both the secretary's story and the typist's story sound true.   _____
12. Neither the secretary's story nor the typist's story sounds true.   _____
13. The battery, the radio, and the antenna are missing.   _____
14. In other words, everything is gone.   _____
15. Neither Mr. O'Day nor Ms. Goldberg will work on it.   _____
16. Each person rides the elevator twice a day.   _____
17. The staff took their seats in the Board Room.   _____
18. The jury arrived at a verdict in two hours.   _____
19. Any one of us can do the job.   _____
20. Both a lawyer and a layman should be present.   _____
21. Half of the pie is gone.   _____
22. Half the pie is gone.*   _____
23. All of the workers are on strike today.   _____
24. All is quiet on the Western Front.   _____
25. All the workers are on strike today.*   _____

See answers in Appendix H.

* Omitting *of* changes *half* and *all* to adjectives and improves the writing style.

SUBJECT-VERB HARMONY: STEP 2

In Read Unit 35 you reviewed how to locate the subject by first finding the verb and then asking who or what did the action. Then you practiced distinguishing between singular and plural subjects. The next step in subject-verb harmony is making the verb agree with its subject in number (singular or plural).

Although most nouns become plural by adding -s, do *not* apply this principle to verbs. As you saw in Units 31 and 32, adding -s to a verb makes it agree with a singular noun or a singular pronoun (except *you* or *I*).

> If the subject is a singular noun or pronoun (except *you* and *I*), add -s to the verb.

PRONOUNS

He run**s** five miles every day.

This mean**s** a great deal to me.

Everyone arrive**s** at 9 a.m.

NOUNS

Ms. Chandler run**s** five miles every day.

This **honor** mean**s** a great deal to me.

Either **Charles or Dolores** arrive**s** at 9 a.m.

> If the subject is a plural noun, plural pronoun, *you*, or *I*, do not add -s to the verb.

PRONOUNS

We run five miles every day.

These mean a great deal to me.

They arrive at 9 a.m.

I arrive at 10 a.m.

NOUNS

Jim and Walt run five miles every day.

The **honors mean** a great deal to me.

The **employees arrive** at 9 a.m.

> When *or* or *nor* joins the elements of a subject, look only at the part of the subject following *or* or *nor*. Then decide which verb form to use.

WHICH IS IT?   Neither Charles nor Dolores (arrives/arrive) at 9 a.m.

HOW TO FIND OUT?   With your finger, cover all words before *Dolores*. Then it's easy to decide: *Dolores arrives at 9 a.m.*

CORRECT FORM   Neither Charles nor Dolores **arrives** at 9 a.m.

WHICH IS IT?	Ms. Pitz, Mr. Schaefer, or two Kensington seniors (represent/represents) Buffalo in the annual contest.
HOW TO FIND OUT?	Imagine omitting all words before *seniors*. Then it's easy to decide: *seniors represent Buffalo in the annual contest.*
CORRECT FORM	Ms. Pitz, Mr. Schaefer, or two Kensington seniors **represent** Buffalo in the annual contest.
WHICH IS IT?	Either Christine or I usually (sort/sorts) the mail at Kensington.
HOW TO FIND OUT?	Imagine starting with "I." Then see which form agrees with "I." I usually sort the mail at Kensington.
CORRECT FORM	Either Christine or I usually sort the mail at Kensington.

> Words separating the subject from its verb usually do not affect the number (singular or plural) of the verb.

RIGHT	The **box** of tools **is** on the table.
WRONG	The **box** of tools **are** on the table.

Why? The subject is the singular noun *box*. Therefore, use the singular verb form *is*. Ignore the prepositional phrase *of tools* when deciding on the number of the verb.

RIGHT	The **supervisors,** as well as the president, **are** here today.
WRONG	The **supervisors,** as well as the president, **is** here today.

Why? The subject is the plural noun *supervisors*. Therefore, use the plural verb form *are*. Ignore the prepositional phrase *as well as the president* when deciding on the verb form.

RIGHT	The **reason** for his difficulties **seems** clear.
WRONG	The **reason** for his difficulties **seem** clear.

Why? The subject is the singular noun *reason*. Therefore, use the singular verb form *seems*. Ignore the interrupting prepositional phrase when deciding on the verb.

Memo from the Wordsmith

The "Queen's English" was fractured when the British Safety Council published a photo of Prince Charles with his arm in a sling after he had fallen off a horse. The caption read "Ouch! One in three accidents are caused by falls."

Recap   Correct the verb in the caption in Memo from the Wordsmith.

Check your answer in Appendix H.

RIGHT   The **reasons** his job was difficult **seem** clear.

WRONG   The **reasons** his job was difficult **seems** clear.

Why? *Reasons* is the plural subject. Therefore, use the plural verb form (no -s). Ignore the clause *his job was difficult,* which separates *reasons* from *seem.*

> The words *here, there,* and *where* are not subjects. In a sentence introduced by *here, there,* or *where,* the subject usually follows the verb.

RIGHT   There **was** a **box** of tools on the table.

WRONG   There **were** a **box** of tools on the table.

Why? The subject is the singular noun *box.* Therefore, use the singular verb form *was. Of tools* is a prepositional phrase.

RIGHT   There **were** several **boxes** of tools on the table.

WRONG   There **was** several **boxes** of tools on the table.

Why? Because the subject is the plural noun *boxes,* use the plural verb form *were.*

RIGHT   Here **is** the **schedule**.

WRONG   Here **are** the **schedule**.

Why? The subject is the singular noun *schedule.* Therefore, use the singular form of the verb *is.*

RIGHT   Here **come** my **sisters**.

WRONG   Here **comes** my **sisters**.

Why? The subject is the plural noun *sisters.* Therefore, use the plural form of the verb *come.*

RIGHT   Where **are** your **sisters**?

WRONG   Where**'s** your **sisters**.

Why? The subject is *sisters.* Use the plural *are* instead of the *'s,* which is a contraction of the singular *is.*

> If *who, which,* or *that* is a pronoun subject, the number (singular or plural) depends on the noun for which the pronoun is substituting.

RIGHT   This is the **man who talks** with you on the phone every day.

WRONG   This is the **man who talk** with you on the phone every day.

Why? *Who* is the subject of the verb *talks*. Since *who* substitutes for the singular noun *man*, use the singular verb form **talks**.

RIGHT   These are the **men who talk** to you on the phone every day.

WRONG   These are the **men who talks** to you on the phone every day.

Why? *Who* is the subject of the verb *talks*. As *who* substitutes for the plural noun *men*, use the plural verb form (without the *-s*).

Replay Unit

37

Here is an opportunity to replay what you studied in both Units 36 and 37. Circle the subject (which may be more than one word). In the blank, write *C* if the verb agrees with its subject. Otherwise, write the verb in the form that does agree with the subject. Remember: Add *-s* to make verbs singular unless the subject is *you* or *I*.

EXAMPLE

_____are_____   Where's the best (places) to buy software?

_____   1. Several groups was invited to participate in the meeting.

_____   2. She don't want to go to the meeting with me.

_____   3. There was several people waiting for the tickets.

_____   4. Warren & Chilson, Inc., have an office in the new building.

_____   5. The latest figures on yesterday's sale is available.

_____   6. The report and the letter were on my desk.

_____   7. A report on the accounts have been completed.

_____   8. Neither he nor they are going.

_____   9. Neither he nor his assistant wrap the parcels carefully.

_____   10. Here are the new machines.

_____   11. Ms. Svendsen rarely arrive late at Bristol.

_____   12. The dean and his assistant drives to Fall River every morning.

_____   13. He usually do his work carefully.

_____   14. The new copier don't work well.

_____   15. My cousin, as well as many of my aunts and uncles, work here.

_____ **16.** Neither the attorney nor the director is able to prepare the report.

_____ **17.** Neither Professor Pribble nor I meets the class today.

_____ **18.** There go the latest models.

_____ **19.** These are the typewriters which has new ribbons.

_____ **20.** The class are finishing their application letters.

_____ **21.** Roberta Simon, as well as all her aides, deserve a raise.

_____ **22.** Another carton of envelopes has just arrived with the return address incorrectly printed.

_____ **23.** Every man and woman in this country want to serve.

_____ **24.** All the calendars was mailed to our customers yesterday.

_____ **25.** One-third of the pies has been sold.

Please check answers in Appendix H.

Read Unit

38   *IF I WERE A MILLIONAIRE*

We've all indulged in fantasies about what we would do if we were someone else or if conditions were enormously different from our present reality. The English language provides a special verb form for the unreal—that is, for expressing ideas contrary to reality. This special form—using the word *were*—is used principally when the subject follows *if, as though,* or *wish.* Use *were* regardless of what the subject is if the statement could not be true.

ORDINARY	**CONTRARY TO REALITY**
I **was** at home yesterday. [true]	If **I were** you, I would accept that position. [I am *not* you.]
Everyone is going to the meeting. **Everyone was not going** to the meeting. [Both statements are true.]	If **everyone were** to go to the meeting, who would mind the store? [Everyone is *not* going to the meeting.]
He was staring at the princess. [true]	John wishes that **he were** a prince. [His parents are not king and queen, and he's not married to a princess.]
It wasn't the fault of the Board of Directors that the company folded. [true]	**If it weren't** for the Board of Directors, this company would fold. [The Board *is* taking care of the situation.]

Replay Unit

38

Make necessary corrections. If the sentence is already correct, write *C* in the blank.

EXAMPLE

_____was_____ If Juanita ~~were~~ at work this morning, she probably picked up the mail. [She might have been. We're not sure.]

_____ 1. If I were not certain of how to get there, I wouldn't give you directions.

_____ 2. If he was in good health, we would offer him the job.

_____ 3. Because he was ill so often last year, he couldn't complete his work.

_____ 4. If he was a faster typist, he could complete that letter on time.

_____ 5. I wish that I was your secretary instead of your wife.

_____ 6. He was a millionaire who spent his money to help the poor.

_____ 7. I wish that I was a millionaire.

_____ 8. When I were your assistant, your office were in the other building.

_____ 9. Cinderella wished that her mother were kind to her.

_____ 10. If I was you, I would hesitate to make that promise.

Answers to this Replay are in Appendix H.
POP QUIZ—Appendix A.

Checkpoint

In the 1600s a mathematician and grammarian named John Willis was disturbed to discover that the words *shall* and *will* had just about the same meaning. He worked out a plan to give them different meanings, and defenseless students have been suffering ever since.

Those of you who studied grammar in the past may be wondering how we could go through this verb section without *will/shall* and *would/should*. Well, the simple truth is that our ever-changing language patterns make this instruction unnecessary. Some people still observe the distinctions between these pairs of words. Others, equally careful writers and speakers in business, politics, and the media, ignore those rules dating back to Mr. Willis.

Only the essential principles of verb usage are included in this section. Therefore, to be confident of your mastery of English for business and professions, concentrate on every item in Section Six. If further details are desired, see the "Grammar Supplement."

Repeat the correct forms aloud until they sound natural. For example, perhaps Unit 38 contains a principle you haven't been careful about following before. In that case, say "If I were you" five times every morning and every evening. Then, using your best theatrical technique, say "If I *was* you," making yourself sound ignorant and uneducated.

Danger

The most serious common verb errors are the following. If your speech or writing contains errors such as these, it's urgent to acquire the *habit* of using the standard English forms.

1. Using the present plural verb form when the past is needed.

   Yesterday Mrs. Jaffe talk to the business class about promptness. [should be *talked*]

2. Not adding *-s* to a verb when it is needed or vice versa—adding *-s* when it should not be there:

   Professor Spannuth **explain** the business English principles carefully. [should be *explains*]
   Ms. Strehlke and Ms. Dorsey **is** members of Theta Alpha Delta, ZETA chapter. [should be *are*]

3. Using the past with a helping verb or the past participle without a helping verb.

   He **had wore** that same shirt yesterday. [should be *worn*]
   I know **he done** a good job because I **seen** it with my own eyes. [should be *did* and *saw*]

Special Assignment

A. First, compose sentences with the present-time form of the listed verbs and any singular subjects except *you* or *I*.

EXAMPLES

beat   **She beats** her husband regularly at tennis.
throw   **Murphy throws** the ball too fast.

1. **go** _____
2. **do** _____
3. **drive** _____

Now compose sentences using the *-ing* form of these verbs. Use them as verbs rather than as some other part of speech.

EXAMPLES

dance   My husband is dancing. [*Dancing* is a verb.]

   NO   My hobby is dancing. [*Dancing* is a noun—your hobby can't dance around the floor.]

   NO   My husband attends dancing school. [*Dancing* is an adjective here.]

1. **run** _____
2. **rise** _____
3. **raise** _____

Now compose sentences using the appropriate form of the listed verbs to show past time **without a helping verb**.

EXAMPLE

talk   **He talked** on the phone for an hour.

1. **win** _____

2. **sing** _____

3. **quit** _____

4. **burst** _____

Now compose sentences using the appropriate form of the listed verbs **with a helping verb** to show past time.

EXAMPLE

drink   The treasurer **had drunk** four cups of coffee before he began to dance in the boardroom.

1. **hide** _____

2. **pay** _____

3. **sink** _____

4. **freeze** _____

Now compose sentences with the *present-time form of these verbs* and any plural subject. **Be sure to use the words as verbs**.

EXAMPLE

give   **They give** shoe polish with all shoe purchases.

1. **cost** _____

2. **ship** _____

3. **equip** _____

This assignment should be completed by _____ (date).

B. Action-word puzzle

ACROSS

1. Simple past and past participle of catch
5. Simple past and past participle of lose
7. Present tense and past participle of run
8. Antonym for down
9. Past participle of see
12. Simple past and past participle of need
15. Simple past of ring
18. Form of beat with singular noun or singular pronoun except you or I
20. Two guys named Ed
22. Present participle of feel

DOWN

1. Past participle of choose
2. Present tense of went
3. Simple past of tear
4. Past participle of ring
6. Present participle of tune
10. Past participle of eat
11. "To _____ or not to _____," wrote Shakespeare
13. Past participle of do
14. Present form of do with a singular noun or singular pronoun except you or I
16. To grow older
17. Present form of be with a singular noun or a singular pronoun except you or I
19. Present form of be—with you, plural pronouns, and plural nouns
21. Past participle of dig

Proofreading for Careers

The names have been changed in this letter from a congressman to his constituent. In addition to name changes, I've planted errors—typing, capitalization, spelling, and grammar—so that you can check your proofreading expertise. Some numbers may also be written incorrectly. Refer to "Numbers in Business" in Appendix F to be sure of writing numbers in the preferred style.

Glide your pen or pointing finger below each line to proofread and correct the letter that follows. Never let any written material leave your desk without proofreading it.

April 19, 19--

Mr. Eric A. Smith

40711 Bendigo Drive

Monroe, LA 71201

Dear Mr. Smith:

Thank you for you're correspondents concerning the nucular issue.

As you no, the house has began debate on this issue.

All american's looks forward to the day Nucular weapons is not a

part of any country's military arsenal. You may wish to read the

entire nucular freeze debate by securing copies of the March 16th

and April 13th congressional records.

Additionaly, I have enclose 2 statements that expresses my views

on this subject.

Thank you for sharing your concerns with me on this important

issue. If you any further thoughts regarding this or any other is-

sues, please write again.

Sincerly,

Daniel J. Monson

Member of Congress

hs

enclosures

After verifying your proofreading and corrections, evaluate your proofreading skill:
Excellent _____ Good _____ Fair _____ Poor

Practice Quiz

Take the Practice Quiz as though it were a real test. Don't look back through Section Six while you take this Practice Quiz. After the quiz is corrected, refer to the appropriate Read Units, shown in parentheses, for explanations of any item you may have missed.

Refer to your dictionary whenever necessary. Circle the correct answer.

1. The Bureau of Mines (is/are) now making preparations to transfer its offices. **(Unit 35)**
2. The people of this country (believe/believes) it can be done. **(Unit 36)**
3. The manager has already (chose/chosen) three people for the job. **(Unit 32)**
4. Mr. Kubik (employ/employs) most extras through the Central Casting Corp. **(Unit 31)**
5. At present 3,800 extras (is/are/be) on the roll of this bureau. **(Unit 34)**
6. If I (were/was) you, I would take advantage of this opportunity. **(Unit 38)**
7. Ms. Jellessd wrote me that I had (did/done) the right thing. **(Unit 32)**
8. I wish that Ed Johnson (was/were) here to see the plans for Fort Worth. **(Unit 38)**
9. You have (broke/broken) one of the rules. **(Unit 32)**
10. We believe that either Tom or James (is/are) to be fired. **(Unit 36)**
11. Each girl and boy (is/are/be) doing well. **(Unit 36)**
12. Accuracy in figures (mark/marks) the expert accountant. **(Unit 37)**
13. A list of names and addresses (come/comes) with the booklet. **(Unit 37)**
14. There (is/are/be) many subjects that you should master. **(Unit 37)**
15. Every one of the bookkeepers (attend/attends) night school. **(Unit 36)**
16. Either a letter or a pamphlet (was/were) sent. **(Unit 36)**
17. He (don't/doesn't) need to go. **(Unit 32)**
18. Have you (took/taken) notes of what he told you? **(Unit 32)**
19. Neither this month nor last month (has/have) been profitable. **(Unit 36)**
20. The systems analyst explained that the new HP computer (is/was) being used now. **(Unit 34)**
21. Both this year and last year (has/have) been profitable for Edna. **(Unit 36)**
22. Everyone who completes the Office Administration major (seem/seems) to pass the test. **(Unit 36)**
23. The results of this experiment in humanistic education (is/are) significant. **(Unit 37)**
24. In the rear of the word processing center (is/are) two electronic typewriters. **(Unit 37)**
25. Before you meet the handsome prince, you (has/have) to kiss a lot of toads. **(Unit 35)**

7

Good

Better

Best

After Completing Section Seven You Will

✔ Use singular and plural pointing adjectives correctly.

✔ Use *a* and *an* correctly.

✔ Use comparative and superlative adjectives and adverbs correctly.

✔ Avoid double negatives

✔ Distinguish between adjectives and adverbs and know when to use each.

*H*ave you ever watched an old movie from the 1940s in which a self-confident woman played by Betty Grable or Barbara Stanwyck teases a man for his "line." "Your graceful movements, pearl-like teeth, star-kissed eyes, petal-smooth skin . . ." he murmurs passionately, while she smiles knowingly, and says, "I'll bet you say that to all the girls." Where would old movies have been without men with lines? And where would lines have been without adjectives and adverbs?

And how about us today? Imagine how dull our language and our lives would be without words like *generous, happily, stingy, cheerfully, prudish, confidently, weaker, meaner, strictest, domineering, shabby, purple, most comfortable.* Describing words—adjectives and adverbs—add precision, character, liveliness, and color to our language.

Communication is difficult at best, for we often misunderstand one another. The skillful writer and speaker draws from a wealth of adjectives and adverbs, using those that most effectively communicate the shade of meaning desired. In fact, others judge our personalities (subconsciously, of course) by the quality of our adjectives and adverbs.

In this section, you review the principles of standard English for adverbs and adjectives. Adverbs modify, or tell about, verbs, adjectives, and other adverbs. Many adverbs are formed by adding *-ly* to adjectives. Other adverbs, however, are completely different words such as *well, often,* or *sometimes.* Adjectives modify, or tell about, nouns and pronouns. The four kinds of adjectives are articles, pointing, limiting, and describing. Limiting adjectives (*one, fifth, any,* and *several*) for example, aren't discussed in this section because adults rarely use them incorrectly. Please review Units 3 and 4 now.

Writing for Your Career

The adverb *very* is probably the most overused adverb in English. When an intensifying word is used too much, it loses its power. William Allen White, famous journalist and writer of the early 1900s, was editor of the *Emporia Gazette,* a well-written Kansas newspaper. To discourage the staff from overuse of *very,* he sent them this memorandum:

If you feel you must write *very,* write *damn.*

Since the copy desk had instructions to delete any of the reporters' profanity, the writing style of the newspaper was improved:

"It was a very fine victory" was written "It was a damn fine victory" and was printed "It was a fine victory."

Read Unit

39

THESE, THOSE, AND THEM

Here are the only reminders you are likely to need for pointing adjectives. Only four words are used as pointing adjectives: *this, that, these, those.* (When a noun does *not* follow these four words, they become pronouns.)

Never use *them* as a pointing adjective; it is a pronoun only.

NO   I plan to give **them boys** a million dollars. [*Them* is used incorrectly as a pointing adjective.]

YES   I plan to give **those boys** a million dollars. [*Those*—or *these*—is correct as a plural pointing adjective.]

YES   I plan to give **them** a million dollars. [*Them* is correct as a pronoun—a substitute for a noun naming some people.]

Use *this* and *that* as adjectives pointing to singular nouns only.

YES   **This kind** of material is too sheer for **that type** of dress. [*This* and *that* are singular pointing adjectives describing singular nouns *kind* and *type*.]

Use *these* and *those* as adjectives pointing to plural nouns only.

NO   **Those kind** of roofs are fireproof.

YES   **Those kinds** of roofs are fireproof. [plural pointing adjective *those* agrees with plural noun *kinds*]

NO   Will **these type** of homes be suitable in this neighborhood?

YES   Will **these types** of homes be suitable in this neighborhood? [plural pointing adjective *these* agrees with plural noun *types*]

Do not use these "combinations": *this here, that there,* and *them there.*

It's not likely that you write these combinations. If, however, you think you might **speak** these expressions, ask a friend or an instructor to listen for them and help you break the habit.

NO   **This here** is my office.

YES   **This** is my office.

NO   **That there telephone** is out of order.

YES **That telephone** is out of order.

NO **Them there paintings** should be hung in the hallway.

YES **Those paintings** should be hung in the hallway.

Replay Unit

Be a "quick-change artist" and correct the following sentences by adding a single letter or by changing a single word.

EXAMPLE

These kind $\overset{s}{\wedge}$ of dogs can be vicious.

1. The purchasing agent ordered those kind of PCs.
2. Them books should be returned to the library.
3. If you are not careful, these type of errors will occur frequently.
4. Those sort of books are extremely interesting.
5. I don't like those type of people.
6. He wants to buy this here book.
7. Please give that there calculator to Michelle Miller of Milwaukee.
8. Tell them there people that they must do the work themselves.
9. That there is the way the cookie crumbles.
10. These kind of advertisements don't attract our customers.

Answers are in Appendix H.

Read Unit

TWO LITTLE WORDS

Another kind of adjective is the *article. The, a,* and *an* are the only three articles. *The* is a "definite" article because it makes the noun that comes after it definite or specific. *A* and *an* are "indefinite" articles. Notice the difference in meaning between "the book" and "a book."

People who are not native speakers of English may experience difficulty learning when to use articles and when to omit them because no rules govern their usage. Look at these two sentences, for example:

Writing for Your Career

- If a singular pointing adjective makes sense, avoid the plural construction. For example, instead of *these* or *those kinds, types,* or *sorts,* use *this* or *that kind, type,* or *sort.*

CORRECT BUT COULD BE IMPROVED

Those kinds of roofs are fireproof.

IMPROVED

That kind of roof is fireproof.

Those roofs are fireproof.

- Avoid the unnecessary *a* or *an* after *kind of, type of,* or *sort of.*

CORRECT BUT CAN BE IMPROVED

This kind of a house . . .

IMPROVED

This kind of house . . .

We are going to school today.

We are going to the office today.

Why don't we use *the* before *school* in the first sentence? Why *do* we use *the* before *office* in the second sentence? These choices "sound right" to a native of an English-speaking country, but no simple rule governs them.

Differences occur even between British English and American English:

BRITISH   She is in hospital.

AMERICAN   She is in the hospital.

For people learning English, the solution is to read English a great deal; listen to the radio, TV, and film; and ask co-workers, teachers, and friends to correct you. Your brain will gradually develop a sense of what "sounds right" in English.

One use of articles, however, can be a problem for native-born speakers of English—the two little words *a* and *an.* Some people use *a* almost exclusively and are not accustomed to using *an* when it's necessary. Nonstandard use of *a* and *an* is very noticeable in on-the-job communication. Since there *are* useful rules to determine whether to use *a* or *an,* correcting this usage is much easier than learning when to use an article and when not to.

Not everyone needs to study the *a/an* rules. Many people automatically use these words appropriately. Complete Replay 40 as a pretest; check your answers to determine whether you need to study all, some, or none of the rules that follow in Unit 41.

Write *a* or *an* in the blank before each word. Choose the answer that comes to you immediately. Don't try to figure out what the right answer should be.

EXAMPLE

__a__ $10 bill

1. _____ adding machine   2. _____ carrot

3. _____ egg   4. _____ apple

5. _____ giant   6. _____ honor

7. _____ heater   8. _____ English teacher

9. _____ hand   10. _____ island

11. _____ manager   12. _____ IBM computer

13. _____ one-day visit   14. _____ European

15. _____ onion   16. _____ FBI report

17. _____ order   18. _____ UN member

19. _____ uncle   20. _____ 2 percent increase

21. _____ 11 percent drop   22. _____ heir

23. _____ X ray   24. _____ unknown admirer

Check your answers in Appendix H.

MANAGING A AND AN

If you had 100-percent accuracy on Replay 40, don't study the rules that follow. Just go directly to Replay 41.

If you made errors in Replay 40, study these rules carefully and **use them as a reference in any writing you do.**

Basic Rule for Managing *A* and *AN*

If the word right after the indefinite article begins with a vowel sound, use *an.* Otherwise use *a.* A vowel sound is a sound usually represented by the letters *a, e, i, o,* or *u.*

Remember, the use of *a* or *an* depends on the **sound** of the word that follows *a* or *an,* not the written letter with which the word begins.

an apple	**a s**ecretary
an Easter egg	**a h**at
an owner	**a b**ookkeeper
an uncle	**a** 10-percent raise [*t* sound]

Because some words beginning with a vowel actually have a consonant **sound**, they take *a*, not *an*.

For example, the sound of *u* in *union* is like the consonant *y* in *you*: *a union*, *a uniform*, *a eulogy*,* and so on. Also, the *o* in *one* sounds like the consonant *w* in *winner*: *a one-cent tax*.

H beginning a word is sometimes silent—as in *honor*. For such words, use *an*.

The first sound of *honor* is *o*, a vowel sound: **an honor, an honest person, an herb garden.**†

When letters are used alone or as part of abbreviations, they take *an* or *a* depending on their sound. Here are two lists.

USE *AN*	**USE *A***
an *A*	a *B*
an *E*	a *C*
an *F*	a *D*
an *H*	a *G*
an *L*	a *J*
an *M*	a *K*
an *N*	a *P*
an *O*	a *Q*
an *R*	a *T*
an *S*	a *U*
an *X*	a *V*
	a *W*
	a *Y*
	a *Z*

Insert **a T** or **an F** in each blank.

He needs **an FBI** report for **a CIA** investigator.

Some abbreviations are pronounced as words instead of individual letters—such as NASA, pronounced **nas** uh. Others are pronounced by the individual letters—such as NAACP.

He was **a N**ASA employee and **an N**AACP member.

(If you're not certain of what NASA and NAACP mean, look them up NOW in your dictionary.)

---

* If you have any doubt as to the meaning or pronunciation of *eulogy*, please look it up now.
† If you pronounce the *h*—like the name Herb rather than "*urb*"—use *a*.

Word to the Wise

Use **a** before a consonant **sound**.

Use **an** before a vowel **sound**.

Replay Unit

41

Write *a* or *an* in each blank.

EXAMPLE

___A___ pessimist sees the difficulty in ___an___ opportunity.

___An___ optimist sees the opportunity in ___a___ difficulty.

1. LaVada Kaufman was given _____ one-day unpaid leave of absence and _____ eight-day paid vacation.

2. _____ union member ate _____ onion daily during _____ 80-day tour of the world.

3. It is _____ unusual combination for someone to be _____ CPA and _____ M.D. also.

4. They left for _____ meeting about _____ hour ago.

5. _____ thesaurus is _____ invaluable tool for those who work with words and ideas.

6. _____ X ray was needed to determine whether there was _____ injury.

7. _____ SEATO representative and _____ NATO representative were seated next to each other at _____ UN meeting.*

8. Flutter is _____ wavering in tape speed that can cause _____ unnatural sound.

9. Each time he received _____ B on _____ report card, he was given _____ $11 gift.

10. He walked down _____ hall to get _____ history book for _____ honest man.

* Pronounce SEATO and NATO as words: **seet** o and **nayt** o. Pronounce UN as two separate letters.

11. _____ heir expected to inherit _____ one-million-dollar mansion.

12. His sister, _____ heiress, was not _____ honest woman.

13. _____ uncle of mine planted _____ herb garden.

14. After receiving _____ AA degree, he earned _____ BA in sociology.

15. _____ European business executive wanted to be _____ CEO in _____ American firm.

Please check you answers in Appendix H.

Read Unit

42

GOOD, GOODER, GOODEST?

If you've been around young children, you've heard talk like "Mine is the goodest of all." Very soon, however, children learn, just from listening to others, to say "best." They don't need any rules. It just happens naturally. This unit reviews those aspects of adjective usage that are often not acquired without specific instruction.

Comparisons

Descriptive adjectives (see Unit 3) let you show a comparison:

> The secretary's typewriter is *newer* than the clerk's. [Adjective *newer* compares one typewriter with another.]
>
> Josephine is the *oldest* girl in the family. [Adjective *oldest* compares the age of Josephine with the ages of the other girls in the family.]

Recognizing Adjectives Reminder

- An adjective modifies—describes, limits, or points to—a noun or pronoun:

  > They are competent. [*Competent* is an adjective describing the pronoun *they*.]

  > They are competent students. [*Competent* is an adjective describing the noun *students*.]

- Articles, reviewed in Units 40 and 41, are also adjectives.
- An adjective generally answers the question What kind? Which? or How many?

Degrees

Descriptive adjectives come in three degrees:

- **Positive degree**—the entry word in the dictionary (*good, bad, high, beautiful*, etc.); describes one noun or pronoun without making any comparison.
- **Comparative degree**—makes a comparison between **two** (*better, worse, higher, more beautiful*, etc.).
- **Superlative degree**—makes a comparison among **three or more** (*best, worst, highest, most beautiful*, etc.).

Forms of Regular Adjectives

A regular adjective has regular, or normal, changes in form for showing comparisons. An irregular adjective does not follow any particular pattern for comparisons.

Positive Degree: No Comparison

This **new** show is at the Bijou Theater.

The show at the Bijou Theater is **new**.

It is **new**.

Comparative Degree: Comparing Two

To compare **two** nouns or pronouns, add *-er* to one-syllable adjectives as well as to two-syllable adjectives ending in *y*.*

Jean is the **older** of the two sisters, but Marian is the **prettier**. [Just two sisters are being compared.]

Dallhold Investments is a **larger** gold producer than St. Joe Gold Company. [Just two gold producers are being compared.]

To compare two nouns or pronouns, use *more* or *less* before an adjective with two syllables *not* ending in *y* or one with three or more syllables.

The new calculator is **more modern**. [Two machines are being compared.]

The old equipment is **less valuable** than the new. [Two types of equipment are being compared.]

Recap Circle the correct choice of the words in parentheses.

Who do you think is (wisest/wiser), the judge or the minister?

Check your answer in Appendix H.

* When an adjective ends in *y*, change *y* to *i* before adding *-er* or *-est*.

Superlative Degree: Comparing Three or More

To compare three or more nouns or pronouns, add *-est* to an adjective with one syllable or with two syllables ending in *y*.

Melvin is the **oldest** child in that family, and he is also the **silliest**. [There are three or more children in that family.]

Yours is the **loveliest** diamond I have ever seen. [I have seen three or more diamonds.]

To compare three or more nouns or pronouns, use *most* or *least* before an adjective with two syllables *not* ending in *y* or before a three-syllable adjective.

Here is the **most recent** letter we have received. [We have received three or more letters.]

The chiffonier is the **least valuable** of all the antiques. [Three or more antiques are being compared.]

Recap　Circle the correct choice of the words in parentheses.

Who do you think is (wisest/wiser), the judge, the minister, or the professor?

Check your answer in Appendix H.

Avoiding Double Comparatives or Superlatives

Never use *more*, *most*, *less*, or *least* before an adjective that ends with *er* or *est*.

HORRORS!!!　He is the **most handsomest** man on the screen today. [double superlative]

Mine is **more better** than hers. [double comparative]

Some one- and two-syllable adjectives are correct with either *-er/-est* **or** *most/most*.

CORRECT　He is the **handsomest** man on the screen today.

CORRECT　He is the **most handsome** man on the screen today.

If you're sure either one sounds right, use whichever you please. You can always avoid error, however, by following the rules given in this unit.

Forms of Irregular Adjectives

When you think the comparison forms of an adjective differ from the ones just reviewed, refer to the dictionary. The irregular forms are next to the entry word, which is the adjective in the positive degree. For example, look up the adjective *good* right now. Next to it, you'll find *better* and then *best* in that order. Other irregular adjectives are *far*, *ill*, *bad*, and *many*.

Writing for Your Career

Avoid the comparative *more* or the superlative *most* before *unique*. Since *unique* means "one of a kind," it isn't logical to say one pie (or anything else) is more unique than any other. *Unique* is an example of an **absolute adjective.** Other absolute adjectives are in the Grammar Supplement (Appendix G).

Dictionary Data

Comparative and superlative degrees are shown in the dictionary (following the positive-degree entry word), in just that order. That is, the comparative form is always before the superlative, thus providing the sophisticated dictionary user with the information for choosing the correct form.

When you look up *ill* in *Webster's New World Dictionary*, here's what you find:

ill (il) adj. worse, worst

This entry signifies that *worse* is the comparative form (for comparing two) and *worst* is the superlative (for comparing three or more).

Replay Unit

42

A. Look up the listed adjectives in the dictionary and fill in the blanks. List any multiple choices the dictionary shows. Because they are irregular, you'll find the comparative and superlative forms next to the positive, which is the entry word.

EXAMPLE

many _____ more _____   _____ most _____

	COMPARATIVE	SUPERLATIVE
1. bad	_____	_____
2. little	_____	_____
3. much	_____	_____
4. good	_____	_____
5. far	_____	_____

B. Correct the adjective errors in these sentences. Write _C_ beside the number of the one sentence that is already correct.

EXAMPLE

                                                                    more
The High Street building is the ~~most~~ valuable property of the two we saw today.

1. When you examine the two diagrams, you discover that the one on the right is biggest.
2. She lives farer away than her partner.
3. The most safest investments are in blue-chip companies.
4. Of the two reports, his is the worst.
5. He is the younger of the two brothers.
6. He is the older of the three brothers.
7. When the work of the two accountants in Puerto Rico was compared, the controller found Mr. Higgins' work to be best.
8. This newly developed alloy is more heavier than any other metal.
9. This file contains recenter information than that one.
10. That trailer is the widest of the two that I saw.
11. Hers is the beautifulest office I have ever seen.
12. He feels worser today than yesterday.
13. She is the least efficient of the two administrative assistants.
14. If you use our detergent and Brand _X_, which one will give you the brightest wash?
15. He's more friendlier than the other office manager.

Answers are Appendix H.
Please take **POP QUIZ** in Appendix A.

Read Unit

TO -LY OR NOT TO -LY, THAT IS THE QUESTION

We add -_ly_ to many adjectives to form adverbs. For example, adding -_ly_ to the adjective _occasional_ results in the adverb _occasionally_. See Unit 4, page 16.

Usually we automatically know when to use an adverb and when to use an adjective. This unit is about only those parts of adjective versus adverb usage that most people need to study in order to use the correct form.

Is It an Adjective or an Adverb?

Most (but not all) words ending in -_ly_ are adverbs.

ADVERBS   prettily   happily   quickly   busily

ADJECTIVES   pretty   happy   quick   busy

Identifying Adverbs Reminder

- An adjective describes a noun or a pronoun by answering the questions Which? How many? What kind?
- An adverb describes a verb, an adjective, or another adverb by answering the questions How? How much? When?
- Use the dictionary when in doubt about whether a word is an adjective or an adverb.

Some *adjectives* end in *-ly* and should not be mistaken for adverbs.

curly   goodly   godly   friendly

If the *-ly* word in question can describe a noun *(curly hair, friendly man)*, you'll know it's an adjective.

Sometimes the same word is used as an adjective or an adverb.

He is a **fast** worker. [*Fast* is an adjective describing the noun *worker.*]

He works **fast**. [*Fast* is an adverb describing the verb *works.*]

Sometimes an adjective and adverb with similar meanings are completely different words.

He is a **good** speaker. [*Good,* an adjective, describes the noun *speaker.*]

He speaks **well.** [*Well,* an adverb, describes the verb *speaks.*]

Which Is Correct: Adjective or Adverb?

Sometimes a descriptive word follows an **existence verb**.*

A describing word after an existence verb is an adjective; it describes the subject of the existence verb.

He **is efficient.** [*Efficient,* which follows the existence verb, is an adjective describing the subject *he.*]

I **look bad** today. [*Bad* follows the existence verb and is an adjective describing the pronoun subject *I.*]

Avoid the adverb *badly* after an existence verb; it would change *look* into an action verb. The sentence above would then mean "I don't do a good job of looking."

Laurie Hamilton **is friendly** and her hair **is curly**. [Adjectives *friendly* and *curly* follow existence verbs *is* and *is.*]

* Also called linking verb or state of being verb.

Recognizing Existence Verbs

Review Unit 1 on verbs.

The most common existence verbs are forms of *be*, such as *is, am, are, was, were, been*. In addition, verbs of the senses are often—but not always—in this category of verbs. The most common verbs of the senses are *appear, become, seem, look, taste, sound, smell, feel*.

■ Here's a way to determine whether a verb of the senses is functioning as an existence verb. Substitute a form of the verb *be*. If the form of *be* makes sense, the verb you substituted for is functioning as an existence verb. For example, *She looks intelligent* makes sense as *She is intelligent* or *She was intelligent. The bosses seem happy* makes sense as *The bosses are* (or *were*) *happy*.

■ Also decide whether the verb is referring to action or to existence (state of being):

She **looks** for the eraser. [action verb because she uses her eyes to look]

BUT

She **looks** sick. [existence verb because she is not doing the action of looking; existence, or state of being, is implied]

The mashed potatoes **taste** delicious. [existence verb—the potatoes are not doing the tasting]

BUT

First, I **taste** the mashed potatoes. [action verb—now taste implies action]

Recap Circle the correct word of the choices in parentheses.

Do you feel (bad/badly) about the incident?

Check your answer in Appendix H.

A describing word after an action verb is an adverb; it tells something about the verb.

He arrived at the office on time and **worked quietly**. [*Quietly* is an adverb telling how he worked. The adjective *quiet* would be incorrect because an adjective does not describe a verb.]

She **knows** English **well**. [*Well* is an adverb telling how she knows. *Good* would be incorrect because an adjective cannot describe a verb.

Word to the Wise

Quick test for adjectives *real* and *sure:* If you can substitute *very,* you need an adverb.

Recap   Circle the correct word of the choices in parentheses

The engine runs (smooth/smoothly).

Check your answer in Appendix H.

Since *real* and *sure* are adjectives, do not use them to describe other adjectives.

Remember that **adverbs** describe adjectives.

WRONG   She is **real smart**. [The adjective *real* cannot correctly describe the adjective *smart;* switch to an adverb such as *really* or *extremely.*]

WRONG   That report is **sure good**. [The adjective *sure* cannot correctly describe *good,* which is also an adjective. Change to an adverb such as *very, certainly, exceptionally,* and so on.)

Recap   Change the incorrectly used adjectives to adverbs.

1. I'm sure happy you decided to buy a new water cooler.
2. We're real disappointed about losing the account.

Check your answers in Appendix H.

Writing for Your Career

Excessive describing words interfere with the effectiveness of a statement. Decide whether to eliminate a *really, surely, extremely, especially, very,* or similar "intensifying" word.

    That report is good may carry more "punch" than *That report is really* (or *very* or *extremely*) *good.*

Word to the Wise

- *-Way* and *-where* compound words are often used as adverbs: *anyway, anywhere, everywhere, somewhere, nowhere.* Adding an *-s* to any of those words is nonstandard; avoid spelling these words with an *-s* or pronouncing an *-s* when you use them in speech.
- The *ily* ending always has one *l*—as in *easily, busily, happily.* The *ally* ending always has two *l*'s—as in *accidentally, occasionally, officially.*

Sometimes adverbs are used without the *-ly* in specialized language such as advertisements and road signs.

> Buy direct.
> Go slow.

This practice is not acceptable, however, in most business writing.

Don't Say It Again!

The adverb and adjective expressions on the left are **redundant**—needlessly repetitive. Avoid redundancies; they make business writing (or any writing) less effective than it should be.

AVOID	USE
repeat again	repeat
return back	return
cooperate together	cooperate
round in shape	round
yellow in color	yellow
modern, up-to-date	modern

REDUNDANT   The document, which is dated in the month of December, is on paper that is yellow in color and heavy in weight.

IMPROVED   The document, which has a December date, is on heavy yellow paper.

Replay Unit

43

A. Concentrate on these directions; then follow one step at a time. All the sentences contain adjectives.

(a) Underline the adjectives that describe.

(b) Circle the word described by the adjective.

(c) If you circled a noun or a pronoun, write *C* (for correct) in the blank.

(d) If you circled a verb, cross out the adjective and write the appropriate adverb in the blank.

EXAMPLE

She (types) careless.   carelessly

1. He walked rapid in order to meet her on time.

2. The fumes from the refinery smell especially bad today.

3. Businesspeople should write clear and correct.

4. Dr. Linville looks beautiful.

5. However, her sister feels bad.

6. Be sure to see that you do the problems careful.

7. The doctor wrote legible.

8. The pie tasted delicious.

9. The manager should think deep about that subject.

10. I hope that you will treat him fair.

11. This one works as good as the new one.

12. We sure wish you would participate in the conference.

13. I know English good.

14. She certainly speaks logical.

15. A rose by any other name would smell as sweet.

B. In the blank, write the words or letter that should be omitted.

EXAMPLE

Our main showroom is now in a modern, up-to-date building.

    up-to-date *or* modern

1. Please repeat that information again in your next speech.

2. We are returning your order back to you.

3. If we all cooperate together, the job will be done quickly.

4. I couldn't find the tool boxes anywheres. _____

5. No matter how hard he worked with the _____

   crew, he got nowheres.

Answers are in Appendix H.

Read Unit

44

COMPARISONS AND GOOD FEELINGS

Shakespeare compared a woman to a summer's day in these romantic lines:

> Shall I compare thee to a summer's day?
> Thou art more lovely and more temperate:
> Rough winds do shake the darling buds of May,
> And summer's lease hath all too short a date.
> But thy eternal summer shall not fade.

Comparing Adverbs

The same three degrees of comparison described in Unit 42 for adjectives—positive, comparative, and superlative—occur with adverbs. As with adjectives, the comparative is for two and the superlative for three or more. Here are the other principles that assure correct adverb comparisons:

Many adverbs are created by adding *-ly* to an adjective. To make these *-ly* adverbs comparative, use *more* or *less* before them. To make them superlative, use *most* or *least* before them.

ADJECTIVE	ADVERB	COMPARATIVE ADVERB	SUPERLATIVE ADVERB
quiet	quietly	more quietly less quietly	most quietly least quietly
active	actively	more actively less actively	most actively least actively
beautiful	beautifully	more beautifully less beautifully	most beautifully least beautifully
polite	politely	more politely less politely	most politely least politely

Use an adverb (not an adjective) to modify a verb, adjective, or another adverb.

WRONG   The new machine works **quieter** than the old one.

RIGHT   The new machine works **more quietly** than the old one. [The adverb *quietly* is required to describe the verb *works*; *quieter* is an adjective and cannot correctly describe a verb.]

WRONG   Of all the businesses with access to the parking lot, our company can obtain parking permits **easiest**.

RIGHT   Of all the businesses with access to the parking lot, our company can obtain parking permits **most easily**. [The adverb *most easily* describes the verb *obtain; easiest* is an adjective and must not be used to describe a verb.]

In speech, substituting an adjective for an adverb in sentences like those above isn't too noticeable and is preferable to fumbling while trying to think of the right word.

Recap   Circle the correct choice of the words in parentheses.

If you drive (speedier/more speedily) than others, stay in the right lane in Great Britain.

Check your answer in Appendix H.

Feeling Good

The irregular adjective *good* and the irregular adverb *well* call for special attention:

	POSITIVE	COMPARATIVE	SUPERLATIVE
ADJECTIVE	good	better	best
ADVERB	well	better	best

The comparative and superlative are easy; you can't go wrong. You don't have to decide whether an adjective or an adverb is needed. As always, however, use the comparative for two and the superlative for three or more:

Our widgets are **better** than yours. [comparing two]

In fact, our widgets are the **best** on the market. [comparing three or more]

To choose between *good* or *well*, decide whether an adjective or an adverb is needed. If an adjective is needed, choose *good*.

You wrote a **good** report. [*Good* describes the noun *report*.]

The report looks **good**. [*Good* describes the noun *report*.]

It looks **good**. [*Good* describes the pronoun *it*.]

Looks is an existence verb in the second and third examples. Therefore, the describing word is an adjective telling about the subject (*report* or *it*), not the verb *(looks)*.

In choosing between *good* and *well*, if an adverb is needed, choose *well*.

He plays the drums **good**. [NO! NO!]

He plays the drums **well**. [The adverb *well* describes the verb *plays*. Using *good* is using an adjective to describe a verb, an error.]

The drums sound **good**. [YES! YES! Now an adjective is describing the noun *drums*, which is followed by an existence verb.]

The rule is that English rules have a reputation for having exceptions. So to prove the rule, here's an exception:

> When referring to health or well-being, *good* and *well* may be used interchangeably. You can't go wrong because *well* becomes an adjective like *good*.

All these are correct adjective usages:

He feels good.   She seems well.
He feels well.   She seems good.

Recap   Circle the correct answer.

1. Marge writes (good/well/either good or well).
2. Do you get along (good/well/either good or well) with people?
3. I hope he feels (good/well/either good or well) today.
4. He spoke (good/well/either good or well) of Ms. Sorenson.
5. The nurse said he's feeling (bad/badly/bad or badly) today, but he was (worse/worser) yesterday.

Check your answers in Appendix H.

Replay Unit

44

These sentences provide practice for Unit 44 as well as Units 42 and 43. Alertness and concentration are required to correct the adjective and adverb errors. If the sentence is correct, write *C* in the answer blank. Otherwise circle the adjective or adverb error and write the correct form in the blank. Use your dictionary whenever it might help.

EXAMPLE

You're doing the work real good.   _____really well_____

1. Ms. Woodall is speaking more logical than anyone else in Franklin.   _____
2. You did satisfactory on all the tests.   _____
3. She appears more calmly than her sister.   _____
4. His work was done the worstest of all.   _____
5. I sure do like your office.   _____
6. Ms. Teller speaks weller than Mr. Keller.   _____

7. These PCs are wider used than the others.   _____

8. Oscar walks faster* than his brother.   _____

9. I did real good in the grammar part.   _____

10. The music on this boat sounds more beautifully than the music on the other boat.   _____

11. He feels badder today than he did yesterday.   _____

12. Mr. Allen, who is a good dictator, enunciates more distinct than does Ms. Stern.   _____

13. The engine in the truck runs smoother than the one in the car.   _____

14. She looks more efficient than the other candidates.   _____

15. Mr. Rosenberg presented his case clearer than the other attorney.   _____

16. Mr. Valenzuela felt more badly about losing to the Mets than about pulling his hamstring.   _____

17. Of the five companies, Digital has the better standing.   _____

18. Nureyev dances more graceful than the others in the troupe.   _____

19. He protested the results the most bitterly of all the contestants.   _____

20. He types the most satisfactory of all the applicants for the job in our Information Systems Department.   _____

Please match your answers with those in Appendix H.

Memo from Grandma Wordsmith

Good, better, best
Never let it rest
Till your good is better
And your better is best.

Read Unit

45

I DON'T WANT NO SPINACH!

When two negative words express one negative idea, the result is a double negative.

CHILD   I **don't** want **no** spinach!

* *Fast* is both an adjective and an adverb. Can you think of a sentence with *fast* as a verb?

PARENT If you don't want **no** spinach, you must want **some** spinach, so eat up!

The idea of a double negative equaling a positive was thought up by an 18th-century British bishop named Robert Lowth. He wrote a book called *Short Introduction to English Grammar* in which he intended to "lay down the rules" and to "judge every form and construction." He based the double negative rule on classical Latin despite the fact that the structure of English is different from that of Latin. He didn't even apply the Latin principle correctly, since double negatives *are* used in Latin for emphasis.

Actually, the use of two negative words to express a single negative idea does not in any way affect your listener's or reader's ability to understand you. You know the child doesn't want any spinach. If your employer asked you what time it is and you reply, "I don't got no watch," she will certainly understand what you mean.

BUT

She will be reluctant to assign you to written or oral communications with her customers. In fact, using double negatives will usually prevent applicants from being hired for better jobs.

It isn't important to identify which negative words are being used as adverbs and which as adjectives. Just remember that two negatives shouldn't be combined to express one negative idea. Here are examples of negative words not to be combined:

no	scarcely	can't
not	rarely	shouldn't
neither	barely	aren't
never	seldom	wouldn't
none	don't	couldn't
nowhere	doesn't	haven't
nobody	won't	hardly

When two of the preceding words are combined, the result is one of the most noticeable nonstandard usages in the English language. It pays dividends to root double negatives out of writing and speech.

This really happened: A student showed me a punctuation quiz before turning it in. "I didn't put no comma there, Ms. Smith," he said, pointing to one of the sentences. Trying to save him from the horrors of a life of double negatives, I said, "I didn't put *any* comma there, Joe." He replied, "Oh, good, you didn't put none there neither," thus increasing his original double negative to a triple.

Memo from the Wordsmith

The *principal* in colonial America was the "principal" teacher in a school with two or more teachers. The principal's job was to keep the records and see that the schoolhouse was kept clean.

Dean was originally the title given to a superior over ten monks. The word comes from the Latin *decanus*, which was derived from the Latin word for ten *(decem)*.

If you suspect you use double (or even triple) negatives, kick the habit by saying them aloud (to yourself) and making them "sound wrong." If you're not sure whether you use double negatives, ask an instructor or friend to listen (and in written work, look) for them. Then, that person can tell you privately whether you have the double negative habit.

Replay Unit

45

Without changing the meaning or the basic sentence structure, correct these sentences so that they conform to standard English. Write *C* next to the one sentence here that has no errors.

EXAMPLE

             some
Don't you want ~~none~~?

1. I scarcely never do that anyways.
2. You don't need no fur coat in the summer in Southern California.
3. Don't put none over there as it might spill.
4. He won't eat no more pizza if he goes to China.
5. If you have a negative attitude, you won't succeed.
6. He don't know nothing about chemistry.
7. Taylor won't go nowheres with me on Saturday.
8. A good student wouldn't never need to cheat.
9. If she eats enough fruits and vegetables, she shouldn't get sick no more.
10. Korey don't need no secretary.
11. Dan ain't never in when you want to see him.
12. Whitney hardly never saw the stock.
13. You couldn't hardly expect Mr. Blank to join such an organization.
14. There's hardly no difference between Eddie Murphy's and Billy Crystal's estimates.
15. Nobody doesn't like Sara Lee Cheesecake.

See Appendix H for answers.
Turn to Appendix A and take the **POP QUIZ**.

Checkpoint
_____

Place a check in the blank after you've reviewed the information and understand it:

Adjectives

_____ Adjectives modify, or tell something about, nouns and pronouns.

_____ Pointing adjectives: *this, that, these, those.*

SINGULAR:	**this** kind	**that** type
PLURAL:	**these** kinds	**those** types

_____ Articles: *a, an, the* Use *a* before a word beginning with a **consonant** sound and *an* before a word beginning with a **vowel** sound.

_____ Limiting adjectives: These limit in the sense of quantity: *42* hats, *several* coats, *few* children, *some* applesauce. Limiting adjectives, identified in Unit 3, are usually used correctly and are therefore excluded from study in this section.

_____ Describing adjectives: These describe the noun or pronoun: *blue* eyes, *black* hair, *good* manners, He is *responsible.*

Adverbs

_____ Adverbs modify, or tell something about, verbs, adjectives, or other adverbs.

eat carefully [*eat* = verb modified by adverb *carefully*]
very good [*good* = adjective modified by adverb *very*]
so softly [*softly* = adverb modified by adverb *so*]

_____ Most adverbs, *but not all*, are adjectives to which *-ly* has been added: *accidental**ly**, happily, cheerfully*—but *well, often, always.*

Degrees

_____ Adjectives and adverbs come in three degrees.

_____ The positive degree modifies without making a comparison.

That stock is **safe**.
That stock is **extremely** safe.

_____ The comparative degree ends in *-er* or is preceded by *more* or *less*. Use the comparative degree to compare two only.

This stock is **safer** than that one.
He writes **more neatly** than his brother.

_____ The superlative degree ends in *-est* or is preceded by *most* or *least*. Use the superlative degree to compare three or more.

This stock is the **safest** one I own.
Of all the managers, he works the **hardest**.

Memo from the Wordsmith

WHICH SENTENCE REFERS TO MENDING A SOCK?
It's darned good.
It's darned well.

WHICH DOG WOULD DO POORLY IN POLICE WORK OR HUNTING?
The dog smells bad.
The dog smells badly.

Adjective/Adverb Hints

_____ A describing word that follows an existence verb is an adjective; it describes the *subject* of the existence verb.

The steak smells **good**. [*Good* is an adjective describing *steak; smells* is an existence verb]

_____ If an action verb is being described, use an adverb:

He plays the saxaphone **well**. [Adverb *well* describes action verb *plays*.]

He plays the saxaphone **loudly**. [Adverb *loudly* describes action verb *plays*.]

_____ Negative words are either adjectives or adverbs, but it isn't important to identify them as such. Just be sure to use only one negative word to express one negative idea.

For additional details about adjectives and adverbs, see the Grammar Supplement in Appendix G.

Special Assignment

Compose a report of 120–150 words (12–15 typewritten lines) comparing two people who differ from each other in some way. Choose a specific difference to write about—such as appearance, personality, character, intelligence, or ability. "Introduce" both people and your subject in the opening sentence. Use simple and concrete language.

Opening Sentences

Start immediately with a **topic sentence** that gets the reader interested instead of writing what you're going to write about. A topic sentence gives the main idea (the topic) of the paragraph. These two examples are **ineffective** opening sentences:

I am going to write about . . .   [We know you're going to write; just get started.]

This is a comparison of two people I know who differ from each other. [Who cares?? Instead, tell me who they are and what they do so that I'll want to know more about them. Be specific and concrete!]

These are good:

Johnson and Stern both make important but different contributions to the success of the basketball team.

Although Dr. X and Dr. Y are both good instructors, their teaching methods differ greatly.

It's hard to believe that Phyllis and Judy are twins because their personalities are so different.

Ellen is a perfect example of how a supervisor should dress for the office, while Janice is just the opposite.

Body

Continue with sentences to "support" your opening statement—or topic sentence. Describe the people with interesting, accurate, and precise words. Anything that doesn't support the topic sentence doesn't belong in the report.

Ending

Conclude with a summarizing type of sentence. Avoid introducing a new subject with the closing sentence.

Submit your report on _____ (date).

Proofreading for Careers

Use proofreading skill and the dictionary to detect and correct spelling, grammar, and typographical errors. Be sure to look up the meaning of any words you don't know. As the letter also has capitalization, number, and abbreviation errors, see Appendix F. Do not change punctuation unless you find a comma splice. Always proofread the entire letter, not just the body. Use a pen or pencil as a pointer and mark errors as you go along.

IDAHO POTATO GROWERS EXCHANGE
COMMONTATER DRIVE
BOISE, IDAHO 83700

March 6th, '85

Ms. Maryann Lamb, Editer

Health Magazine

1300 5th St.

Wenatchee, Wash. 98801

Dear Ms. Lamb:

In response to you Feb. 27 letter, we are please to share the following facts about potatos with you:

Potatos is composed of 78% water, about eighteen per cent carbohydrate, and about two percent protein. Their a good source of iron and vitamines.

It is a errogeneous idea that poatoes is fatening. Nutritionists recognize that all foods eaten in excess are fattening. Actualy potatoes aren't no more fattening than most items in the daily american diet. Potatoes alone are more lower in calories per pound than bread and many other foods. When fryed or served with butter and sour cream; however, the total caloric intake is high.

Potatoes has a high satiety value and imparts a full feeling that checks overeating. Sodium content is so slight that the American Heart Association reccomend potatoes for low-salt diets, in addition they taste well.

The enclosed pamplet was wrote by Nancy Borden who lives in Southwick, a area known for their potato industry. Also enclosed are 2 recipes; we think the Potatoes Granada recipe would be the best for your publication.

Please let us know if we can be further help to you.

Very truely yours,

Mike Rothstein

lr

enclosures

After checking with the corrected version of this letter, evaluate your skill. Excellent _____ Good _____ Fair _____ Poor _____ Other? _____

Practice Quiz

A. In the blank, write the letter that identifies the correct answer. Use the dictionary when in doubt.

EXAMPLE

___b___ (a) A (b) An eager history professor assigned 200 pages.

_____	**1.** (a) A (b) An union official would probably	**(Unit 41)**
_____	**2.** refuse (a) a (b) an hourly wage.	**(Unit 41)**
_____	**3.** Of the two designs we have considered, the first seems (a) best (b) better (c) more better.	**(Unit 42)**
_____	**4.** Of all the colors we have considered, brown is (a) more appropriate (b) most appropriate (c) appropriatest (d) appropriater.	**(Unit 42)**
_____	**5.** She doesn't want to lose (a) a (b) an $82 commission.	**(Unit 41)**
_____	**6.** If he doesn't understand the work, he will get (a) a (b) an F on the test.	**(Unit 41)**
_____	**7.** (a) A (b) An European businessperson would probably	**(Unit 41)**
_____	**8.** consider this award to be (a) a (b) an honor.	**(Unit 41)**
_____	**9.** Since both brands are equally good, please order the (a) less (b) least expensive.	**(Unit 42)**
_____	**10.** Which is (a) easier (b) easyer (c) easiest (d) easyest for you to type, a report or a tabulation?	**(Unit 42)**
_____	**11.** Mr. Shue is a (a) faster (b) more faster typist than Mr. Woo.	**(Unit 42)**
_____	**12.** I would prefer to have Harold rather than Richard assist me, as Harold is (a) patientist (b) most patient (c) more patient (d) patienter.	**(Unit 42)**
_____	**13.** Her work is even (a) badder (b) worse (c) worser (d) worster than her sister's.	**(Unit 42)**

B. Cross out adverb or adjective errors, and write the correct word or words in the blank. If the sentence is correctly written, write *C* in the blank.

EXAMPLE

___slowly___ Ms. Tomlan walked ~~slow~~ to the store.

_____	**14.** The class was asked to sit quiet anywheres.	**(Unit 43)**
_____	**15.** The flowers smell good.	**(Unit 43)**
_____	**16.** I hope you won't do no more work on that job.	**(Unit 45)**
_____	**17.** Ms. Yuden spoke brief and to the point when she addressed the club.	**(Unit 43)**
_____	**18.** The new modem operates smoother than the old one.	**(Unit 44)**
_____	**19.** Of all our stores in the city, this one is managed the poorest.	**(Unit 44)**
_____	**20.** Brenda furnished the office different from what I would have expected.	**(Unit 43)**
_____	**21.** The chemicals don't smell as bad today as they did yesterday.	**(Unit 43)**

_____ 22. The business machine show isn't open no more, but it   **(Units 43 and 45)**
                will reopen again in May.

_____ 23. It seems that Marvin wrote this prescription clearer than usual.   **(Unit 44)**

_____ 24. The accountant and the auditor were real unhappy about   **(Unit 43)**
                the figures.

_____ 25. This report was typed the most accurate of all the reports.   **(Unit 44)**

The Taming of the Apostrophe

After Completing Section Eight, You Will

✔ Write possessive nouns and nonpossessive plurals correctly.

✔ Write contractions correctly.

✔ Use the apostrophe correctly in special plural forms.

✔ Use the apostrophe symbol correctly to express feet, minutes, years, and quotations within quotations.

*T*he shrew (a scolding, nagging woman) in Shakespeare's *Taming of the Shrew* didn't "know her place" and didn't know how to behave as a dutiful wife until her husband "tamed" her—a concept quite unacceptable today.

Our concern, however, is with the taming of the apostrophe. When apostrophes are untamed, they appear in the wrong places and are missing from the right places. The result is unclear or distracting writing.

It's important to know exactly where to use apostrophes in order to avoid the common error of using them where they don't belong. Take advantage of the opportunity to master the use of this little mark. Since the apostrophe is all you concentrate on in this section, you'll always be confident in the future of your ability to place the mark correctly.

Read Unit

46 *THE UBIQUITOUS S*

It's here again. But then that's what *ubiquitous* means—"seeming to be everywhere at the same time." The letter *s* begins more words than any other letter in the alphabet and is the second most frequently used consonant (*t* is the first).

In Section Four you worked with the ubiquitous *-s* while it played the original numbers game—plurals. The *-s* also makes nouns possessive. For that reason, be careful to avoid confusing plurals with possessives. Use an apostrophe in possessive nouns, as well as an *-s*.

BUT

Do not use an apostrophe in nouns that are **just plain plural** and not possessive.

Conscientious students who are aware of the need for apostrophes sometimes sprinkle them like raindrops wherever an *s* happens to end a word. Studying this section ensures you will *not* be an apostrophe sprinkler and that you *will* use apostrophes where needed.

Distinguishing between Plurals and Possessives

Possessive Nouns

Possession in grammar terminology refers to a relationship between one noun and another. When the first noun shows who possesses and the second shows what is possessed, the relationship is made clear by use of an *-s* and an **apostrophe** in the first noun. Study the various possessive relationships on page 211.

Memo from the Wordsmith

WHICH BUTLER WOULD GET FIRED?

The butler stood at the doorway and called the guests names.
The butler stood at the doorway and called the guests' names.

PERSONAL	Karen's brother	the manager's friend.
OWNERSHIP	the men's hats	a girl's pen.
PLACE OF ORIGIN	Nebraska's population	Ohio's weather
AUTHORSHIP	the president's speech	the auditors' report
TYPE OR KIND	children's clothes	women's studies
TIME	two months' delay	a week's vacation

(Wait for Unit 47 to decide whether to place the apostrophe before or after the *s*.)

A possessive noun replaces a prepositional phrase. Compare the prepositional phrases in bold type below with the possessive expressions using apostrophes above. (Whether a prepositional phrase or an apostrophe with *s* is used, showing possession is the result.)

the brother **of Karen**	the friend **of the manager**
the hats of **the men**	a pen belonging **to the girl**
the population **of Nebraska**	the weather **in Ohio**
a speech **by the president**	a report **by the auditors**
the clothing **of the children**	studies **about women**
a delay **of two months**	a vacation **of one week**

Writing for Your Career

Whenever possessives sound natural, use them rather than the prepositional phrase. If the result sounds awkward or changes the meaning, use the prepositional phrase. For example, *the interior of the house* sounds better than *the house's interior*. In *The Star Spangled Banner*, however, *the dawn's early light* is smoother than *the early light of the dawn*.

The sentences that follow show how a prepositional phrase is eliminated by using a possessive noun. The results are more concise and clearer. Notice it's always the noun naming the possessor (or owner) that gets the apostrophe.

PREPOSITIONAL PHRASES (without apostrophe)	POSSESSIVE NOUNS (with apostrophe)
The **records prepared by the accountants** were taken to the office of the secretary.	The **accountants' records** were taken to the secretary's office.
The **population of Nebraska** is smaller than the **population of Rhode Island**.	**Nebraska's population** is smaller than **Rhode Island's**.
Clothes for children are on the fifth floor, and **clothes for infants** are on the fourth floor.	**Children's clothes** are on the fifth floor, and **infants' clothes** are on the fourth floor.
A **delay of two months** would be disastrous to this project.	**Two months' delay** would be disastrous to this project.

In the sentence about Nebraska, "population" is understood but not stated after the possessive *Rhode Island's*. This is an example of an "incomplete possessive."

To find out whether an apostrophe is needed with two nouns when the first one ends in *s*, reverse the order of the nouns and put *of* between them.

Karens brother—brother of Karen

If the reversal and insertion of *of* delivers your intended meaning, the original expression is possessive and the first noun needs an apostrophe:

Karen's brother

Recap   Circle the complete possessive expressions; that is, the possessor and the possessed. Write in the "understood" word in sentence 2.

1. "Five minutes' planning might save an hour's work on New Year's Day," said Jose's mother.
2. In 1867, the purchase of Alaska was called Seward's Folly, but history has proved the foolishness was his critics' rather than Secretary of State William H. Seward's.

Check your answers in Appendix H.

Plural Nouns

Just because a noun ends in *s* doesn't mean it needs an apostrophe. Most plural nouns end in *s*.

Use the apostrophe only for a possessive noun.

The example sentences have plurals that end in *s*; no possessive idea is shown. Apostrophes would be **incorrect.**

Memo from the Wordsmith

Study the difference in meaning. What part of speech is *work* in each sentence?

1. We would like you to see our students' work.
2. We would like you to see our students work.

The **brothers** are **partners** in a plumbing supply business.

The **girls** each own several **books**.

The **ladies** wore straw **hats**.

Your **records** include several errors made by the **auditors**.

New **accountants** are needed in our office.

Three of the **secretaries** go to lunch at one o'clock.

All of the **factories** they own are in small **towns**.

In two **months** we hope to start selling the new **disks**.

When a noun that ends in *s* is followed by another noun, the first noun is usually possessive. The nouns ending in *s* in the sentences above are not followed by other nouns. Hence they are not possessive and do not require apostrophes.

Replay Unit
46

Some nouns in the following sentences are possessive. The apostrophes, however, are left out. First underline the noun that is "possessed" or "owned." Then circle the noun that is the "possessor" or "owner" (the word that needs an apostrophe). Please do **not** insert apostrophes—just circles and underlines. Write *C* for correct beside the sentences that don't require an apostrophe.

EXAMPLE

The (artists) books were left in (Mr. Foxs) office.

1. The Williamses have sent four sopranos to try out for the chorus.
2. The new editors stories pleased his readers greatly.
3. His brothers-in-law manage the office.
4. His brother-in-laws manager has been transferred to the Guam offices.
5. The Barneses owned several pieces of property in the swamp lands of Brazil.

6. All the attorneys offices are in the new buildings.

7. South Dakotas resources are listed in the back pages of the *Almanac*.

8. Mens and womens clothes are on sale in all the stores today.

9. Have you shipped Mrs. Lopezs orders yet?

10. One of the film industrys talented directors, Steven Spielberg, will deliver several lectures at UCLA.

11. The crews strength was spent in a useless maneuver.

12. Even at their peak, the gold mines in California were less profitable than the orange groves.

13. Californias vineyards are the source of more than 75 percent of the nations wine and almost all of its raisins.

14. In three months we hope to see Saschas greatest invention.

15. Claremont Mens College is one of about fifty privately supported institutions of higher education in Southern California.

16. Oral communication in business includes making introductions, giving directions, greeting visitors, making announcements, and other speaking tasks.

17. Claudes instruction book was used for several weeks before the errors were noticed.

18. Several weeks work was completed in less than three days.

19. Extremely important to James Cash Penneys success was his attitude toward employees.

20. We all look forward to Sandys visit and hope she will enjoy the sights of Fort Lauderdale.

Answers are in Appendix H.

Read Unit

47

BEFORE OR AFTER?

Several hundred years ago, writers showed possession by using the pronoun *his* after the first noun. Instead of writing *the clerk's desk*, they wrote *the clerk his desk*. If you say this old-fashioned possessive form fast, you'll find you hardly hear the first two letters of "his." Therefore, people of that day, when spelling was much more individualized than it is today, began spelling the expression *the clerk s desk*. Since the apostrophe had previously been used to show that one or more letters had been omitted, writers began to use this mark to show that the first two letters had been left off "his." That's how we ended up with the modern form, *the clerk's desk*.

If more than one clerk shared the desk, the original expression would have been *the clerks their desk*. This, in turn, was shortened to *the clerks' desk*—the apostrophe coming after the *s* to show that the word *their* was left out after the plural word *clerks*.

You can still use this method to determine whether to place the apostrophe before or after the *s*: Once you've decided that the noun is posses-

Word to the Wise

Words do not normally become plural by adding apostrophe and *s*.

NO   The Jones's are both server's at our new restaurant's.

YES   The Joneses are both servers at our new restaurants.

sive, as explained in Unit 46, then decide whether it is singular or plural. If it's singular, put the apostrophe where the word *his* would have been in the 1700s. If it's plural, insert the apostrophe where the word *their* would have fit.

Although the *his* and *their* trick works every time, here are some simple rules for added confidence that you're forming possessives correctly.

Rule 1—Singular Nouns

Add *'s* to make a singular noun possessive.

One-Word Possessives

The **engineer's** desk is on wheels. [one engineer]
We do not believe the **witness's** testimony. [one witness]
Please send the **technician's** report to the lab. [one technician]
The **city's** needs for extra funds have not been met. [one city]
Mr. Gaines's office is around the corner. [one Mr. Gaines]

Exception: If adding apostrophe + *s* to a *singular* noun makes the word hard to say, just add an apostrophe. You may choose this alternate method when a proper noun has two or more syllables and ends with an *s* sound.

Mr. Stettinius' wife was not active in Washington social life.
Joyce Simmons' office is on the main floor.
Moses' journey is described in *The Bible*.
Steinmetz' discoveries made him famous.

Compound Possessives

If a singular compound noun is possessive, add the apostrophe and *s* to the end.

All words, whether individual words or compounds, form possessives at the end, not somewhere in the middle:

The reporters were amused by the **editor in chief's** remarks.
My **brother-in-law's** appetite amazes me.

Recap   Add the needed apostrophes.

1. Mr. Smiths and Ms. Perkins secretaries will take minutes at the board meeting.
2. My son-in-laws business is bankrupt.

Check your answers in Appendix H.

Rule 2—Plural Nouns Ending in *s*

Add only an apostrophe to make a plural noun that ends in *s* possessive.

One-Word Possessives

The **engineers'** desks are on wheels. [more than one engineer]

The **witnesses'** statements are false. [more than one witness]

Send the **technicians'** report to the lab. [more than one technician]

Throughout the nation, the **cities'** needs have not been met. [more than one city]

The **Gaineses'** home is in Sioux City. [more than one person named Gaines]

Exception

There is none! The exception rule under the "Singular Nouns" heading is for **singular** possessives only—**not** for plurals.

Rule 3—Plural Nouns not Ending in *s*

Add *'s* to make possessive a plural noun that does not end in *s*.

Notice that the irregular nouns *in italics* are plural but don't end in *s*.

Men's suits are very colorful this year.

The **children's** assets are held by the trustee.

The **alumni's** contributions were small.

Compound Possessives

Apply the same rule to plural compound nouns. As you studied in Section 4 and can look up in the dictionary, some compound words become plural by adding *s* to the first word—like *sons-in-law*. This plural word does not end in *s* but in *w*.

If a plural compound is possessive, first spell the plural form. Then add the possessive to the end of the compound.

Reporters from the five newspapers listened attentively to all five **editors in chief's** speeches. [The *s* after *editor* makes the compound expression plural. The *'s* after *chief* makes it possessive.]

My **brothers-in-law's** appetites amaze me. [plural possessive]

Word to the Wise

The preceding rules require that before placing the apostrophe, you decide whether the possessive noun is singular or plural. Then make certain this noun is correctly and completely spelled before making it possessive.

the ladies' purses [possessive noun is plural]
the lady's purses [possessive noun is singular]

It doesn't matter whether the second noun—the possessed—is singular or plural. Just look at the first—the possessor—and decide whether it's singular or plural.

Recap Please insert *s, es,* and apostrophes where needed. Correct sentence 1 so that we can tell I have more than one brother; then make Lopez plural.

  1. The meeting was held at my brother office, and both the Lopez attended.

Sentence 2 needs three possessives.

  2. The old saying "Women work is never done" has affected women and men roles in society.

Correct this sentence so that it means the business belonging to your daughters' husbands is bankrupt.

  3. Your son-in-law business has gone into bankruptcy.

Check your answers in Appendix H.

Special Case

When the name of an organization includes a possessive form, just see how the organization writes it and do the same. Just as in spelling a person's name (Stephen/Steven), follow the preference of the person or organization.

These two organizations do not use apostrophes in their names: Silverwoods (department store), Columbia Teachers College. *Ladies' Home Journal,* however, does have an apostrophe.

The Last Word

Men's, women's, children's, man's, woman's, and *child's* are always written with ' **before the -s** to show possession. No exceptions!

Writing for Your Career

If a possessive sounds clumsy, rephrase the sentence to avoid the possessive form. Don't compromise by using incorrect forms.

Instead of

My **brothers-in-law's** huge appetites amaze me. [correct but clumsy]

Rephrase:

My **brothers-in-law** have appetites that amaze me. [nonpossessive sounds smoother and is correct]

This version is incorrect:

My **brother-in-laws** appetites amaze me. [According to the dictionary, the *s* follows *brother* to make it plural. The possessive—if used—belongs at the *end* of a compound word.]

Replay Unit

47

A. Write the singular possessive, the plural, and the plural possessive. Follow the rules in the Read Unit.

SINGULAR EXAMPLE	SINGULAR POSSESSIVE	PLURAL	PLURAL POSSESSIVE
lawyer's	lawyer's	lawyers	lawyers'
1. freshman			
2. week			
3. witness			
4. James			
5. country			
6. employee			
7. clerk			
8. goose			
9. wife			
10. father-in-law			
11. congresswoman			
12. minute			
13. fox			
14. hour			

15. Wolf   _____   _____   _____

16. wolf   _____   _____   _____

17. principal   _____   _____   _____

18. boss   _____   _____   _____

19. lady   _____   _____   _____

20. child   _____   _____   _____

B. Insert an apostrophe and an *s* wherever needed. Show clearly whether the apostrophe is before or after the *s*. Three sentences do not require any apostrophes.

If the grammar and meaning indicate a noun is plural but not possessive, add -*s* only; make any necessary spelling change. Remember that subjects and verbs should agree in number. Do not change the form of any verb; if necessary, add an -*s* to a noun. Read each sentence carefully before deciding on the corrections.

EXAMPLE

Mr. Williams_∧[,] book is the personnel manager_∧^{'s} choice.

1. The boy sweater was torn during the football game.
2. Several new member were initiated into the club.
3. Each of the community has a civil defense program.
4. Two year interest is due on the note.
5. A person health is his most valuable possession.
6. I think men fashion change almost as quickly as women.
7. This new company asset are limited.
8. The two editor in chief remark were helpful.
9. Be prepared to come at a minute notice.
10. Mr. Perkins signature was needed two day ago.
11. The store was having a sale on lady coat.
12. The Goldstein of West Palm Beach will join us in two day.
13. San Diego population has increased during the past five year.
14. Mr. Jones desk is to your right.
15. The chairman report included several detail on the proposed worker cafeteria.
16. We studied Keats poetry in our literature class.
17. Montreal and Quebec are in Mr. Knox territory.
18. Fritz brother is chairman of the board.
19. I don't believe Hendrix story.
20. The butler stood at the doorway and called all the guest name.

C. Rewrite sentence 8 from part B so that it becomes a smoother-sounding sentence.

Check answers in Appendix H.
Turn to Appendix A for **POP QUIZ** on Units 46–47.

Read Unit

48

MORE APOSTROPHES

Contractions

In the dictionary section you observed how moving an accent mark can change not only the pronunciation but also the meaning of a word. The word *contract*, for example, with the accent on the first syllable means an agreement. With the accent on the second syllable, it means to reduce in size by drawing together. Hence, the word *contraction* refers to a word that has been shortened by removing one or more letters.

Contraction also means joining two or more words together and leaving out a letter or two. The apostrophe is placed at the exact point the letters are omitted. Do not use a period at the end of a contraction unless it ends the sentence.

Here are some words frequently contracted in business writing. Look at them carefully and remember that the apostrophe belongs where the missing letter or letters would have been.

is not = isn't	are not = aren't
was not = wasn't	were not = weren't
have not = haven't	would not = wouldn't
should not = shouldn't	could not = couldn't
will not = won't	cannot = can't
has not = hasn't	do not = don't
does not = doesn't	of the clock = o'clock
I have = I've	you have = you've
we have = we've	I shall or will = I'll
we shall or will = we'll	You will = you'll
he is = he's	I am = I'm
we are = we're	you are = you're
that is = that's	they are = they're
it is = it's	what is = what's
	she is = she's

These contractions are acceptable and desirable in ordinary business writing and speech. Whenever the contraction sounds natural to you, use it. However, in extremely formal writing, avoid contractions.

Contractions other than the types listed above—such as *nat'l* for *national, sec'y* for *secretary*—are used only in informal notes or in tables where saving space is important.

Plurals

Apostrophes normally makes words possessive, not plural. The following categories, however, show when to use and when not to use apostrophes in special circumstances. These principles are based on ease of readability. (Reference books do not agree with one another on some of these rules.)

Plural of Letters

Use an apostrophe for the plural of letters.

Please be sure to dot your **i's**.
The applicant's college transcript showed four **F's** in various math classes.

Plural of Numbers and Words

An apostrophe is unnecessary when forming the plural of numbers or of words.

The temperature in Akron is in the 70s.
A young child will sometimes write 3s backwards.
Please omit all *therefores*. [plural of word]

Plural of Abbreviations

A handy reference for abbreviations used in business is in Appendix F.

Capital Letter Abbreviations   Capital letter abbreviations are often, but not always, written without the periods.

An apostrophe is unnecessary to form the plural of capital letter abbreviations.

All CODs should be sent to my office.
There are two YWCAs in Toledo.

Lowercase Abbreviations   Do use an apostrophe to form the plural of lowercase abbreviations that might be misread without the apostrophe:

All c.o.d.'s should be sent to my office.
Too many *etc.*'s usually mean the writer isn't sure of the facts.

In such documents as a table, chart, or invoice, these abbreviations are appropriate: yds., gals., ctns., and so on (no apostrophes). Within sentences of a business letter or report, however, spell out words such as *yards, gallons, cartons*.

Possessive Abbreviations

When an abbreviation is possessive, use the apostrophe—the same as with any other noun:

The AMA's position is clear. [singular possessive—Make a singular noun possessive by adding apostrophe and *s*.]

The R.N.s' uniforms at this hospital are yellow. [plural possessive—First make *R.N.* plural by adding *s* and then make it possessive by adding an apostrophe to a plural noun ending in *s*.]

Miscellaneous

As a symbol, the apostrophe has several meanings. The most common are for feet and minutes, for years with the century numbers left out, and to mark quotations within quotations.

FEET AND MINUTES

4′ [four feet]   4′ [four minutes]

Use this style for feet and minutes only in technical work, tables, charts, and so on; otherwise, spell out *feet* or *minute(s)*.

The apostrophe *may* be used in class graduation years, well-known historical years, and decades: *During the '60s much upheaval took place in our society.*

Ordinarily, however, use the full number for the century: *In **1995** our company will celebrate 25 years in business.*

QUOTATION WITHIN A QUOTATION

The candidate said, "It was Abraham Lincoln who referred to 'government of the people, by the people, and for the people'; and that is also my credo."

Replay Unit

Insert apostrophes or numbers where needed. Write *C* next to the sentences that do not require a correction.

EXAMPLE

He͚'s likely to remember that Churchill was in his 80s in ^19^54.

1. I couldnt meet you at five oclock.
2. Please be sure to dot your is.
3. All CODs should be referred to the receiving manager.
4. In 22 America was prosperous and optimistic about the future.
5. Its hoped that the late 90s will be an era of full employment.
6. Dont forget that all R.N.s uniforms are yellow.
7. Several M.D.s have their offices on the third floor.
8. There are too many *ands, ifs,* and *buts* in your composition.
9. In 89 the class of 75 held its reunion at the finest hotel in the city.
10. There were many suicides following the stock market crash of 29.
11. There are three CPAs in this building.
12. The Gay 90s was a period when workers suffered while the wealthy had lavish parties.
13. If you cross your ls, theyll look like sloppy ts.
14. Wont you please marry me?
15. Only five As were recorded.
16. In the early 1900s, women wore long dresses.

17. Whats the difference between Stock No. 234 and No. 235?
18. Youve only two forms left.
19. Arent you going to hire that mechanic?
20. Couldnt you make your 9s look less like 7s?

Answers are in Appendix H.

Checkpoint

Tame apostrophes, like pets, obey the rules and are in the right place at the right time. After completing the Practice Quiz, Proofreading, and the Special Assignment according to Units 46–48, you'll be sure your apostrophes are ready for company—any company you work for.

Test your mastery of the apostrophe principles just studied by placing a check next to each one you are sure of. If your conscience will not permit the check mark at first, reread the explanations in the unit.

_____ Apostrophes are used in singular and plural possessive nouns.   **(Unit 46)**

Maria's office and the managers' offices are always open.

_____ If a plural noun isn't possessive, don't use an apostrophe.   **(Unit 46)**

The managers have offices on the 5th floor.

_____ To form the plural of a lowercase abbreviation or of a capital **or** lowercase single   **(Unit 48)**
letter, use an apostrophe.

If you mind your p's and q's and don't use too many e.g.'s, your grades will be A's.

_____ A possessive noun ends with *s* and precedes another noun or an "understood"   **(Unit 46)**
noun.

Charley's aunt is eccentric.

Of all the aunts in the room, Charley's is the most eccentric. [*Charley's* is an incomplete
possessive; *aunt* is understood.]

_____ To test for possessives, reverse the order of the two nouns and insert "of"   **(Unit 46)**
between them—*aunt of Charley* is written as *Charley's aunt*.

_____ Make a singular noun possessive by adding *'s*.   **(Unit 47)**

Shinji's job pays well.

_____ If adding *'s* to a singular noun results in a possessive that is awkward to   **(Unit 47)**
pronounce, the *s* may be omitted. When in doubt, add the *s*; you won't go wrong.

Watkins' home is near mine.
Morris's home is near mine.

_____ Make a plural noun that ends in *s* possessive by adding an apostrophe only.   **(Unit 47)**

The Joneses' stores are all in good locations.

_____ Make a plural noun that does **not** end in *s* possessive by adding *'s*.   **(Unit 47)**

Children's toys should not encourage violence.

_____ An apostrophe is inserted within a contraction at the exact place where letters   **(Unit 48)**
are left out.

A toy gun isn't a good gift for a child.

_____ The apostrophe is the symbol used for feet, minutes, centuries, and quotes inside quotes.   **(Unit 48)**

_____ You have studied possessive nouns in this section. Now is a good time to review possessive pronouns in Unit 27. Look over the difference between possessive pronouns and contractions with pronouns; for example, is it *your* or *you're, its* or *it's, someones, someone's,* or *someones'*??

For further details about apostrophe usage, see Section 8 of the Grammar Supplement in Appendix G.

Special Assignment

A. In Replay Unit 46, you were asked to circle the words that require apostrophes. List those words below and insert the apostrophes. When no change is required in a sentence, just write "None" in the blank.

EXAMPLE

_____ artist's, Fox's _____

1. _____   11. _____
2. _____   12. _____
3. _____   13. _____
4. _____   14. _____
5. _____   15. _____
6. _____   16. _____
7. _____   17. _____
8. _____   18. _____
9. _____   19. _____
10. _____   20. _____

B. Write sentences in which you shorten these phrases by using a possessive noun.

EXAMPLE

son of Mr. Ames Mr. Ames's son is the auditor. _____

1. books of Patricia _____
2. wife of Mr. Adams _____
3. vacation of one week _____
4. home of the Adamses _____
5. books belonging to the boys _____
6. toys of the children _____
7. problems of the members _____
8. commissions of the salespeople _____
9. work of two years _____
10. office of my father-in-law _____

8

11. words of Moses _____

12. streets of Houston _____

13. report of the auditor _____

14. notice of ten minutes _____

15. expense accounts of the supervisors _____

C. Correct the following sentence:

Student's who put apostrophe's into plain plural's may receive shock's when they get grade's on the examination's in a few day's.

This assignment should be completed by _____. (date)

Proofreading for Careers

This short essay requires the addition of eight apostrophes. Also be on the lookout for two misspellings of nouns you studied in Section 4, two capitalization errors, and one comma splice which requires a capital letter for correction.

WHISTLER'S MOTHER

In the worlds most famous museum, the louvre in Paris, hangs a painting by Americas celebrated artist, James McNeill Whistler. This paintings formal title is "An Arrangement in Gray and Black," but it is better known by the simple name "Whistlers Mother."

Many studies have been made in an effort to explain the basis of this portraits almost universal appeal. But what criterions can the art Critic use in judging a painting?

The critic is not like a scientist, he or she cannot set up a controlled experiment wherein a number of stimulus are shot into a subject and data collected on the subjects reaction. No, the art critic must rely on inner emotions and sensitivity when analyzing a painting.

Analyses of a painting is very personal. If you looked at "Whistlers Mother," what would you see? Would you, like most of us, be left wondering about the source of this portraits greatness?

After verifying your corrections, choose an adjective to evaluate your skill today: _____
Do you need to review
Apostrophes? _____
Section Four singulars and plurals? _____
Section Two comma splice? _____

Practice Quiz

After reading each sentence, indicate the correct forms of the words listed below the sentence.

EXAMPLE

The chairmans report included details on the proposed workers cafeteria.

___b___ **1.** (a) chairmans (b) chairman's (c) chairmans'

___a___ **2.** (a) details (b) detail's (c) details'

___c___ **3.** (a) workers (b) worker's (c) workers'

The camp directors view was that drastic changes had to be made in Johns outlook. (This camp has one director.)

_____ **1.** (a) directors (b) director's (c) directors'   **(Unit 47)**

_____ **2.** (a) changes (b) change's (c) changes'   **(Unit 46)**

_____ **3.** (a) Johns (b) John's (c) Johns'   **(Unit 47)**

It was agreed that new desks should be installed in the salesmens office.

_____ **4.** (a) desks (b) desk's (c) desks'   **(Unit 46)**

_____ **5.** (a) salesmens (b) salesmen's (c) salesmens'   **(Unit 47)**

Yesterdays techniques cannot succeed in todays market.

_____ **6.** (a) Yesterdays (b) Yesterday's (c) Yesterdays'   **(Units 46 and 47)**

_____ **7.** (a) techniques (b) technique's (c) techniques'   **(Unit 46)**

_____ **8.** (a) todays (b) today's (c) todays'   **(Unit 46)**

Davon has one weeks time to accept or reject this companys offer.

_____ **9.** (a) weeks (b) week's (c) weeks'   **(Units 46 and 47)**

_____ **10.** (a) companys (b) company's (c) companie's   **(Unit 47)**
     (d) companys' (e) companies'

The managers, at last Wednesdays meeting, agreed to rebuild the executives recreation room.

_____ **11.** (a) managers (b) manager's (c) managers'   **(Unit 46)**

_____ **12.** (a) Wednesdays (b) Wednesday's (c) Wednesdays'   **(Unit 47)**

_____ **13.** (a) executives (b) executive's (c) executives'   **(Unit 47)**

Michael hasnt read the minutes of the meeting yet.

_____ **14.** (a) hasnt (b) has'nt (c) hasn't (d) hasnt'   **(Unit 48)**

_____ **15.** (a) minutes (b) minute's (c) minutes'   **(Unit 46)**

The PTAs paper supply is in the top drawer.

_____ 16. (a) PTAs (b) PTA's (c) PTAs'   **(Unit 48)**

The presidents of five PTAs were invited to the reunion of the class of 75.

_____ 17. (a) presidents (b) president's (c) presidents'   **(Unit 46)**

_____ 18. (a) PTAs (b) PTA's (c) PTAs'   **(Unit 48)**

_____ 19. (a) 75 (b) '75   **(Unit 48)**

My sister-in-laws manager left college after two years work.

_____ 20. (a) sister's-in-law (b) sister-in-law's (c) sister-in-laws'   **(Unit 47)**
            (d) sisters'-in-law

_____ 21. (a) years (b) year's (c) years'   **(Unit 47)**

Yamada and Jones is one of the citys finest firms.

_____ 22. (a) Jone's (b) Jones (c) Jones'   **(Unit 47)**

_____ 23. (a) citys (b) cities (c) city's (d) cities' (e) citie's   **(Unit 47)**

_____ 24. (a) firm's (b) firms (c) firms'   **(Unit 46)**

Houstons streets are safe at night.

_____ 25. (a) Houstons (b) Houston's (c) Houstons'   **(Units 46 and 47)**

Memo from the Wordsmith

DOORMATS IN SUBURBIA

A stroll through any middle-class suburb reveals incorrect apostrophes on doormats, mailboxes, and even in elaborate wrought iron signs. Notice the unneeded apostrophes in the names that identify the owners of the homes:

The Smith's   The Jone's   The Anderson's   The Fox'es

To form the plural of proper nouns, merely add *s* or *es*:

The Smiths   The Joneses   The Andersons   The Foxes

NOTES

After Completing Section Nine, You Will

✔ Use commas in the way that improves the accuracy and clearness of your writing.

✔ Use commas according to principles established for effective business writing.

*W*hen you're talking with someone, brief pauses between certain words help the listener follow the ideas you are expressing. If you don't pause at exactly the right places, the listeners let you know they're not sure of what you mean. Then you repeat or even change the order of the words to make sure your listener understands.

Writing, however, needs to be understood immediately by readers since they cannot easily ask for a repeat or rephrasing. When you're writing, punctuation marks replace the pauses.

Good writers have developed a system for placement of these pausing symbols—or punctuation marks. Although punctuation through hearing (placing some mark wherever it seems there should be a pause) is helpful, it's too inexact by itself for a business letter, a report, instructions, and so on. When you know the rules in this section and the next, you no longer rely on a kind of guesswork. Instead, your ability to punctuate by hearing will be increased by your understanding of the logical rules that follow. This section explains the system established for the most commonly used punctuation mark—the comma.

A Warning

As you complete these replay units, be sure to insert a comma only when the rule applies. If you punctuate without at least mentally referring to the rules each time, you will continue to make whatever comma errors you made in the past. In short, you will waste time doing this work if you don't practice applying the rules.

Read Unit
49

WINE, WOMEN, AND SONG

Johann Voss, an 18th-century poet, who may have been a bit of a reprobate,* wrote:

> Who does not love wine, women, and song
> Remains a fool his whole life long.

Wine, women, and song is an example of a series. A series means three or more words, phrases, or clauses.

Use commas to separate items in a series.

* Look it up now before you forget.

WORD SERIES   He filed all the letters, reports, invoices, and purchase orders.

PHRASE SERIES   Joe believes in government of the people, for the people, and by the people.

CLAUSE SERIES   Scot does the typing, Robin does the filing, and Dawn keeps the books. [independent clauses]

We believe that your intentions were good, that you planned carefully, and that you had a good product. [dependent clauses]

Notice the commas between the items in the series as well as before *and* or *or* that precedes the last item.*

If a conjunction precedes each item in the series, commas are not used.

NO COMMAS   Engineers **and** physicists **and** chemists are working on the project.

Replay Unit

49

Apply the comma rule for series by inserting commas in these sentences; if you are tempted to use a comma for any other reason, **don't**! If no comma is needed, write *C* in the blank.

EXAMPLE

We ordered stationery, envelopes, message pads, and memo forms for the new office.

_____   1. Meetings will be held on June 12 July 6 and August 19 to plan the operation of the new office.

_____   2. Our agent and our accountant and our broker are all needed for consultation before decisions can be made.

_____   3. Chevrolets Fords Plymouths and VWs have always been lower priced than Chryslers Cadillacs and Lincolns.

_____   4. We looked under the desk in the trash and everywhere else we could think of but still couldn't find the report.

_____   5. First we studied the report then we investigated its accuracy and finally we decided to buy the stock.

_____   6. During the 1980s such companies as General Motors Acme-Cleveland Corporation and National Semiconductor made staff cuts of between 10 and 25 percent.

_____   7. Find out what kind of world you want to live in what you are good at and what you need to work at to build that world.

* Business English experts recommend the use of that final comma, although some literary writers and journalists omit it.

_____ 8. The job of a top manager is to set broad objectives formulate strategies to meet them and decide among alternate possibilities.

_____ 9. Then the manager must determine which task should be performed first second and so forth.

_____ 10. International Business Machines General Motors American Telephone and Telegraph and other major business organizations reported a drop in earnings this year.

See Appendix H for answers.

FOR ADJECTIVES ONLY

The Unit 49 rule concerns comma use with _three_ or more items in a series. With **adjectives**, however, use a comma between just _two_ or more when they describe the same noun.

To test for whether or not a comma is needed, imagine _and_ between the adjectives. If it makes sense, a comma is needed. The comma replaces the word _and_, which is understood but omitted.

And Imagined Test

They died during the **long, severe** winter. [The adjectives _long_ and _severe_ describe _winter. And_ makes sense between them—_long and severe winter_; therefore, use a comma.]

They died during the **long and severe** winter. [_And_ is between _long_ and _severe_; therefore, no comma is needed.]

She is an **intelligent, loyal** employee. [A comma replaces _and_ between _intelligent_ and _loyal_.]

She is an **intelligent and loyal** employee. [_And_ is between _intelligent_ and _loyal_; therefore, no comma is used.]

Reversal Test

Another test that may help decide whether to use a comma between two adjectives is to reverse the order of the adjectives. If they make sense reversed, you need a comma.

She is a **loyal, intelligent** employee.
She is an **intelligent, loyal** employee.

Since the sentence makes sense either way, a comma is used between the adjectives.

No Comma Between Adjectives

Sometimes one word really describes two other words; in such cases, *and* does not make sense between the adjectives, and no comma is used. Also try reversing the adjectives; if the reversal doesn't make sense, omit the comma.

AND-IMAGINED TEST   Many elderly people died during the long, severe winter. ["Many and elderly people" doesn't make sense; therefore, no comma is needed.]

REVERSAL TEST   Elderly many people died . . . [The reversal doesn't make sense, further proof that a comma shouldn't be used.]

Betty Van Meter drives a yellow sports car. [Since "sports yellow car" doesn't make sense, a comma should not be used between the adjectives.]

Now you try both the *and*-imagined and reversal tests with the adjectives shown in bold type. You'll see why commas are not used between them.

Our **new advertising** booklet was completed last week.

The **annual financial** report was prepared by a famous cost accountant.

Replay Unit
50

Apply the comma rules for "adjectives only" and for series by inserting commas where needed. When you are tempted to use a comma for any other reason, **don't**! If the sentence needs no comma, write *C* in the blank.

EXAMPLE

The company needs a strong, aggressive salesperson for that job.

_____ 1. Her pleasant friendly personality is an asset to this office.

_____ 2. She is wearing a new red dress and looks clean and neat.

_____ 3. He asked why you came what you wanted and what you expected to do.

_____ 4. Our office is located in a small elegant building in the new part of Denver.

_____ 5. Eric Smith is an ethical knowledgeable investment counselor specializing in socially responsible investing.

_____ 6. Susan and Kevin will travel with you to Paris Brussels and Munich.

_____ 7. John Sculley's marketing expertise in a profitable highly competitive industry was what Apple sought.

_____ 8. Sculley was wooed away from Pepsico with a million dollar bonus a million dollar salary and stock options.

_____ 9. Payment will be made by certified personal check.

_____ 10. The Middle East sheikdom of Bahrain had a settled well-educated population.

Answers are in Appendix H.

Read Unit

51

INDEPENDENTS DAY

No, the title isn't spelled wrong, but then neither is it July 4. This unit is about independent clauses and reviews Section Two.

> Use a comma between independent clauses joined by a coordinating conjunction—*and, but, or, nor, for,* and sometimes *yet.* Place the comma before the conjunction.

Although *so* is also a coordinating conjunction, avoid using it in business writing.

INDEPENDENT CLAUSES WITH COMMA

The clerk filed copies of all the outgoing letters, but she forgot to file copies of the invoices. [Two independent clauses joined by *but.*]

The clerk filed copies of all the outgoing letters but forgot to file copies of the invoices. [Because a clause does not follow *but,* no comma is used. A clause requires a subject and a verb. The entire sentences is one clause: *clerk* is the subject and *filed* and *forgot* are the two verbs.]

I am proud Evan is one of us, and I want him to know that we appreciate his work. [Two complete thoughts are joined by *and.*]

I am proud Evan is one of us and want him to know that we appreciate his work. [Since a complete thought, or independent clause, does not follow *and,* no comma is used.]

> For a short sentence (no more than about 10 words), omit the comma when *and* or *or* joins the independent clauses.

If *but, nor, for,* or *yet* is the joining word, use a comma before it regardless of sentence length.

INDEPENDENT CLAUSES WITHOUT COMMA

He won and I lost.

Did she type or did she file?

Francine wants the job and she will do it well.

BUT AND *YET* SHORT INDEPENDENTS WITH COMMA

He won, **but** I lost.

Ms. J. Mack is a member, **yet** she didn't attend.

Replay Unit

51

Apply the comma principles from Units 49–51 to these sentences. If you are tempted to insert a comma for another reason, **resist!** Write *C* next to the three sentences that do not require any commas.

EXAMPLE

She bought her husband a microwave oven for Christmas,and he bought her the same.

_____ 1. I have thought the problem over carefully and I shall give you the answer in an hour.

_____ 2. Peter spoke with Amy today but he couldn't persuade her to do the research.

_____ 3. Mrs. Jaffe will teach the shorthand class in the mornings but is unable to teach any afternoon classes.

_____ 4. A well-educated person is needed to manage the new marketing division and Mr. Chandra might be just the man for the job.

_____ 5. Either you may make a 20 percent down payment or you may pay the entire amount now.

_____ 6. J. C. Penney treated his employees as he would want to be treated were the situations reversed.

_____ 7. Doris lives in Rochester but she visits Florida often.

_____ 8. Lucille was a creative conscientious teacher but is now retired and living in Oceanside.

_____ 9. Are the summers warmest in Miami Fort Dade or Jacksonville?

_____ 10. An advertising agency acts as an intermediary between a company that wants to advertise and the various media that sell space and time.

Check your answers in Appendix H.

Read Unit

52

CURTAIN RAISERS

A curtain raiser is a short play presented before the principal performance. The "curtain raiser" for a sentence is a word or several words presented before the main part of the sentence. **This introductory expression is always dependent**; that is, it cannot stand alone as a complete thought any more than the theatrical curtain raiser can be presented without the main show. The audience would want their money back.

Many, but not all, introductory expressions are separated from the main idea of the sentence by a comma.

Introductory Expressions

Place a comma after the following one-word introductory expressions: *Yes, No, Well, Oh.*

Yes, we'll be glad to ship ten dozen toasters to Harley.

Place a comma after an introductory that names the person you're writing to.

This is called "direct address." Direct address, when it's not a sentence opener, is referred to again in the next unit.

Joelene, will you help me?

Place a comma after an introductory expression containing any form of a verb.*

If you attend the meeting, be sure to take notes for Ann.

Recap   Insert commas after introductory expressions that have a verb or a verb form.

1. Because Twileen and George wanted to be discreet they met in out-of-the-way places.
2. Several weeks ago George had plans to meet Twileen at their favorite rendezvous.
3. When he got to his car he found a note on the windshield.
4. Being in a hurry to meet Twileen he didn't read the note and quickly stuffed it into his pocket.
5. Had he read the note he would have taken his time getting to the rendezvous.

Check your answers in Appendix H.

Place a comma after an introductory expression of five or more words—whether it has a verb form or not.

Because of the unusual circumstances, we shall encourage Twileen to stop seeing Jesse.

Under the sponsorship of George and Jesse, a conference on hypnosis and psychosomatic medicine will be held on July 2.

When a introductory expression has fewer than five words and no verb form, use a comma only if needed for clearness.

---

* Do not use a comma if a verb form (verbal) is the subject; for example, **To know you** is a joy.

Commas are not required after short "place" and "time" introductories—unless a comma clarifies the meaning or contributes needed emphasis.

> **Once inside,** the man requested food. [comma required for clearness]
>
> **For a while,** longer skirts will be worn. [comma required for clearness]
>
> **Within a month** Professor Hanawell will know the results of this unfortunate office romance. [comma unnecessary in this "time" introductory]
>
> **In Alaska** the winter nights are long. [comma unnecessary in this "place" introductory]

Replay Unit

52

Insert commas where needed. Apply the rules included so far in Section Nine. If tempted to use a comma for some other reason, be strong—**don't**! Write *C* next to the four sentences that need no commas.

EXAMPLE

Although George didn't know it,Twileen and Jesse often worked late on the same projects.   ∧

_____ 1. If Ms. Sorenson places an order now she'll receive the software in ample time for the new semester.

_____ 2. In our attractive modern office on Wall Street you will find a courteous staff at your service.

_____ 3. As we all know real merit is hard to conceal.

_____ 4. Since you have not seen the report you and your staff should not be criticizing it.

_____ 5. You'll receive the goods in ample time for the sale if you place your order now.

_____ 6. Being an alert salesperson he noticed the prospect's gesture of annoyance.

_____ 7. No he hasn't called on us either this month or last month.

_____ 8. Mrs. Lee we are unable to repair your washer dryer toaster and coffeepot all in one day.

_____ 9. Please write a note to the conference leader if you cannot attend.

_____ 10. If it is to be it is up to me.

_____ 11. No one in the world has more self-control than the person who can stop after eating one peanut.

_____ 12. Working quickly he carefully organized the information.

_____ 13. Although the furniture arrived on time telephone service was not immediately available.

_____ **14.** Francine and Evan think Emerson would be a good location for the factory but the client feels it would be too far from Cherry Hill.

_____ **15.** In Chicago many people sunbathe on the cement beach near Lake Michigan.

Answers are in Appendix H.
POP QUIZ—Appendix A.

Read Unit
53   PARENTHETICALS

A parenthetical expression adds an extra idea but doesn't change the main idea of the sentence. (You can picture the expression in parentheses.) When the parenthetical expression "interrupts" the main idea, commas are used before and after. Naturally, if the parenthetical expression—or extra information—is at the beginning or the end of the sentence, only one comma is needed. When the parenthetical expression is at the beginning, it might also be called an introductory expression. It doesn't matter what you call it, as long as you use the comma.

If removing the expression from the sentence makes the meaning unclear or changes the meaning of the sentence, it is not parenthetical; do not use commas. Reading the sentence aloud may help to determine whether the expression is parenthetical.

Parenthetical Words, Phrases, Clauses

Use a comma (or commas) to separate a parenthetical—that is, a nonessential—word, phrase, or clause from the rest of a sentence.

Each parenthetical expression in the examples is in bold type. If you cover the parenthetical words, the rest of the sentence keeps its original meaning.

WORDS AND PHRASES

Marty is an expert in this field, **however**, and will lead the discussion.

Anything, **little or big**, becomes an adventure when the right one shares it with you.

Joseph Kleinberg is, **of course**, an expert in this field.

Janet, **an expert in this field**, will lead the discussion.

CLAUSES

*Marci, **who is an expert in this field**, will lead the discussion. [Compare with starred (*) sentence on page 239 under heading "Not Parenthetical."]

Several features of this proposal are unsatisfactory, **we believe**, and need to be rewritten.

We shall definitely meet you at 5 p.m., **although we cannot remain for long**.

Recap Insert commas around parenthetical expressions.

1. Home where I learned to walk and talk holds a special place in my heart.
2. The guidebook is divided into two parts Job Content and Work Environment the two main aspects of work to be considered.
3. The exact job you want however may not be available when you want it.
4. The new records management system which was devised by the American Records Management Association eliminates considerable waste motion.
5. Mr. Davidson who was a national authority on Ninja Turtles has recommended the purchase of this software.
6. The guide gave us a fascinating tour and told us about the history of the courthouse even though he was worried about his wife's health.

Check your answers in Appendix H.

Not Parenthetical

Commas do not belong around words that are essential to a sentence's meaning—that is, not parenthetical.

Cover the words in bold type in the examples; notice how the meaning of the rest of the sentence is distorted when these words don't appear.

A person **who is an expert in this field** should lead the discussion. [Compare with starred (*) sentence about Marci on page 238.]

Someone **like you** should lead the discussion.

The document **that is dated June 12** should supersede all others.

Memo from the Wordsmith

Both the following sentences are punctuated correctly. However, the commas making "thought Ron" parenthetical make a big difference:

Bradley thought Ron was very generous.
Bradley, thought Ron, was very generous.

Word to the Wise

Most prepositional phrases are not parenthetical and should not be set off with commas:

NO   We saw your sales representative, **at the conference,** Thursday.

NO   The Board of Directors, **of ABC Software,** is considering mail order sales.

Take out all commas in both these sentences; the comma-enclosed expressions aren't parenthetical and thus shouldn't *be* comma enclosed.

Will you please bring your resume with you **when you come to my office**?

A national organization **with a research and service bureau** stands behind our product.

Any pedestrian **who doesn't obey the caution signals** should be fined.

A city **that can qualify as a depressed area** is eligible to receive state and federal aid.

The ones **who complain the loudest** are generally those **who contribute the least**.

An Arizona mapmaker was fired **because he had no sense of Yuma**.

A woman student must not enter men's rooms **without a chaperone approved by the principal or her representative**. *Oxford Intercollegiate Rules for Women, 1924.*

Recap   Insert commas needed for parenthetical expressions. If no comma is needed, write *C* in the blank:

_____ 1. Sales representatives who increase sales by 50 percent will win a Caribbean cruise for two.

_____ 2. The vice president and the general manager who usually meet in the sales manager's office are meeting today in the president's office.

_____ 3. The shipment arrived at our Receiving Department before we telephoned the cancellation.

_____ 4. We have referred your memo of January 6 to the IRS auditor.

_____ 5. How you handle customers on the phone can either increase sales or turn customers away.

Check your answers in Appendix H.

Writing for Your Career

Trained correspondents use "direct address" because it's courteous and because readers generally like to be personally addressed in a business letter:

Thank you, Ms. Ross, for showing me around Heald Colleges.

Overuse of the technique, however, appears insincere.

To Comma or Not To Comma
Names

When the name of the person you're writing to is used in direct address, the name is parenthetical; use commas.

Notice how you pause before the name when saying the sentence aloud.

DIRECT ADDRESS

We're sorry we cannot pay you for giving the lecture, **Mr. Simmons**.

Because of your expertise, **Harry**, we would appreciate your leading the discussion.

Sandra, we would appreciate your leading the discussion because of your expertise in this field. [It doesn't matter whether you call *Sandra* parenthetical or introductory.]

Now, **ladies and gentlemen**, I'll show you a simple experiment in physics.

When the parenthetical name* is not a direct address, use commas if the name consists of more than one word.

PARENTHETICAL   My former neighbor, **Pat Greenland,** is a talented artist.

My former neighbor, **Mrs. Greenland,** is a talented artist.

BUT

If just the first name is used, it's often not parenthetical and commas are not, therefore, required. Notice that you don't pause before the name when saying these sentences aloud.

NOT PARENTHETICAL   My former neighbor **Pat** is a talented artist.

My sister-in-law **Bea** will lead the discussion.

Your brother **Sid** will meet you in Detroit.

If a name is essential—that is, not parenthetical—don't use commas.

* These constructions are often referred to as **appositives** or **nouns in apposition**.

I believe that **Professor Joanne Murcar** lives in Spokane.
Professor Chan-Nui is from Wenatchee.

Titles

If a title of a publication is parenthetical—or nonessential—use commas.

TITLES WITH COMMAS

Bergerud and Gonzalez' book**, *Word Processing: Concepts and Careers*,** is being studied in colleges throughout the country.

The two new training videos**, *Banking for Older Customers*** and ***It's Just Good Business*,** may now be borrowed from the employee library.

BUT

If the title just flows into the rest of the sentence—or is essential— do not use commas.

TITLES WITHOUT COMMAS

Have you read the book entitled ***Word Processing: Concepts and Careers***?

The video ***Dealing with Angry Customers*** presents a simple method for dealing effectively with angry customers.

Replay Unit

53

Insert commas according to the principle explained in Unit 53 only. Decide on the main idea intended by the writer of these sentences.

First, read the sentence with the questionable words omitted.

If the meaning changes, the questionable words are essential and should not be enclosed in commas. Write *C* beside the eight sentences that do not require addition of commas.

If, however, the meaning remains the same when you leave out the questionable words, those extra words are parenthetical; **do** use commas.

EXAMPLE

George, who was supposed to be giving the party, was locked out of his home. [Commas are used because the meaning of the main part of the sentence remains the same even without the extra information: "George was locked out of his home." The clause "who was supposed to be giving the party" is additional information; it could be another sentence.]

_____ **1.** In the Newark office however this plan saved the company a great deal of money.

_____ **2.** The operating costs as he probably told you are too high.

_____ **3.** Two of our employees Mr. Siegel and Ms. Washington are attorneys.

_____ 4. My office Room No. 103 is in this building.

_____ 5. The Credit Department which is on the third floor will be open all day.

_____ 6. Martin Simon the auditor found a $100,000 error.

_____ 7. The woman wearing a red dress is my sister-in-law.

_____ 8. The boys who stole the bicycles were arrested.

_____ 9. Your work therefore is better than anyone else's.

_____ 10. We are happy to accept this proposal Ms. Odland.

_____ 11. Jane will lead the discussion today even though she knows more about other divisions.

_____ 12. The new equipment which I haven't even learned to operate yet is out of order.

_____ 13. Ted Banta will lead the discussion tomorrow although we might ask Meriam to co-chair.

_____ 14. My friend Alberta works in the field of property management.

_____ 15. The merchandise will we believe be shipped by the end of next week.

_____ 16. George isn't that Stella Glitter signing autographs in the lobby?

_____ 17. Coaches who fail to inspire their players should be replaced.

_____ 18. My sister-in-law Bette lives in Plantation.

_____ 19. The textbook we use in the office administration course is called *Machine Transcription and Dictation*.

_____ 20. Openness fosters growth and establishes an important feeling of worth which motivates everyone to do the best possible job.

_____ 21. Harold Simon is the attorney who will try the case.

_____ 22. This instruction booklet which gives you complete information can be purchased for $3.95.

_____ 23. Barry Hicks enjoys effective and correct use of the English language although he is not a purist.

_____ 24. A great idea it has been said comes into the world as gently as a dove.

_____ 25. The book *In Praise of English* was written by Joseph T. Shipley.

Please check your answers in Appendix H.

Read Unit

54

THREE EASY COMMAS

The three principles of comma usage in this unit are easy. Just about all you have to do is read through the unit and complete the Replay; then you'll be sure of these commas.

States

Almost everyone remembers the comma between city and state. It's the one *after* the state that some people forget.

Use commas before and after the state when it follows the name of the city.

BEFORE AND AFTER

I lived in Springfield, Massachusetts, when I was young.

The art festival in Laguna Beach, California, attracts many tourists.

Dates

Another principle that almost everyone remembers is the comma between a date and a year. But a comma after the year some people forget.

When a date is used within a sentence, a comma is needed *after* the year as well.

BEFORE AND AFTER

The meeting was held on April 5, 1990, in Canton, Ohio.

When a specific day of the month isn't used, commas are optional. Use both or none.

Word to the Wise

Do not use a comma—
- after a date without the year:

  The March 6 meeting was a long one.

- between the state and the ZIP code:

  Seattle Central Community College is at 1701 Broadway, Seattle, Washington 98122.

OPTIONAL

The meeting was held in April 1988 in New Orleans.

The next meeting will be in May, 1995, at the branch office.

Enclose a date that explains a preceding day. Be sure to use commas both before and after the date.

BEFORE AND AFTER

On Wednesday, January 3, we shall begin the training sessions.

Abbreviations with Names

Use commas before and after college degrees that follow a name.

BEFORE AND AFTER

Pam Nguen, M.D., and Fran Smith, Ed.D., have been elected to the Board of Directors of City of Hope Hospital.

Commas sometimes set off *Jr., Sr., II, III, Inc.,* or *Ltd.* If a comma is used before these titles, another comma follows the title, unless it ends the sentence.

OPTIONAL

Charles Davis, Jr., and his son Charles Davis, III, have worked for Metromedia, Inc., for the past five years.

If the Davises and the company choose not to use commas . . .

Charles Davis Jr. and Charles Davis III formerly worked for Avco Inc.

Replay Unit

54

Insert commas where needed. Write *C* next to the five sentences that don't need a comma. If you are tempted to use a comma but can't think of the reason for it, **don't!**

EXAMPLE

Rexburg, Idaho, is the home of Ricks College.

1. We received your order on March 9 1992 and acknowledged it the same day.
2. Mara Simmons started to work for us in April 1989 and has been with us ever since.
3. Steven Smith Ph.D. is in charge of the Industrial Arts Department in the Saratoga School District.
4. Billy Crystal started his career as a comedian in a Long Beach New York nightclub.
5. The deposition was taken on Friday January 4 1989 with all witnesses present.

6. We hope to attend the Mardi Gras in New Orleans next year.

7. Little Rock Arkansas was the scene of tragedy and strife in the 1960s.

8. Goldfinger's Variety Stores, Inc. closed the White Plains New York store in 1973.

9. Windsor Woolens Ltd. carries mostly imports from Edinburgh Scotland and from London.

10. Susan Smith will begin interviewing on February 5 for the job of executive director.

11. F. W. Woolworth suggested to his boss the owner of a hardware store that he open another store to sell only nickel and dime items.

12. Woolworth's boss was not enthusiastic because he thought there weren't enough items to sell for a nickel or a dime.

13. The young Woolworth was disappointed but eventually went ahead on his own and made a fortune out of the idea.

14. Analysts said many traders were concerned that the stock market which hit record highs recently was due for a more pronounced pullback than has already occurred.

15. Intel which used to be owned by IBM is a major manufacturer of semiconductors microprocessors and microcomputers.

Check your answers in Appendix H.

Read Unit

55 NOTES ON QUOTES

Note 1

Use a comma to separate a direct quotation from the rest of the sentence. If the quotation has 3 or more lines, however, use a colon instead of a comma.

Some people place an apostrophe directly over an *s* because they don't know whether it goes before or after. Another kind of fence sitter places quotation marks directly over a comma. The correct placement is very easy to learn by reading Note 2.

Note 2

Always place a comma or period *before* the quotation mark, never after—no exceptions!

QUOTE AT END OF SENTENCE

Years later his former boss complained, "Every word I used in turning Woolworth down has cost me a million dollars."

QUOTE AT BEGINNING OF SENTENCE

"Money is the root of all evil," he replied.

QUOTE AT MIDDLE OF SENTENCE

George whispered, "I love you," and then fainted.

QUOTE THAT IS INTERRUPTED

"Money," Jesse explained, "is the root of all evil." [*Is* begins with a small letter as it is not the beginning of the sentence.]

Note 3

Don't add a comma when a quotation ends with a question mark or an exclamation mark.

"Will you arrive early?" asked Miss Alvarez.
"I don't believe it!" exclaimed Mr. Ripley.

Note 4

No comma is used before a quotation that is not a complete sentence but is woven in with the remainder of the sentence.

We all sang "Happy Birthday" when Twileen entered the room.
Jonathan answered the big question with a simple "no."

Replay Unit

55

The best way to remember the four Notes of Unit 55 is to compose sentences to apply them.

1. Compose sentences that include the following:

    (a) a quote at the end of the sentence _____

    _____

    (b) a quote at the beginning of the sentence _____

    _____

    (c) a quote at the middle of the sentence _____

    _____

    (d) a quote that is interrupted _____

    _____

2. Now write a sentence beginning with a quotation that is a question or an exclamation. _____

    _____

3. Should commas be added to the sentences that follow?

Yes _____ No _____ Maybe _____

(a) My teacher has told me over and over again to "keep my eyes off the keyboard."

(b) Scarlett O'Hara wanted to do everything "tomorrow" in *Gone With the Wind.*

Please check your answers in Appendix H.

Read Unit 56

KISS ME ONCE AGAIN, BUT NOT NOW

"Kiss me once, kiss me twice, and kiss me once again" is a line from a romantic ballad of the 1940s. Many activities do improve with repetition. Sometimes repetition of a word results in an improved sentence because of added emphasis.

Use a comma between two identical words that appear together.

SAME WORD TWICE

Many, many years ago romantic ballads were much more popular than they are today.

He who cries, cries alone.

Use a comma before a sharply contrasting or opposite expression. These expressions are generally introduced by not, never, seldom, or but.

OPPOSITES

Be sure to send for his brother, not his sister.

He has often considered leaving his job, never his wife.

Kiss me once again, but not now.

Memo from the Wordsmith

This punctuation blooper was part of a newspaper advertisement:

House for rent. View takes in five counties, two bedrooms.

It was Ms. Hernandez, not Mr. Cheng, who spoke at the meeting. [When the "opposite" expression is in the middle of the sentence, you could call it a parenthetical. It doesn't matter what you call it as long as you use two commas.]

Replay Unit 56

Insert commas where necessary. If you cannot apply one of the rules presented in Units 49–56, don't use a comma.

EXAMPLE

She worked up the courage and finally asked‸"Will you marry me?"

1. He arrived at 10 p.m. not a.m.
2. Yes he was a quiet efficient worker.
3. I want to urge you however not to worry.
4. On February 7 1964 the Beatles landed in New York for the first time.
5. For the next six years they reigned as kings of rock'n'roll.
6. "I know" he said "that you will be there on time."
7. I am very very happy that you received the promotion.
8. He works out at the gym every morning never in the afternoon.
9. If you decide to run run fast.
10. Although the quality is excellent the price is too high.

Answers are in Appendix H.

Read Unit 57

A COMMA MEDLEY

A medley usually refers to a musical arrangement that includes several different melodies. In other words, it's a mixture. This unit is a medley of comma rules.

A comma replaces omitted verbs or other important words that are easily understood from the way the rest of the sentence is worded. This type of construction usually occurs in a clause following a semicolon.*

VERB REPLACED WITH COMMA

A used machine costs $1,245; a new one, $2,300. [The comma replaces the verb *costs*.]

---

* Remember that a semicolon is used between independent clauses not joined by *and, but, or, nor,* or *for*—Unit 12.

Twileen is in Cleveland; George, in Alaska.

Twileen qualified for promotion to upper management; George, for transfer to Alaska.

A comma separates thousands, millions, billions when the number refers to a quantity.

Starting from the right, count by threes and then insert the comma.

COMMAS AND NUMBERS

$2,000   167,823 widgets   1,321,000 shmitchiks

However, commas are not used in numbers that "identify," such as addresses, serial numbers, page numbers, and so on.

page 1247   19721 Victory Boulevard   No. 23890

Commas separate the parts of an address that appear in sentence form.

COMMAS IN ADDRESSES

They had lived at 1114 Fteley Avenue, Bronx, New York, for many years.

Please return the gold charm bracelets to Robert Stern, Inc., 7 Tappan Terrace, Ardsley, New York 10502, before next week. [Never place a comma before the ZIP.]

Replay Unit
57

All the commas in these sentences are correct. On the blank line below each sentence, briefly state the rule (in my words or yours) covering each sentence's comma(s).

EXAMPLE

Jesse will see her this week or, if she prefers, next week.

Use commas before and after a parenthetical expression.

1. If you need more information, please let us know.

   _____

2. Please send the equipment to our distributor: Easy Street, 328 North Palm Drive, Palm Springs, California 90036.

   _____

3. Our home office is at 6413 Third Avenue, but we have offices all over the world.

   _____

4. Please ship 167,823 shmitchiks and weblows to us at once.

_____

_____

5. Carol, Eric, and Harley ran up the stairs, along the hall, and into the office.

_____

_____

6. In September we hired a new secretary; the following month, a typist; and in November, a bookkeeper.

_____

_____

7. Geographic information for the three years ending October 31, 1989, is on page 1465.

_____

_____

8. After eating, my brother washed the dishes.

_____

9. The novelist Ernest Hemingway once lived here.

_____

_____

10. No, you have the wrong number.

_____

_____

Answers to this Replay are in Appendix H.
A **POP QUIZ** on Units 53–67 is in Appendix A.

Checkpoint

Commas are written signals that, when correctly used, are almost as effective as a speaker's pauses and voice inflections. Misplaced commas or omitted commas can make a sentence difficult or impossible to understand or can completely change the meaning.

Memo from the Wordsmith

Look up the meanings of _misogynist_ and _philogynist_ to find out why they each punctuate the following sentence differently:

MYSOGYNIST   Women are pretty generally speaking.

PHILOGYNIST   Women are pretty, generally speaking.

In addition to enabling us to write clearly, the correct use or omission of commas is an important segment of Standard written English—because it happens in every sentence you write.

Place a check in the blank next to each comma rule you clearly understand. Review the ones you're not sure of.

_____ Use commas between the items in series as well as before the conjunction that precedes the last item.   **(Unit 49)**

_____ Use a comma between two adjectives when *and* is omitted but understood.   **(Unit 50)**

_____ Use a comma before *and, but, nor, or, for,* and sometimes *yet* when one of those conjunctions joins independent clauses (complete thoughts).   **(Unit 51)**

_____ Use a comma after an introductory expression: **(Unit 52)**

_____ (a) with a verb form in it

_____ (b) with five words or more

_____ (c) when necessary for clearness

_____ (d) consisting of *yes, no, well,* or *oh*

_____ (e) when addressing a person by name

Use commas around nonessential, or parenthetical, words.   **(Unit 53)**

_____ Use commas before **and after** a state name directly following the name of a city.   **(Unit 54)**

_____ Use commas before **and after** the year when it follows a specific date.   **(Unit 54)**

_____ Use commas before and after dates that explain preceding days.   **(Unit 54)**

_____ Use a comma after an abbreviation following a name IF a comma is used before the abbreviation.   **(Unit 54)**

_____ Use commas to separate a direct quotation from the rest of the sentence unless the quotation ends with an exclamation mark or a question mark.   **(Unit 55)**

_____ Use a comma before a word that is a repeat of the previous word when a pause or emphasis is desirable.   **(Unit 56)**

_____ Use a comma before a sharply contrasting or opposing expression. These often begin with a word such as *but, seldom, never,* or *not.*   **(Unit 56)**

_____ Use a comma to replace omitted words. This comma usually occurs in a clause following a semicolon.   **(Unit 57)**

_____ Use commas to separate thousands, millions, billions when the number refers to a quantity.   **(Unit 57)**

_____ Use commas between parts of addresses that appear within sentences.   **(Unit 57)**

Grammar explanations for some of the comma rules appear in Section 9 of the Grammar Supplement in Appendix G.

Special Assignment

Insert commas in the sentences below. Always think of the rule before inserting the comma. Four sentences don't require commas. Complete this assignment by _____. (date)

1. Mr. Munoz thought the problem over carefully and will give you the answer tomorrow.   **(Unit 51)**

2. I talked with Ann Rosenberg today and you should receive a call from her by Thursday. **(Unit 51)**

3. We received your letter yesterday Mr. Chin and will ship your order by the end of the week. **(Unit 53)**

4. Shortly before eight thirty men appeared. **(Unit 52)**

5. After we had eaten Max took a walk through Atlanta. **(Unit 52)**

6. If the only tool you have is a hammer you tend to see every problem as a nail. **(Unit 52)**

7. "A man's best friend is his ape" said Tarzan. **(Unit 55)**

8. The teacher said "The most important asset is the will to study." **(Unit 55)**

9. "The law" said the speaker "is broken every minute of the day." **(Unit 55)**

10. If you will take the matter up with our coach Mr. James Heffron you will be given full information. **(Unit 52)**

11. There is a good opportunity of course to market our stationery envelopes and business forms to your most exacting trade. **(Units 49 and 53)**

12. Mr. Kuwahara if you decide to take out any life insurance in the future the premium will be more than you are now paying. **(Unit 52)**

13. We believe that the owner The Robinson Realty Company will accept $750. **(Unit 53)**

14. Each alteration omission or addition costs us a great deal of money. **(Unit 49)**

15. We shall temporarily suspend service on your telephone 345-6789 from December 1 1993 until further notice. **(Units 53 and 54)**

16. Henry F. Albert Jr.* of Cincinnati Ohio is the author of the new book. **(Unit 54)**

17. The publisher's price on this new book *America's Supreme Opportunity* is $18.95. **(Unit 53)**

18. The word "accommodate" has two *c*'s and two *m*'s. **(Unit 53)**

19. White and fancy colored leather shoes are selling fast but how are your customers keeping their delicate footwear clean? **(Units 50 and 51)**

20. The assessment for March 2 1992 amounted to $26; for May 2 $32; and for June 4 $35. **(Unit 54)**

21. Automobiles that do not have brakes are hard to stop and should not be driven in Chaosville after midnight December 31 1994. **(Units 53 and 54)**

22. Yes I expect to meet Inez Valdez who is the president of Premier Electronics Inc.* at two o'clock on March 6. **(Units 52, 53, and 54)**

23. We are very very sorry that you suffered from such a long hot summer in Panama. **(Units 50 and 56)**

24. We expect to receive this order by the first of October not December. **(Unit 56)**

25. David Bowie the manager believes that no one is exempt from this ruling. **(Unit 53)**

26. Because you visited the office and talked with Mr. Chang we will expect a brief report not a book. **(Units 52 and 56)**

27. Upon hearing the evidence Mr. Wong felt she was guilty. **(Unit 52)**

28. Phyllis Ross formerly of 2245 Prospect Avenue Bronx New York 10923 is now offering interior design service from the Miami Beach address shown below. **(Units 53 and 57)**

29. In two or three more weeks The Grateful Dead and Pink Floyd will be here. **(Unit 52)**

30. In some ways you cannot understand her viewpoint. **(Unit 52)**

31. Mr. Kelly if you have already received the goods no reply to this letter is necessary. **(Unit 52)**

32. This practice I believe is bringing about results that could not be obtained in any other way. **(Unit 53)**

33. Samantha falls in love with every Tom Dick and Harry. **(Unit 49)**

* Henry (item 16) and Premier (item 22) use the commas.

34. In Seattle the large amount of rain results in lush foliage.   **(Unit 52)**
35. Many years ago my family and I began to meditate twice daily.   **(Unit 52)**

Proofreading for Careers

As you proofread this letter to an Eagle Scout, correct commas, apostrophes, spelling, sentence construction, grammar, and capitalization:

Dear Fellow Eagel:

Thank your for extending you membership in the National Eagle Scout association.

There have never been a time in the history of our Country when Scouting* was needed more. Scouting needs it's Eagle Scouts, regardless of age to maintain high standards and to strengthen the program.

As a dedecated Eagle Scout I urge you to carryon with the mission of NESA and to strengthen Scouting on an local level. Scouting has enriched our lifes in so many ways, it is our challenge to reach, and touch the lives of other with a quality Scouting program. Noone has a deeper understanding of the aims and purposes of the Boy Scouts of America than do Eagle Scouts.

Expect nothing from the NESA accept pride in membership the opportunity to serve Scouting and an association with Americas finest citisens. The National Eagle Scout association is designed to give back to Scouting not to continue to receive from it.

Sincere best wishes,

Frederick St. Amour, Director

After verifying your corrections, choose an adjective to evaluate your proofreading and English skills. _____

* It is acceptable for an organization to capitalize its "product." Capitalization adds importance and emphasis to a word.

Practice Quiz

If the commas are correctly placed, write *C* in the blank; otherwise, write *N* and make the corrections.

_____ 1. The English language is full of traps and pitfalls and it can be harder to write a clear sentence, than to keep a clear conscience.—Jack Smith, Columnist for *Los Angeles Times*

_____ 2. Did he finish the accounting report on Tuesday or, did he attend the controllers' meetings?

_____ 3. First you should type all of today's letters, and then you should file the copies of yesterday's letters.

_____ 4. If you are going to leave footprints in the sands of time, you had better wear workshoes.

_____ 5. Homemakers who watch TV all day probably serve many TV dinners to their families.

_____ 6. Although, he rarely achieves his goals, Mr. O'Connor tries very hard.

_____ 7. If a dependent clause precedes an independent clause put a comma after the dependent clause.

_____ 8. Yes, Jack Smith and I love the English language more than flowers and wine.

_____ 9. A factory closing usually means the community loses jobs, tax revenues, and retail sales.

_____ 10. The manager, Amy Lieb, believes that no one is exempt from this ruling.

_____ 11. We have mailed you a copy of the first volume, and hope it will reach you this week.

_____ 12. The copies dated June 12, 1989 are being sent to you today, not tomorrow.

_____ 13. The basic factors for business success are materials, money and management.

_____ 14. "In Dayton, Ohio, we have two factories," said Henry Kissinger, Jr. to his father.

_____ 15. The convention will begin on March 28, but you don't have to be there, until the next day.

_____ 16. The pleasant cheerful young woman knows how to type, file and take dictation.

_____ 17. Please visit us in August if you can't make it in July.

_____ 18. Because of a serious misunderstanding we lost the customer, and discharged one of our best salespeople.

_____ 19. We need 5000 cheese pizzas for the employees, although I personally prefer pepperoni.

_____ 20. Please ship the pizzas by refrigerated air freight to our plants in Akron and in Oakland.

_____ 21. Ron, have you met my cousin Chuck?

_____ 22. Avoid commas, that are not necessary.

_____ 23. All the students in the class who had not handed in their term papers failed.

_____ 24. "Very well," Steve said "I'll obtain the papers by Friday."

_____ 25. In August Ellen plans to reduce the prices on oak furniture.

NOTES

Punctuation Potpourri

10

After Completing Section Ten, You Will

✔ Use 11 punctuation marks with precision: semicolon, colon, period, exclamation, question, hyphen, dash, comma, quotation, apostrophe, parentheses.

*R*otten pot is the literal translation of the French word *potpourri*. In American usage, the word refers to a combination or mixture. The combination or mixture referred to here is made up of useful dots, lines, and curves. Look up *potpourri* in your dictionary to see whether you are pronouncing it correctly, and while you're there, notice its definitions.

Leaving the French now, we move to a 15th-century Italian named Aldus Manutius, the man chiefly responsible for systematizing punctuation. The principles he developed enabled both writers and readers to interpret a sentence in the same way. Although his system has been modernized through the years and adapted to various languages, its purpose remains the same: to enable a reader to better understand a writer.

One of the best-known examples of double meaning caused by the absence of punctuation is the written reply of the prophets to the Roman soldiers. The soldiers had asked whether they would return from the war. Since death was often the punishment for an inaccurate prediction, the soothsayers understandably took great care with their words: *ibis et redieris non morieris in bello* ("you will go and return not die in war").

As a punctuation system had not yet been devised, the reader could interpret it both ways—with a pause either before or after "not." That way the soothsayers could keep their heads no matter how the war turned out.

If you want to "keep ahead" in business, modern punctuation expertise helps you communicate effectively and confidently. Today's punctuation system includes marks *required* in certain places, as well as some punctuation dependent on the writer's judgment. To apply judgment, first determine the exact shade of meaning to communicate. When you understand punctuation rules and have business writing experience, you develop a "sense" of how to apply a variation of a particular rule. In the meantime, punctuation rules enable you to punctuate with precision and without risk of criticism. In a few cases, you're offered a choice where you must use your judgment. The rules are, however, sufficiently specific to provide you with confidence in the correctness of your writing.

Punctuation affects meaning, clearness, ease of reading, reader's emotions and mood, and how important or unimportant an idea seems to the reader.

Writing for Your Career

Punctuation expertise adds professional polish to your business writing.

Read Unit

IN CONCLUSION . ! ?

Let's begin with the end—the end of sentences. The three marks that end sentences are the period, the exclamation mark, and the question mark.

Use a Period*

. Use a period after a statement that is a sentence or an expression that stands for a sentence.

We sent you the bill last week.
Yes, of course.

. Use a period after a sentence that is a command or a courteous request.

Pay your bill this week. [command]
Please pay your bill this week. [courteous request]

. Use a period after a sentence that is a courteous request, even though it is worded like a question. If action is desired rather than a reply, use a period.

For example, after asking a customer to pay a bill, the seller wants the money, not a "yes" or "no" answer.

Will you please pay your bill now.
Would you please pay your bill now.

. Use a period after a sentence that is an indirect question.

I asked whether he would pay his bill.
I wonder whether you will pay your bill.

. Use just one period after an abbreviation that ends a sentence.

Please send the purple widgets c.o.d.

Use a Question Mark

? Use a question mark after a direct question that is a sentence or an expression that stands for a sentence. A direct question requires a reply.

* See "Read and Replay Reference Manual" regarding periods in abbreviations and in money.

Memo from the Wordsmith

Which one gets the job?

He'll wear nothing that might discourage them from hiring him.
He'll wear nothing. That might discourage them from hiring him.

Will you pay the bill this week or next?
Do you intend to pay this bill?
If so, when?
Why?

? Use a question mark after a sentence that might be considered presumptuous if punctuated as a courteous request.

Would you please handle my mail while I'm away? [as part of a memo to your supervisor]

BUT

Would you please handle my mail while I'm away. [courteous request, as part of a memo to your subordinate]

? Use a question mark in parentheses in very informal business (or personal) writing to express humor or uncertainty. In most business writing obtain precise information or rephrase the sentence.

Although our new accountant (?) can't count, he is the boss's nephew. [personal message]
The Michigan representative called on us five (?) times last year. [okay in informal business communication, such as a memo]

? Use a question mark after questions in a series.

Have you visited London? Paris? Rome?

Use an Exclamation Mark

! Use an exclamation mark to express strong feeling at the end of a sentence or an expression that stands for a sentence.

Send your check today!
He paid!
I can't believe it!
What great pizza!
Wait!

Writing for Your Career

- The exclamation mark is often used in advertising copy and sales letters. Don't use it often in other types of business writing. Overuse of the exclamation mark causes it to lose its effectiveness—just as the parent who yells at the children all the time finds that the children are no longer affected by the yelling.
- Avoid using an exclamation mark to knock the reader over the head with how wonderful, cute, or funny something is.

The exclamation mark following what looks like a statement, command, or courteous request enables the reader to sense some strong emotion or urgency. If the expression is spoken instead of written, voice and facial expression transmit the strong feeling to the listener. Read these correctly punctuated sentences aloud:

Will you please order the pizza.

Will you please order the pizza!

Replay Unit

58

Add periods, question marks, and exclamation marks. Change commas to periods where necessary, and capitalize when necessary. (Beware of run-ons and comma splices, which are described in Units 11 and 12.)

1. I wonder whether he will attend the conference
2. The pizza is good, but where's the pepperoni
3. Would you please ship our order by air express
4. Will you be at the convention
5. Management makes important policies and decisions, I just carry them out
6. He asked me whether I would be at the convention
7. Would Thursday or Friday be more convenient for you
8. Buy UNEEDA now
9. Will you please file these letters
10. Wonderful
11. May I hear from you by return mail
12. Will you come
13. He asked if you would come
14. Your house is on fire
15. A winner says he fell, a loser says somebody pushed him

Check answers in Appendix H.

Memo from the Wordsmith

Which sentence has the exclamation mark in the proper place?

Woman! Without her, man would be uncivilized.
Woman without her man would be uncivilized!

Read Unit

59   *THE HALFWAY MARK*   ;

The semicolon (;) might be called a halfway mark: It's the punctuation midway in "pausing value" between the comma and the period, explaining perhaps why it is made up of one of each.

> ;   Use a semicolon to join two closely related complete thoughts not joined by *and, but, or, nor,* or *for. Yet* may be preceded by either a semicolon or a comma.

There is no way to peace; peace is the way.

Transition words—such as *however, nevertheless, then,* and *therefore*—often join the two closely connected ideas. Use a semicolon before these transitional expressions when they join **independent clauses.** Since transition words are usually parenthetical, or nonessential, use a comma after them. However, when the transition is a short word—*then, thus, hence, still, yet, also*—omit the comma.

First she typed the letters; then she made the phone calls.

He was upset by the criticism; therefore, he refused to discuss the matter.

We're unable to offer him full-time employment; however, we can hire him on a part-time basis.

Each of the preceding examples would be correct with a period (and capital letter) instead of the semicolon. When you wish to *separate* the two thoughts, use a period. If you're not sure whether to join with a semicolon or separate with a period, use your judgment. Either way will be correct, but one way will read more smoothly than the other.

; Use a semicolon between independent clauses that are joined by one of these conjunctions—*and, but, or, nor,* or *for*—if the sentence already has two or more commas.

Sally Strelke, who is an expert in this field, will show the African slides; but we expect the others to participate also.

As a matter of fact, his work has been good; and considering his extensive training, we think he will progress rapidly.

We would like to buy that valuable property; but the owner, Cathy Allen, will not sell it.

Recap   Join the independent clauses with a semicolon. Be sure the clauses are independent before inserting the semicolon.

1. Employment is at an all-time high however, you'll find a job quickly.
2. The unemployment rate is high nevertheless, your skills will enable you to be placed quickly.
3. Here's a surefire way to double your money fold it in half and put it in your pocket.
4. Because the recession has bottomed out, jobs will now be more plentiful.

Place a semicolon before a coordinating conjunction that joins independent clauses when two or more commas are already in the sentence. Be sure the clauses are independent before inserting the semicolon.

1. My employer, Mr. Anton, was upset by the harsh criticism and he refused to discuss the issue with my accountant.
2. Mr. Perez, we're unable to offer you full-time employment here but we do have an opening in Springfield, Massachusetts.
3. The recession, which began last year, has bottomed out and jobs in your field will now be more plentiful.
4. England's famous naval hero, Lord Nelson, suffered from seasickness throughout his entire life but did not let it interfere with his career.

Check your answers in Appendix H.

; Use a semicolon after an independent clause that precedes *for example* or *namely* or *that is* when the expression is before a list or an explanation that ends the sentence. (Independence is not required for the list or explanation.)

Dr. Baity needs additional equipment to complete the project; for example, several drawing boards and at least two compasses would help.

Jennifer Crystal Imports, Inc., is conveniently located; that is, just two blocks south of the Long Beach exit of the Long Island Expressway.

; Sometimes a series already has commas *within* the items of the series. In such cases, use semicolons *between* the items.

AMTRAK stops at Schenectady, New York; Newark, New Jersey; and West Palm Beach, Florida.

The new officers of the corporation are Ms. May Stern, President; Ms. Mildred Sweet, Vice President; and Mr. Myron Siegel, Secretary-Treasurer.

Replay Unit

59

A. Insert semicolons were needed. If the sentence does not require a semicolon, write *C* in the answer blank.

1. Ms. Dorsey believes desktop publishing is the answer to rising costs of corporate publications. _____

2. Although Ruth wants to stay, she must return to her work on the newsletter. _____

3. Our records indicate, Mr. Alvarez, that we filled six orders for you last year and every one of them was delivered within three days. _____

4. Our records indicate, Mr. Mendoza, that we filled six orders for you last year. Every one of them was delivered within three days. _____

5. Use the semicolon properly, always place it where it's appropriate and never where it isn't. _____

6. He has one overpowering ambition, namely, to fly a jet plane. _____

7. Kim has many assets that most people are not aware of, for example, he has a law degree. _____

8. Carolinda graduated from Shimer College, which is in Illinois, therefore, she would be ideal for the job. _____

9. The president of a big corporation generally earns a higher salary than the President of the United States. _____

10. A large business is highly complex and difficult to understand, it is divided into many departments in which people perform specialized functions. _____

11. As long as the government has the power to tax and private citizens still have considerable wealth, the government will not go bankrupt. _____

12. His typing and shorthand speeds are low, however, he was hired as a secretary because of his excellent English and mathematics skills. _____

13. This year Standard Packaging might declare a dividend,   _____
    that is, a portion of the company's earnings paid to
    stockholders.

14. From a study of old newspapers, I find that business   _____
    conferences were held in this building on March 19,
    1902, April 11, 1913, and September 2, 1945.

15. Typewriters were first patented in 1714, but they didn't   _____
    become practical to use until the 1860s.

16. I am a great believer in luck, and I find that the harder I   _____
    work, the more I have of it.

17. Although I am a great believer in luck, I find that the   _____
    harder I work, the more I have of it.

18. I believe, however, that you are right.   _____

19. It isn't hard work that kills, it's worry.   _____

20. The materials arrived late, therefore, the secretary didn't   _____
    type the report today.

Please check the answers in Appendix H.

B. If you don't believe this event took place, insert one semicolon and
one comma.

Charles the First walked and talked half an hour after his head was cut off.

Read Unit 60

AN EASY MARK :

The rules for the colon (:) are easy to learn.

> : Use a colon after a sentence when a second sentence, a
> phrase, or even a single word explains or supplements the first
> sentence.

Just one word describes him: cruel.

In an 1899 issue of the *Literary Digest*, a prediction was made
about the horseless carriage: It was that automobiles would never
come into as common use as bicycles.

Heed this warning: Punctuation marks cannot save a poorly constructed sentence.

When a complete sentence follows a colon, capitalize the first letter.

> : Use a colon when a complete sentence introduces a quotation
> and after any words that introduce a quote of more than two
> lines.

He added this statement to the contract: "The housesitter must provide food and affection to my 18 cats."

Elwood Chapman said: "Although most organizations require many raw materials, machines, equipment, buildings, and much money, a business is made up primarily of people."

:   Use a colon after a complete sentence (or independent thought) when a listing follows.

The secretary needs these supplies: carbon paper, envelopes, and letterheads.

His goals are clear: health, wealth, and love.

BUT REMEMBER

Use that colon only if the introduction to the list is a complete sentence. That's why the following sentences do not have colons:

His goals are health, wealth, and love. [Look again at the similar example above, where the word *clear* makes all the difference!]

The personality traits he was most interested in were initiative, loyalty, honesty, and dependability.

BUT

If the items are listed on separate lines, do use the colon even though the introduction isn't a complete sentence.

The personality traits he was most interested in were:

>   Initiative
>   Loyalty
>   Honesty
>   Dependability

BUT

Do not use a colon before the list if another sentence follows the introductory sentence:

Please send the following people to the office. I need to speak with them immediately.

>   Shuzu Itakara
>   Elsie Linares
>   Kim Yong

:   Use a colon after the salutation of a business letter when *mixed,* or *standard,* punctuation is used. **Standard punctuation** calls for a colon after the salutation *and* a comma after the complimentary close.

Ladies and Gentlemen:
Sincerely yours,

Open punctuation calls for *no* punctuation after salutation and complimentary close.

Ladies and Gentlemen
Sincerely yours

: Use a colon between hour and minutes and in proportions.

The pizza was delivered at 12:30 p.m.
The ratio is 3:1. [in technical documents]

: Use a colon between a title and a subtitle of a book.

English for Careers: Business, Professional, and Technical is popular in Guam.

After typing a colon, space twice—except in ratios (see preceding example) and between hours and minutes. (When you are typing ratios or hours and minutes, do not space on either side of the colon.) In printed material, such as books and newspapers, however, spacing after a colon differs from the two-space rule.

Replay Unit

60

A. Insert colons where needed. Write *C* in the blank if the sentence is correctly punctuated.

_____ 1. Please ship the following two dozen Style No. 308 and three dozen Style No. 402.

_____ 2. He has just one goal in life revenge.

_____ 3. Please send these items to Detroit, Chicago, Seattle, and San Diego.

_____ 4. In three words I can sum up everything I've learned about life It goes on.   ROBERT FROST

_____ 5. We plan to visit these cities Portland, Miami, Seattle, and San Diego.

_____ 6. These are two important things you can do to prevent shoplifting Place mirrors in strategic locations and post special warning signs.

_____ 7. Our school is in a lovely community in the San Fernando Valley Mission Hills.

_____ 8. Here is something worth thinking about A small idea that produces something is worth more than a big idea that produces nothing.

_____ 9. Judges have a double duty They are supposed to protect the innocent and punish the guilty.

_____ 10. Sherrill Frank wrote, "Appearance counts greatly when a person is to be chosen from among a number of people."

B. Insert appropriate punctuation in the next 5 sentences. You will need 2 colons, 1 semicolon, 1 period, 1 question mark, and 1 exclamation mark.

1. Amy made an important decision yesterday She decided to hire a new secretary

2. Peter, her present secretary, doesn't type well but he has a great deal of charm, which is why everyone likes him.

3. The new secretary will need these qualifications 100-words-a-minute dictation speed, 60-words-a-minute typing speed, excellent spelling, and a comprehensive knowledge of punctuation.

4. Do you think we can find someone with those qualifications

5. What a difficult job for the Personnel Office

Please check your answers in Appendix H.

Read Unit

61 GOOD MARKSMANSHIP — ( )

The business writer with good marksmanship hits exactly the right spot with even the less frequently used marks—the dash and the parentheses.

Insecure writers tend to use the dash (in handwritten work) like a security blanket. When not sure of whether to use period, comma, semicolon, or colon, they use a dash and hope the reader will assume the writer was in a hurry. Although parentheses errors are rare, some suggestions for appropriate use are included here as a guide.

— Use dashes to emphasize a parenthetical expression that would ordinarily be enclosed with commas.

( ) To de-emphasize such an expression, use parentheses.

The president of this company, a man who once earned $50 a week as a janitor, is one of the richest men in the world. [ordinary parenthetical expression]

The president of this company—a man who once earned $50 a week as a janitor—is one of the richest men in the world. [emphasis of parenthetical expression]

The president of this company (a man who once earned $50 a week as a janitor) is one of the richest men in the world. [de-emphasis of parenthetical expression]

In the sentence above, a good writer would choose the dashes to emphasize an interesting point. However, the commas and parentheses also result in correctly punctuated sentences.

In the next example, to emphasize that the supervisor is a holography expert, choose parentheses to enclose the de-emphasized information:

Our supervisor (he's a new employee) is a holography expert. [de-emphasis of parenthetical expression]

To emphasize that the supervisor is new on the job, choose dashes to set this information off:

Our supervisor—he's a new employee—is a holography expert. [emphasis of parenthetical expression]

Do not choose commas for the parenthetical information because it is an independent clause:

NO   Our supervisor, he's a new employee, is a holography expert. [awkward because the parenthetical expression is an independent clause]

— Use dashes to separate a parenthetical (or nonessential) expression that contains one or more commas.

( ) To de-emphasize the word group, use parentheses. Do not use commas.

The officers of this corporation—the president, the vice president, the treasurer, and the secretary—are in complete agreement about the new budget. [Parentheses would also be all right, but not commas. Notice how this sentence could be misinterpreted if a comma were used after *corporation*.]

My plan saved the company thousands—no, it was nearer tens of thousands—of dollars last year. [Use dashes around a parenthetical expression that has a comma.]

— Use a dash after a series or a single word that comes *before* a complete thought. The dash is required for this kind of construction.

Writing for Your Career

Construct a typewriter or computer dash by keyboarding two hyphens. In handwriting, make a dash twice as long as a hyphen. The printed dash is a solid long line.

TYPED   A diamond is the hardest stone--to get.

HANDWRITTEN   *A diamond is the hardest stone-- to get.*

PRINTED   A diamond is the hardest stone—to get.

Dependability, loyalty, and efficiency—those are the qualities we look for in an employee.

BUT

These are the qualities we look for in an employee: dependability, loyalty, and efficiency.

OR

The qualities we look for in an employee are dependability, loyalty, and efficiency.

Reaganomics—did it work?

BUT

Did Reaganomics work?

( )   Use parentheses to enclose directions.

The profits (see chart, page 7) were the highest in the history of the company.

Replay Unit

61

Insert dashes, parentheses, or colons. If there's more than one correct way to punctuate, use your judgment to make a choice as long as you use only dashes, parentheses, or colons. Write *C* beside the correctly punctuated sentence.

1. Harbor Office Supply Company I'll check the address has ordered ten Ace Calculators.
2. *Roget's Thesaurus* a treasury of synonyms, antonyms, parallel words, and related words was first published in 1852 by Peter Mark Roget. Look up the pronunciation of Roget.
3. These fine machines they are the best money can buy are offered to you for only $99 each.
4. Money, beauty, intelligence, and charm she has all of them.
5. She has money, beauty, intelligence, and charm.
6. She has all these attributes money, beauty, intelligence, and charm.
7. We must see him at once not tomorrow.
8. The job requires the following skills shorthand, filing, typing, and bookkeeping.
9. His check for $152 not $156 was returned by the bank.
10. Roosevelt Island was supposed to be New York City's ideal place to live a crime-free, auto-free, dog-free new island right in the East River.

11. The owner plans to put all the profits for the year $100,000 back into the business.

12. Knowledge of DBase and Lotus 1, 2, 3 those are the requirements for the job.

13. The majority of new jobs created in America are in small companies where fewer than one hundred persons are employed.

14. We are not interested not now at least in your proposition.

15. The three departments of our government the executive, the legislative, and the judicial derive their authority from the Constitution.

Answers are in Appendix H.
The **POP QUIZ** for Units 58–61 is in Appendix A.

Read Unit

PLAGIARISM'S ENEMY " "

If you're not sure of what *plagiarism* means, look it up now to see why **quotation marks** are its enemy.

> When repeating someone else's exact words, you are using a *direct quotation*. To avoid being accused of plagiarism, use quotation marks before and after a direct quotation.

Direct Quotations and Paraphrases

DIRECT QUOTATION

He added, "I don't believe we can proceed in an organized manner."

PARAPHRASE (OR INDIRECT QUOTATION)

He added that he didn't believe we could proceed in an organized manner.

No quotation marks are used because this is not a direct quotation; this is a **paraphrase**—a rewording that gives the meaning but not the exact words of the person being quoted.

> When paraphrasing or quoting someone indirectly, you put the statement in your own words and do not enclose it in quotation marks, but you must name the author and the work, in your sentence or a documentation note, to avoid plagiarism.

DIRECT QUOTATION

"A business," Elwood Chapman writes, "is an organization that brings capital and labor together in the hope of making a profit for its owner or owners."

PARAPHRASE (OR INDIRECT QUOTATION)

Elwood Chapman writes in *Getting into Business* that the principal aim of a business is to make a profit for its owners.

Writing for Your Career

Better writers often avoid starting the sentence with the introduction to the quotation. Instead start with the words being quoted; and then find a suitable place, as shown in the Elwood Chapman quotation, to insert the source of the statement.

No quotation marks are used because Elwood Chapman's words are paraphrased. Chapman's idea is conveyed, but not in the words he used.

Other Uses for Quotation Marks (and Underlines)

" "   Use quotation marks to show a reader that slang or an informal expression was used for special effect where it might otherwise seem out of place.

Frankly, I'm too "chicken" to invest in a venture that seems so risky.

" "   Use quotation marks to show that a word or expression is being used to draw attention to that word rather than as part of the vocabulary of the sentence.

Many people find it difficult to distinguish between "effect" and "affect."

The underline or italics may be used for this purpose instead of quotation marks: effect and affect or *effect* and *affect*.

" "   Use quotation marks to enclose titles of subdivisions of published works—such as titles of articles appearing in magazines or titles of chapters. Also use quotation marks for names of films, plays, shows, poems, songs, lectures, and so on.

"Dances with Wolves" won several Academy Awards in 1991.

Refer to "Notes on Quotes," page 246, to review the use of the comma with quotation marks and capitalization with quotation marks.

Italicize, underline, or type in all capital letters* the titles of full-length published materials (books, magazines, newspapers).

* If keyboarding, underline or italicize titles of full-length published materials (rather than use all capital letters) in scholarly, or academic, writing.

In print, italics replace all caps or underlining.

> GETTING INTO BUSINESS by Elwood Chapman is used as a text in college-level introductory business courses. [All caps—easier when typing.]

> *Getting into Business* by Elwood Chapman is used as a text in college-level introductory business courses. [Underline—easier when handwriting.]

More Notes for Quotes

These "notes" review some of Unit 55 as well as introduce additional aids for quotation marks.

." ," When a period or a comma is needed with the closing quotation mark, *always* (no exceptions) place the quotation mark *after* the period or the comma.

"Some publishers are born great, some have greatness thrust upon them, and others merely survive television," said John H. Johnson of *Ebony* magazine.

In 1972 Mr. Johnson received the Magazine Publishers Association award for "Publisher of the Year."

"; ": When a colon or a semicolon is needed with the closing quotation mark, place the quotation mark *before* the colon or the semicolon.

The following scientists were quoted in the article entitled "Rediscovering the Mind": Elizabeth Doble, Claire Thompson, Carl Sagan, and Georgi Lozanov.

When we expressed concern, the bookkeeper explained, "The check was accidentally postdated"; however, we have still not received a correctly dated check from him.

Sometimes a question mark or exclamation mark is needed with a closing quotation mark.

Decide whether the quotation itself is the question or exclamation; if so, type the question or exclamation mark before the closing quotation mark.

He said, "Do you love me?" [The quotation is the question; therefore the question mark comes first.]

If the question mark or exclamation mark is for the rest of the sentence, type the quotation marks first.

Did you know that he said, "I love you"? [Quotation is not a question; the rest of the sentence is the question.]

When both the quotation and the rest of the sentence are questions or exclamations, use the appropriate mark first; then type the quotation mark.

Did he ask, "Do you love me?" [Both parts of the sentence are questions.]

Replay Unit

62

A potpourri of punctuation marks is required in these sentences—on your mark, get set, go!

1. He shouted Your house is on fire

2. Your house is on fire he shouted

3. She whispered Are you sure you love me

4. Are you sure you love me she whispered

5. Do you know whether he said I love you

6. Since many people are price-conscious, we must look at more cost-efficient methods said Dave Young the spokesperson for Chevron

7. Do you know what the phrase negotiable instrument means

8. The following information is quoted from the letter The train departs Chicago at two p m and arrives in Springfield at 5 p m

9. Was it Mr. Higgins who said Results are what count

10. Its important that Craig doesn't think you are too pushy

11. Barbara Bankston said she would send the graphs from Oakland to your office by fax.

12. I believe that Elaine and Michelle will be considered for the management positions Rosemary will receive the diplomatic post

13. Alexander Smith who lives in Toronto will write the screenplay for us

14. Please tell the chef how many tacos you need for the company party

15. This shipment of stationery the manager clearly stated will arrive in time for the January sale

16. I have this to say regarding his "abject poverty" It is fictitious

17. Are you all right asked Ann

18. Yes groaned Len as he lifted the box of posters that had fallen

19. Bach Suite No. 2 in B Minor is first on the program at the Laredo Junior College Music Festival.

20. Ms. Sumner whispered Did you know that the item marked 'fragile' was broken on arrival in Sacramento. (Review page 222 for single quote use.)

Please check your answers in Appendix H.

Read Unit

63

HALF A DASH   -

Half a dash equals one hyphen (-). The hyphen and the dash are two separate and distinct marks of punctuation. Unit 61 includes information on the dash. This unit is about the hyphen.

In Unit 22, you reviewed compound nouns and observed that hyphens are used in some of them. Here are suggestions to help you recognize other compound words and determine whether to use a hyphen.

Words Spelled with a Hyphen

-   Compound numbers from twenty-one to ninety-nine are spelled with a hyphen.

BUT

The numbers *one hundred, five million,* and the like are not hyphenated.

-   When *self* is used before a *word*, include a hyphen.

self-control   **self**-respect   **self**-propelled

The only exception is *selfsame.* (Of course, *selfish* is not hyphenated because *ish* is not a word.)

-   When *non, over, under, semi,* or *sub* is a prefix, write the whole word without a space or hyphen:

nonfat   overpayment   underexposed
semisweet   subhuman

If the prefix *re* results in a word that might confuse the reader, use a hyphen. (Most *re* words do not need the hyphen.) When the prefix *re* precedes an *e,* the hyphen is optional.

HYPHEN BECAUSE OF POSSIBLE MISUNDERSTANDING

re-cover [to cover again]

BUT

recover [get better from illness or get something back that had been lost]
re-collect [to collect again]

BUT

recollect [to remember]

OPTIONAL HYPHEN BECAUSE *E* FOLLOWS *RE*

re-enter *or* reenter *and* re-examine *or* reexamine [As you can see, they're easier to read with the hyphen.]

NO HYPHEN

recheck   rediscover   reheat   restate

When in doubt about other words, consult your dictionary. The tendency over the years has been to drop hyphens from words. Many words that used to be hyphenated are now written solid. The only complete guide is an up-to-date dictionary.

Words spelled with hyphens have hyphens shown in the entry word. When a dot or an accent mark appears between the syllables, write the word "solid," as one word.

Recap   Consult your dictionary to see how the following entry words appear. Write the dictionary form in the blank.

1. b r o t h e r i n l a w _____
2. v i c e p r e s i d e n t _____
3. i n a s m u c h a s _____
4. d o u b l e b o i l e r _____
5. u p t o d a t e _____
6. o f f t h e r e c o r d _____

Check your answers in Appendix H.

The five principles listed and illustrated above refer to words **spelled** with hyphens.

Compound Adjectives

Hyphens are also used in a way that cannot be verified in the dictionary; that is, to join the elements of a **compound adjective**. Since the dictionary is of no help in such cases, it is important to understand the principles that follow.

An adjective describes or explains a noun or a pronoun. Sometimes the description is two or three closely related words. A hyphen or two makes such an expression easier to read. Because this kind of adjective consists of more than one word, it is called a **compound adjective**.

a **blue-white** diamond

one-story house

first-class report

Notice that if any part of the compound adjective is omitted, either the meaning changes or what remains doesn't make sense.

- Use a hyphen (or hyphens) in a compound adjective that comes *before* the noun being described—or if the expression is spelled with a hyphen in the dictionary.

Buy your **back-to-school** clothes now. [Use hyphens because the compound adjective appears *before* the noun *clothes.*]

BUT

Buy your clothes now for going **back to school.** [no hyphens]

They wanted to develop **easy-to-use** software for the project. [Use hyphens because the compound adjective appears *before* the noun *software*.]

BUT

They wanted to develop software that would be **easy to use** for the project. [no hyphens]

Often, when the compound adjective is moved away from the noun it describes, the part of speech changes; it is no longer an adjective. Being aware of this grammar change is unimportant. Just remember to hyphenate when the describing expression comes *before* the noun or if the expression is spelled with a hyphen in the dictionary.

If the first word of the compound expression ends with *ly, er,* or *est,* the hyphen is usually not required. If, however, the *ly* word is an adjective, do use the hyphen.

The **fashionably dressed** executive carried a leather bag. [*fashionably* = adverb]

My employer is a **friendly-looking** man. [*friendly* = adjective]

We found out that she is the **highest paid** executive in Detroit.

Word Division

The third major use of the hyphen is to divide words at the end of a line. The most important rule is this:

Divide between syllables.

When a word is divided elsewhere (*fl-ower*), the effect of the entire piece of work can be destroyed as the reader wonders, "*Where* did that writer go to school?" or "*Did* that writer go to school?"

Word to the Wise

Avoid distracting the reader by word division that might amuse or momentarily confuse:

UNWISE DIVISIONS

Please send me your cat-
alog.

Just over the horizon-
tal line, you'll find a number.

He had a blind date with a dog-
matic woman.

Other specific rules are required for written work to look professional. These rules are in "Read About Word Division" in the Reference Section at the end of the book. If you keep that page and a dictionary close by (and refer to them) when writing, you'll get to know the word division rules well.

Replay Unit

63

A. Complete the Word Division Read and Replay in Appendix F.

B. Use compound adjectives to write more concisely. The following sentences are written correctly. However, they could be more concise. Rewrite these sentences so that they include compound adjectives requiring hyphens. Do not change the meaning.

EXAMPLE

Lionel Barrymore was an actor who was well known.
Lionel Barrymore was a well-known actor.

1. I work in a building that has ten stories.

_____

2. I need a ladder that is 10 feet.

_____

3. My father is a man who works hard.

_____

4. The comment she made was off-the-record.

_____

5. The case against the company that is based in Dallas was handled in Seattle.

_____

C. Some of these sentences contain words spelled with a hyphen or with space between the parts. When in doubt, use the dictionary. Write the correctly spelled word in the blank, or write *C* in the blank if no correction is needed.

1. The artist feels that recreation of the entire scene is possible.

_____

2. What is your favorite form of recreation? _____

3. Our overall objectives are similar, but our methods differ. _____

4. You should report underpayments as well as over-payments. _____

_____

   5. My fatherinlaw acts like a commanderinchief. _____

   6. Uncle Jack made an off the record comment about being a
      selfmade millionaire. _____

   7. Do you think our country will ever produce enough oil to be
      selfsufficient? _____

   8. Her goal is to have one hundred pairs of shoes by the time she is
      twenty one. _____

   9. Dr. Kaufman was a Johnny come lately whose effect on the market
      is overstated. _____

  10. A person who acts as though intellect and reason are not very im-
      portant to solving world problems is often called an antiintellectual.

      _____

D. Refer to the word division rules when necessary. Use a diagonal (/)
to show the correct place to divide these words at the end of a line. **It is
essential to use your dictionary as well as the rules.** If a word should
not be divided at all, place the diagonal at the end of the word.

function	believe	horizontal	wouldn't
thousands	punctuation	aligned	impossible
interrupt	syllables	stopped	guesswork

Answers are in Appendix H.

Read Unit

64

WILD APOSTROPHES

Our punctuation potpourri could not be complete without a reminder
about avoiding "wild" apostrophes and using apostrophes exactly where
they belong. This unit is an opportunity to review possessive nouns, as
studied in Section Eight. (The other uses of the apostrophe are not repeated
here.)

   A possessive noun shows ownership, authorship, place of origin, type
of use to which something is put, and time relationship. A possessive noun
always ends with an apostrophe and an s. These principles determine
whether the apostrophe is placed before or after the s.

> To make a singular noun possessive, add 's.

The boss's office   Frank's notebook
Ms. Jones's secretary   a week's vacation

> When the singular proper noun has two or more syllables and
> ends in an s or a z sound, you may omit the added s, to avoid a
> hard-to-pronounce word.

Socrates' disciples
Ms. Perkins' report

To make a plural noun possessive, first look at the last letter of the plural noun.

If the last letter is *s*, add only an apostrophe.

REGULAR PLURALS

The Adams**es'** factory   three week**s'** work
ladie**s'** clothes   all the attorney**s'** offices

If the last letter is not *s*, add *'s*.

IRREGULAR PLURALS

the alum**i's** contributions
me**n's** hats
the childre**n's** rooms

Use an apostrophe only if the possessive relationship of two nouns is evident.

The Joneses own factories all over the world. [*Jonses* is the plural subject of the sentence. *Own* is the verb. No possessive relationship between two nouns is shown.]

BUT

The Joneses' factories are all over the world. [*Joneses'* tells *whose* factories and is therefore possessive. *Factories* is the plural subject of the sentence.]

Replay Unit 64

A. Insert apostrophes where they are needed.

1. This agents approach to sales is to get a clerks opinion of the presently used office machines.

2. These comments are taken from Patricia Hills pamphlets. [her name is Hill]

3. Our womens and girls jackets are on sale for prices that will fit your pocketbook.

4. Heres an extract from Beths lecture: "It takes more than moneys worth to satisfy buyers—a fact that must be implanted in every salespersons mind."

5. Ms. Perkins memos refer to the conferences for planning next years meeting.

B. As you read the daily newspaper, a magazine, or a book, be on the lookout for apostrophes. Cut out or copy (include source) any five sentences that contain apostrophes. Below each, indicate whether the apos-

trophe is correct. State (in your own words or mine) the rule applied or
that should have been applied.

Sentence 1: _____

_____

Is apostrophe used correctly? _____ Rule _____
                                  yes/no

_____

_____

Sentence 2: _____

_____

Is apostrophe used correctly? _____ Rule _____
                                  yes/no

_____

_____

Sentence 3: _____

_____

Is apostrophe used correctly? _____ Rule _____
                                  yes/no

_____

_____

Sentence 4: _____

_____

Is apostrophe used correctly? _____ Rule _____
                                  yes/no

_____

_____

Sentence 5: _____

_____

Is apostrophe used correctly? _____ Rule _____
                                  yes/no

_____

_____

Answers for Part A are in Appendix H.
Now take the **POP QUIZ** in Appendix A.

Checkpoint

Whenpeoplestartedwritingtheyputonewordafteranother. Later writers separated words with spaces.
Eventually they began to mark their writing with dots, dashes, and curves. Today we know punctuation is the most important single device that leads to easy reading. Punctuation enables a
writer to imitate spoken language on paper.

All punctuation marks except for the comma are included in this section. Check off the ones you are confident about using, and review the appropriate units for those that seem a bit difficult.

_____   Use a period, question mark, or exclamation mark at the ends of sentences.   **(Unit 58)**

_____   Use a period after a courteous request, even though it might be worded like a   **(Unit 58)**
question.

_____   Four reasons are given for correct use of the semicolon. Do you know what   **(Unit 59)**
they are?

_____   Use a colon after an _independent_ clause when: **(Unit 60)**
(a) words that explain the clause follow it.
(b) a list follows it.
(c) a quotation follows it.

_____   Use a colon after the salutation of a mixed- (or standard-) punctuation letter,   **(Unit 60)**
between the hour and the minutes, and between the numbers of a ratio.

_____   Use dashes to set off: **(Unit 61)**
(a) a parenthetical expression to be emphasized or that already has commas
in it.
(b) a series that already has commas within the items.
(c) a series preceding a complete thought.

_____   Use parentheses to enclose: **(Unit 61)**
(a) directions
(b) a supplementary expression
(c) an expression to be de-emphasized.

_____   Use quotation marks around direct quotations and around subdivisions of   **(Unit 62)**
published works. Underline, use all capital letters, or italicize to designate
titles of full-length materials.

_____   Use quotation marks around certain slang expressions and around an   **(Unit 62)**
expression used to draw attention to itself.

_____   Three rules determine whether the quotation mark is before or after another   **(Unit 62)**
mark of punctuation. Do you know them?

_____   The hyphen is used: **(Unit 63)**
(a) as part of the spelling of a word (in which case, it is shown in the entry
word in the dictionary).

Sign in Boarding House

Punctuate so that tenants won't bathe the landlady.

Please Clean Tub After Bathing Landlady

(b) in a compound adjective preceding the noun being described.

(c) for word division at the end of a line.

_____   The apostrophe shows ownership, authorship, kind, and time relationships.   **(Unit 64)** What rules determine whether to place the apostrophe before or after an *s?*

_____   Unit 48 shows the apostrophe in other than possessive nouns. Take a moment to review these now.

Additional punctuation principles are explained in Appendix G, the Grammar Supplement, in the back of the book.

Special Assignment

Select ten punctuation principles from Sections Nine and Ten. Write each principle as briefly as you can. Then compose a sentence that applies the rule. By applying more than one principle within the same sentence, you may write fewer sentences. Read the examples below before you begin. Submit this assignment, preferably typed, to your instructor on _____. (date)

PRINCIPLE   Use commas to separate the items of a series.

SENTENCE   Alan, Lois, Mimi, and Jack met at 1025 Fifth Avenue.

PRINCIPLE   A semicolon may join two independent clauses.

SENTENCE   An executive needs to make decisions quickly; in fact, decisions are often necessary before all the facts are available.

COMBINATION METHOD

PRINCIPLE 1   Use commas to separate the items of a series.

PRINCIPLE 2   A semicolon may join two independent clauses.

SENTENCE   A decision had to be made at once; therefore, Ms. Cates, Ms. Chandler, Ms. Denova, and Mr. Heffron were notified.

Proofreading for Careers

For skillful proofreading, use a closed pen to "underline" each line as you read it. Another proofreading trick is to use a "window": Cut a slit in an index card; make the slit big enough to see four or five words at a time.

Read for content as well as for correctness so that you can spot any kind of error. Use your dictionary and the Reference Manual in the back of this book. When you think you've found all errors, read the document from the bottom up. Often additional "typos" and spelling errors can be spotted this way.

Proofread and correct this article. Look for errors in the application of principles studied in this course so far.

AMERICA'S DEPARTMENT STORES

Door-to door peddling is'nt one of the high status jobs but many famous people got there start there, according to Robert Hendrickson, author of, The Grand Emporiums, a book published by Stein & Day.

Cyrus McCormick, first sold his reapers on the road. Benedict Arnold peddled stockings in the Hudson river Valley before he became this countrys best known traiter. Even the early Rockefellers were roadies of a sort. John D.s father billed hisself as "Dr. William A. Rockefeller the celebrated cancer specialist. Among the very best of the 19th century peddlers was Gimbel, Saks and Field, who eventually opened 3 of the 1st department stores.

Mr. Hendrickson tells us that store-keepers have helped shape our language as well as our economy. Calling dollars bucks is traced to early trading in deerskins. "Getting down to brass tacks comes from country merchants who hammered brass headed tacks into their sales counter's to measure lengths of cloth.

Mr. Woolworth often made unannounced visits to his own stores posing as a customer. He also frequently sent telegrams to each of his stores. One of them read, Good morning. Did you say Good morning to each customer this morning? Frank W. Woolworth.

John Wanamaker opened his first store in Philadelphia in 1861. He set up a huge gong at the front door to welcome each customer but it scarred people out of their minds and he had it removed. Mr. Wanamaker and most other store keepers learned that retailing is a visual eye catching kind of business.

The Neiman-Marcus catalog has included such items as: a 30 thousand dollar solid gold omelet pan, a 3 hundred dollar mink sling for the lady who breaks her arm, and a mouse ranch.

The Grand Emporiums is a lively book and certainly worth reading, however, the author does include some errogenous information: The books states that Arthur Wood a retired chairman of Sears, is the son of Gen. Wood who ran Sears from '28 through '54.

While its true that they had the same name and job, they were not in the same family.

The book has 78 pp of photographs and unusually interesting information about department stores, the people who run them and there customers.

After checking your corrected article with a key or with your instructor, answer these questions: What kinds of errors, if any, did you make in completing this proofreading practice (e.g., punctuation, numbers, overlooked typos, abbreviations, overlooked wrong words)?

How do you evaluate your career English and proofreading skills?

Excellent _____ Good _____ Fair _____ Needs Improvement _____ Other? _____

Practice Quiz

Take the Practice Quiz as though it were a real test. Don't look back through the book while you take it. This quiz includes application of principles from Sections Two, Four, Eight, Nine, and Ten. If the sentence is correctly punctuated, write *C* to the left; otherwise, make the necessary changes.

_____ **1.** Obviously upset by the criticism he refused to make the necessary changes.

_____ **2.** Have you read the article entitled "Increase Your Vocabulary"?

_____ **3.** In the Hartford office, for example, this plan saved the company; thousands of dollars every year for the past five years.

_____ **4.** His itinerary provides for stopovers in Springfield, Massachusetts, Chicago, Illinois, and Houston, Texas.

_____ **5.** The personality traits that we were most interested in were; initiative, loyalty, and dependability.

_____ **6.** Elizabeth, who is a good listener, never once interrupted while I read what must have seemed to be a never ending story.

_____ **7.** When Good Queen Bess, who could swear like a sailor enjoyed one of her rages, the whole Court trembled.

_____ **8.** This little booklet contains forty six important facts, and much useful information.

_____ **9.** The supervisor said, "Fire him"!

_____ **10.** He told us that he had allowed his usual discount; namely, 8 percent off for a cash payment within ten days.

_____ **11.** "The sale of mens' and boys' coats will be held next week, said the manager."

_____ **12.** Mr. Robertson's automobile was stolen, then his wife ran away with his best friend.

_____ **13.** Both events occurred on May 11, 1988 and he wondered whether this might have been his unlucky day?

_____ **14.** Ms. Mitzner called Dr. Stitt in and questioned her about the transaction?

_____ **15.** Lily and Roger the two managers of Housewares have requested these items, one additional cash register, a supply kit for the packing table, and two shipping carts.

_____ **16.** "The man who lies down on the job," so the lecturer said, "deserves to get run over."

_____ **17.** Our enclosed brochure is self explanatory, and may be of interest to you and your employee's.

_____ **18.** We have sent you a copy of Fundamentals of Business, you may return this textbook at your convenience.

_____ **19.** The roads were slippery; therefore, we proceeded with caution.

_____ **20.** I warn you I know Im right that the new treasurer is dishonest.

_____ **21.** John Wanamaker believed that the American system of storekeeping was the most powerful factor yet discovered to compel minimum prices.

_____ **22.** The prices of our greeting cards and desk sets see page 46 of the catalog are subject to a discount.

_____ **23.** We hope to hear from you by the first of January; but if we don't, we shall immediately place the account with our attorney's.

_____ **24.** Many of today's corporations started in the 1800s.

_____ **25.** The competition among business organizations at that time was so fierce that only the strong and aggressive survived.

NOTES

A Business Dictionary

Assets

Amalgamation

Ergonomics

Equity

Capitalism

Overhead

Bull Market

Disbursements

After Completing Section Eleven, You Will

Verbatim

Quorum

Liquidate

✔ Know the meanings of the words listed in "A Business Dictionary."

*E*veryone who plans a career in business should be familiar with the terms of the trade. In fact, everyone who does not plan a career in business should be familiar with the terms included in this section. These words contribute to understanding and dealing with life in the closing years of this century.

If you're experienced in business or are taking other business classes, these words are already in your vocabulary. If, however, most of the words are new to you, now is the time to become sufficiently familiar with the expressions so that you will understand them in print or in conversation.

These words, of course, do not represent a complete business dictionary. Make it a point to increase your business vocabulary through reading the business section of a newspaper and of a weekly news magazine. A good vocabulary pays off not only in job success but also in handling personal finances.

Whether or not you work in business, you are involved in business all your life. A good understanding of business terminology helps you to make intelligent decisions about your bank accounts, purchase of a home, all kinds of insurance, services of an attorney, credit buying, voting, and investments. It is difficult to obtain information and advice about the foregoing subjects without an appropriate vocabulary.

If a number of words in this section are unfamiliar to you, prepare 3-by-5 cards for ease in studying. Write the word on one side of a card and the definition on the other. Carry the cards with you, shuffle them, and frequently test yourself: look at the definition side and try to name the term on the back before looking at it.

Your own experience or referring to the dictionary will make clear that the following pages contain, in many cases, only some of the definitions of the terms. For example, look up *audit* (word number 12 in Read Unit 65) in a college or an unabridged dictionary. You'll find other definitions besides the one given here. To successfully complete this section, you are responsible only for the definitions and explanations that appear within the next pages.

Read Unit

65

ADJUSTER *THROUGH* CAPITALISM

1. **adjuster**   a representative of an insurance company who investigates claims, losses, or damages and determines the amount to be paid to the insured person.

2. **affidavit**   a statement in writing sworn to before a notary public; a person authorized by law to administer oaths.

3. **agenda**   a summary of the business to be taken up at a meeting; a copy of an agenda is often given to each person attending a meeting.

4. **amalgamation**   a joining of two or more businesses into a single body; a **merger**.

5. **annual report**   a printed yearly message to stockholders providing information about the progress of a corporation; for example, earnings of the past year, prospects for the future, new products or methods.

6. **appraisal**   determination of property value by an expert.

7. **appreciate**   to increase in value.

8. **arbitration**   asking a third party to settle a dispute; for example, before a strike is called, officials of both the union and the company might agree to abide by a decision made through the process of arbitration.

9. **arrears**   an amount overdue and still unpaid is referred to as being "in arrears."

10. **assets**   all the property owned by a business or an individual.

11. **attachment**   seizure of property for failure to meet obligations; a court order authorizing such a seizure.

12. **audit**   an examination of the financial records of a business to determine correctness; such an examination is made by an **auditor**.

13. **balance sheet**   a statement of assets, liabilities, and net worth as of a certain date.

14. **bear market**   the stock market when prices are declining and many stockholders want to sell their stock because they think prices will continue to decrease.

15. **beneficiary**   a person designated to receive the benefits from an insurance policy, annuity, will, or trust fund.

16. **bid**   an offer to buy or sell services or goods at a certain price.

17. **bill of lading**   a form made out by a transportation company (issued to the shipper as a receipt) listing goods to be shipped.

18. **bit**   the smallest unit of information in a computer's memory.

19. **bull market**   the stock market when prices are increasing and many people want to buy stock because they think prices will continue to rise. "Bull" is the opposite of "bear." (*Memory Device:* Notice the second letter of *bull* and *buy* is *u* while the second letter of *bear* and *sell* is *e*.)

20. **byte**   a group of bits equal to a unit of information in a computer's memory.

21. **by-product**   an article manufactured from material that would otherwise be wasted when the original product is made.

22. **capitalism**   an economic system based on individual, rather than government, ownership of the means for producing and distributing goods and services.

Replay Unit

65

Insert the appropriate number in the blank.

1. adjuster	9. arrears	16. bid
2. affidavit	10. assets	17. bill of lading
3. agenda	11. attachment	18. bit
4. amalgamation	12. audit	19. bull market
5. annual report	13. balance sheet	20. byte
6. appraisal	14. bear market	21. by-product
7. appreciate	15. beneficiary	22. capitalism
8. arbitration		

a. _____ a form made out by a transportation company listing goods to be shipped

b. _____ a number of bits making up a unit of information in a computer's memory

c. _____ an article manufactured from material that would otherwise be wasted when the original product was made

d. _____ a pessimistic stock market

e. _____ representative of an insurance company who investigates claims, losses, or damages and determines the amount to be paid to the insured person or company

f. _____ seizure of property for failure to meet obligations or a court order authorizing such a seizure

g. _____ a determination of the value of property by an expert

h. _____ to increase in value

i. _____ a statement in writing sworn to before a person authorized by law to administer oaths

j. _____ an amount overdue and still unpaid

k. _____ summary of business to be taken up at a meeting

l. _____ the smallest unit of information in a computer's memory

m. _____ all the property owned by a business or an individual

n. _____ a person designated to receive the benefits from an insurance policy, annuity, will, or trust fund

o. _____ an examination of the records of a business to determine their correctness

p. _____ a statement of assets, liabilities, and net worth as of a certain date

q. _____ a joining of two or more businesses into a single body; a merger

r. _____ an offer to buy or sell services or goods at a certain price

s. _____ a printed message to stockholders providing information about the progress of a corporation

t. _____ asking a third party to settle a dispute

u. _____ an optimistic stock market

v. _____ economic system based on individual ownership of the
means for production and distribution

Answers—Appendix H

Read Unit
66

CASHIER'S CHECK *THROUGH* ERGONOMICS

23. **cashier's check** a check drawn on a bank by its cashier; the person
who "buys" this check gives the money plus a small fee to the cashier
or other bank employee.

24. **cash discount** a reduction in payment allowed a customer for
prompt payment of a bill.

25. **certified check** a check guaranteed by the bank to be worth the
amount for which it is written.

26. **clone** a computer made by another manufacturer to IBM's specifications, with the intention of offering additional features or lower prices.

27. **collateral** property offered as security for payment of a loan.

28. **corporation** an artificial "person," created by law, operating under a
charter granted by a state government and authorized to do business
under its own name.

29. **credit memorandum** an itemized statement of the allowance given
a buyer for goods returned to the seller.

30. **database** a computerized collection of information dealing with a
particular function of a business.

31. **defendant** the person against whom a legal action is brought.

32. **deficit** a shortage of money; the opposite of surplus.

33. **depreciation** decline in value of property because of wear and age;
the opposite of appreciation.

34. **desktop publishing** the use of personal computers and "desktop"
printers for typesetting, layout, artwork, and printing of documents
that previously required expensive typesetting equipment and personnel.

35. **direct mail** advertisements (such as sales letters, catalogs, or other
printed pieces) mailed directly to homes or businesses.

36. **disbursements** money paid out.

37. **dividend** a payment to a stockholder of a portion of a corporation's
profits.

38. **Dow Jones Average** the average, computed daily, of the closing
prices of 65 specific stocks on the New York Stock Exchange.

39. **down time** time during which machinery is out of operation for ad-
justment or repair.

40. **embezzlement**   fraudulent taking of property by someone to whom the property had been entrusted; for example, when a banker steals a depositor's money.

41. **employee profit-sharing**   setting aside a portion of a company's profits for distribution to the employees.

42. **endorsement**   a signature on the back of a check (or other negotiable paper) that enables the check to be cashed by someone else or deposited in the signer's own account.

43. **equity**   the amount a purchaser has actually paid toward the total price of the item being purchased.

44. **ergonomics**   the study of equipment, furniture, and physical environment to make the workplace safe, comfortable and healthful, and equipment easier to use.

Replay Unit

66

Insert the appropriate number in the blank.

23. cashier's check	34. desktop publishing
24. cash discount	35. direct mail
25. certified check	36. disbursements
26. clone	37. dividend
27. collateral	38. Dow Jones average
28. corporation	39. down time
29. credit memorandum	40. embezzlement
30. data base	41. employee profit-sharing
31. defendant	42. endorsement
32. deficit	43. equity
33. depreciation	44. ergonomics

a. _____ amount purchaser has actually paid toward total price of item being purchased

b. _____ check guaranteed by bank to be worth amount for which it is written

c. _____ reduction in payment allowed customer for prompt payment of bill

d. _____ shortage of money; opposite of surplus

e. _____ computer similar to an IBM but made by another manufacturer with the intention of competing for sales with IBM

f. _____ signature on back of check enabling check to be cashed

g. _____ setting aside a portion of company's profits for distribution to the employees

h. _____ publishing of documents with personal computers that previously required much more expensive typesetting equipment and personnel

i. _____ money paid out

j. _____ study of the workplace to enable workers to be more productive, safer, and more comfortable

k. _____ time during which machinery is out of operation

l. _____ a check drawn on a bank by its cashier

m. _____ property offered as security for repayment of loan

n. _____ the daily average of the closing prices of 65 specific stocks traded on the New York Stock Exchange

o. _____ a collection of information specific to a particular business or other organization

p. _____ person against whom legal action is brought

q. _____ statement sent a buyer for goods that have been returned

r. _____ artificial "person" authorized by state to do business

s. _____ advertisements mailed directly to homes or businesses

t. _____ fraudulent taking of property by someone to whom the property had been entrusted

u. _____ payment to stockholder of a portion of a company's profit

v. _____ decline in value of property

Answers—Appendix H
POP QUIZ—Appendix A

Read Unit 67

EXEMPTION *THROUGH* LITIGATION

45. **exemption**   a specified amount of money not subject to taxation, such as an exemption from taxable income for money used to support a dependent.

46. **fax**   technology for transmitting documents, photographs, drawings, signatures, etc. over telephone lines to a receiving machine (short for facsimile).

47. **fiscal year**   any period of 12 months between one annual balancing of accounts and another (an "annual report" is prepared at the end of a fiscal year).

48. **fluctuation**   a rise and fall, as of prices.

49. **foreclosure**   taking over property when a debtor does not keep up payments on a mortgage.

50. **good will *or* goodwill**   value of public relations of a business.

51. **gross**   (a) the total, such as gross income, gross profit, gross weight; (b) 12 dozen.

52. **hardware**   the equipment that constitutes a computer system (see **software**).

53. **input**   data fed into information processing systems.

54. **insolvent**   unable to pay one's debts.

55. **inventory**   a written list of merchandise in stock at a given time.

56. **itinerary**   a written plan of travel showing arrival and departure dates and times, as well as hotels where reservations have been made.

57. **jobber**   a wholesale dealer who buys from manufacturers or importers and sells relatively small quantities to retail merchants.

58. **journal**   a book in which financial transactions are recorded as part of a bookkeeping system.

59. **K**   the unit of measure for computer memory (for example, 32K, 64K); 1K = 1,024 bytes.

60. **lapsed policy**   insurance that has expired because payments have not been kept up-to-date.

61. **liabilities**   the obligations or debts of a business or a person.

62. **libel**   a statement, usually published, that is untrue and that injures another's reputation.

63. **lien**   a claim against property that prevents the owner from selling it until a debt (such as taxes) is paid.

64. **liquidate**   to close the affairs of a business and sell the assets; to turn assets into cash.

65. **list price**   price of an article as given in a price list or catalog; discounts are often subtracted from a list price.

66. **litigation**   the process of engaging in a lawsuit, or legal action.

Replay Unit

67

Insert the appropriate number in the blank.

45. exemption	51. gross	57. jobber	62. libel
46. fax	52. hardware	58. journal	63. lien
47. fiscal year	53. input	59. K	64. liquidate
48. fluctuation	54. insolvent	60. lapsed policy	65. list price
49. foreclosure	55. inventory	61. liabilities	66. litigation
50. good will	56. itinerary		

a. _____ book in which financial transactions are recorded

b. _____ process of engaging in a lawsuit

c. _____ rise and fall, as of prices

d. _____ wholesale dealer who buys from manufacturers or importers and sells small quantities to retail merchants

e. _____ taking over property when a debtor doesn't keep up payments

f. _____ published statement that is untrue and that injures another's reputation

g. _____ a sum of money not subject to taxation

h. _____ 12-month period between one annual balancing of accounts and another

i. _____ written plan of travel

j. _____ value of public relations a business has developed

k. _____ data fed into data processing or word processing systems

l. _____ price of article as given in catalog or price list

m. _____ claim against property that prevents its sale until a debt is paid

n. _____ 1,024 bytes

o. _____ to turn assets into cash

p. _____ technology for transmitting documents over telephone lines

q. _____ unable to pay debts

r. _____ equipment making up a computer system

s. _____ list of the merchandise in stock

t. _____ obligations or debts

u. _____ insurance that has expired because payments have not been kept up

v. _____ 12 dozen; total

Answers—Appendix H
POP QUIZ—Appendix A

Read Unit 68

LOSS LEADER *THROUGH* PROGRAMMER

67. **loss leader** a retailing strategy of advertising an item below cost to attract customers to the store. The advertiser expects customers to buy other items at full price.

68. **markup** the difference between the cost price and the selling price.

69. **microcomputer** a very small computer used in business and professional offices as well as in homes; now usually called a "PC."

70. **middleman** one who buys in bulk from producers and resells in smaller quantities; may be a wholesaler or a jobber (a jobber is a middleman willing to sell smaller quantities of an item than is a wholesaler).

71. **modem** a device to transmit computerized messages via telephone lines.

72. **monopoly** exclusive control of the supply of a commodity or service.

73. **mortgage** a pledge of property (real estate) as security for a loan.

74. **muitinational corporation** a company that has subsidiaries or other operating units in many nations.

75. **negotiable** transferable to a third person; for example, checks are negotiable if they are made out to "cash."

76. **net** the amount remaining after all deductions are made; for example, net profit is the balance after all expenses have been deducted from gross profit.

77. **notary public** a public officer empowered to administer oaths, witness signatures, and certify copies of legal papers.

78. **option** a promise to hold an offer open for a specific time. (If Mr. Alvarez agrees to sell a lot to no one but Ms. Wang within the next ten days, Ms. Wang has an option on that lot.)

79. **output** a computer term to describe information after it has been processed; for example, the answers to mathematical problems or business letters ready to be signed and mailed.

80. **overhead** the general costs of running a business, such as taxes, rent, heating, lighting, and depreciation of equipment.

81. **per annum** by the year.

82. **per capita** by the head, or by the person.

83. **per diem** by the day.

84. **petty cash** a small amount of money kept on the premises of a business to pay for minor purchases.

85. **plaintiff** a person who starts a legal action; one who sues.

86. **postdated check** a check dated later than the date on which it is written; such a check cannot be cashed or deposited until the date written on the check.

87. **power of attorney** the right granted by one person to another to represent him or her legally; also the legal document granting this right.

88. **programmer** a person who writes the statements necessary to produce the information to be obtained from a computer.

Replay Unit

68

Insert the appropriate number in the blank.

67. loss leader	78. option
68. markup	79. output
69. microcomputer	80. overhead
70. middleman	81. per annum
71. modem	82. per capita
72. monopoly	83. per diem
73. mortgage	84. petty cash
74. multinational corporation	85. plaintiff
75. negotiable	86. postdated check
76. net	87. power of attorney
77. notary public	88. programmer

a. _____ by the head, or by the person

b. _____ difference between cost price and selling price

c. _____ exclusive control of the supply of a commodity

d. _____ by the year

e. _____ promise to hold an offer open for a certain time

f. _____ advertising an item at a lower price than the seller paid for it so that customers will come in and buy other higher priced items

g. _____ check dated later than date on which it is written

h. _____ right granted to represent someone legally

i. _____ by the day

j. _____ general costs of running a business

k. _____ information that has been processed through a computer or word processing equipment

l. _____ one who buys in bulk from producers and resells in smaller quantities

m. _____ company that has operating units in many nations

n. _____ device to transmit computerized messages via telephone lines

o. _____ very small computer suitable for home as well as business use

p. _____ small sum of money kept to pay for minor purchases

q. _____ one who sues

r. _____ pledge of property as security for a loan

s. _____ public officer empowered to administer oaths, witness signatures, and certify legal papers

t. _____ amount remaining after all deductions are made

u. _____ transferable to a third person

v. _____ person who writes the statements necessary to produce the information to be obtained from a computer

Answers—Appendix H
POP QUIZ—Appendix A

Read Unit
69

PROXY *THROUGH* VOID

89. **proxy**   a written authorization by a stockholder for someone to vote in his or her place at a stockholders' meeting.

90. **quorum**   the number of members of an organization required to be present in order to constitute a formal meeting at which business may be transacted.

91. **ream** 500 sheets of paper.

92. **reconciliation** comparing and bringing into agreement a bank's records—as presented on a form called a "statement"—with the depositor's own record of transactions.

93. **remittance** money sent to pay a bill.

94. **reprographics** methods and equipment for making copies; also called copy processing, reproduction, or duplicating.

95. **requisition** within an organization, a written request made for supplies.

96. **retainer** a fee paid to a lawyer for services to be rendered in the future.

97. **rider** an addition attached to the end of a document.

98. **royalty** money paid to the holder of a patent or copyright for the right to use it.

99. **software** programs and instructions used to operate a computer (see **hardware**).

100. **solvent** having the funds necessary to pay all debts.

101. **speech recognition** ability of a computer to accept speech and transform it into characters on a screen; also known as voice recognition.

102. **tariff** a duty (tax) on imported items.

103. **telecommunications** high-speed communication via wires or phone lines enabling computers to "converse" at a distance.

104. **terminal** equipment compatible with the main computer. Data can be put into or requested from a computer by an operator who selects the appropriate keys on a terminal.

105. **turnaround time** time elapsed between the initiation of a task and the completion of that task.

106. **underwriter** a company or person in the insurance business.

107. **vendor** manufacturer, wholesaler, or importer from whom goods may be purchased.

108. **verbatim** word for word; for example, a *verbatim* report.

109. **via** by way of; often printed on invoices or orders next to a blank space for indicating the method of shipment.

110. **void** of no legal effect; not binding; for example, a check made out improperly is void. (*Void* may also be used as a verb: *to void a check*.)

Replay Unit

69

A. Insert the appropriate number in the blank.

89. proxy	97. rider	104. terminal
90. quorum	98. royalty	105. turnaround time
91. ream	99. software	106. underwriter
92. reconciliation	100. solvent	107. vendor
93. remittance	101. speech recognition	108. verbatim
94. reprographics	102. tariff	109. via
95. requisition	103. telecommunications	110. void
96. retainer		

a. _____ equipment compatible with the main computer

b. _____ ability of a computer to recognize speech

c. _____ 500 sheets of paper

d. _____ of no legal effect; not binding

e. _____ number of members required to be present in order to transact business

f. _____ authorization by a stockholder for someone else to vote in his or her place at a stockholders' meeting

g. _____ the bringing into agreement of a bank's statement with the depositor's records

h. _____ by way of

i. _____ written request within an organization for obtaining supplies

j. _____ time elapsed between starting and completing a task

k. _____ word for word

l. _____ money sent to pay a bill

m. _____ a seller or supplier of goods

n. _____ fee paid to a lawyer for services to be rendered

o. _____ programs and instructions used to operate a computer

p. _____ company or person in insurance business

q. _____ high-speed communication at a distance

r. _____ addition attached to end of a document

s. _____ able to pay all debts

t. _____ money paid to holder of patent or copyright for right to use it

u. _____ duty on imported goods

v. _____ methods and equipment for making copies

B. Learn the principles of abbreviating in business writing. Do "Read and Replay Abbreviations". You don't need to memorize the items on the abbreviations list; just be able to recognize them and have an idea of what they mean.

Answers—Appendix H
POP QUIZ—Appendix A

Checkpoint

The 110 words in the "Business Dictionary" are included at least once in the sentences that follow. By reading the sentences, you'll increase your familiarity with these terms as used in a business sense. Check back to the definition if in doubt about the meaning of any word in bold type.

If you use your dictionary as an aid to learning some of these words, be sure to locate the business definitions of the word. Many of the words have several definitions and in some cases even more than one business definition.

1. An **adjuster** was here yesterday to make an **appraisal** of the losses from the fire.

2. The **annual report** provides details about our planned **amalgamation** with Harley David, Inc.

3. We believe that this property will **appreciate** even before **escrow** is completed.

4. Lela Powers is the **notary public** who administered the oath for the **affidavit**.

5. A copy of the **balance sheet,** which had already been **audited,** was attached to the **agenda**.

6. Management suggested the **employee profit-sharing** plan before the dispute went into **arbitration**.

7. When I see an ad for a dozen eggs for 39 cents, I know this is a **loss leader**.

8. Since they are in **arrears**, their **assets** are being **attached** by the Court.

9. In fact, there is already a **lien** for unpaid taxes on their Beverly Hills mansion.

10. After the **audit**, the company purchased computer **hardware** and **software**.

11. The city requires that several **bids** be received before a **vendor** is selected.

12. A copy of the **bill of lading** is attached to the invoice.

13. One of the **by-products** of tuna processing and canning is used as fertilizer.

14. His sons were to have been the principal **beneficiaries** of his **lapsed** policy.

15. The economic system of the United States is called **capitalism**, while that of Sweden is socialism.

16. The key punch operators trained to become **programmers**.

17. A **cash discount** of 7 percent may be taken if your **certified check** accompanies your order.

18. The creditors are all requesting **certified checks** or **cashier's checks**.

19. By hitting a few keys at his **terminal**, he was able to obtain the information from the **database**.

20. We offered ten shares of AT&T stock as **collateral**.

21. A big corporation is the **defendant** in that trial, and a customer is the **plaintiff**.

22. After you return the merchandise, we'll send you a **credit memorandum**.

23. **Bit** is an acronym for BInary digiT. An acronym is a word formed from a letter or two of several words that make up a term.

24. Certain employees with long service to the company can retire at the end of the **fiscal year** with **profit-sharing** benefits of over $100,000.

25. Profits of a **corporation** are distributed to the owners of the company (stockholders) through **dividends**.

26. The **defendant** in the **embezzlement** trial had made inaccurate entries in the **journal** in an attempt to conceal the theft.

27. **Microcomputers**—IBM PCs as well as **clones** and other types—perform a variety of tasks, including **desktop publishing**.

28. **Depreciation** on the equipment and **disbursements** for **overhead** expenses totaled $500,000, resulting in a **deficit**.

29. The **Dow Jones Industrial Average** is more often referred to as simply the Dow Jones average. The average is based on 30 industrial stocks, 15 public utility stocks, and 20 transportation stocks; and it is computed at the close of every trading day.

30. **Direct-mail** advertising pays off in new accounts even though many recipients call our letters "junk mail."

31. Before purchasing a **modem**, we should find out what the **down time** is likely to be.

32. Your **endorsement** on the check from the insurance company constitutes acceptance of the settlement for the injuries received in the accident.

33. Although they have $5,000 **equity** in the property, **foreclosure** will be necessary if they don't continue to make the payments.

34. The **per diem** traveling expenses of the salespeople are deducted from the **gross** income of the company when preparing the tax return.

35. His **itinerary** includes several stops designed to enhance **goodwill**.

36. Mr. Chandra had an **option** to buy the Pioneer Chicken franchise in San Pedro.

37. All the employees worked overtime to complete the **inventory**, and the manager reimbursed them for their dinner expenses from the **petty cash** fund.

38. During a **bear market** many investors are eager to sell, thus forcing prices down.

39. **Fluctuation** in **per capita** expenses for patients is typical at this hospital.

40. The **jobber's markup** was so low that he couldn't meet his **overhead** expenses, and he was soon **insolvent**.

41. **K** is equal to 1,024 **bytes**.

42. Since **liabilities** have remained greater than **assets** for the past two years, we have no choice but to **liquidate**.

43. Although the **list price** is $25, your **net** price would be $18.

44. Hewlett-Packard has been involved in **litigation** several times this year.

45. A free market cannot exist when **monopolies** are permitted.

46. Farmers often complain that **middlemen** receive too big a share of the profits from farm work.

47. An insurance policy is not a **negotiable** instrument.

48. A **rider** on our homeowner's policy protects our jewelry from loss, theft, or damage.

49. A **proxy** form accompanied the **annual report**.

50. Please type a **requisition** for a **ream** of letterhead paper.

51. The **remittance** consisted of a **postdated check** and a **void check**.

52. The attorney insisted on a **retainer** before she would take the **libel** case.

53. Business could not be conducted at the meeting because a **quorum** was not present.

54. Evan Simon was able to sign the contract since he has a **power of attorney** for his sister Francine.

55. Mr. Omori clearly marked on the order, "Ship **via** Railway Express."

56. Since he quoted an entire chapter **verbatim** from *Toronto Giants*, he must pay a percentage of his **royalties** to Alex Smith.

57. After Lois completed the **reconciliation** of their bank statement, she realized that she and Alan are **solvent**.

58. A limitation of **speech recognition** technology is that it cannot yet deal with various types of accents.

59. In an information processing system, the **input** is "characters," and the **output** is the completed document.

60. **Reprographics**, also known as reproduction or duplication, and **fax** represent other forms of **word processing output**.

61. **Telecommunications** hookups make it possible to transmit documents at incredibly high speeds.

62. The information processing supervisor hopes to improve techniques for decreasing **turn-around** time; she thinks more **terminals** will be required.

63. Pepsico, Safeway, and Nissan Motors are examples of **multinational corporations**.

64. During a **bull market**, stock prices increase because investors are buying.

65. **Software** refers to a system or program to achieve efficient use of a computer, while **hardware** refers to the computer equipment itself.

Special Assignment

"Business Dictionary" Puzzles

A. Review "Read and Replay Abbreviations" in Appendix F.

B. Here's a crossword puzzle for you to do.

ACROSS

1. a claim against property that prevents the owner from selling it until a debt is paid

6. the year between one annual balancing of the accounts of an organization and the next

9. the economic system of the United States

11. a unit of information stored in a computer's memory

12. a highly trained accountant (abbreviated)

13. price of an article as shown in a catalog (2 words)

16. abbreviation for the relationship between a business and the public

17. abbreviation of Connecticut

19. relationship between an organization and its customers and community is known as _____ will

20. an investor who is buying because of the belief that prices will increase

22. 12 dozen

23. the amount remaining after all deductions are made

25. a small amount of money kept in office or shop to pay for minor expenses (2 words)
27. the _____ report is sent yearly to stockholders
30. fixed expenses of an organization, such as rent and utilities
33. by the day (2 words)
34. abbreviation of Michigan
36. an amount that is overdue
40. a president of a large corporation (abbreviated)
41. examination of the records of a business to determine their correctness
44. abbreviation of Colorado
45. abbreviation of pages
47. a supplier of merchandise; a seller
48. a duty (tax) on goods imported
49. an investor who sells stocks because of the belief that prices are going down
50. Japan's unit of money (see currency or money page in your dictionary)

DOWN
 1. written statement that injures another's reputation
 2. Bachelor of Arts degree
 3. advertisements sent by mail
 4. technology for transmitting graphics by phone
 5. something added to the end of a document
 7. data fed into information processing equipment
 8. to go out of business by turning what's left into cash
10. exclusive control of the supply of a product or service
14. able to pay one's bills
15. 500 sheets of paper
18. time when equipment is out of order
20. abbreviation for bill of lading
21. a policy that has expired because the premium was not paid
24. National Aeronautics and Space Administration acronym
26. outline of the business to be taken up at a meeting
28. To increase in value
29. by the person (2 words)
31. abbreviation for horsepower
32. by way of
35. abbreviation for foot or feet
37. money paid for use of a patent or copyright
38. amount purchaser has paid toward the total price
39. by the year is per _____
42. a middleman who sells to retailers
43. a promise to hold an offer open for a certain time
46. statement allowing someone to vote in another's place at a meeting
47. of no legal effect; not binding

C. The student I assigned to type this list of business terms failed the typing course. Will you please rewrite the dwors.

		Unit				Unit	
1.	bilel	67	_____	14. funluctotia	67	_____
2.	niel	67	_____	15. scimogreno	66	_____
3.	dib	65	_____	16. ramkup	68	_____
4.	setsdisburmen	66	_____	17. readhove	68	_____
5.	pitun	67	_____	18. flipfaint	68	_____
6.	ticifed	66	_____	19. ontiop	69	_____
7.	zztemnbeleme	66	_____	20. quaildite	67	_____
8.	yetqui	67	_____	21. ten	68	_____
9.	roujaln	67	_____	22. polyonom	68	_____
10.	pexetionm	67	_____	23. traineer	69	_____
11.	sorgs	67	_____	24. direr	69	_____
12.	ebty	65	_____	25. yxorp	68	_____
13.	ntrirayie	67	_____			

D. Because so many new business and business technology terms are being added to our language, books cannot keep up with them. The only way to keep up-to-date is to read about business and technology in newspapers and magazines (periodicals). Write five current business terms not listed in Section 11 and briefly define them. Look for these words in the *Wall Street Journal*, the business section of your local newspaper, or any business or computer periodical.

Word and Source   **Meaning**

1. _____   _____

   _____   _____

2. _____   _____

   _____   _____

3. _____   _____

   _____   _____

4. _____   _____

   _____   _____

5. _____   _____

   _____   _____

Proofreading for Careers

Proofread one word at a time—the opposite of speed reading. Proofreading is one of the most important skills of an office professional.

THE BUSINESS OF AMERICA

Business has a basic purpose in society, it must furnish the things people want and need, and it must do that at a cost people can afford to pay. If a company cannot meat this challenge, it declines and fails. If a nations businesses collectively cannot continue to provide goods and service's at ever increasing levels of efficiency, the nations standard fo living stagnates or declines.

In business, efficiency of production is known as productivity. The productivity of american business has been increasing steadally since even before the United States became a country.

Our History is starred with men like Eli Whitny, who invented the cotton gin, Samuel Colt, who developed the consept of standardized parts, Cyrus McCormick, whose reaper almost tripled the output of the wheat former, and Henry Ford, who's assembly lines cut the cost of an automobile in 1/2.

Because of them, and countless others like them 2/3 of our nations' economic growth has come from increases in productivity. As a result, American's now live better then any other people in the history of the world.

—GEORGE B. POTTER

After verifying your corrections with a key or with your instructor, select an adjective to evaluate your business English and proofreading skills today. _____

Practice Quiz

Take the Practice Quiz as though it were a real test. Don't look back through Section Eleven while you take this Practice Quiz. Mark these statements *T* (true) or *F* (false).

EXAMPLE

___F___ Tariff is the traveling expenses of salespeople.

_____ 1. An agenda is a summary of business to be taken up at a meeting.

_____ 2. A postdated check can be cashed at once.

_____ 3. A rider is a means of transmitting interoffice memorandums.

_____ 4. A bid is a promise to hold an offer open.

_____ 5. The fiscal year is the bookkeeping year.

_____ 6. A cash discount is an amount added to the original price.

_____ 7. In business, the term *appreciate* means to increase in value.

_____ 8. Stock prices are generally rising during a bull market.

_____ 9. A lien is property in need of repair.

_____ 10. The person buying goods is referred to as the vendor.

_____ 11. A monopoly often results in a higher price than would be possible in a competitive market.

_____ 12. Per diem is a written list of merchandise in stock at a given time.

_____ 13. To liquidate a business means to improve the efficiency of the office procedures.

_____ 14. A verbatim report is a summary of the full report.

_____ 15. A quorum is 500 sheets of paper.

_____ 16. A published statement that is untrue and that damages another's reputation is called slander.

_____ 17. A request for supplies is called a requisition.

_____ 18. Most people would rather be insolvent than solvent.

_____ 19. A lapsed policy is insurance that has expired because the payments have not been kept up-to-date.

_____ 20. An itinerary is a plan of travel.

_____ 21. The general cost of running a business is known as underhead.

_____ 22. A company that has operating units in many parts of the world is known as a multinational corporation.

_____ 23. An underwriter is a person trained as an expert in reprographics.

_____ 24. Software means the program and instructions used to operate the hardware.

_____ 25. Power of attorney is a set of weights used by attorneys to develop their biceps.

Sail
Sale

Suit
Suite

Wave
Waive

Bow
Bough

*T*he words we use tell a listener or reader much about us. They make us appear to be foggy or clear thinkers; they make us appear well informed or ignorant. They affect how a listener or reader reacts toward us or the organization we represent.

Word power enables us to communicate clearly and confidently. You have probably heard people say, "I know what I mean, but I just can't explain it." Those who want to express themselves clearly can develop this ability if it is important to them. The methods are no secret:

- Read books, magazines, and newspapers on a variety of subjects.
- Listen to articulate and well-informed speakers (radio, TV, lectures, etc.).
- Converse with well-informed people.
- Develop a larger and more precise vocabulary.

This section provides the information you need on how to choose, spell, or say the word that most accurately and precisely expresses your meaning.

Read Unit 70

CONFUSING PEARS

Confusing *pears* with *pairs* is what happens when a writer chooses the wrong spelling of soundalikes. In this unit and the next, you'll review some pairs of soundalikes; when you've finished, it will be easy to select the correct word.

accept	agree to receive.
except	excluding, as in *everyone except me.*
access	ability to enter, to communicate, or to make use of something.
excess	more than is needed or wanted.
ad	a noun, short for *ad*vertisement.
add	a verb that means "to join"; has two *d*'s, like *ad*dition.
affect	a verb that means "to change; to influence." [A decrease in salary may **affect** the quality of his work.]
effect	a verb that means "to bring about; to result in." [We can **effect** no changes without your consent.]
effect	a noun that means "result"; only the noun can have *the* or *an* before it. [We all know the serious **effect** of his actions.]

310

Memo from the Wordsmith

Here's how the bikini got its name: During World War II, the atomic bomb was tested on the tiny atoll of Bikini in the Marshall Islands. The shock effect of this explosion was recalled several years later when women started to stroll along the French Riviera wearing a shocking new swim-suit style.

alter	The groom said, "Don't try to alt**e**r [verb meaning change] me
altar	after we leave the alt**a**r [noun meaning place for sacred rites]."
bazaar	a sale or marketplace
bizarre	odd, grotesque, strange
capital	a noun that means "wealth; a city; an upper-case letter"; an adjective that means "involving execution," as in *capital punishment.*
capitol	The *building* where legislators (lawmakers) do their work. **This is the only meaning for the *-ol* word.**
cite	a verb that means "to summon to court; to honor; to quote."
sight	a noun or a verb that refers to vision.
site	a noun that means "a location."
coarse	rough; of poor quality; crude.
course	school subject; portion of meal; place where golf is played; a direction taken.
counsel	as a noun, a lawyer or advice; as a verb, to give advice.
council	a group that meets to discuss, plan, or decide action.
die	to pass from life. (dying)
dye	to change a color. (dyeing)
dissent	disagreement. (Notice that the first three letters are the same in both **diss**ent and **dis**agreement.)
descent	a noun meaning "a downward movement." (The verb meaning "to go down" is *descend.*)
here	at this place.
hear	There's an *ear* in *hear.* (Proofread carefully to avoid careless errors with *hear* and *here.*)
heir	person who inherits. A female who inherits a fortune is an *heiress.*
air	the mixture of gases that surrounds us. (*Heir* and *air* are pronounced exactly the same.)
illicit	not legal, prohibited, improper.
elicit	to draw forth or to bring out.
fiscal	adjective pertaining to financial affairs.
physical	adjective or noun pertaining to the body.

Replay Unit

70

Write the correct word in the blank.

accept
except

1. We'll _____ deliveries every

2. day _____ Sunday.

access
excess

3. He has _____

4. to the _____ materials.

ad
add

5. We hope to _____ several people to our staff.

6. We'll place an _____ in the paper.

affect
effect

7. The _____ was startling to all the visitors.

8. We cannot _____ a change on such short notice.

9. His appearance will not have any _____ on his ability.

10. Did the failure of the business _____ you personally?

alter
altar

11. We cannot _____ the circumstances.

12. The _____ was prepared for the ceremony.

bazaar
bizarre

13. I wore a _____ hat

14. to a _____.

capital
capitol

15. I'll meet you on the steps of the C_____.

16. Please use a _____ letter at the beginning of the word.

17. The _____ of New York is Albany.

cite
site
sight

18. She needed to _____ several cases that had been tried in the past.

19. The _____ for the new factory has not yet been selected.

coarse
course

20. His manners are _____ and so is burlap.

21. The first _____ of the banquet was

22. served overlooking the golf _____.

counsel
council

23. The _____ for the defense is Richard Braverman.

24. The Springfield City C_____ meets every Friday morning.

die
dye

25. The flowers will _____

26. if you spray them with that _____.

dissent
descent

27. Peaceful _____ should be encouraged in a democracy.

28. The _____ was made with great difficulty.

here
hear

29. Can you _____ me?

30. Amy and Susan are working _____ today.

heir
air

31. Lee Stevens, the mathematician, is the _____ to the fortune.

illicit
elicit

32. We cannot _____ any more information

33. about the _____ affair.

fiscal
physical

34. Karen had planned to be a _____ therapist.

35. Our _____ year begins April 1 and ends the last day of March.

Answers are in Appendix H.

Read Unit

71 AN APPLE HAS A PEEL

The spelling checker in most word processing software won't signal that *a peel* should be *appeal*. Only careful human proofreading can catch errors resulting from misused soundalikes.

it's with the apostrophe—the contraction for *it is.*
its without the apostrophe—a possessive pronoun.

led past participle of the verb *lead.*
lead present time form of verb; also the metallic element.

minor under 18, unimportant.
miner worker in a mine. (The spelling difference is easy to remember because *mine* ends with *e.*)

naval having to do with a navy.
navel the depression in the middle of the abdomen.

passed past time form of the verb *pass.*
past a period before the present; beyond or at the farther side of; used as noun, adjective, preposition, or adverb—but not as verb.

peace the absence of conflict.
piece a portion. (Think of a **pie**ce of **pie**.)

pear a fruit.
pair twosome; a couple.
pare to peel or to cut.

peddle to sell.
pedal to operate by foot; a lever operated by foot.

principal your **pal** at school; **ma**in or most important; money invested—capi**ta**l.

principle a ru**le**; moral or ethical assumption.

Writing for Your Career

- Contractions such as *they're* and *you're* are appropriate for business writing. Make it a point to use some contractions in your reports, memos, and letters. Trained business writers know that an informal, conversational tone is desirable in today's business communication in the United States. However, avoid contractions and use a more formal tone in international communication.

- Better writers usually avoid beginning sentences with *there*. "**There's** a box of disks in the top drawer" should be rewritten: "A box of disks is in the top drawer."

raise	to lift; to increase.
raze	to destroy down to the ground; to demolish.
residents	people who live in some area or in a particular home.
residence	a place where people live.
role	behavior pattern—the one you play Saturday night is different from the one you play Monday morning.
roll	you get down a hill fast that way; you butter it; the teacher takes it.
stationery	paper on which letters are written. (Notice **er** ending of *paper* and *letter*.)
stationary	cannot be moved; st**a**nds in one place. (Notice the **a** in st**a**nds.)
their	possessive pronoun.
there	a place (notice the word *here* is in *there*) or a way to begin a sentence in which the subject follows the verb: *There goes my money.*
they're	the contraction for *they are*.
waist	where you usually wear your belt.
waste	to use extravagantly.
waive	to give something up voluntarily, as a legal right.
wave	a hand signal or greeting.
your	possessive pronoun.
you're	the contraction for *you are*.

Replay Unit
71

Write the correct word in the blank.

its
it's

1. I_____ necessary to hire someone who can type 60 words a minute.

2. The hurricane took _____ toll in destroyed property.

led
lead

3. He _____ the parade in a magnificent float.

4. Babies sometimes develop _____ poisoning as a result of eating paint.

5. We asked Eric Smith to _____ the Photographer's Guild.

minor
miner

6. The coal _____ has a hazardous job.

7. Spencer can't enter into that contract because he is still a _____ .

naval
navel

8. The ensigns at the N_____ Academy

9. eat _____ oranges.

past
passed

10. She _____ the test just before

11. she _____ out.

peace
piece

12. The _____ in our office will not last long.

13. Give me a _____ of pie.

pear
pair
pare

14. We need to _____ expenses if we are to balance the budget.

15. There are only two _____s of scissors in the stock room

16. It's a _____-shaped device.

pedal
peddle

17. He plans to _____ fresh pears at the park.

18. Old sewing machines are operated by a foot lever called a _____ or a treadle.

principal
principle

19. The _____ problem is lack of funds.

20. The _____s of English grammar are easy to learn.

21. The amount of money still owed on the mortgage is called the _____ .

raise
raze

22. The workers will _____ the old building today.

23. I asked the boss for a _____ .

residents
residence

24. The _____ of this apartment house are angry about the rent increase.

25. The White House is the _____ of the President.

roll
role

26. The principal's _____ in discipline is important.

27. Which _____ did she play in the movie?

28. A _____ing stone gathers no moss.

stationery
stationary

29. That kind of envelope is available in the local _____ store.

30. The operator will find a _____ machine easier to use.

their
there
they're

31. T_____ offices are on the third floor.

32. You'll also find my office _____.

33. T_____ going to start typing the reports now.

waste
waist

34. Food if you diet goes to _____,

35. and if you fry it, it goes to your _____.

waive
wave

36. As he leaves with his suitcase filled with money, he will _____ good-bye.

37. The lawyer advised him to _____ his right to a jury trial.

your
you're

38. Y_____ the best student I have ever had.

39. The lawyer will take _____ deposition.

40. I think _____ going to do _____ own laundry at camp.

See answers in Appendix H.

Read Unit

72   *LOOK-ALIKES*

The words in this section might look alike at first glance. With the second glance, however, the difference in spelling is apparent. They are also pronounced differently. When you're not certain of the difference in pronunciation, refer to the dictionary.

adapt	to change to meet the needs of different circumstances.
adopt	to accept or to take through choice.
adept	adjective that means "skillful."
advise	verb that means "to suggest; to counsel." The *s* sounds like a *z*.
advice	noun that refers to the suggestions received when someone advises. The second syllable rhymes with "dice."
beside	by the side of; near; next to.
besides	in addition to.
bibliography	a list of books, pamphlets, periodicals, or other printed matter all dealing with a specific subject.
biographical	pertaining to a written history of a person's life.
conscience	the part of us that hurts when we do something wrong. (Notice that *science* is in this word.)
conscious	alert; awake; aware.

chose	past time form of verb *to choose*. (The *o* in *chose* is pronounced like "oh.")
choose	present time. (the *oo* in *choose* is pronounced with the same sound as in "pool.")
desert	accent on 1st syllable—where camels live.
desert	accent on 2nd syllable—to leave behind, to abandon.
dessert	the last course of a meal. ("Taking **second**s on dessert" is the memory hook for the second **s**.)
device	noun meaning "a machine, tool, or method designed to achieve or to do something." The second syllable rhymes with "nice."
devise	verb meaning to plan; to figure out.
defer	to put off or to postpone (accent on 2nd syllable).
differ	to be of unlike or opposite opinion.
eligible	having met the qualifications to participate.
illegible	difficult to read or not readable.
eminent	well known; famous; generally used to describe people known for their accomplishments.
imminent	about to happen; often used for a threatening event, such as a hurricane. (Notice the 2 *m*'s.)
envelop	to enclose or to surround (accent on 2nd syllable—en VEL op)
envelope	you put a letter in it.
human	the species to which you and I belong.
humane	considerate of other human beings or animals.
irregardless	this is not standard English. Do **not** use it. Use the word without the *ir* beginning.
regardless	this is standard English meaning "without regard."

Replay Unit
72

Write the correct word in the blank.

adapt
adept
adopt

1. They will _____ the plan exactly as it is written.

2. They will _____ the plan to their needs.

3. He is an _____ shipwright.

advise
advice

4. The lawyer will _____ you not to sign the contract.

5. She didn't want any _____ .

6. I _____ you to take the _____ of the counselor.

beside
besides

7. No one _____ Miss Muffet sits on tuffets.

8. Along came a spider, however, who sat down _____ her.

9. B_____ the antiques already listed, we chose a mahogany table.

biographical
bibliography

10. I read a _____ sketch of Julio Iglesias.

11. On the last page of the biography was a

_____ .

conscience
conscious

12. In another children's story, Pinocchio had a

_____ named Jiminy Cricket.

13. The patient was not _____ when the doctor arrived.

chose
choose

14. In my dream I _____ a lavender and orange computer terminal.

15. What color would you _____ ?

desert
dessert

16. Did you ever eat _____

17. in the _____ ?

device
devise

18. Can you _____ a plan for paring the budget?

19. With that _____ , you can pare an apple in two seconds.

defer
differ

20. They decided to _____ plans for going into business until after the wedding.

21. Although they agree on the goal, they _____ on the strategy.

eligible
illegible

22. His handwriting is _____ .

23. She is _____ for the volleyball team.

eminent
imminent

24. In 1940 most Americans knew that war was

_____ .

25. Some experts believe that the _____ statesman Winston Churchill used the English language more effectively than anyone else in this century.

envelop
envelope

26. I believe that fog will _____ the entire peninsula before morning.

27. Please give me a piece of stationery and an

_____ .

human
humane

28. The H_____ Society is concerned about cruelty to animals.

29. "To err is _____ ; to forgive, divine," wrote Alexander Pope, the 18th-century poet.

regardless
irregardless

30. He plans to attend _____ of the consequences.

Check your answers in Appendix H.

Read Unit 73

MORE LOOK-ALIKES

lose	to misplace; to be unable to locate (pronounce the *s* like a *z*).
loose	not tight; not fastened.
moral	a conception of right behavior.
morale	spirit; a sense of common purpose.
personal	private.
personnel	people who work for a particular company or who make up a group.
perquisite	a privilege or a benefit; a payment or profit in addition to regular salary. Usually used in the abbreviated form *perk* or the plural *perks*.
prerequisite	something required beforehand.
persecute	to mistreat or to injure, often because of belief or way of life.
prosecute	to take legal action against someone accused of some kind of wrongdoing.
perspective	the ability to see objects in terms of their relative distance from one another or to consider ideas in terms of their relative importance to one another.
prospective	expected; likely to happen in the future.
proceed	to go ahead; to advance.
precede	to go before; to be earlier.
quite	positively; completely.
quiet	without noise.
realty	real estate; property.
reality	what is real or true.
recent	just before the present time; modern; new.
resent	to feel or show hurt, annoyance, or anger.
respectfully	with respect. Used as a complimentary close when writing a letter to someone deserving unusual respect because of position or age; for example, the president of the United States.
respectively	in the order named.
suit	clothing consisting of a jacket and trousers or a jacket and skirt, and sometimes a vest.
suite	a group of items forming a unit, such as a set of matched furniture for a room; a group of rooms, such as an apartment or several adjoining offices that together form a suite.
then	at that time; next; following that.
than	used in making comparisons: *better **than**, rather **than**, more **than**,* and so on.

through across; from one side to another.
thorough with attention to detail; complete.
thought what is in the mind; past time of verb *think*.
whether a word indicating a choice or alternative conditions.
weather condition of the atmosphere.
were past time of verb *are*.
we're contraction of *we are*.
where a word referring to a place or location.

Replay Unit

73

Write the correct word in the blank.

lose
loose

1. Robin Hood was about to _____ his arrow.

2. All the clothing is too _____.

3. Beth Simmons is confident that she will not

_____ the account to our competitors.

moral
morale

4. M_____ is excellent in our office this year.

5. The executives of this company try to make

_____ decisions.

personal
personnel

6. The mail clerks are not to open envelopes marked

"P_____."

7. The morale of our _____ is excellent.

perquisite
(perk)
prerequisite

8. The _____ for History II is History I.

9. The job offers many _____s.

persecute
prosecute

10. The District Attorney will _____ the case to
the best of his ability; however, the evidence isn't
clear.

11. Before and during World War II, the Nazis

_____d people for many reasons, including
religious and political beliefs.

perspective
prospective

12. Seen in _____, the incident was not too serious.

13. One thousand _____ customers received our
catalog.

14. His _____ improved after he studied drawing
at the Art Institute.

proceed
precede

15. The chairman suggested that we _____ with
the meeting.

16. Speeches will _____ the festivities.

17. You may _____ to the next question.

quite
quiet

18. Are you _____ sure that it will be

19. _____ enough for you to work here?

realty
reality

20. A _____ company should be consulted before a site for a new factory is selected.

21. R_____ is often stranger than fiction.

recent
resent

22. The managers _____ your taking such long lunch breaks.

23. They expressed their _____ment

24. in their _____ memo.

respectfully
respectively

25. I _____ request a month's paternity leave.

26. When I wrote to the British Prime Minister, I signed the letter, "_____ yours, Wanda Stitt."

27. The first, second, and third place winners are Louise Peebles, Joan Teufel, and Paul Lomax,

_____.

suit
suite

28. A _____ is appropriate attire for either a man or a woman to wear to a job interview.

29. The lawyers rented a _____ in the Empire State Building.

then
than

30. Mark Allen _____ asked whether he should broadcast more details

31. about word processing _____ about data processing activities.

32. We do more for our clients _____ other attorneys do.

through
thorough
thought

33. Mr. McGuiness _____ he had done a

34. _____ job of explaining the business principle.

35. However, he went _____ the explanation again.

weather
whether

36. The meteorologists said they didn't know

_____ the

37. _____ would change before tomorrow.

were
we're
where

38. W_____ wondering whether you

39. _____ planning to spend the winter

40. someplace _____ it's warm.

Answers are in Appendix H.

Read Unit

74

THE SMALL WORDS

The small words that show how a noun or a pronoun relates to some other word in a sentence are called **prepositions** (please briefly review Unit 5 now). A preposition is the first word of a prepositional phrase—a word group *without* a subject and verb.

Here are some nonstandard usages of prepositions, along with corrections for business and professional communication.

Omit unnecessary prepositions.

AVOID   Where are you going **to**?

USE   Where are you going?

AVOID   Where has he been **at**? *or* Where's he been **at**?

USE   Where has he been?

AVOID   It fell off **of** the table. *or* It fell off**a** the table.

USE   It fell off the table.

AVOID   I live near to the building.

USE   I live near the building.

Never write the preposition *of* in the combination shown in the NEVER column. Instead, write the verb *have,* as shown in the USE column.

In speech, it's okay to slur these words together; the listener cannot normally distinguish between "of" and "have." In writing, however, the substitution is a serious error.

NEVER	USE
could of	could have
would of	would have
should of	should have
might of	might have
may of	may have
must of	must have

Use the preposition *from* (not *off* or *off of*) when something is going from one person to another.

NEVER   Did you get that ring **off** him?

NEVER   Did you get that ring **off of** him?

USE   Did you get that ring **from** him?

NEVER   Tell Fred to get the papers **off** the accountant.

NEVER   Tell Fred to get the papers **off of** the accountant.

USE   Tell Fred to get the papers **from** the accountant.

Use *among* for three or more and *between* for two.

The three men talked among themselves. [more than two]
The money was divided between Marci and Joseph. [two]

Use *for* (not *on*) after the verb *wait* when the meaning is "to await."

NEVER   I've been **waiting on** you for two hours, and I can't wait any longer.

USE   I've been **waiting for** you for two hours, and I can't wait any longer.

Wait **on** refers to service.

I **waited on** several grouchy customers today.

When a pronoun follows a preposition, remember to use the object—not the subject—form of the pronoun (see Unit 25). The object forms are *me, you, him, her, it, us, them, whom.*

NEVER   This is just between you and **I**. [*Between* is the preposition.]

USE   This is just between you and **me**.

NEVER   I received letters from Joe and **she**. [*From* is the preposition.]

USE   I received letters from Joe and **her**.

NEVER   Everyone was in Rocklin except Ms. Sumner and **I**. [*Except* is the preposition.]

USE   Everyone was in Rocklin except Ms. Sumner and **me**.

Sometimes *but* is used as a preposition to mean about the same as *except*. Use the object pronoun after *but* when it means "except."

NEVER   Everyone **but I** agreed to the plan.

USE   Everyone **but me** agreed to the plan.

USE   Everyone agreed to the plan **but me**.

But me is a prepositional phrase.

Replay Unit

74

Correct the preposition errors by crossing out unnecessary ones and changing incorrect words. Write *C* next to the correct sentences.

EXAMPLE

Everyone but Brenda and ~~he~~ him took the Lotus 1,2,3 course.

1. While he was painting the house, he fell off of the roof.
2. Take a picture of Ms. Yamamoto and I.
3. I might of known that Ms. Peebles would promote another secretary instead of me.
4. Where will the sales meeting be held at this year?
5. Between you and I, they have made a mistake in the plans for the new building.
6. Dr. Inacker drove near to the auditorium.
7. A letter was given to Louise and he.
8. The letter is for she and I.
9. Where are you sending the package to?
10. There was no one to appeal to.
11. I took the book off of the salesperson.
12. Mar-Sue should of typed the report herself.
13. Where are you going to this afternoon?
14. I bought a car off of a used car dealer in Peoria.
15. Who between the three of you is willing to go to South Carolina next week?
16. They divided the assets between the five partners.
17. I'm tired of waiting on you; why can't you be more prompt?
18. We have no secrets among the two of us.
19. You could of gone if Charles Payne had bought the tickets off of the agent.
20. Everyone but Brenda Baity and me read the report.

Please check your answers in Appendix H.
Then take **POP QUIZ** in Appendix A.

Read Unit

75

SAY IT RIGHT

Here are some words that are sometimes mispronounced. Knowing you pronounce these words correctly increases your confidence when conversing in business and professional situations. Please use the dictionary when in doubt about any of the pronunciations. Select the ones you may have been saying incorrectly; say each one aloud, and then repeat it within the sentence. Next you might ask your instructor to listen to whether you now pronounce them all correctly.

Dictionary-type phonetics are not used here. Instead I direct your attention only to correction of common mispronunciations. The syllable receiving the most emphasis is capitalized. The common mispronunciation is in parentheses after the sample sentence. The x beside it will remind you **not** to pronounce the word this way.

accessories	ak SES a rees *The interior designer selected the accessories for the offices last.* ×(uh SESS a rees)
affluence and **affluent**	AF loo ent and AF loo ens *Palm Beach and Santa Barbara are affluent communities.* ×(af LOO ent and af LOO ens)
arthritis	ar THRI tis *Mr. Lee is retiring because of his painful arthritis.* ×(ar ther IT is)
asked	ASKT *He asked four questions.* ×(AST *or* AXT)
athletics	ath LET iks *Participation in athletics contributes to good health.* ×(ath e LET iks)
debris	de BREE *After the storm, debris was everywhere.* ×(DEB ris)
Des Moines	de MOYN *The site for our new factory is in a suburb of Des Moines.* ×(de MOYNZ)
etcetera	et SET e ra or et SET ra *Usually abbreviated to etc. The King of Siam was fond of saying "etcetera, etcetera, etcetera."* ×(ek SET e ra)
February	FEB ru e ree *Valentine's Day is in February.* ×(FEB u e ree)
genuine	JEN u in *The stock certificates are genuine, but the checks are forgeries.* ×(JEN u wine)
grievous	GREEV us *A grievous crime has been committed, and the police were looking for the perpetrator.* ×(GREEV e ous) Yes, *perpetrator;* please look it up if you're in doubt.
height	HIT *The height of the new building has not yet been determined.* ×(HITH)
Illinois	ill i NOY *That salesperson's territory is the entire state of Illinois.* ×(ill i NOYS)
incomparable	in COMP er abul or in COMP ra bul *Our widgets are incomparable.* ×(in com PAR abul)
irrelevant	ir REL a vint *That course is irrelevant to your major, but it is related to your hobby.* Note *rel* in **rel**ate and **rel**evant. ×(ir REV a lint)
irrevocable	ir REV e ka bul *An irrevocable decision is one that cannot be reversed.* ×(ir ree VOK abul)
Italian	i TAL yin *You will need to learn how to speak Italian.* ×(eye TAL yin)
jewelry	JOO el ree *Many jewelry manufacturers are located on 45th Street.* ×(JOOL er ee)

library	LI brer ee *Be sure to pronounce both r's in library.* ×(LI ber ee)
mischievous	MIS chiv us *Some mischievous children were here on Halloween.* ×(mis CHEEV i us)
naive	ni EEV *He is naive to think he will get that raise without asking for it.* ×(NAV)
pageant	PAJ nt *A fishermen's pageant takes place in San Pedro, California, every year around Christmastime.* ×(PAGE nt)
picture	PIK cher *Pictures of all the past presidents are hanging in the galley.* ×(PICH er)
preferable	PREF er abul *or* PREF rabul *The old equipment would be preferable to the new items, which are cheaply made.* ×(pree FER abul)
preface	PRE fis *Have you read the preface to this book?* ×(PREE face *or* PREE fis)
picnic	PIK nik *I'm looking forward to meeting your husband at the company picnic.* ×(PIT nik)
probably	PROB ub lee *Most employees will probably be there.* ×(PROB e lee *or* PROB lee)
pronunciation	pro NUN see A shun *In order to spell and pronounce pronunciation correctly, remember that the second syllable is nun.* ×(pro NOUN see A shun)
realty	REE ul tee *Several new realty offices opened last year in Fort Lauderdale.* ×(REE li tee)
relevant	REL e vint *Mr. Goldfinger included only relevant statistics in his report.* ×(REV e lint)
statistics	sta TIS tiks *All the sales statistics are included in Ms. Gomez' report.* ×(sis TIS tiks)
subtle	SUT l *The personnel director was so subtle that Jason didn't understand he had been fired.* ×(SUB tl)
superfluous	soo PER floo us *Those items are superfluous and therefore wasteful.* ×(soo PER ful us *or* soo per FLOO us)
versatile	VER suh til *Marty Isozaki is the most versatile leader we have ever had.* ×(VER suh tile)

Writing for Your Career

Etc. is appropriate only in very informal writing. Better writers usually precede a list with *such as* or *for example*, then stop after naming three or four examples, and do not add *etc.* Another alternative is to use *and so forth* or *and so on* instead of *etc.* if *such as* or *for example* isn't used.

Replay Unit
75

Say each word aloud before answering the question.

A. How many syllables do each of these words have?

1. athletic _____
2. arthritis _____
3. mischievous _____
4. probably _____
5. naive _____

B. Which letters are silent (not sounded at all) in these words?

1. Des Moines _____
2. Illinois _____
3. subtle _____
4. debris _____
5. pageant _____

C. Write *T* (true) or *F* (false) in the blank.

1. Pronounce *affluent* with the accent on the 1st syllable. _____
2. The *i* in *versatile* is pronounced the same as the alphabet sound of

   i. _____
3. When saying *preferable*, the accent is on the first syllable. _____
4. The capital *i* in *Italian* sounds like the alphabet sound of *i.* _____
5. The word *height* ends with a *th* sound. _____
6. *Jewelry* should be pronounced *jool'e ree.* _____
7. *Realty* should be pronounced *reel' i tee.* _____
8. The first two syllables of *accessory* are pronounced like the word

   assess. _____
9. The second syllable of *pronunciation* sounds different from the sec-

   ond syllable of *pronounce.* _____
10. The first syllable of *statistics* includes a *t* sound. _____
11. One can remember how to pronounce (and spell) *irrelevant* and *rel-*

    evant by noticing their connection with the word *RELate.* _____
12. *Picture* is pronounced the same as the word for a baseball player

    who pitches. _____
13. *Irrevocable* has the primary accent on the third syllable. _____

14. The second syllable of *preface* rhymes with *place*. _____
15. When you pronounce *genuine* correctly, the end of the word sounds like the name of a beverage made from fermented grapes. _____

Answers—Appendix H.

Checkpoint

Which does the sick man hope is right?

(a) A glass of brandy at this time will **affect** his recovery.
(b) A glass of brandy at this time will **effect** his recovery.

Which required more cleverness and originality?

(a) He **adapted** the plan.
(b) He **adopted** the plan.

Which theater was almost deserted?

(a) In the theater there were five people **beside** me.
(b) In the theater there were five people **besides** me.

Review the words in this section now to be sure you know the appropriate use of each one. Take advantage of this opportunity to increase your vocabulary and to use more words correctly.

Some Useful Definitions

- **Synonyms**   Words with similar meanings (*satisfied, contented*).
- **Antonyms**   Words with opposite meanings (*rich, poor*).
- **Homonyms**   Words pronounced alike but different in meaning; they may be spelled alike (swimming *pool* and *pool* table) or spelled differently (*to, two, too*).

Memo from the Wordsmith

An acronym is a word formed by combining the first letter (or letters) of the words in a compound expression:

scuba   **s**elf-**c**ontained **u**nderwater **b**reathing **a**pparatus
radar   **ra**dio **d**etecting **a**nd **r**anging
laser   **l**ight **a**mplification by **s**timulated **e**mission of **r**adiation

Special Assignment

A. Fun with Words

This article wasn't really in the Bridal Section of a local newspaper.

> The bride dissented the isle in an off-white satin gown crowned with a wastelength tool vale and carrying lavendar orchards.

If you were the editor of the paper, you would probably fire the reporter. Then you'd make some changes in the article. What would they be?

This assignment is due on _____. (date)

B. Words that Mean Business

Goals

- To increase your knowledge of business activities
- To increase your vocabulary
- To improve your ability to speak and listen effectively on business subjects

Assignment

Prepare and present a brief oral report. Listen attentively and critically to the reports of others.

1. Read an article from the front page of the *Wall Street Journal*. If obtaining the *Wall Street Journal* is inconvenient, select an article from the business section of a weekly magazine such as *Newsweek, Time, Fortune, U.S. News & World Report,* or any other approved by your instructor.

2. For about three minutes tell the class about what you read. Just share the information in the same way as you might tell a friend about something you heard on the radio or read in the local newspaper. Practice the presentation in advance so that you will be able to explain the article clearly in the time alloted. (*Warning:* If you select an article that isn't clear to you, you won't be able to explain it to someone else.)

3. Be sure to know the meaning of all the words in the article by the time of your presentation.

4. Select one word from the article that might be unfamiliar to some students. Write the word on the board, give an easy-to-understand definition, and read aloud the sentence in which the word appeared.

The date of your oral presentation is _____.

Evaluation

The other students may judge the presentation as shown below, and your instructor might base your grade on the scores they indicate.

Assign points for each question as follows: 4 = Excellent, 3 = Good, 2 = Fair, 1 = Poor.

POINTS

1. Was the speaker's voice loud and clear enough so that you could hear without strain? _____

2. Were the ideas expressed clearly enough so that you could understand what the article is about? _____

Memo from the Wordsmith

Student: I've been trying to think of a word for two weeks.
Wise Guy: How about fortnight?

3. Was the material presented in an interesting way? _____
4. Did the speaker maintain good eye contact with the members of the audience? _____

TOTAL _____

Do you have any comments that might be helpful to the speaker?

_____

_____

Proofreading for Careers

Proofread and correct the following article. Refer to the Reference Manual, Appendix F, as well as to your dictionary.

PRODUCTIVITY AND THE COMPUTER

Researchers have been concerned over the fact that their apparently is a limit to the nations ability to continue too increase productivity at the rates demonstrated through-out the 20th century.

For one thing, virtually all are increases have been in manufacturing and agriculture; industry's that make up a proportionately smaller part of the economy each year. We have now entered the post industrial age, in which more than sixty % of the people employed in the United States are in service oriented industrys, such as medicine, law, education, marketing, ect. Thus any productivity incrases in manufacturing will have a comparatively smaller affect on the nations' over-all economic growth.

Its easy to see how developement of a tractor that pulls 2 plows instead of 1 doubles the no. of acres a farmer plows in a day. It is difficult; however, to visualize the development of a similiar tool or technique to double the productivity of a lawyer, or a window washer, or a teacher.

A 2nd factor is more subtle. Many people in service oriented jobs are professionals doctors managers data processors who are not accustomed to thinking about there duties in terms of increasing efficiency. Dealing primarily with skills rather than things, workers in service industries, tend to view attempts to increase their productivity as some how de-humanizing.

Many economists beleive the computers arrival on the business scene is giving productivity a boost at exactly the write time to maintain the healthy mementum the nation has enjoyed over the passed century. While the impact of automation have been most visible in the mfg. sector of the economy, computer based systems has been steadily moveing into service industries as well.

GEORGE POTTER

After verifying the completeness and accuracy of your corrections, choose an adjective to evaluate your business English and proofreading skill and alertness. _____

Practice Quiz

Take the Practice Quiz as though it were a real test. Don't look back through Section Twelve while you take this Practice Quiz. After the quiz is corrected, refer to the appropriate Read Units, shown in parentheses, for explanations of any item you may have missed.

A. Fill in the blank with the letter indicating the correct word.

1. Your _____ is hardly necessary now. (a) advice (b) advise **(Unit 72)**

2. The _____ of the war was felt in every home. (a) affect (b) effect **(Unit 70)**

3. The professor presented the fundamental _____ of astronomy. (a) principles (b) principals **(Unit 71)**

4. _____ at the university has been low since the Padres lost the game. (a) Moral (b) Morale **(Unit 73)**

5. I can't tell _____ figures to believe. (a) who's (b) whose **(Unit 27)**

6. _____ in the habit of arriving late every day. (a) They're (b) Their (c) There **(Unit 71)**

7. He will probably _____ all his credits. (a) lose (b) loose **(Unit 73)**

8. John Hay was an _____ statesman of his day. (a) imminent (b) eminent **(Unit 72)**

9. That song has lost _____ popularity. (a) it's (b) its **(Unit 71)**

10. The _____ for the defense asked for a recess. (a) council (b) counsel **(Unit 70)**

11. Sue Rubenstein is opposed to serving hospital patients _____ made with sugar. (a) desserts (b) deserts **(Unit 72)**

12. Harley invented this _____. (a) device (b) devise **(Unit 72)**

13. A _____ is not allowed to vote. (a) minor (b) miner **(Unit 71)**

14. The District Attorney has enough evidence to _____ for burglary. (a) prosecute (b) persecute **(Unit 73)**

15. _____ customers should be treated more courteously. (a) Perspective (b) Prospective **(Unit 73)**

B. If the sentence contains a preposition error or a preposition-related error, make the needed correction. Otherwise, write *C* in the blank.

_____ 16. Mr. McMullen could of taught the accounting class if he had known about it in time. **(Unit 74)**

_____ 17. Jacob said that he bought it off Mr. Ng. **(Unit 74)**

_____ 18. We shipped the furniture from our factory in Topeka to our warehouse in Detroit. **(Unit 74)**

_____ 19. Please divide all the work between Steve, Ellen, and Phyllis. **(Unit 74)**

_____ 20. However, all the money should be sent to Chuck and I. **(Unit 74)**

C. Say the word aloud before writing *T* or *F* in the blank.

_____ 21. *Preferable* should be pronounced with the accent on the second syllable. **(Unit 75)**

_____ **22.** The second syllable of *February* begins with a *u* sound.   **(Unit 75)**

_____ **23.** The *s* in *debris* is silent.   **(Unit 75)**

_____ **24.** *Superfluous* should be pronounced sup ERF a lus.   **(Unit 75)**

_____ **25.** *Picnic* should be pronounced PIT nik.   **(Unit 75)**

NOTES

Sentence Power 13

Parallel Power

*Y*ou have, in Sections One through Twelve, studied standard English usage as well as increased the number of words you spell, understand, and use intelligently. In short, you have increased the power of your words. Now here's the opportunity to increase the power of your sentences by:

- Analyzing common faults that weaken sentences and
- Practicing how to eliminate the faults.

While writing or dictating on the job, a person usually concentrates on the content of the message. As a result, a writer not trained to recognize common sentence faults may become careless about sentence construction. The reader of the business letter, report, or memo is probably in a hurry and has many other communications competing for his or her attention. That's why sentences in business communications must be written for easy and quick comprehension—clearly, correctly, logically, and concisely.

Poorly written sentences result in such problems as these:

A reader is annoyed because he or she wastes time rereading a sentence or even a paragraph in order to understand it.

A reader is amused by an error that sounds funny and thus is distracted from the important message.

A reader writes or phones for clarification. The time of several people is wasted.

The reader misunderstands the message to such an extent that it contributes to the failure of a business transaction.

In this section you'll further your chances for a successful career by learning to recognize and correct the most common sentence faults.

Writing for Your Career

Vary the length of sentences within a report or a letter, but rarely exceed 25 words in one sentence.

SECRET REVIEW

The "Secret Life of a Sentence" was revealed in Section Two. Unit 76 reviews that entire section.

Be able to distinguish between phrases and clauses, as well as between dependent and independent clauses.

A **phrase** is a word group with no subject and verb: *Having no one to turn to, Under the old apple tree.*
A **clause** is a word group that *does* have a subject and a verb.
A **dependent clause** begins with a dependent conjunction such as when, as, if, since (see page 38 for others):

sub. v.
When he had no one to turn to.

A clause is *independent* if it can stand alone as a sentence. An **independent clause** does *not* begin with a dependent conjunction:

sub. v.
He stood alone under the old apple tree.

A sentence may have one or more phrases and clauses, but it must have at least one independent clause: *When he had no one to turn to, he stood alone under the old apple tree.*

Use complete sentences, not fragments, in most business writing.

For definitions of fragments, run-ons, and comma splices, see Section 2 Checkpoint, page 54.

Fragments and Corrections

A fragment lacks a subject, a verb, or independence.

FRAGMENT Rolling Hills Mayor Thomas Heinsheimer, a world-renowned hot-air balloon expert. [no verb]

subject v.
CORRECT Rolling Hills Mayor Thomas Heinsheimer is a world-renowned hot-air balloon expert.

subject
CORRECT Rolling Hills Mayor Thomas Heinsheimer, a world-renowned hot-air balloon expert, does research for NASA.

FRAGMENT By accepting the idea of limitation. [no subject or verb]

sub. v.
CORRECT We accept the idea of limitation.

CORRECT   By accepting the idea of limitation, $\overset{\text{sub.}}{\text{you}}$ $\overset{\text{v.}}{\text{limit}}$ yourself unnecessarily. [*By accepting the idea of limitation* = phrase]

Eliminate run-ons and comma splices by using a period and a capital letter or a suitable joining device.

Suitable Joining Devices for Clauses

1. Use a semicolon between independent clauses.

Ms. Alderman suggested this addition; we're glad that it's feasible.

2. Use a comma plus *and, but, or, nor, for,* or sometimes *yet* between independent clauses.

Ms. Alderman suggested this addition, and we are glad it is feasible.

If the sentence is very short and *and* or *or* is the joining word, the comma is unnecessary.

Ms. Alderman suggested this and we're glad it's feasible.

3. Change one of the independent clauses to a dependent clause or to a phrase.

Because Ms. Alderman suggested this device, we'll reduce expenses by $5,000 next year. [a dependent clause followed by an independent clause]

Because of Ms. Alderman's suggestion, we'll reduce expenses by $5,000 next year. [a phrase followed by an independent clause]

Run-ons, Comma Splices, and Corrections

Run-ons and comma splices consist of two or more incorrectly joined independent clauses.

RUN-ON   The word *marketing* needs explanation you may have first heard it used about grocery shopping.

COMMA SPLICE   The word *marketing* needs explanation, you may have first heard it used about grocery shopping.

CORRECT   The word *marketing* needs explanation. You may have first heard it used about grocery shopping.

CORRECT   The word *marketing* needs explanation; you may have first heard it used about grocery shopping.

COMMA SPLICE   The professional term *marketing* means everything connected with the distribution of a product or service, therefore, it includes transporting and advertising.

CORRECT   The professional term *marketing* means everything connected with the distribution of a product or service; therefore, it includes transporting and advertising.

CORRECT   The professional term *marketing* means everything connected with the distribution of a product or service. Therefore, it includes transporting and advertising.

CORRECT   Since the professional term *marketing* means everything connected with the distribution of a product or service, it includes transporting and advertising.

RUN-ON   Many college students major in marketing it is a field of study that encompasses a variety of interesting activities.

COMMA SPLICE   Many college students major in marketing, it is a field of study that encompasses a variety of interesting activities.

CORRECT   Many college students major in marketing, for it is a field of study that encompasses a variety of interesting activities.

CORRECT   Many college students major in marketing; it is a field of study that encompasses a variety of interesting activities.

CORRECT   Many college students major in marketing because it is a field of study that encompasses a variety of interesting activities.

Summary

- Avoid fragments by remembering that a complete sentence not only has a subject and a verb but also is independent.
- Both a run-on and a comma splice consist of independent clauses **not** joined by *and, but, or, nor, for,* or *yet.* The comma splice has a comma between the independent clauses. The run-on does not have a comma between the independent clauses.
- Avoid run-ons and comma splices by remembering that two complete sentences may be:
  (a) Joined with *and, but, or, nor, for,* or *yet.**
  (b) Joined with a semicolon.
  (c) Joined by making one of the clauses dependent.
  (d) Separated by a period followed by a capital letter to begin the second sentence.

Writing for Your Career

Choose the (c) option explained above to de-emphasize the information or idea in one of the clauses; that is, create a dependent clause for the idea you want to seem less important. To give equal emphasis to the ideas in both clauses, choose (a), (b), or (d) depending on length and smooth readability.

* Use a comma before the conjunction if the resulting sentence is long. A comma isn't required if the resulting sentence is short and is joined with *and* or *or.* (See unit 234 to review the comma rule).

Replay Unit

76

A. Use the period method of correcting the business letter on page 341.

B. Add commas and/or semicolons where needed.

1. I no longer maintain an office downtown therefore please call me at home.
2. I do have people supposedly working on it but nothing has happened so far.
3. The movement of money is the fuel that keeps the machinery of our economic system working economists call this phenomenon "money flow."
4. The U.S. business scene is a very complicated process and few people can understand all aspects of it.
5. Most people agree however that the system *produces*.
6. Socialism can take many forms but basically it is a system in which the government owns and operates the means of production and distribution.
7. Sometimes our system is not stable that is we have periods of high prosperity followed by periods of recession or decline.
8. Many perhaps most Americans feel however that we can keep our present economic system and still build a much better society.
9. Few Americans believe that our present system is perfect most agree that abuses exist.
10. Corporations must meet their responsibilities to their employees stockholders and society and still show a profit.

C. In the blank write *F* for fragment, *R* for run-on, *S* for comma splice, or *C* for correct.

1. _____ As I no longer maintain an office downtown, please call me at home.

2. _____ Although I do have people supposedly working on it, nothing has happened so far.

3. _____ Looking forward to hearing from you soon.

4. _____ Thanking you for your interest in my map.

5. _____ Because corporations must meet their responsibilities to their employees, stockholders, and society and still show a profit.

6. _____ Since U.S. business is a very complicated system, few people can understand all aspects of it.

7. _____ Turkey raised prices of sugar, cement, iron, and steel, it is expected to announce other increases tomorrow.

8. _____ Think of all the beauty that's still left in and around you, and be happy.   ANNE FRANK, *The Diary of Anne Frank*

J. McFadden
DECORATIVE ARTS
666 First Avenue
Oak Park, Illinois 60024

June 2, 19__

Mr. Leonard S. Rubenstein
Vice President
People's Gallery
5746 Sunset Boulevard
Los Angeles, CA 90028

Dear Mr. Rubenstein:

I was happy to hear from you again Jeff Strausberg has
been relating some of the great things to me that you
have been doing with the People's Gallery.

Regarding the map, I do have people who are supposedly
working on it, but so far nothing has happened I would
be happy to have your friend try his luck with it, ask him
to call me when he's in Chicago next month.

As I no longer maintain an office downtown, please write
to me at my home, I have been working full time
for one of my old clients, Marsha Karl & Associates, Inc.,
since February of this year.

                    Sincerely,

                    Jean McFadden

xx

9. _____   It's easier to go down a hill than up however, the view is from the top.

10. _____   The son and daughter who own the firm are responsible businesspeople, they aren't dependent on their parents for funds to keep the dealership going.

Turn to answers in Appendix H.

Read Unit

77

DON'T LET YOUR VERBALS DANGLE IN PUBLIC

A dangling verbal is a phrase containing a verbal that hangs loosely, or dangles, in a sentence.

> A verbal is not a verb; it looks like a verb but isn't functioning as a verb. If the word group in question has a verb, it cannot be dangling.

The dangling verbal phrase usually opens the sentence. A clause follows this opener. The subject of this clause should tell who does the action named in the verbal; otherwise, the verbal phrase is dangling, and the sentence may amuse, confuse, or distract the reader.

Sentences with Danglers

$\overline{\qquad\text{verbal phrase}\qquad}$ sub.
To get the most out of our time together, the session will include discussion of the day-to-day problems we face.

Writing for Your Career

You can improve a correct sentence by omitting an unnecessary *that* before a dependent clause. Be sure the resulting sentence is clear and easy to understand.

GOOD   We are glad that the new system works.

BETTER   We are glad the new system works.

A further improvement for business writing is to use contractions often.

BEST   We're glad the new system works.

See example sentences 1 and 2, page 338.

The verbal is *to get*. It looks like a verb, but a verb can always have a subject; a verbal cannot have a subject. You wouldn't say, "I to get the most out of our time." It would have to be "I want to get . . ." with *want* as the verb.

An infinitive (***to*** + **a verb form**) is a verbal—never a verb.

After noticing that the sentence begins with a phrase containing a verbal, find the subject of the clause that follows the verbal phrase.

The subject is **session**. Then ask, "Is the *session* to get the most out of our time together?" No, it's you and I who want to get the most out of our time together. Therefore, the verbal phrase is dangling. To stop it from dangling, the subject must identify **who** is to get the most out of our time together:

CORRECT   To get the most out of our time together, **we** will include in the session discussion of the day-to-day problems we face.

CORRECT   To get the most out of our time together, Ms. Hamilton and I will include in the session discussion of the day-to-day problems we face.

DANGLER   ┌──────── verbal phrase ────────┐
Having made too many errors on the typing test, the
            subject
personnel director did not hire him.

Since it was not the personnel director who made the errors on the test, the opening phrase is dangling. To stop the verbal *(having made)* from dangling, change the subject to the person who did make the errors:

CORRECT   Having made too many errors on the typing test, **Joe** did not get the job.

Notice that *having made* is a verbal, not a verb, because you can't give it a subject. You wouldn't say, "I having made errors."

DANGLER   While flying over the jungle at an altitude of 2,000 feet, the villagers could be seen hunting and fishing.

The opening phrase includes the verbal *flying*. Notice that *flying* **can't** be a verb unless it has a helping verb preceding it. You can't say, "They flying over the jungle." The subject following the phrase is *villagers*. To decide whether the opener is dangling, ask, "Are the villagers flying over the jungle?" Since the answer is "no," correct the sentence so that the subject tells who is flying:

CORRECT   While flying over the jungle at an altitude of 2,000 feet, I could see the villagers hunting and fishing.

DANGLER   After looking at the cars for a while, the salesman approached me.

After looking at the cars for a while is dangling. Was the salesman looking at the cars? To make this sentence clear, immediately explain who is doing the looking:

CORRECT   After looking at the cars for a while, I was approached by the salesman.

DANGLER   Topped with whipped cream, the minister quickly ate a piece of Dad's delicious pecan pie.

Since the minister wasn't topped with whipped cream, stop the verbal *(topped)* from dangling by using a subject telling **what** was topped with whipped cream.

CORRECT   Topped with whipped cream, Dad's delicious pecan pie was quickly eaten by the minister.

Recap   Rewrite this sentence so that the verbal no longer dangles. The subject of the independent clause should be the person doing the verbal action; for example, the subject could be *you.*

While strolling along the beach, unusual shells and pebbles can be found.

CORRECT: _____

_____

_____

Check your answer in Appendix H.

You can use other methods for correcting a dangling verbal, too.

DANGLER   ┌────── dangling verbal phrase ──────┐   sub.
While swimming in a river near his farm, his clothes were stolen.

Since his clothes were not swimming in the river, rewrite the sentence to change the dangling verbal phrase to a dependent clause—that is, a dependent conjunction followed by a subject and a verb—as the opener. Then the independent clause does not have to be changed.

CORRECT   While he was swimming in a river near his farm, his clothes were stolen.

Be careful of trying to correct a dangler by moving the beginning of the sentence to the end. Usually the result will be a dangler at the end of the sentence instead of at the beginning:

DANGLER   subj.   ┌────── dangling verbal phrase ──────┐
His clothes were stolen while swimming in a river near his farm.

The sentence still reads as though his clothes were swimming in the river because the verbal phrase is still dangling.

DANGLER   Topped with whipped cream, the minister quickly ate a piece of Dad's delicious pecan pie.

Another way to correct this dangler you saw before the Recap is to begin the sentence with an independent clause.

Writing for Your Career

Express your ideas in a variety of ways. Good business writers vary sentence construction to keep the reader's interest. The sample sentences in this unit could have been corrected in several ways besides those shown. You probably thought of other ways to revise the sentences. Only the simplest corrections appear so that you can see how easy it is to keep verbals from dangling.

CORRECT The minister quickly ate a piece of Dad's delicious pecan pie, which had been topped with whipped cream.

DANGLER Having been sick for two weeks, his father took him to the doctor.

Father is the subject; *his* is a possessive pronoun. Father was not sick for two weeks. Therefore, *having been sick for two weeks* is dangling. The correction below changes the opener to a dependent clause.

CORRECT Because he had been sick for two weeks, his father took him to the doctor.

DANGLER Having made too many errors on the typing test, the personnel director did not hire him.

CORRECT **Because Jim** made too many errors on the typing test, the personnel director did not hire him.

DANGLER After looking at the cars for a while, the salesman approached me.

CORRECT **After I had looked** at the cars for a while, the salesman approached me.

CORRECT The salesman approached me after I had looked at the cars for a while.

BUT

Simply reversing the parts of the sentence usually results in moving the dangler—from the beginning to the end of the sentence—but not correcting it. The following has the same dangling verbal as the original sentence and is equally **incorrect**:

Recap Rewrite this sentence so that the verbal no longer dangles. This time change the verbal phrase to a dependent clause. Start with a dependent conjunction such as *because*. Leave the independent clause as is.

Being one of our most discriminating customers, we invite you to attend this private showing.

CORRECT: _____

_____

Check your answer in Appendix H.

DANGLER   The salesman approached me after looking at the cars for a while.

After looking at the cars for a while is dangling. The sentence reads as though the salesman is looking at the cars.

Replay Unit

77

Write *D* in the blank if the sentence has a dangler. Otherwise, write *C* for correct.

_____ 1. To keep the machine running in perfect condition, it was oiled once a month.

_____ 2. On examining the goods, we found them to be defective.

_____ 3. After opening the window, I felt cold and damp.

_____ 4. Having recovered from his illness, his mother took him to Europe.

_____ 5. To keep the machine running in perfect condition, we oiled it once a month.

_____ 6. Before going to lunch, this report must be typed.

_____ 7. This report must be typed before going to lunch.

_____ 8. Walking quickly down the aisle, her skirt caught on a nail.

_____ 9. While working at the daily chores, a fire started in the barn.

_____ 10. Handing me the $50,000 order, his face broke into a broad smile.

_____ 11. Upon being told to dive into the pool, I experienced a sickening feeling of fright.

_____ 12. After looking the cars over for a while, the saleswoman approached me and asked how I liked them.

_____ 13. Looking marvelously glamorous in a midnight green gown adorned with baguette rhinestones, her husband accompanied her to the performance.

_____ 14. Upon arriving in Dallas, his friends met him at the airport.

_____ 15. While buying a pair of shoes at the Belzer Bootery, Brenda suddenly realized she had missed her appointment with Marvin.

_____ 16. When looking up a word, you should notice its pronunciation, its derivation, and its various uses.

_____ 17. Being in dilapidated condition, she was able to buy the building very cheaply.

_____ 18. After climbing out of the seat, my legs wobbled and my knees shook.

_____ 19. If you are going to be a serious student of business, you should understand advertising, promotion, and sales.

_____ 20. Confused by the crowds of students rushing from one building to another, the freshman was happy to see a familiar face.

_____ 21. You should understand advertising, promotion, and sales if you are going to be a serious student of business.

_____ 22. After standing and repeating the pledge, the meeting began.

_____ 23. While walking home, a hundred dollar bill suddenly appeared before me.

_____ 24. While I was walking home, a hundred dollar bill suddenly appeared before me.

_____ 25. It began to rain after being on vacation for two hours, and it didn't stop for two weeks.

Answers are in Appendix H.

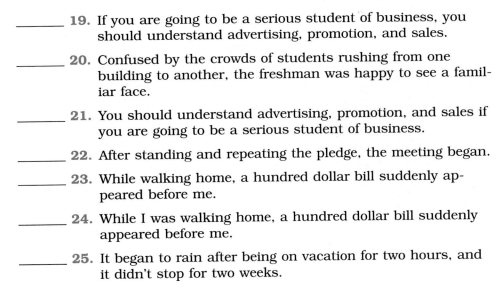

Read Unit

78 LADIES WITH CONCRETE HEADS AND PARALLEL PARTS

The late James McSheehy, a member of the San Francisco Board of Supervisors, was speaking to a group of women about his work on a finance committee. "Ladies," he said, "I have here some figures that I want you to take home in your heads, which I know are concrete."

Of course, Mr. McSheehy meant that the _figures_ were concrete. To avoid errors of this kind in your writing, be on the lookout for misplaced ideas when proofreading. Words, phrases, or clauses not appropriately positioned in a sentence are somewhat different from danglers but also result in a confused or amused reader (or listener). Here are some examples, along with suggested revisions:

Misplaced Words

Ms. Henneman hung a picture on the wall painted by Rembrandt. [Rembrandt painted the wall?]

CORRECT   Ms. Henneman hung on the wall a picture painted by Rembrandt.

INCORRECT   He only arrived in the city with $5. [All he did was arrive?]

CORRECT   He arrived in the city with only $5.

INCORRECT   The spectators in the stands watched the home team win the big game with jubilation and cheers. [They won with jubilation and cheers?]

CORRECT   With jubilation and cheers, the spectators in the stands watched the home team win the big game.

Writing for Your Career

Improved wording for the Rembrandt example on page 347 could be:

Ms. Hamilton hung a Rembrandt in the president's office.

Notice how unnecessary words are omitted, and additional information may be included in one concise sentence.

INCORRECT	We sat there listening to his singing in awed silence. [He sang in awed silence?]
CORRECT	In awed silence, we sat there listening to his singing.
INCORRECT	Margery Meadows worked for IBM during her vacation in the Information Systems Department. [She vacationed in the Information Systems Department?]
CORRECT	During her vacation, Margery Meadows worked for IBM in the Information Systems Department.

Recap   Find the misplaced words in each sentence and move them to where they belong; write the correct sentence in the blank:

1. Genevive Astor died in the home in which she had been born at the age of 96.

   _____

   _____

2. The fire was brought under control before much damage was done by the fire department.

   _____

   _____

Check your answers in Appendix H.

Parallel Parts

Using the same part of speech for similar sentence elements is a technique of good writing called **parallel construction**. Parallel parts enable the reader to understand immediately how two or more parts of the sentence are related. Good writers express parallel ideas in the same grammatical form. In the following example, the cat chased the mouse in three places; those three places are expressed in parallel form.

The cat chased the mouse **through the barn, over the fence, and into the yard**.

The parallel parts *through the barn, over the fence,* and *into the yard* are all prepositional phrases.

Below are sentences that lack parallel construction. Each has parts that should be parallel but are not:

NOT PARALLEL   He was **tall**, **dark**, and **had a handsome face**.

Make all three describing expressions parallel by using three adjectives and omitting the superfluous words:

PARALLEL   He was **tall**, **dark**, and **handsome**.

NOT PARALLEL   His two ambitions were **to join** a good fraternity and **becoming** a football player.

Make his two ambitions parallel by using *to* + verb (infinitive form) before each ambition:

PARALLEL   His two ambitions were **to join** a good fraternity and **to become** a football player.

Or make his two ambitions parallel by using the *-ing* form for each ambition:

PARALLEL   His two ambitions were **joining** a good fraternity and **becoming** a football player.

NOT PARALLEL   She is an expert not only in sketching but is also an expert painter.

Make the parts parallel by using *in* and an *-ing* word for each area of expertise:

PARALLEL   She is an expert not only **in sketching** but also **in painting**.

NOT PARALLEL   Typing accurately is more important than to type fast.

Here are four possible corrections that demonstrate parallel parts:

PARALLEL   **Typing accurately** is more important than **typing fast**.

PARALLEL   **To type accurately** is more important that **to type fast**.

PARALLEL   **Accurate typing** is more important than **fast typing**.

PARALLEL   In typing, **accuracy** is more important than **speed**.

Recap   Rewrite the following sentences so that the parts are parallel:

1. Linda is a full-time securities analyst, and her husband Tom is working part time as an insurance agent.

_____

_____

2. We are particularly interested in learning your views on how to introduce change, controlling quality, and the motivation of employees.

_____

_____

Check your answers in Appendix H.

Replay Unit

78

Write _P_ in the blank if parallel parts are needed. Write _M_ in the blank if the sentence has a misplaced word or group of words. If the sentence has neither of these errors, write _C_ for correct.

_____ **1.** The man is in the office now whom I want for the job.

_____ **2.** He is very much interested in science, math, and literature.

_____ **3.** George began a frantic search for his notebook in the library which was missing.

_____ **4.** The orange is an important source of vitamins, which is not mentioned in your report.

_____ **5.** The woman suggested that we fill out the form and to leave it with her.

_____ **6.** Classified Ad: For Sale: Piano by lady with fancy carved legs.

_____ **7.** I believe that playing a good game of chess is a greater accomplishment than to play a good game of bridge.

_____ **8.** If you want to type mailable letters, you must spell correctly and punctuation is important too.

_____ **9.** Her hobbies are painting, to go to concerts, and the collection of diamonds.

_____ **10.** The function of a wholesaler is to buy in large quantities and to sell in small quantities.

_____ **11.** The man sat down in an easy chair to tell his children about his childhood after dinner.

_____ **12.** We have in stock the equipment you inquired about in your letter of May 15.

_____ **13.** Do you advise me to go to the conference tonight or that I go right home?

_____ **14.** More than 90 percent of the Fortune 500 companies have complete in-plant printing departments, according to the In-Plant Printing Management Association of Chicago.

_____ **15.** We would like to hear your ideas on motivating employees and how to introduce change.

_____ **16.** That program has too much sex, violence, and the language is bad.

_____ **17.** Free ears pierced here.

_____ **18.** Friendship means forgetting what one gives and remembering what one receives.

_____ **19.** Norma said she believed him as well as having faith in him.

_____ **20.** Professor Vara told us to read the story, then we had to answer some questions about it, and write a book report.

See answers in Appendix H.
Please turn to Appendix A for **POP QUIZ** on Units 76–78.

Read Unit 79

THE BEELINE

Do you know someone who makes a beeline for the snack table upon arriving at a party? This food fancier moves in a straight and direct path just as a bee flies to its chosen flower. When a sentence is written in beeline style, it is direct and to the point. This is the type of sentence most often written by effective business writers. The business or professional person is likely to react more favorably to a direct style of writing.

In addition to your friend who makes a beeline for the refreshments, you probably know others who eventually get to the snack table; but they take their time about it. Skillful business writers sometimes use the indirect style, but they get there eventually too.

In the **direct** and to-the-point style of writing, the subject *does* the action stated by the verb. (Active voice is the traditional name for the direct style.)

Craig kissed Rosemary.

Memo from the Wordsmith

LITTLE GIRL I met a man with a broken leg named Smith.

MARY POPPINS Oh, what's his other leg named?

The subject of the sentence *(Craig)* is doing the action *(kissed.)*

In the **indirect** style of writing, the subject *receives* the action stated by the verb. (Passive voice is the traditional name for the indirect style.)

Rosemary was kissed by Craig.

The subject *(Rosemary)* receives the action *(was kissed).*
Since the basic ingredients of a sentence are subject, verb, and independence, we can write a sentence in the indirect style without mentioning who did the action.

Rosemary was kissed.

The sentence is complete because it has a subject and a verb and is independent.

DIRECT STYLE   Roberta Chandra made an error in the transportation report. [Subject—*Roberta Chandra*—did the action—*made.*]

INDIRECT STYLE   An error was made by Roberta Chandra in the transportation report. [Subject—*error*—received the action—*was made.*]

INDIRECT STYLE   An error was made in the transportation report.

The sentence is complete because it has a subject and a verb and is independent; yet the doer of the action (the one who made the error) is not mentioned.

DIRECT   The auditor presented the report to the stockholders.

INDIRECT   The report was presented to the stockholders by the auditor.

OR

The report was presented to the stockholders.

By using the indirect style, the doer of the action (the auditor) may be omitted if desired.

Use of Direct and Indirect Styles

Use the direct style for most business writing because fewer words are required, and it takes the reader from point *A* to point *B* in a straight line. $A \longrightarrow B$

Use the indirect style for any of the following purposes: tact, emphasis, or variety.

Tact   You may want the reader to know an error was made, but you want to leave the culprit's name out of it:

INDIRECT   An error was made.

Emphasis When you want to emphasize the receiver of the action because it is more important than the doer of the action, use the indirect style. Then the most important words appear at the beginning of the sentence instead of at the end. The report is more important than the auditor in the following sentence:

INDIRECT   A report was presented to the stockholders by the auditor.

INDIRECT   A report was presented to the stockholders.

Variety One way to write more interestingly is to construct a sentence in the indirect style occasionally for variety in sentence structure.

Instant Test to Distinguish Direct from Indirect Style

If the expression "by someone" can be inserted after the verb, the style is indirect. Of course, if "by someone" is already there, then you *know* the style is indirect.

The book was purchased last week.

INSTANT TEST   The book was purchased (by someone) last week.

Since "by someone" can be inserted, we're sure the sentence is in the indirect style.

Laurie Hamilton purchased the book last week.

INSTANT TEST   Laurie Hamilton purchased (by someone) the book last week.

Since "by someone" after the verb doesn't make sense, the sentence is direct.

Writing for Your Career

When a sentence has two clauses, they should usually be parallel.

$$\text{Since } \overset{\text{sub.}}{\text{we}} \ \overset{\text{v.}}{\text{know}} \text{ of your interest in business, the}$$

$$\overset{\text{sub.}}{\textit{Wall Street Journal}} \ \overset{\text{verb}}{\text{will be sent}} \text{ to you as a gift. [not parallel]}$$

CLAUSE 1   Since we know of your interest in business, [direct]

CLAUSE 2   the *Wall Street Journal* will be sent to you as a gift. [indirect]

Revise so that both parts are either direct or indirect; for example, direct and preferable for this sentence:

DIRECT   Since we know of your interest in business, we will send you the *Wall Street Journal* as a gift.

Replay Unit

79

Write *D* next to each sentence that is written in the direct style and *I* next to each that is in the indirect style.

_____ 1. More errors were discovered by the supervisor today.

_____ 2. The surface has barely been scratched for the possible uses of personal computers.

_____ 3. Some evening classes at Oak Park Community College were taught by Mr. Rand.

_____ 4. Last year we paid more than $300,000 for typography services.

_____ 5. You should move that equipment to our Indianapolis factory.

_____ 6. Companies such as Avon Products and the Fuller Brush Company employed neighborhood sales representatives.

_____ 7. My clothes were stolen.

_____ 8. Importers and exporters are constantly moving merchandise from one country to another.

_____ 9. The plants were watered every day during your vacation.

_____ 10. All freight changes must be verified before they are paid.

_____ 11. He misspelled *Mississippi* in every paragraph.

_____ 12. *Mississippi* was misspelled in every paragraph.

_____ 13. These tools are manufactured in Toronto.

_____ 14. We mailed that statement to you on May 5.

_____ 15. The statement was mailed to you on May 5.

Answers are in Appendix H.

Memo from the Wordsmith

If you were the editor of the classified ads, what would you do to this one?

For Sale: Crystal chandelier by lady, slightly cracked.

DICK AND JANE

Do you remember Dick and Jane from elementary school reading books? When children write a letter or a composition, they are taught to compose short, simple sentences like those in their readers. This writing style is an important stage in learning written expression.

Sometimes, however, these "choppy" writing habits appear in the work of adults because of carelessness or because of never having learned an appropriate style.

Here are techniques to convert "Dick and Jane" writing into polished writing:

> Join—instead of separate—two independent but closely related clauses that seem to be equal in importance. Insert a coordinate conjunction.

CHOPPY   Jane likes to work. Dick likes to play.

SMOOTH   Jane likes to work, but Dick likes to play.

> Combine two ideas by joining an independent clause with a dependent clause. Insert a dependent conjunction.

CHOPPY   Jane likes to work. Dick likes to play.

SMOOTH   Although Jane likes to work, Dick likes to play.

> Use phrases and describing words instead of expressing every idea with a clause.

CHOPPY   Jane is wearing a new dress. She looks very pretty. She approached Dick. She is shy.

SMOOTH   Jane, looking very pretty in her new dress, shyly approached Dick.

> Use a transition expression between two complete sentences.

A transition is like a bridge that enables the reader to cross over from one thought to the next.

CHOPPY   Dick and Jane like to read. Dick and Jane like to dance.

SMOOTH   Dick and Jane are very much alike. For example, they both enjoy reading as well as dancing.

Notice that the vocabulary in the following sentences is adult, but the writing style of each original sentence is choppy. The revision that follows each sentence shows one way to improve the writing. You will probably think of other ways.

CHOPPY	He wears glasses for reading. They have a tortoise-shell frame.
REVISION	For reading, he wears glasses with a tortoise-shell frame.
CHOPPY	You write in code. In this manner you convey the information secretly.
REVISION	By writing in code, you convey the information secretly.
CHOPPY	The dean's office is next to the reception room. It is on the first floor.
REVISION	The dean's office is next to the reception room on the first floor.
CHOPPY	Ira Simon has a collection of butterflies. It is large and varied. He has acquired it gradually over a period of years.
REVISION	Over a period of years, Ira Simon has acquired a large and varied collection of butterflies.
CHOPPY	Industrial output is comparatively easy to measure. Measuring the "output" of our education system is difficult.
REVISION	While industrial output is comparatively easy to measure, measuring the "output" of our education system is difficult.
CHOPPY	Some manufacturers engage in wholesale trade. They are not regarded as wholesalers. Their primary function is that of manufacturing.
REVISION	Some manufacturers engage in wholesale trade. They are not, however, regarded as wholesalers because their primary function is that of manufacturing.
CHOPPY	Retail establishments come in all sizes and varieties. The grandfather of retailing is the traditional department store.
REVISION	Retail establishments come in all sizes and varieties, but the grandfather of retailing is the traditional department store.
CHOPPY	He finished dinner. He returned to work.
REVISIONS	First he finished dinner. Then he returned to work. After finishing dinner, he returned to work. He finished dinner and then returned to work.
CHOPPY	Market research and analysis is a highly specialized field. Excellent career opportunities exist in marketing for statisticians.
REVISION	Market research and analysis is a highly specialized field. For example, excellent career opportunities exist in marketing for statisticians.
CHOPPY	The story is full of action, and Dumas is the author.
REVISIONS	This story by Dumas is full of action. Dumas' story is full of action.

Dick and Jane versus Gobbledygook

The preceding examples show various ways to join ideas for more effective writing. Sometimes, however, a writer will join too much. Then the sentences are too long and complicated to allow efficient reading. The result may be gobbledygook—talk or writing that is pompous, wordy, and hard to understand:

> Merchants in the Middle Ages kept track of merchandise they sold on "tally sticks," on which they made a notch on a stick which was then broken in half, with the merchant retaining half and the other half being presented to the customer in order to have a record of the data for the merchant and the customer.

The sentence above is too long and clumsy. The improved version below has three sentences:

> Merchants in the Middle Ages kept track of transactions with "tally sticks." After the data had been notched on a stick, the stick was split. The merchant kept half and gave the matching half to the customer, thus providing duplicate records.

TLC for Pronouns

To use pronouns with tender loving care, provide the reader with a clear, immediate reference to all pronouns used. Pronouns must refer to specific nouns, not to words or ideas *implied* (but not stated) in a sentence. Be sure each pronoun means to the reader exactly what you intend it to mean. The bold-type pronouns below have not received TLC. For clear sentences, replace the vague pronouns with appropriate nouns or recast the sentence.

POOR   Ms. Senterfitt is interested in good writing, **which** she acquired from a communication expert in industry.

GOOD   Ms. Senterfitt is interested in good writing, an interest she acquired from a communication expert in industry.

POOR   If washing machines have been tearing your fine linens and laces, let us do **it** for you by hand.

Writing for Your Career

For good business writing, vary the length and construction of sentences. Often a short, simple sentence is exactly right and doesn't sound like "Dick and Jane."

GOOD   If washing machines have been tearing your fine linens and laces, let us do your laundry for you by hand.

POOR   Jose's father is a successful doctor, and I'm sure **he** will be rich some day. [Who will be rich?]

GOOD   Jose's father is a successful doctor, who I'm sure will be rich some day.

GOOD   Jose's father is a doctor, and Jose will surely be rich some day.

Replay Unit

A. Combine these short, choppy sentences into one smooth sentence.

1. I like biscuits. I especially like them hot. Also I like to have plenty of butter and honey with them.

_____

_____

_____

2. Ella mashed her finger with a hammer. It was the index finger of her left hand. She mashed it while repairing a table.

_____

_____

_____

3. On that side of the room is a college pennant. There is also a picture by Millet. There is also a medical diploma. All these hang on the wall.

_____

_____

_____

4. Claude and Alex walked to the telephone company office. From there they walked to the gas company office. They then walked to the electric company office. They were paying their bills. It took them all afternoon [Condense to one or two sentences.]

_____

_____

_____

5. An animal paced restlessly back and forth in the cage. It appeared to be a hyena.

_____

_____

_____

B. Improve the construction of these sentences.

1. A house sits far back among the trees, and it needs painting.

_____

_____

_____

2. From a door of the house a stairway leads to the housekeeper's room, and it is the rear door.

_____

_____

_____

3. A tall man came forward, and he was the owner of the garage.

_____

_____

_____

4. Hams hung in the smokehouse, and they were well cured.

_____

_____

_____

5. Shari and Peter saw the coat and it belonged to their father. They knew the man was a thief.

_____

_____

_____

6. Respectable lady seeks comfortable room where she can cook herself on an electric stove.

_____

_____

_____

7. FOR SALE: The First Presbyterian Church women have discarded clothing of all kinds. They may be seen in the church basement any day after six o'clock.

_____

_____

_____

8. For those of you who have small children and don't know it, we have a nursery downstairs.

_____

_____

_____

9. This is the friend of Ms. Mosson who lives in La Jolla.

_____

_____

_____

10. We can't allow the children to visit the neighbors, for they are mean and intolerant.

_____

_____

_____

Answers are in Appendix H.
Please turn to Appendix A for **POP QUIZ** on units 79 and 80.

Checkpoint

An accountant doesn't prepare a report just for the fun of it. A manager doesn't write instructions just to pass the afternoon. A secretary doesn't write a letter to get more typing practice. Business writing should always have a **specific objective**. To succeed in this objective, the writing must have power. The letter, report, or instructions can't be effective if the sentences are weak.

The power of a business communication may be judged by the degree to which it makes the reader feel, think, or act how the writer wants him to feel, think, or act. For example, if the credit manager writes to a customer about an unpaid bill, the letter is a success if a check arrives by return mail. The letter is even more successful if the customer's order for more merchandise accompanies the check. To accomplish that magic, you must first think about your goals for any business communication.

Overcoming common sentence faults is a major step toward accomplishing your purposes in business writing. By keeping in mind the pointers discussed in this section, your writing will improve. Along with that improvement will be an increased opportunity for a successful career in any field where communication is part of the job (and it's part of the job in any field!).

Place a check in the blank when you can recognize these characteristics of sentence construction:

_____ run-on sentence

_____ comma splice

_____ fragment

_____ dangler

_____ misplaced word, phrase, or clause

_____ nonparallel construction

_____ direct style of sentence construction

_____ indirect style of sentence construction

_____ immature writing style

_____ gobbledygook

_____ unclear pronouns

Sections 2 and 13 of the Grammar Supplement in the back of the book present additional details about sentences.

Special Assignment

A. Sentence Revision Practice

From Replay Unit 77 Revise the *D* sentences so that they no longer have danglers. Danglers are not the same as misplaced parts. Don't correct a dangler by moving it to the end of a sentence. Frequently that moving process results in a verbal dangling at the end instead of the beginning. Review the instructions for correcting danglers.

From Replay Unit 78 First, revise the *M* sentences so that they no longer have misplaced words or word groups. Correct these by moving the misplaced part to a logical position in the sentence. Then, revise the *P* sentences so that the similar parts are parallel.

From Replay Unit 79 Select three *I* sentences and change them to the direct style.

Prepare this assignment by _____. (date)

B. Sentence Power Practice

Your objective in this part of the Special Assignment is to write clear, concise, logical, and correct directions.

In 100 to 150 words explain how to do something that you understand very well. The process should be simple enough so that a reader with average, everyday (rather than specialized) skills can perform the task by following your written instructions. Examples of such tasks are sewing on a button, changing a tire, checking the oil in a car, or answering a business call and taking a message.

In so short a paper, a formal introduction is inappropriate. Get right into your subject. Use complete sentences with smooth transitions.

SAMPLE OPENING SENTENCE

Sewing on a button is easy if you have the right tools and follow six easy steps.

C. Revision

Rewrite these ads so that they say what they mean and mean what they say:

Wanted: Boy to deliver fish and oysters with good references.
Now you can buy six different products to protect your car from your Mobil dealer.
Need man to take care of horses that can speak German.
Now on the market: a Norco Shaver for women with three heads

Submit this assignment on _____. (date)

A Word to the Wise

The Reference Section of this book provides information on numbers, capitalization, word division, and abbreviations. See Appendix F.

Proofreading for Careers

Please proofread and correct this article.

GROWTH OF COMPUTERS

Howard Aikens, a mathematics instructor at Harvard university, working under a grant from IBM, produced the Mark 1 computer in '44. This machine, which worked on a combination of mechanical, electrical and electronic principals, was the first to perform all the functions of a true computer.

In 1945 University of Pennsylvania Professor's John W. Mauchly, and J. Presper Eckert completed ENIAC (Electronic Numerical Integrator and Calculator), the first all electronic computer. 2 years' later they formed their own Corporation to construct UNIVAC (UNIVersal Automatic Computer), the worlds 1st commercial computer, it was delivered to the United States bureau of the Census in Spring of 1951.

Since the first UNIVAC, computer development has not been the steady smooth advance that characterizes the growth of most inventions. Instead, successive technological break-throughs have propelled computers forward in a series of great leaps. Each breakthrough have created computers far advanced over previous computers and have brought about radical changes in our concepts of data processing. These new family's of computers have become known as the computer generations.

Their is no doubt, that computers will cintinue to grow in number, and they are becoming faster, and have better memory capacity. They will be physically smaller, virtually troublefree, and less expensive. New methods of in-put and out-put will make it far easier for more people to use them for a variety of tasks.

Another kind of revolution has all ready started, and it will continue indefinitly, it is the "user revolution", and mankind will be the winner. Vast new areas of computer applications will be developed that will provide computer power to make our daily lives more pleasant, more convient, less dangerous, and more filled with leisure and fun.

GEORGE B. POTTER

After verifying corrections with your instructor or with a key, evaluate your English for careers and proofreading skills. Excellent _____ Very good _____ Good _____ Fair _____ Need improvement in spotting errors _____ Need improvement in the following English skills

_____

_____

Practice Quiz

A. Take the Practice Quiz as though it were a real test. Don't look back through Section Thirteen while you take this Practice Quiz. After the quiz is corrected, refer to the appropriate Read Units, shown in parentheses, for explanations of any item you may have missed. Write the appropriate letter in the blank according to these instructions:

a Properly constructed sentence
b Fragment or unclear pronoun
c Run-on or comma splice
d Lacks parallel parts or is choppy
e Has dangler or misplaced parts

_____ 1. The chairman is waving her arms and attempting to get our attention. **(Unit 78)**

_____ 2. The new drug has proved to be highly effective, it has no side effects. **(Unit 76)**

_____ 3. He is an extremely capable worker, however, he lacks seniority. **(Unit 76)**

_____ 4. To get the most from your employees, it is important to be sympathetic. **(Unit 77)**

_____ 5. The angry instructor began stamping his foot and to pound the desk. **(Unit 78)**

_____ 6. When completing the invoice, one item was omitted. **(Unit 77)**

_____ 7. I am fully acquainted with the situation; in fact, I know too much about it. **(Unit 76)**

_____ 8. After going over the work more carefully, more errors were discovered. **(Unit 77)**

_____ 9. He is very much interested in science, which he acquired from his cousin who is a chemist. **(Unit 76)**

_____ 10. Working accurately is more important than to work fast. **(Unit 78)**

_____ 11. The main problem for people who grow African violets is that they stop blooming. **(Unit 80)**

_____ 12. She types letters and reports faster than anyone else. She makes many errors. **(Unit 80)**

_____ 13. The bank approves loans to reliable individuals of any size. **(Unit 78)**

_____ 14. The English teacher was sitting on a bench with his dog reading Shakespeare. **(Unit 78)**

_____ 15. Even though I went to town this morning and later went to the farm. **(Unit 76)**

_____ 16. She is very much interested in science, math, and likes good books. **(Unit 78)**

_____ 17. Mara heard Beth talking to her boyfriend on the phone. **(Unit 80)**

_____ 18. After voting on several issues, the meeting was adjourned. **(Unit 77)**

_____ 19. The three steps for making peanut butter are: **(Unit 78)**
    (a) Picking the nuts
    (b) Roasting the nuts
    (c) To squeeze the oil from the nuts

_____ 20. Learning to fly is challenging and a thrill. **(Unit 78)**

B. Write *D* in the blank if the sentence is written in the direct style and *I* if it is in the indirect style.

(Unit 79)

_____ **21.** The report was carelessly prepared.

_____ **22.** The already low prices were reduced for regular customers.

_____ **23.** Fast-food restaurants offer their customers many advantages.

_____ **24.** The meeting was adjourned.

_____ **25.** The attorney questioned the witness.

NOTES

14

**Getting set
to win!**

✔ The basics of
business
stationery.
✔ The language style
of business letters.
✔ The format of
business letters
and envelopes.
✔ Appropriate
salutations,
complimentary
closes, and
signatures for
business letters.
✔ Business letter
paragraphing.

*S*incerely Yours is the section I'm using to sign off to you. Now that you've mastered the mechanical aspects of English for business, I recommend you study business communication. In that valuable course, you'll compose many kinds of business letters, as well as reports, memos, and other types of communications.

In 1930 the Dartnell Institute of Business Research conducted the first of its annual surveys of the cost of an average business letter. At that time the cost was 30 cents. As of this writing it is about $10 for an average letter of about 190 words. Since the cost has increased each year since 1930, by the time you read this page, the $10 letter is likely to be history. Notice that this figure is the average and not the maximum. It's hard to imagine that letters are so expensive when we think of the postage and stationery costs. But consider also the hourly pay of the persons composing and typing the letter, the electronic equipment, and other incidentals. Long-distance telephoning is often less expensive than sending a letter.

Although actual letter cost continues to increase, the percentage of increase has been declining because of computerized typing technology.

Despite the high cost, more and more letters continue to be written. Writing instead of telephoning has several advantages. One is that a letter provides a permanent record for both the sender and the receiver. Another is that a phone call might occur when the recipient is busy with another matter, while a letter's arrival doesn't interrupt the receiver.

Although preparing and sending a letter is expensive, this expense can be multiplied many times by a poorly prepared letter that results in lost business. On the other hand, a well-prepared letter can result in considerable profit for the sender.

Employees who write good business letters are exceedingly important to the success of an organization. In this section, you will learn and practice the basics of modern letter preparation. These basics are the finishing touch to your study of English for your career, as well as the introduction to your potential future study in business communication.

Word processing has created new methods of producing business letters in most organizations. With computers and electronic typewriters, correspondence is produced, edited, revised, and corrected and then stored in the electronic memory of the machine. In Section 14 you learn how to make the message, style, and format as effective as the technology that produces the letter.

Read Unit

81

LOOKING GOOD

A first consideration in preparing effective letters is to be sure they look good:

- Appropriate stationery should be used.
- Neat, legible file copies are required.
- Letters must be proofread carefully.
- Letters need to be properly folded and inserted into envelopes.
- Numbers, abbreviations, word division, and capitalization should be handled appropriately for business communication.

Stationery

Business Letters

Most business letters are typed on attractive, good quality $8\frac{1}{2}$ by 11* letterheads and are mailed in matching envelopes. Somewhat smaller stationery is often used in professional, top executive, and diplomatic offices. Although some companies do use color, white or light beige letterhead stationery is typical.

Personal Business Letters

A personal business letter deals with personal transactions rather than those of your company. You might write to your insurance company, to the motor vehicle department about your license, to an employer when

* European business stationery is called "A4" (for size designation) and is $8\frac{1}{4}$ by $11\frac{1}{2}$.

you're looking for a job, to a department store about errors in your bill, and so on. Personal business letters should usually be typed on plain 8½ by 11 paper without a company's letterhead. On page 27 in Unit 7, you can see a personal business letter I sent to Chevrolet Motor Division in Detroit. (P. S. I received a courteous response from Detroit and a refund from the dealer.)

Envelopes

Two sizes of envelopes are commonly used in offices for correspondence: the small business envelope (No. 6¾) for one-page letters without enclosures and the large business envelope (No. 9 or 10) for two or more pages or for letters with enclosures. Many firms, however, prefer the large one for all 8½ by 11 letters, whether one or more pages.

No. 6 3/4 envelope (small or business size).

```
Your Name
Street Address
City, State ZIP


                    First National Bank
                    711 Campus Drive
                    Alberta, VA 23821
```

Envelope for personal business letter — your name and address typed in upper left.

No. 9 or No. 10 envelope (large or legal size).

```
    GOLDFINGER & SIMON
       30711 Ganado Drive
 Rancho Palos Verdes, California 90274




                    LAMAR UNIVERSITY
                    P O BOX 1043
                    BEAUMONT, TEXAS 77710
```

Envelope or business letter— Letterhead printed in Upper left.

Capitals, Numbers, Abbreviations, Word Division

For the preferred ways to write numbers, capitalize, divide words, and abbreviate in business letters, review pages in Appendix F.

Copies

At least one neat and accurate copy of each letter, usually on less costly paper than the original, should be on file. Photocopies or computer printer copies are the most common forms for filed duplicates of letters. When you don't have ready access to electronic copying, use carbon paper to make copies.

Proofreading and Signing

Be sure the letter is carefully proofread and errors are neatly corrected. Then it should be signed with a pen.

Folding and Inserting

To insert an $8\frac{1}{2}$ by 11 sheet in a small envelope, fold it in half from the bottom up. Then fold it in thirds, starting from the right. To insert it in a large envelope, fold the letter in thirds from the bottom up and then from the top down. Please take a moment now to practice folding for both envelope sizes. Use $8\frac{1}{2}$ by 11 paper for this practice.

Replay Unit

81

1. What is the standard size stationery used for letters?
   _____ by _____

2. A small envelope is called a No. _____.

3. A large envelope is called a No. _____ or a
   _____.

4. At least one _____ should be made of every business letter.

5. What should be handwritten on a business letter before inserting it in the envelope? _____

6. When a properly folded letter is removed from a large business envelope, it has _____ folds.

7. When a properly folded letter is removed from a small business envelope, it has _____ folds.

8. True or False: Business letters must always be written on white stationery. _____

9. After a business letter is typed, it must be carefully _____.

10. Reads and Replays for expressing numbers, abbreviations, capitalizing, and word division are on pages _____.

Check answers in Appendix H.

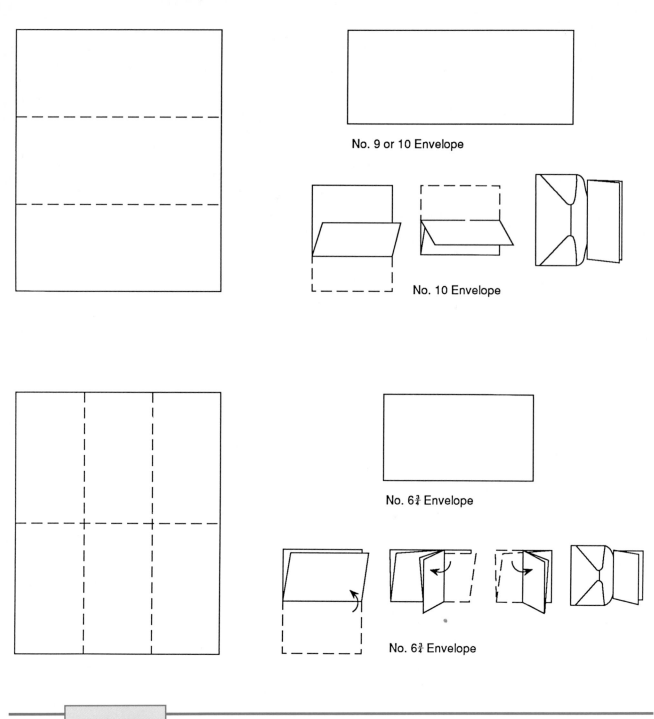

No. 9 or 10 Envelope

No. 10 Envelope

No. 6¾ Envelope

No. 6¾ Envelope

THE PARTS

In this unit you review the parts of a personal business letter and a regular business letter. The difference between the two is that in the *personal* business letter the sender's address is typed above the date. The *regular* business letter on letterhead stationery *begins* with the date—since the printed

letterhead provides the name, address, phone number, and often other information, such as the nature of the business and a logo. The parts are discussed in order from beginning to end.

Printed Letterhead or Typed Address of Sender

If letterhead stationery isn't used, the writer's street address comes first. Spell out words such as *Street, Road, Avenue, Boulevard*. The writer's city, state, and ZIP code are on the next line. Only if the official postal abbreviation is used, should the state name be abbreviated. The ZIP code follows the name of the state:

2166 Clinton Avenue
Bronx, NY 10406

Date

Two styles are commonly used:

June 2, 199-   2 June 199-

Notice that the day doesn't have *nd, th,* or *st,* added to it. The style on the right (day-month-year) is standard for government, military, and international correspondence.

Inside Address

The inside address is the typed name and address of the person or company to receive the letter. When writing to an individual, precede the name with a courtesy or professional title such as *Mr., Mrs., Miss, Ms., Dr., Professor, Father, Rabbi,* etc. If there's no professional title and you can't tell whether the letter is being sent to a man or a woman, omit the courtesy title. For example, Whitney Blake could be the name of a male or a female, and Phoung Do is a Vietnamese name, which most Americans cannot identify as masculine or feminine.

Avoid abbreviations in the inside address also, except for Mr., Mrs., or Dr. and the postal state abbreviation. (See the list in Appendix F.)

Attention Line

Use of an Attention line is being discontinued by people with recent business communication training. For traditionalists who continue its use, be sure that the first line of the inside address is the name of a company or other organization and that the Attention line also appears on the envelope (see the envelope on page 386).

```
El Dorado College
451 Mustang Circle
Austin, TX 78727

ATTENTION: MS. MELANIE LIPMAN

El Dorado College
ATTENTION: MS. MELANIE LIPMAN
451 Mustang Circle
Austin, TX 78727
```

For a more up-to-date appearance for your business letters, I recommend you omit the Attention line and simply write the name of the person as the first line of the inside address and the company name as the second line:

```
Ms. Melanie Lipman
El Dorado College
451 Mustang Circle
Austin, TX 78727
```

Salutation

The salutation is the usual way for the letter writer to greet the letter receiver. The first line of the inside address and the salutation should agree. If the first line is an organization name, the salutation is *Gentlemen:, Ladies:, Ladies and Gentlemen:,* or *Gentlemen and Ladies:.**

* Use of the colon depends on the punctuation style as explained on page 380 (in Read Unit 83).

WITH AN ATTENTION LINE

Singer Business College   Singer Business College
135 Rollingwood Drive   135 Rollingwood Drive
Athens, GA 30605   Athens, GA 30605

ATTENTION Ms. Nita McKenzie   Gentlemen and Ladies

Ladies and Gentlemen:

If the first line is a person's name, the salutation is *Dear Ms. Chavez, Dear Mr. Chavez,* or *Dear Kim,* depending on the relationship between the sender and the receiver of the letter. If you know the name of the person to whom you are writing, choose this style:

Ms. Nita McKenzie
Singer Business College
Address
City, State ZIP

Dear Ms. McKenzie: [or Dear Nita,]

If you can't use a courtesy title before the individual's name in the inside address, type the salutation to agree, as follows. (Trained business writers use this format only if they don't know the sex of Leslie Caron.)

Leslie Caron
Drake School of Business
Schuster Boulevard
Ames, Iowa 50010

Dear Leslie Caron

If you know a job title for the person you wish to write to but cannot find out the name, use the title:

Plant Manager
University of Puerto Rico
23 Avenida Del Norte
Mayaguez, Puerto Rico 00617

Dear Plant Manager:

The simplified letter style, developed by the American Management Society, requires no salutation at all. Please see this letter style on page 382.

Subject Line

When a subject line, which states the letter's main topic, is used, it serves as a heading for the body of the letter. That's why the best place for it is between the salutation and the body. The subject line lets the reader know at a glance the topic of the letter. (A subject is always included in the simplified letter as shown on page 382.)

Mr. Bob Wallace
United College of Business
Street Address
City, State ZIP

Dear Mr. Wallace:

JOB PLACEMENT OF GRADUATES

The five United graduates listed below received high scores on
our employment test and . . . .

Body

The body of a letter states the message. Single-space the message and
double-space between paragraphs.

Complimentary Close

The complimentary close is, as its name suggests, a polite conventional phrase such as *Sincerely yours* or *Very truly yours* that signals the
end of the message. Only the first word of the complimentary close is capitalized. The complimentary close is not used on a memo or on a simplified
letter.

Company Name

Some companies want their name (exactly as it appears in the letterhead) a double space below the complimentary close in all capital letters.
This letter part is not often used anymore.

Sincerely,

LINCOLN LAND INDUSTRIES

Dick Williams

Dick Williams, Vice President

Handwritten Signature

Sign with a pen. Do not give yourself a courtesy title.

YES   *Joan Musé*

NO   *Mrs. Joan Musé*

Writer's Name and Titles

The writer's name is a typed version of the signature. Unless there's a
special need for it, a courtesy title is not used. It's acceptable, but not necessary, to precede the name with *Mr.* and *Ms.* **only** if the reader can't tell
from the name whether the writer is male or female. It's a better solution to
spell out Chris to Christine or Christopher or to include a middle name—
Whitney Anne Blake. Those devices enable the reader to know whether to
use Mr. or Ms. when communicating with the letter writer. Also, in a business letter, there's rarely a need for a woman to indicate her marital status
in the handwritten and typed signature lines.

Official job titles are important to include. A job title is typed directly below the writer's typed name (or on the same line in the simplified letter).

Sincerely,

Janet S. Arena
Curriculum Director

Initials

Initials are used to identify the typist when someone else authored the letter or memo. When you type a letter for your own signature, do not use initials. The most popular style today is to show the typist's initials in lower-case letters below the writer's name.

Sincerely,

Carolyn Wendell
Vice President

lrs

Enclosure

Enclosure Notation

If something is to be enclosed with the letter, *Enclosure* is typed two spaces below the typist's initials (or below the writer's name or title if there are no typist's initials). The name of the item enclosed may also be stated. Spelling out *Enclosure* is preferable to abbreviating it.

Copy Notation

A notation is used when a copy of a letter is to be sent to someone in addition to the person to whom the letter is addressed. The *c* may be followed by a colon. Do **not** use the notation when just a file copy is being made.

c Mr. Bill Speers   c: Mr. Bill Speers

The following notation means *blind copy:* the letter writer doesn't want the person receiving the original to know a copy has been sent to someone else. Therefore, type *bc* only on the copy going to Mr. Nguyen and on the file copy, not on the original letter.

bc Mr. Tom Nguyen   bc: Mr. Tom Nguyen

A *c* or *bc* notation, if needed, is the last information on the page, unless there's a postscript.

Postscript

When a postscript is used, it is the final item typed on the letter. The letters *P.S.* or *PS* are correct, but not required, before the message. Postscripts often appear in sales letters for emphasis. Avoid them in most other letters, however, as they give the impression of inadequate planning.

Spacing and arranging of letters are explained briefly in Unit 83. For further details about letter parts, spacing, and arranging of business letters, see the latest edition of an office reference manual.

Replay Unit

82

A. Write *T* (true) or *F* (false) in each blank.

_____ 1. Whenever a copy of a letter is made, type a copy notation.

_____ 2. The typist's initials should be typed in capital letters preferably.

_____ 3. Be sure to use a courtesy title before the letter writer's name.

_____ 4. The *bc* notation should not appear on the original letter.

_____ 5. A correct way to type the date in a business letter is 6/2/95.

_____ 6. The letters *PS* (or *P.S.*) are not required before a message that appears below the initials.

_____ 7. The preferred place for the subject line is between the salutation and the body of the letter.

_____ 8. The company name is not required as part of the signature block.

_____ 9. If the first line of the inside address is an organization name, an Attention line may be used.

_____ 10. If the first line of the inside address is "Mr. Peter Settle," an appropriate salutation would be "Gentlemen."

B. Fill in the blanks below the letter with the names of the parts.

1. _____   6. _____

2. _____   7. _____

3. _____   8. _____

4. _____   9. _____

5. _____   10. _____

Check answers in Appendix H.

1. **KmS** FINANCIAL SERVICES, INC.

    1125 DENNY BUILDING/SEATTLE, WASHINGTON 98121-1866 / Seattle (206) 441-2885

2. May 3, 19__

3. Mr. and Mrs. Sean McDonald
    8051 Corliss Avenue N.
    Seattle, WA 98103

4. Dear Mr. and Mrs. McDonald:

5. Here's the information on Calvert's Social Investment Fund that
    you requested. The enclosed materials describe four Calvert
    Social Investment Funds:

    Managed Growth (balanced fund)
    Bonds (income)
    Equity (growth stocks)
    Money Market (liquid or shorter term fund)

    Before you invest, please review the enclosed prospectus, bro-
    chure, and performance literature.

    I think you'll be pleased with your Calvert investments.
    Calvert also offers an excellent IRA arrangement for your tax
    benefit. These same investments are used by many large retire-
    ment plans and other serious investors. Many investors also use
    the Calvert "Moneyvest" savings plan for convenient periodic
    investment.

    Mr. and Mrs. McDonald, when you wish information on how to get
    started or are interested in the many other socially responsible
    investment opportunities, please call me at 206-441-2885,
    Extension 219.

6. Sincerely,

7. Eric Andrew Smith
    Socially Responsible Investing

8. lr

9. Enclosures

10. c Ms. Heidi Perreault

Read Unit

83

THE ARRANGEMENT

In this Read Unit you'll learn about letter format by reading letters arranged in the format being described. Study both aspects—the information and the arrangement.

READ THIS LETTER DESCRIBING:

- Full block style
- Open and standard punctuation

NOTICE:

- Subject line
- Postscript

MODERN BUSINESS LETTERS, INC.
Street Address
City, State ZIP

June 1, 19__

Mr. Billy Crystal
711 Wilshire Boulevard
Hollywood, CA 90210

Dear Billy,

THE FULL BLOCK LETTER STYLE

You reviewed the parts of business letters in Unit 82 of your
ENGLISH FOR CAREERS textbook, and you studied a well-arranged
letter in the Replay. Please refer to Units 7, 14, and 76 to see
other well-arranged letters.

Two types of arrangements, or styles, are used most often: the full
block style and the modified block style. This letter is arranged
in the full block style.

A clean, contemporary appearance results from beginning all lines
at the left margin. Some reasons for selecting this style are:

1. It's faster to type.

2. The modern looking style tends to carry over to the
    psychological image of the company and its products or
    services.

3. It might look better with the design of the letterhead.

Choose either open or standard (also called *mixed*) punctuation
This letter has the standard style, which means a colon or comma
after the salutation* and a comma after the complimentary close.
Perhaps you'll decide on the block letter style when replying to
your fans.

Best wishes,

Leila R. Smith

PS Regards to Janice, Jennie, and Lindsay.

READ THIS LETTER AND REVIEW:
- Modified block letter style
- Open punctuation

NOTICE:
- Subject line
- Typist's initials
- Copy notation

COMMUNICATIONS CONSULTANTS
315 Stevens Hall
Oreno, ME 04469

                                        March 19, 19___

President Keshia Mary Washington
The White House
Washington, DC 20500

Dear Madam President

Subject: Modified Block Style

In the modified block style letter, the date and closing begin at
the center of the page.

The first word of each paragraph may begin at the left margin as
in this letter, or it may be indented five to ten spaces.
Blocked paragraphs are now more popular than indented.

Reasons for using this style include:

        It is more traditional looking.

        As a more conservative, traditional style, it may
        be appropriate to the image the company desires
        for its products and services.

        It creates a more balanced appearance.

As shown above, listed items may be double indented; that is,
indented five spaces from the left and from the right.

This letter, Madam President, is written with the open style of
punctuation, which means your secretaries won't use a colon or a
comma after the salutation nor a comma after the complimentary
close. Standard punctuation, however, would be equally correct.

I hope these instructions will help when you answer the many
letters you receive from the people of America.

                        Respectfully,

                        Leila R. Smith

ec

c: Secretary of State Sasha Gross

READ THIS LETTER DESCRIBING:

- Simplified letter style

NOTICE THAT THE SIMPLIFIED LETTER STYLE:

- Omits the salutation
- Omits the complimentary close

January 3, 19__

Mr. Eric A. Smith
Investment Planner
Queen Anne Square, Suite 102
200 West Mercer Street
Seattle, WA 98119

SIMPLIFIED LETTER STYLE

The full block and the modified block letters are the most frequently seen arrangements. The simplified letter was developed
by members of the American Management Society to improve business
letters.

The AMS said that salutations and complimentary closes do not
contribute to the effectiveness of a letter, are meaningless, and
should be omitted. They chose the full block style because it
saves time for the typist, as does the omission of the complimentary close and the salutation.

Other characteristics of the simplified letter are the use of a
subject, which is a triple space below the inside address. Notice that the subject and the writer's name and title at the end
of the letter are in all capital letters. The writer's name and
title are placed about five spaces below the last line of the
body.

Although this letter style was developed a number of years ago,
most businesses were not ready for so drastic a change. Now,
however, the simplified style provides an appropriate solution to
the "Gentlemen" or "Ladies and Gentlemen" issue.

The simplified style is also used to address an individual. In
that case, the person's name is included in the first sentence of
the letter; for example, "Thank you, Mr. Nielson, for visiting
our showroom yesterday." This technique personalizes the letter
even more than a conventional salutation.

I would be happy to answer your questions about business letter
arrangement in exchange for hot tips on the market.

G. FRANCES CATES, PROFESSOR OF OFFICE ADMINISTRATION

kco

READ THIS LETTER DESCRIBING:

■ Personal business letter style

NOTICE:

■ First line is writer's address

■ Writer's name at end only

■ Standard (mixed) punctuation; open punctuation is also appropriate

■ Modified block style format; full block is also appropriate

---

30 Christanna Street
Alberta, VA 23921
January 4, 19___

Ms. Hazel Flora
General Manager
Designing Women
203 Lamar Street
Beaumont, Texas 77710

Dear Ms. Flora:

It's a pleasure, Ms. Flora, to provide you with information about
the personal business style letter.

Use this style with confidence when corresponding about your
personal business, such as your insurance, credit, job applications, charitable functions, and comments to government officials.

Because you use plain paper with no letterhead, start with your
street address, followed by city, state, and ZIP. Next type the
date. The rest of the letter is the same as any other business
letter. Type your name below the complimentary close, allowing
three or four spaces for your signature. Sign your name with a
pen, never a pencil. Do not use identification initials.

I expect to be in Beaumont next month and look forward to
visiting you in your new showroom.

Sincerely yours,

David Shade

Placement of Letter Parts for Block and Modified Block Styles

Whether to use block, modified block, or simplified depends on your preference or your employer's. Regardless of the style selected, be sure to center the letter attractively on the page.*

Here's a method that results in a well-centered letter:

1. Estimate the length of the letter to determine left and right margins.

    Short letter (under 100 words) . . . 50-space line.
    Medium letter (100 to 200 words) . . . 60-space line.
    Long letter (200 or more words) . . . 70-space line.

2. Type date 2 or 3 spaces below the bottom of the letterhead.

3. Begin inside address 4 to 10 lines below date; the number of blank lines after date depends on the length of letter.

4. Double space between all other parts of letter, except before the writer's name, where 3 blank lines are left for the handwritten signature. Single space the body of the letter, but double space between paragraphs. (The arrangement of the simplified letter differs, as shown on page 382.)

5. As you approach the end of the letter, if it doesn't look well centered, cheat! Here are the cheating rules: (a) allow up to 5 or as few as 2 blank lines before the typed signature, (b) allow one more or fewer blank lines before initials and other closing details.

Interoffice Memorandums

Memos are usually typed on special forms that include the organization's name at the top and spaces for inserting the receiver's name, the sender's name, and the subject of the memo. Begin the message a triple space below the heading. Do not use a complimentary close.

Read the memo on page 385 and study the format.

Placement of Envelope Parts

Begin to type the address on a small envelope about 2 inches from the top (the 12th line down) and about $2\frac{1}{2}$ inches from the left edge. On a large envelope start typing on the 13th or 14th line and about $4\frac{1}{2}$ inches from the left.

The Postal Service prefers that envelope addresses be typed in all capital letters without punctuation. This style allows for computerized reading of the address at the Post Office and speeds delivery of high-volume mailings.

Many businesses, however, still prefer that envelopes for ordinary correspondence be typed to match the style of the inside address: upper and lower case letters as well as needed punctuation. This traditional style can be read by the Postal Service OCR (optical character recognition) computer if addresses are keyboarded on a standard typewriter or word processing

---

* A few employers require the same placement for all letters and do not want centering techniques used.

```
                         VALLEY COLLEGE
                      INTEROFFICE MEMORANDUM


TO:    Coach Musselman          DATE:  April 1, 19__

FROM:  Ben Wisenheimer          SUBJECT:  Every Coin Has Two
Sides

       English Department
```

Remembering our discussions of your football players who were having troubles in English, I have decided to ask you, in turn, for help.

We feel that Paul Barebones, one of our most promising scholars, has a chance for a Rhodes Scholarship, which would be a great thing for him and for our school. Paul has the academic record for this award, but we find that the aspirant is also required to have other excellences and, ideally, should have a good record in athletics. But he does try hard.

We propose that you give some special consideration to Paul as a varsity player, putting him if possible in the backfield of the football team. In this way, we can show a better school record to the committee deciding on the Rhodes Scholarships. We realize that Paul will be a problem on the field; but as you have often said, cooperation between our department and yours is highly desirable. Of course, we do expect Paul to try hard. During intervals of study, we shall coach him as much as we can.

His work in the English club and on the debate team will force him to miss many practices, but we intend to see that he carries an old football around to handle (or whatever one does with a football) during intervals in his work.

We expect Paul to show entire good will in his work for you, and though he will not be able to begin football practice until late in the season, he will finish the season with good attendance.

software (six lines to an inch), rather than on special addressing plates and equipment.

When possible, use a courtesy title before the name (Dr., Mr., Ms., Captain, etc.). Special notations such as PERSONAL or ATTENTION DR. BRAD ROSENBERG are typed 2 or 3 spaces below the return address or on the line just below the organization name in the outside address. Mailing instructions such as Special Delivery are typed or rubber stamped below the postage location—about $1\frac{1}{2}$ inches from the top edge.

ERIC A. SMITH, INVESTMENT PLANNER
Queen Anne Square, Suite 102
200 West Mercer Street
Seattle, WA 98119

ATTENTION MS. JUDITH BLACKMAN   SPECIAL DELIVERY

Time International
5 Ottho Heldringstraat
1066 AZ Amsterdam
THE NETHERLANDS

BAY PATH JUNIOR COLLEGE
Longmeadow, Massachusetts 01106

Mr. Albert Encinas
Valley Memorial Hospital
1801 Panorama Drive
Bakersfield, CA 93305

Notice in the illustrations that the addresses are single-spaced. Never punctuate between the state and the ZIP, and always keep the ZIP on the same line with the state. (Use 9-digit ZIP codes when you know them.) The city may be on a line by itself if necessary.

These envelopes illustrate the style preferred for general business correspondence. For information on other styles of preparing envelopes, see a reference manual of office procedures.

Replay Unit

83

Write *T* (true) or *F* (false) in each blank.

_____ **1.** In the modified block style, all lines begin at the left margin.

_____ **2.** Paragraphs may be indented when a letter is in the full block style.

_____ **3.** For open style punctuation, use a semicolon after the salutation.

_____ **4.** The ZIP code should be typed on a line by itself on the envelope if there isn't enough room after the state.

_____ **5.** A triple space is used between the subject line and the body of a modified block letter.

_____ **6.** The body of a business letter should nearly always be double spaced.

_____ **7.** It's all right to vary slightly the spacing between certain parts at the bottom of the letters.

_____ 8. Always leave six blank lines between the date and the inside address.

_____ 9. A long letter should be typed on a 70-space line.

_____ 10. When an attention line is used, it should be typed in the upper right corner of the envelope.

_____ 11. The most frequently seen business letter styles are full block and modified block.

_____ 12. The only difference between open punctuation and standard is that a comma is placed after the complimentary close in the standard style.

_____ 13. In the modified block style, the date may be typed to the right of the center of the page.

_____ 14. The full block style is more modern looking than the modified block.

_____ 15. In a personal business letter, the writer's name and address should be typed above the date.

_____ 16. In the simplified letter style, both the salutation and the complimentary close are omitted.

_____ 17. The simplified style should not be used when addressing a letter to an individual.

_____ 18. When typing the simplified letter style, triple space after the subject before beginning the body.

_____ 19. The writer's name and title should be in all capital letters in the simplified letter.

_____ 20. When typing the mailing address on a large envelope, begin about $2\frac{1}{2}$ inches from the left edge.

See Appendix H for answers.

Read Unit 84

SOUNDING GOOD

The Message
Use an Informal Tone

Write the message in a friendly, conversational tone. Today's good business writers use shirt-sleeve English rather than stuffed-shirt English. Here are two versions of a letter that show what I mean.

This one belongs in an antique collection:

Dear Sir:

Enclosing your policy and trust same is in order. If I can be of any service along the insurance line, kindly advise me. With appreciation, for your patronage, we remain,

　　　　　　　Respectfully yours,

Writing for Your Career

Untrained business writers think a formal tone sounds successful and educated, but they end up sounding pompous and insecure.

Here's a modern version of the same note:

Dear Mr. Marvin:

Your new policy is enclosed. Whenever I can be of help to you, please let me know.

Sincerely,

The grammar, punctuation, spelling, and sentence construction of your letters should be Standard English. But that's not enough. In addition, make the reader feel that a warm human being wrote the letter, not an impersonal corporation or a computer. Don't select words because they sound "businesslike" or because they have many syllables and sound impressive. Instead, select words that contribute most effectively to delivering your message and to building a good relationship between you (or your company) and the reader.

STUFFED-SHIRT ENGLISH

This company sincerely regrets any inconvenience caused you by our inadvertently miscalculating the extensions on our invoice to you.

This letter is to advise you that the dozen gold birthday charms you ordered are out of stock. We, therefore, cannot ship same to you until next month.

SHIRT-SLEEVE ENGLISH

We're sorry about the error on our Invoice No. 2482.

Thank you for your order for one dozen gold birthday charms. Because this charm sells fast at many fine shops like yours, we're temporarily out of them. We will be pleased, however, to send them to you the first week in March.

Recap   Which is the better sentence for business correspondence? Circle (a) or (b) for each pair.

1. (a) I am writing to inform you that I have received the book you sent me, and I sincerely appreciate your kindness.
   (b) Thank you for the book.

2. (a) In accordance with your request, we are herewith enclosing the price list.
   (b) Enclosed is the price list you requested.

Check your answers in Appendix H.

Emphasize Positive Ideas

Try to write about what you and your company **can do** instead of what you **can't do**. People respond better to positive ideas. Even if you have something negative to write about, you can usually find a positive way to express it.

NEGATIVE	POSITIVE
We cannot conduct this seminar with fewer than ten students.	We'll conduct this seminar with ten or more students.
We're sorry we can't extend more than $3,000 credit to you.	You can charge up to $3,000 worth of widgets and whatnots.

Recap   Using a positive tone, rewrite these negatively expressed sentences.

1. We hope you will not be disappointed.

   _____

2. We are not open after 8 p.m. during the week or on weekends after five.

   _____

   _____

Check your answers in Appendix H.

Say It Once

Although it can be effective occasionally to repeat an idea for emphasis, for most business communication, express a concept just once. Needless repetition of an expression using a slightly different word or words is called being *redundant*.

Word to the Wise

Success comes in cans.

REDUNDANCIES	**SAYING IT ONCE**
It is absolutely essential that each and every widget be round in shape.	It is essential that each widget be round.
The consensus of opinion is that although the whatsit is only 4 feet long in size, we can see it at a distance of 50 feet.	The consensus is that although the whatsit is only 5 feet long, we can see it from 50 feet.

Recap   Rewrite these sentences by eliminating the redundancies.

1. First and foremost you should pack the basic essentials.

   _____

2. Final completion of the research investigation study revealed and showed that the UFO is small in size, triangular in shape, and purple in color.

   _____

   _____

Check your answers in Appendix H.

Salutation

The choice of salutation (and complimentary close) is part of the business writing trend toward less formality and more friendliness.

The ultraformal *Dear Sirs* or *Dear Sir* is rarely used by knowledgeable writers. If the first line of the inside address is a company name, the preferred salutation is *Ladies and Gentlemen* or *Gentlemen and Ladies*. Never write *Dear* before *Gentlemen* or *Ladies and Gentlemen.*

> Alondra Electronics
> 2030 Bay Shore Drive
> Durham, North Carolina 27701
>
> Ladies and Gentlemen:

If an Attention line is included, the salutation is still *Ladies and Gentlemen* because the salutation is based on the first line of the inside address (as explained in Unit 78). Never use an attention line with the personal salutation.

ATTENTION MR RICHARD BARNHART

NO   Dear Mr. Barnhart:

YES   Ladies and Gentlemen:

Rather than an Attention line, however, address the individual in the first line of the inside address. Precede the name with a courtesy title and repeat the name in the salutation:

Mr. Richard Barnhart
Alondra Electronics
2030 Bay Shore Drive
Durham, North Carolina 27701

Dear Mr. Barnhart:

Here are examples of addresses and salutations when you can't obtain a person's name.

Human Resources Department   Training Director
Citibank Inc.   Trimfit Company
400 South Primrose   2415 K Street
Englewood Cliffs, NJ 07632   New Paltz, NY 12561

Gentlemen and Ladies   Dear Training Director

Complimentary Closes

The most popular complimentary closes are those using *Sincerely: Sincerely yours, Yours sincerely,* or *Sincerely. Cordially* closings—*Cordially yours, Yours cordially,* or *Cordially* also create a friendly tone. The least formal closings are expressions like Regards, Best wishes, Thanks again, or Happy new year. Do use this kind of closing whenever it seems appropriate.

For a formal letter, a *truly* closing is suitable: *Very truly yours, Yours very truly,* or *Yours truly.* The *Respectfully* closings are not suitable for ordinary business correspondence. *Respectfully* may close a letter to a high-ranking government official or religious leader or someone whom you wish to give an unusual degree of deference. Capitalize only the first word of the complimentary close.

Paragraphs

Paragraphing in a business letter is based on judgment. Since many well-written business letters are about one subject only, a new paragraph begins whenever the writer wants a longer pause than occurs after just a period. The opening and closing paragraphs are often the shortest in the letter. One-sentence opening and closing paragraphs are not unusual. A brief, meaningful opening tells the reader what the letter is about or, when possible, gives the reader some good news:

> **First Paragraph:** The two dozen gold birthday charms requested in your February 3 order will be on their way to you tomorrow.
>
> **Middle of Letter:** One or two longer paragraphs might follow providing information the customer requested about a related product.
>
> **Last Paragraph:** If you want us to send the silver charms next month, just complete and return the enclosed order blank.

You can develop confidence in your ability to paragraph by reviewing the paragraphing of the sample letters in this book. There is no "right" or "wrong" to paragraphing business letters, only good or poor judgment. Avoid the "chopped-up" look of too many short paragraphs one right after the other. Long paragraphs (more than nine lines) look difficult to read and discourage the busy person from concentrating on the letter. Use the preceding hints plus your common sense to vary the length of paragraphs in a sensible way.

Replay Unit
84

Write *T* (true) or *F* (false) in each blank.

_____ 1. The use of long words is effective in business writing so that your reader will think you're well educated.

_____ 2. Stuffed-shirt English means that the sentences are too long.

_____ 3. Shirt-sleeve English means writing that appeals to the "working class" because it includes commonly made grammar errors.

_____ 4. *Very truly yours* is probably the most popular business letter closing in use today.

_____ 5. When writing a business letter to a customer you had lunch with last week, *Respectfully* would be the preferred closing.

_____ 6. If the line *Attention Ms. Doris Eames* is used, the salutation should be *Dear Ms. Eames.*

_____ 7. When the first line of the inside address is the name of a man, the preferred salutation is *Dear Sir.*

_____ 8. Good letter writers follow specific rules for paragraphing.

_____ 9. The last paragraph in a letter should usually be the longest.

_____ 10. The appearance of a letter can be improved by having all the paragraphs approximately the same length.

_____ 11. The following is written in stuffed-shirt English: We wish to inform you that we can forward to you gold and silver charms next week if you will advise us as to the quantity you desire us to ship.

_____ 12. The following is written in shirt-sleeve English: Both gold and silver charms will be available next week. How many of each would you like?

_____ 13. Using a series of very short paragraphs will result in a friendly-looking, attractive letter.

_____ 14. When the first line of the inside address is the name of a company, use *Dear Sirs* as the salutation.

_____ 15. The following is a positive expression: About half the flowers in my garden have died.

_____ 16. The following sentence has a redundant expression: Measure the width of the four-sided square.

_____ 17. The following is a positive expression: We believe you won't have any trouble with our newly designed widgets.

_____ 18. The following is a positive expression: About half the flowers in my garden are still blooming.

_____ 19. This is typical of a good sentence to end a business letter: Please do not hesitate to contact us whenever we may be of further service to you in the future.

_____ **20.** This is typical of a good sentence to end a business letter: Please call or write if you have any questions.

Answers—Appendix H.
CONGRATULATIONS! You have finished the last Replay.
Now take **POP QUIZ** in Appendix A.

Checkpoint

This course provided a review of English usage important to people in business, professional, and technical careers. Applying what you studied occurs almost every time you speak and write, usually without your being aware of it. Section Fourteen deals with the most common written application of English for careers, the business letter. The art of writing good business letters requires:

- Knowledge of business procedures
- Understanding of human behavior
- Mastery of English fundamentals
- A good vocabulary
- Knowledge of letter parts and arrangement

In a letter and report writing class, you learn to transform the preceding five ingredients into letters that get and keep business for your company and result in promotions for you. You should now, however, be confident of your ability to compose and set up simple or routine business letters in a satisfactory manner.

Place a check next to each item when you are sure of what it is and where it belongs in a letter.

_____ Return address on personal business letter or letterhead on business stationery

_____ Date

_____ Inside address

_____ Attention line (optional—but not recommended)

_____ Salutation (omitted in simplified style)

_____ Subject line (optional but required in simplified style)

_____ Body

_____ Complimentary close (omitted in simplified style)

_____ Company name (optional)

_____ Handwritten signature

_____ Typed name of writer and title

_____ Typist's initials (not used when the same person composes and types the letter)

_____ Copy notation

_____ Blind copy notation

_____ Enclosure notation

_____ Postscript

The two most popular styles of arranging business letters are full block and modified block. Open and standard (also called "mixed") are the two most used punctuation styles. Effective business correspondents use a conversational and informal style, express themselves positively, and avoid redundancies. A warm tone is also applied to choice of salutation and complimentary close. The length of paragraphs in business letters should vary. It is desirable to use some very short paragraphs (particularly at beginning and end) and to consciously avoid very long paragraphs.

If the letter is to be centered attractively on the page, determine margins based on the length of the letter.

For correct word-division, capitalization, abbreviation, and number-writing styles, refer to Appendix F when you're writing business letters.

Special Assignment

On April 20 you ordered a pen-and-pencil set from the Sunrise Mail Order Catalog. You sent a check for $30 ($28.50 plus $1.50 for mailing) along with the order form. It is now May 25 and you still haven't received the merchandise, which is described in the catalog as No. 777 Chrome Plated Pen and Pencil Set. Type a letter and envelope to send to Sunrise Mail Order Company, 711 Lucky Street, Las Vegas, Nevada 40232. Sign, fold, and insert the letter into the envelope.

Submit the letter _____. (date)

Proofreading for Careers

Please proofread and redo this letter from a store called The Women's Corner. Check everything from the first line of the letterhead to the last typed line.

Dear Student: I hope you've found the proofreading practice in each section to be a challenge and a bit of fun. You would, of course, be unlikely to find so many errors in a real-life letter, or would you?! Please remember: Before submitting anything in writing to an instructor, a colleague, a client, or?— Proofread, **Proofread**, **PROOFREAD**. If possible put the letter or report away for an hour or a day. Then reread it with a fresh eye.

LRS

THE WOMENS' CORNER
406 INDIAN WELL STREET
LAS CRUCES, NM 88001
(505) 373-5711

January 12, 19__

Joy D. Schuhmann
International Business Coll.
Las Cruces, New Mex. 88001

ATTENTION Ms. Joy D. Schuhmann

Dear Ms. Schuhmann:

Effective 3/1/9_, the Womens' Corner will have new owners. They
have asked us to reduce drasticly the size of our inventory
before they take over on March, the first.

Your normal charge priveledges will continue; making it easy for
you take advantage of our closing sale. Starting now, every
peice of fashion marchandise in the store is on sail!

We take this opportunity to express our most warmest thanks
and appreciation, for all your passed business. It has been our
pleasure to serve you, and we hop that this has been a mutualy
satisfactory relationship.

All our regular personal will be on hand to assist you during this
sale, which starts January 15th. We will be open 7 days a
week from 9 AM to 9 pm., come early for the best selections.

Respectfully,

The Women's Corner

Mrs. Leila R. Smith

Practice Quiz

Write *T* (true) or *F* (false) next to each sentence.

_____ 1. The average business letter costs about $5. **(Introduction)**

_____ 2. Completion of Section Fourteen means you should be an expert business **(Unit 84)**
letter writer.

_____ 3. The principal advantage of writing letters rather than telephoning is **(Introduction)**
that letters are less expensive than long-distance calls.

_____ 4. Most business letters are typed on 8½ by 11 paper. **(Unit 81)**

_____ 5. It's a good idea to use a sheet of your employer's letterhead stationery to **(Unit 81)**
write to your own insurance company about an automobile accident.

_____ 6. Since the writer's typewritten name should appear at the end of a business **(Unit 82)**
letter, a handwritten signature is unnecessary.

_____ 7. Before inserting a letter in a large business envelope, fold in thirds starting **(Unit 81)**
from the bottom.

_____ 8. When you write a personal business letter, your name should not appear **(Unit 83)**
above your address on the letter.

_____ 9. Smaller-than-usual size letterhead paper is used only by companies that **(Unit 81)**
want to save money on stationery.

_____ 10. Whenever you make a copy of a letter, type the letter *c* below the initials. **(Unit 82)**

_____ 11. In business letters and reports, spell out all numbers up to 100. **(Unit 84)**

_____ 12. The best place for a subject line in a block or modified block letter is a **(Unit 82)**
double space below the salutation.

_____ 13. *September 25th, 1993* is one of the acceptable styles for writing the date in **(Unit 82)**
a business letter.

_____ 14. The modified block style of arranging a letter is more conservative than the **(Unit 83)**
full block style.

_____ 15. If the letter includes the line ATTENTION MS. RODRIQUEZ, the salutation **(Unit 82)**
could correctly be *Ladies and Gentlemen*.

_____ 16. Let's meet at 4 p.m in the afternoon. is an example of redundancy. **(Unit 84)**

_____ 17. A comma is correct between the state and the ZIP code. **(Unit 82)**

_____ 18. If the first line of the inside address is the name of a company, *Ladies and* **(Unit 84)**
Gentlemen is an appropriate salutation.

_____ 19. Trained business writers use a more formal style for letter writing than was **(Unit 84)**
used in the past.

_____ 20. *Very truly yours* is one of the friendlier sounding, less formal **(Unit 84)**
complimentary closes.

_____ 21. The simplified letter always has a subject line. **(Unit 83)**

_____ 22. The writer's name and title are typed in all capital letters in a simplified **(Unit 83)**
letter.

_____ **23.** Whenever possible use a courtesy title in the signature of a business letter.   **(Unit 82)**

_____ **24.** A 50-space line is appropriate for typing a short letter.   **(Unit 83)**

_____ **25.** Whenever possible use a courtesy title in business letters before the name of the addressee.   **(Units 82 & 84)**

The Final Rehearsal, Appendix E, provides you with a review of *English for Careers.*

Appendices

Pop Quizzes

Unit Nos.	Page	No. Right	Out of
1–3	400	_____	25
4–6	402	_____	25
8–10	404	_____	25
11–13	405	_____	13
15–18	406	_____	15
19–21	407	_____	30
22–24	408	_____	20
25–27	409	_____	25
28–30	410	_____	25
31–33	411	_____	25
34–38	412	_____	25
39–42	413	_____	25
39–45	414	_____	25
46–47	415	_____	25
49–52	416	_____	25
53–57	417	_____	25
58–61	418	_____	25
62–64	419	_____	25
65–66	420	_____	15
65–67	421	_____	20
65–68	422	_____	15
65–69	423	_____	20
70–74	424	_____	30
76–78	425	_____	20
79–80	426	_____	12
81–84	428	_____	10

Pop Quiz for Units 1-3 (Section One)

Please insert nouns in the blanks.

1. The _____ types all the _____.
2. In _____ the _____ is two feet deep.
3. _____ wants a new _____.
4. _____ is the best _____.
5. Our _____ is closed on _____.

Please insert verbs in the blanks.

6. She _____ all the way to the office.
7. He _____ the letter and _____ it.
8. Dorothy Dietz _____ chairman of the Board of Directors until last year.
9. The students at Diablo Valley College _____ the colorful garden.
10. The Internal Revenue Service _____ our tax return.

Please insert pronouns in the blanks.

11. The clerks _____ can do word processing earn high salaries.
12. Thank _____ for writing to _____ about the problem _____ have with _____ copier.
13. _____ wrote to _____ about _____.
14. When _____ goes wrong with _____, what will _____ do?
15. Give _____ to _____ will take _____.

Please insert adjectives in the blanks.

16. Our _____ copier makes life easy for _____ operator.
17. Please reserve _____ rooms for our _____ members.
18. Vince Martin presented an _____ plan for teaching our _____ courses.
19. The _____ chairs and the _____ desks will be used in Carolyn Wardell's _____ office.
20. Alvarez and Shay read a _____ report to _____ participants.

Convert these nouns to adjectives:

21. help _____ **22.** incident _____ **23.** beauty _____

24. wonder _____ **25.** occasion _____

Name: _____ **Date:** _____

Pop Quiz for Units 4–6 (Section One)

Please insert prepositions in the blanks and then place parentheses around the prepositional phrases in each sentence.

1. The book is _____ the desk _____ the water cooler.

2. New carpeting is needed _____ our office and _____ the lobby.

3. _____ exactly 5 p.m. the mail was delivered _____ Joyce Tarr _____ Pleasant Hill.

4. Everyone _____ him walked _____ the corner.

5. He looks _____ his brother _____ head _____ toe.

Insert conjunctions in the blanks.

6. More _____ more firms realize the advantage of microfilm.

7. He could qualify for a good job _____ he knew shorthand.

8. _____ he knows shorthand, he can qualify for a good job.

9. You may apply for a job as either an administrative secretary _____ as an executive secretary.

10. Career paths sometimes become limited _____ supervisory positions may not exist.

Convert these adjectives to adverbs. Use the dictionary when in doubt about spelling.

ADJECTIVE	ADVERB	ADJECTIVE	ADVERB
11. happy	_____	14. true	_____
12. loud	_____	15. busy	_____
13. accidental	_____		

Insert adverbs that do not end in *ly*.

16. Linda Diamond _____ works efficiently.

17. It costs _____.

18. Barbara Riva does _____ need a stapler for her birthday.

19. Launa Huddleston dresses _____.

20. Jane Scott is _____ good at inventory control.

What part of speech is the underlined word?

21. Shopping is his favorite activity when he's on vacation. _____

22. Lou Phillips, however, prefers swimming. _____

402

23. They provided the child with <u>swimming</u> lessons. _____

24. Joan Teufel <u>is shopping</u> for software. _____

25. They must raise the money <u>before</u> they hire an architect. _____

Name: _____ **Date:** _____

Pop Quiz for Units 8–10 (Section Two)

_____ 1. To be a sentence, a group of words requires (a) identity (b) action (c) independence (d) none of these (e) a, b, and c

_____ 2. The identity requirement of a sentence means that every sentence must have (a) a subject (b) a verb (c) independence (d) a, b, and c

_____ 3. The action requirement of a sentence means that every sentence must have (a) a subject (b) a verb (c) independence (d) none of these

Write *T* for true or *F* for false.

_____ 4. *If, because, since, when, although* and *as* are examples of words that make a clause dependent.

_____ 5. An independent clause cannot stand alone as a complete sentence.

_____ 6. If a dependent clause is joined to an independent one, the result may be a complete and correct sentence.

_____ 7. A prepositional phrase contains a subject and a verb.

_____ 8. A fragment might be an independent word group, or clause.

_____ 9. The verb tells what the subject does or is or has.

_____ 10. If a word group has a subject and a verb, it is always independent.

Write *F* for fragment or *S* for complete sentence.

_____ 11. Among the interests during the Civil War period.

_____ 12. As soon as the students arrived and the parents and faculty had gone.

_____ 13. Since the establishment of this plan.

_____ 14. The architect was seated at her desk.

_____ 15. More than any other single segment of society.

_____ 16. Industry holds the answers to these questions.

_____ 17. Devouring his lunch in a piglike fashion.

_____ 18. In a research study funded by the U. S. Office of Education.

_____ 19. We are all required to attend the training program.

_____ 20. Norma Baker, while viewing the slides on the large new screen in the San Diego facility.

_____ 21. The workers, having been on strike for more than three months.

_____ 22. Photography, now popular as an art as well as a hobby.

_____ 23. Please show Mr. Vergara where the computer is, and then introduce him to the clerks.

_____ 24. Ms. Lafitte was seated at her desk.

_____ 25. The lecture began after Ward Macauley arrived.

Name: _____ **Date:** _____

A. In the blank write **a** for complete sentence, **b** for fragment, **c** for run-on, or **d** for comma splice.

_____ 1. He's the purchasing manager she is the assistant manager.

_____ 2. He's the purchasing manager, she is the assistant manager.

_____ 3. He's the purchasing manager, but she is the assistant manager.

_____ 4. Although he's the purchasing manager, she is the assistant manager.

_____ 5. Even though she is the assistant manager.

B. In the following paragraph, eliminate the comma splices by replacing the incorrectly used commas with periods. If a comma doesn't create a comma splice, leave it alone. Capitalize the first word of new sentences.

To help concentration, take frequent breaks, take breaks before you get tired, do desk work for no more than 30 minutes at a time, then take a mini holiday of one to two minutes, use that time for some physical activity such as walking into several rooms and looking out the windows, juggling two or more balls, running up a flight of steps, or organizing items on a high shelf, using these short breaks to snack, however, is not advisable.

C. Write four comma splices about yourself or members of your family. For example: I attended Theodore Roosevelt High School in the Bronx, my husband went to DeWitt Clinton High School.

6. _____

_____

7. _____

_____

8. _____

_____

9. _____

_____

In Units 11–13, you practiced four methods of correcting a comma splice. One way is to **separate** the independent parts as explained in Read Unit 11. Two ways of **joining** the independent parts are explained in Read Unit 12, and one more joining method is presented in Read Unit 13. Please correct one of the comma splices you wrote above. Use at least three of the four different correction methods.

10. _____

_____

11. _____

_____

12. _____

_____

13. _____

_____

Name: _____ Date: _____

Pop Quiz for Units 15–18 (Section Three)

Use your dictionary.

1. What is a synonym for the word *responsible?* _____

2. Show the pronunciation for the city of *Vallejo.* _____

3. What does it mean if a word doesn't have a usage label? _____

_____

_____

4. What is the etymology of the word *shrewd?* _____

5. *Abstract* is used as what parts of speech? _____

6. What does the abbreviation ILGWU mean? _____

_____

7. Show the pronunciation given for *faux pas.* _____

8. Is there a usage label in your dictionary for the meaning of the underlined word? If so, what is it? How is the word defined?

    The play <u>bombed</u> in New Haven.
    verb

_____

_____

9. Referring to your dictionary, divide these words into syllables by drawing a diagonal (/) at the end of each syllable:

    w o r k e d   b e e t l e   g e t t i n g   f u l l n e s s   c o n t a g i o n

10. The treasurer dis_____rsed (*pe* or *bu?*) all the funds before declaring bankruptcy.

True or False

_____ 11. *It's* and *its* are both correct forms but have different meanings.

_____ 12. Antonyms are words that mean almost the same.

_____ 13. Beethoven died at age 45.

_____ 14. A pocket dictionary is an example of an unabridged dictionary.

_____ 15. Dante was a British playwright.

Name: _____ **Date:** _____

406

Pop Quiz for Units 19–21 (Section Four)

Spell the plurals of these nouns. Use your dictionary when in doubt.

1. inventory _____
2. testimony _____
3. valley _____
4. motto _____ or _____
5. scarf _____ or _____
6. louse _____ or _____
7. money _____ or _____
8. moose _____
9. loaf _____
10. genius _____ or _____
11. Adams _____
12. Gates _____
13. stepchild _____
14. plaintiff _____
15. bacterium _____
16. trousseau _____ or _____
17. tomato _____
18. academy _____
19. knife _____
20. statistics _____
21. Chinese _____
22. ox _____

Cross out the incorrect words in parentheses.

23. Civics (was/were) the most interesting course in the seventh grade.
24. The news (is/are) good today.
25. Shift on the 9 key to type the left (parentheses/parenthesis).
26. Ms. Strain has to handle several (crisis/crises/criseses) at one time in Riverside.
27. Your clothes (is/are) all over the place.
28. Even though the factory is on strike, the goods (was/were) shipped yesterday.
29. I typed five (memoranda/memorandas/memorandum) this morning.
30. The president of the Society for Psychic Research introduced two new (medias/media/mediums).

Name: _____ **Date:** _____

Pop Quiz for Units 22–24 (Section Four)

Based on your study of Units 22–24, proofread this page and make the needed corrections. Please use your dictionary.

1. We have two applicants for the Accounting job from Miami-Dade Community College.
2. The College is in the south of Florida.
3. The young lady who works for me is studying engineering at night.
4. When the authoress of this book is presiding over a meeting, she prefers to be called the "chairman" rather than the "chairperson."
5. We visited the Empire State building, which is in New York city.
6. We should have a Social committee to plan parties and to buy gifts for special occasions.
7. Last winter we arranged for my brother-in-laws to attend the conference in the Spring.
8. A has been and a name dropper gave the commander in chief a bouquet of forget me nots.
9. A poetess, a lady doctor, and a woman bank president were among the parents who agreed to serve as officers of the PTA.
10. The attorney general took two spoonsful of honey before he began the cross examination.
11. The tour of the west includes visits to the grand canyon and to Yellowstone national park.
12. Sean Chandra has just been elected to the senate and he will soon see his cousin Rachel Rothstein, who is a woman senator.
13. What will you do with the proceed from last year's sales?
14. Copys of all his itinerarys are in the portfolioes.
15. A government order prohibiting trade with a particular country is called a tariff.
16. The king of denmark visited the house of representatives.
17. The allys in this strange coalition drove up and down the allys.
18. The board had a short circuit that resulted in the time clock not working.
19. Any self respecting sharp shooteress would have more self control.
20. A catholic lady kissed the pope's ring, while the man she was with was repairing the run down car.

Name: _____ **Date:** _____

Pop Quiz for Units 25–27 (Section Five)

Please make the necessary corrections. Write *C* next to the three sentences that are already correct.

1. Please tell me when you plan to visit Jack Cassidy and myself in San Francisco.
2. You're application for credit has been rejected.
3. Do you really think he is better informed on the subject than her?
4. You're taking a leave of absence during the busiest time of the year.
5. The supervisor regrets this incident even more than I.
6. Marg Taylor is better qualified than her for the job.
7. No workers are more respected than them.
8. The ream of stationery on the counter is your's.
9. If you prefer hers', you could request an exchange.
10. The new member should be seated between Gladys Horton and I.
11. The engineer requested the help of a draftsman and myself to determine where to set the boundarys.
12. Those blueprints are our's.
13. Him and Ozelle will discuss it at the forum.
14. The owner and me discussed working conditions for the assemblers.
15. Us older employees always try to help the newer workers.
16. You are a better painter than him.
17. After conferring with Henry and they, he left.
18. Us men are out on the field practicing every day.
19. You will hear from either the treasurer or myself within two weeks.
20. Jill and her are the two best soloists.
21. You must remember that our opponents want to win as much as us.
22. Marian married a man who was as critical and intolerant as herself.
23. She herself was the first one to admit it.
24. The coach had a long talk with each of we halfbacks.
25. He asked Shirley Castain and I to change the tire for him.

Name: ———————————————— **Date:** ————————————————

Pop Quiz for Units 28–30 (Section Five)

Make the necessary pronoun corrections. If the pronoun is correct, write *C* in the blank. Don't make a change unless the pronoun is INCORRECT.

_____ 1. Someone left his books on my desk.

_____ 2. We may hire a zone manager whom Burroughs Corporation just discharged.

_____ 3. Whom do you suppose will lead the district in sales this month?

_____ 4. Whom do you think we should select for the job of district manager?

_____ 5. It was probably Mr. Mceachern whom you heard speak in Glendale.

_____ 6. The company filed it's suit last week.

_____ 7. Did he say who he wanted to see?

_____ 8. The program was designed by Jerry Tufteland, whom we all recognize as a superior systems analyst.

_____ 9. We don't know who is to blame.

_____ 10. Mr. McMullen said everyone of the students did well on the accounting test.

_____ 11. Each girl qualified for the secretarial job will receive an application blank, which they will be asked to fill out.

_____ 12. One man after another took his place in line.

_____ 13. Every one of the programmers had his or her own idea on the subject.

_____ 14. We all respect the woman to whom we dedicated this building.

_____ 15. We met Kathleen Young of Moorpark, who had not been in the bank for years.

_____ 16. Every body in this office is being asked to contribute to the fund.

_____ 17. If any customer would like a brochure, they may have one.

_____ 18. The Board of Education moved their offices to Canal Street.

_____ 19. The old company closed their doors yesterday for the last time.

_____ 20. Each employee is to indicate when he wants his vacation.

_____ 21. A student needs to improve their grammar so that he or she can talk and write properly on the job.

_____ 22. Everyone in the new accounting department has their own phone.

_____ 23. The committee finally made their decision.

_____ 24. The best executive is the one whom picks good men to do the job he wants done.

_____ 25. It's a rare person who doesn't get discouraged occasionally.

Name: _____ **Date:** _____

410

In the blank, write the correct form of the verb given in parentheses. Please use your dictionary as necessary. Spelling counts. Some are correct already.

_____ 1. How often has this mistake (occur) in the past year?

_____ 2. The mirror was (break) when it was delivered.

_____ 3. Many elderly people have (benefit) from her work.

_____ 4. Transportation charges on both shipments were (prepay).

_____ 5. Mr. Bautista has been (transfer) to our Seattle office.

_____ 6. Yesterday Sheela Danielle (begin) an in-depth study of the plan.

_____ 7. For two years the business has been (lose) money.

_____ 8. Do you know who (precede) Marcia Karl in this position?

_____ 9. This branch is well (equip) to give good service.

_____ 10. Phenomena of this kind (show) the weakness of our system. (present)

_____ 11. Mr. Bond has (lay)* the matter before the board.

_____ 12. The balance sheet has been (lie)* here for a week.

_____ 13. The weather bureau has (forecast) snow for tomorrow in Milwaukee.

_____ 14. How long do you think this carton has (lie)* here?

_____ 15. Yesterday Uriah (order) more produce for the Miami store.

_____ 16. Our new discount policy (improve) our sales. (past)

_____ 17. All our employees (enjoy) the annual barbecue. (present)

_____ 18. Last week Jesse (refer) to increased sales.

_____ 19. They now (deny) having made any comments regarding the new bonus plan.

_____ 20. The manager is (transfer) most of the new employees to the Anchorage branch.

_____ 21. He is, however, (permit) me to remain in Orlando.

_____ 22. I am not (imply) that you approve of the plan.

_____ 23. The chairman of the book club felt that *How Green Was My Valley* (was) an exciting novel.

_____ 24. Carol Hagel will (defer) shipment of your order until next week.

_____ 25. It (cause) his blood pressure to rise. (present)

* Look up the verbs *lie* and *lay* in the dictionary.

Name: _____ **Date:** _____

Pop Quiz for Units 34–38 (Section Six)

Each of these sentences contains one verb error. Write the correct verb in the blank.

_____ 1. Every one of the stenographers do her best.

_____ 2. Ms. Dale and Mr. Kennedy is rapid typists.

_____ 3. Neither the instructor nor the student are here.

_____ 4. Ms. Cates, as well as Mr. Heffron, attend every meeting.

_____ 5. Neither the salesman nor the managers was in the office.

_____ 6. On my desk is four letters for Mr. Sandell.

_____ 7. Half of the envelopes was on my desk.

_____ 8. None of the paper were on my desk.

_____ 9. Everyone who completes the medical transcription classes are qualified to take the examination.

_____ 10. The results of this new expression of democracy in education is impressive.

_____ 11. Either of these two procedures are practical.

_____ 12. Ruth, along with her assistants, do desktop publishing in Carson.

_____ 13. A carton of books be there since last week.

_____ 14. Congress are for this legislation.

_____ 15. I wish that she was more assertive.

_____ 16. If he was the manager, he would fire everybody.

_____ 17. His educational background, experience, and personality is well suited for the job.

_____ 18. The statement of assets and liabilities were prepared yesterday.

_____ 19. A list of names and addresses were sent out last week.

_____ 20. Although the report were received last week, I've not yet read it.

_____ 21. If I was you, I would ask Bill Palmer for a transfer.

_____ 22. The firm of Blackman, Blackman, and Braverman have been chosen to represent the plaintiff.

_____ 23. The contestant in the blue suit had never swam that distance before.

_____ 24. I use to drive race cars in Indianapolis.

_____ 25. This series of mistakes are bound to cause problems.

Name: _____ **Date:** _____

Pop Quiz for Units 39–42 (Section Seven)

In the blank, write the correct form of the adjective that is in parentheses. When in doubt, use the dictionary.

_____ 1. Which of the two teams do you think has the (good) chance of winning the World Series?

_____ 2. The sloppy, poorly dressed man is the (young) of the five cousins.

_____ 3. Two employees were in the same accident, but the older one suffered the (bad) injury.

_____ 4. In the 25 years of our business, she is the (careful) seamstress we have had.

_____ 5. Which is the (much) beautiful city, Dallas or Miami?

_____ 6. As the (heavy) woman on the team, Darla was asked to diet.

_____ 7. Of all the hockey teams in the country, which do you consider to be the (good)?

_____ 8. This is the (bad) display of sportsmanship that I've ever seen.

_____ 9. Of all the cars in the race, the Porsche traveled the (far).

_____ 10. This pen-and-pencil set costs the (little) of all those pictured in the catalog.

Correct the errors.

11. That there lady weighs 450 pounds and it's a honor to know her because she is a star of a circus.
12. Those kind of oranges and them pears would make a good salad.
13. These type of people are a irritation to me when I need a X ray.
14. Which would be more profitable, a $11 increase or a 1 percent increase?
15. Please write a *U* in the first blank and a *S* in the second.

List the four pointing adjectives: Write *a* or *an* in the blank.

16. _____   20. _____ union member

17. _____   21. _____ one-inch ruler

18. _____   22. _____ heiress

19. _____   23. _____ hairline fracture

Write the comparative and the superlative in the blank.

24. pretty _____ _____

25. beautiful _____ _____

Name: _____   **Date:** _____

413

Pop Quiz for Units 39–45 (Section Seven)

Most of these sentences contain adjective or adverb errors. Show the corrections in the blanks or write *C* if the sentence is correct. Use the dictionary.

_____ 1. Hardly nobody likes that course because it don't offer no challenge.

_____ 2. You can't never make no money in those kind of businesses because the overhead is so high.

_____ 3. Lindsay Crystal has worked harder in this sales campaign than anybody else.

_____ 4. Which of the twins has the best personality?

_____ 5. He is angryer than I've ever seen him.

_____ 6. Remember that the most safest rule is to drive within the speed limit.

_____ 7. He plays the piano good.

_____ 8. Sean is a good piano player.

_____ 9. May Paquette feels real good today.

_____ 10. Professor Sunayama seems different today.

_____ 11. Smoking is the least of the two evils.

_____ 12. The accountant's report is more better than the controller's.

_____ 13. Ms. Dowd typed the letters as good as possible under the circumstances.

_____ 14. His voice sounds too softly without the microphone.

_____ 15. When you strike the bar quicker, the machine operates better.

_____ 16. The children all sat quiet through the ceremony.

_____ 17. She dresses too casual for the office.

_____ 18. Ms. Day of United was busyier than anyone could have expected.

_____ 19. Pat Garner was asked to be carefuller in the hiring procedures.

_____ 20. We needed an one-cent stamp an hour ago.

_____ 21. Anywheres you go, you'll find that there kind of person.

_____ 22. A apple a day keeps the doctor away.

_____ 23. Although she returned back to the hospital two weeks ago, she still feels badly.

_____ 24. The food at the new restaurant tasted and smelled badly.

_____ 25. While preparing coffee for his boss this morning, he accidentaly overturned the sugar bowl.

Name: _____ **Date:** _____

Pop Quiz for Units 46–47 (Section Eight)

Fill in the blanks with the correct forms of the nouns that are in parentheses. One of them is already correct.

1. From Mr. (Sax) letter we learned that prices have advanced 11 percent since Ms. (March) article was published. _____ _____

2. If (Schultz) gets the layout into Mr. (Austerlitz) hands today, the advertisement will be run on time. _____ _____

3. The signature on the contract isn't my (brother-in-law). _____

4. Has Mr. (Fingles) committee reached its quota of contributions in the (PTA) annual fund-raising campaign? _____ _____

5. During the convention, Ms. (Janowicz) committee will be in charge of registration, and Mr. (Dickens) group will usher. _____ _____

6. The (Governor) correspondence is being handled by two (secretary).

   _____ _____

7. A successful business considers every (customer) requirements. _____

8. The (Commissioner) office issues each (driver) license. _____

   _____

9. This building was planned for (doctor) offices. _____

10. It is our (agency) duty to ascertain all our (customer) desires. _____

    _____

If the possessive is incorrectly shown, write the correct form in the blank. If the possessive is correct, write *C* in the blank.

11. President Zeitlin visited *Ms. Jackson's business English class.* _____

12. *Girl's and women's coats* are on sale today. _____

13. *My mother-in-law's will* was probated in Tucson. _____

14. *A notaries' seal* appears on the bill of sale. _____

15. *Our chairman's decision* was omitted from the minutes. _____

16. There will be a *few day's delay* in filling orders. _____

17. After *a week's consideration,* I've decided to sign the contract. _____

18. *A creditor's meeting* will be held on March 2. _____

19. *Passenger's baggage* should not be placed in the aisle. _____

20. I conducted the *salespeoples' conferences* last year. _____

21. The conclusion is the *secretarys.* _____

22. The statements do not represent *Mr. Jones's beliefs.* _____

23. *Beginner's class's* start today. _____

24. They have a large inventory of *children's clothing.* _____

25. Addresses of subscribers cannot be changed without *two weeks advance notice.* _____

Name: _____ **Date:** _____

Pop Quiz for Units 49–52 (Section Nine)

Apply the comma rules in Units 49–52. Write *C* next to the seven correct sentences.

1. In the autocratic style of management the manager draws a very narrow firm discipline line.
2. Before the Hawthorne experiments management felt certain that the way to improve production was to improve the machinery reduce unnecessary hand motions provide better lighting reduce fatigue and so on.
3. As a result of research such as the Hawthorne experiment employers have found that individual recognition opportunity to learn treatment as an individual personal involvement and many other factors are also vital.
4. Personality conflicts are upsetting and cause serious drops in productivity.
5. Some employees find little satisfaction in their personal lives and have a deep need to enjoy rewarding relationships with those they meet at work.
6. If the foregoing ideas are interesting to you perhaps you should take courses in human relations or in industrial psychology.
7. You might discover that you have a career interest in such a position as personnel director industrial psychologist or human relations consultant.
8. Some important morale factors are satisfaction with the job itself opportunity to learn and compatibility with co-workers.
9. In a corporation having several thousand employees top-level managers seldom know more than a small fraction of those on the payroll.
10. The personnel department is responsible for the activities that concern employees and it advises other departments and management regarding personnel matters.
11. The clerk blushed and handed the message to the tall stern general.
12. Formal courses will not of themselves make you effective but they will help you learn about supervision and management.
13. If becoming a supervisor sounds promising you should start to prepare now.
14. Some decisions may seem trivial to you but the quality of each decision is important to the success of a department.
15. Yes you will need to talk seriously with your people.
16. A supervisor must learn how to conduct group meetings to discipline and terminate employees and to be a good member of the management team.
17. Roberta Simon manages a variety store in a middle-class section of Hartford.
18. The store did more than $750,000 in sales last year and is considered successful by the other merchants.
19. Six months ago Brian and Rachel were assigned stores to manage.
20. Yesterday Jordan decided that he wanted to get into management.
21. He may not know everything about motivating others but he is willing to learn.
22. The supervisor must learn early in her career that what others do under her guidance is more important than the actual work she does herself.
23. Should you move into a supervisory job from a technical one you must quickly become a people-oriented individual.
24. Whenever you can take at least a few management courses.
25. If you are interested in becoming a manager maintain a courageous open-minded attitude toward your problems.

Name: _____   Date: _____

Pop Quiz for Units 53–57 (Section Nine)

Applying the rules from Units 53–57, insert commas in these sentences. Write *C* next to the sentences that don't require additional commas.

1. We noticed that Professor Lingo changed her methods not her objectives.
2. The typing test was given to all the applicants; the shorthand test to a selected group in Bakersfield.
3. Payment for half the purchase price $250,000 is due on June 1; the balance on October 15.
4. We need an electronic calculator, not a 10-key adding machine.
5. Your report was submitted to Fresno officials on June 3; D. Scanio's on June 16.
6. The name of the book is How to Catch a Wolf.
7. On January 3 1998 we shall meet in Longmeadow Massachusetts to discuss the marketing plan for the 21st century.
8. Please send the scripts to my nephew Alex who lives in Toronto near his parents.
9. You will need two new writers for the offices in Vance, Canada and in Calgary, Canada.
10. I believe Phil that a more experienced person is needed for the job.
11. The average wage earner in 1914 worked 12 hours a day for about $800 a year.
12. They live at 40536 Picket Fence Road Levittown Pennsylvania in an older home that is in very good condition.
13. The textbook used this semester *Word Processing: Concepts and Careers* will inform you of new career paths and how to train for them.
14. It was the expense of the work not its difficulty that made us refuse to begin the project.
15. Wrestling not modern dance was the physical education class I wanted.
16. "You must study during the winter vacation," stressed Oralee Clark "because final examinations begin in January."
17. Please telephone Casey Kubik when the costumes are ready.
18. Ms. Green who is Mr. Williams' administrative assistant is able to take dictation at 120 words a minute and is a CPA.
19. They replied "We think we are within our rights."
20. "Do you think so?" she asked.
21. All birds, especially those that migrate fascinate me.
22. It is I'm pleased to report, a promising idea.
23. Parenthetical words however should be enclosed in commas.
24. I tell you Mr. Marino there is no other way to settle this case.
25. Professor Roche said that during the summer of 1988 he left the College of the Desert.

Name: _____ **Date:** _____

Pop Quiz for Units 58–61 (Section Ten)

( ) . ? ! — ; : Parentheses, period, question mark, exclamation mark, dash, semicolon, colon

Please insert only the punctuation marks shown above. I've put the commas in already. Write *C* beside the one sentence that is already correct.

1. Sales last year were well over ten million dollars the best year in our history.
2. A lawn mower, a rake, and a hose these are the implements I must buy next.
3. In the United States men own an average of three coats, an overcoat, a topcoat, and a raincoat and five pairs of trousers.
4. May I hear from you by return mail
5. In the course of the tour, we shall visit four points of interest in Washington
   Library of Congress
   White House
   Capitol
   Smithsonian Institute
6. Everything seems favorable for increased production The workers are experienced, the morale is excellent, and the machinery is new.
7. Campers must take these items pillows, blankets, linens, and cooking utensils.
8. Yesterday we sent you this night letter "Make shipment to our Harrisburg factory."
9. Our prices are reasonable for example, $9.50 for a ream of heavyweight typing paper and $4.42 for 500 envelopes.
10. Get a better job then you will earn more money.
11. There are three requirements for the job speed, accuracy, and intelligence.
12. "Do not use hyperbole, not one writer in a million can use it effectively," wrote Dr. Alan Dundes with tongue in cheek.
13. Consumer demand can be changed or influenced in other words, you can be influenced to select one item over another.
14. The judges had rejected all but three of the dogs a cocker spaniel, a boxer, and an Irish setter.
15. His phenomenal success is due to one thing hard work.
16. I plan to visit Oakland, California Homewood, Illinois and Omaha, Nebraska.
17. My assistant and I wish to stay however, Mr. Allen feels we should leave.
18. Will you please answer this letter immediately
19. Do your records indicate, Mr. Green, that we filled six orders for you last year and that every one of them was delivered within five days
20. He has an overpowering ambition namely, to fly a jet plane.
21. The mayor said, "Our city is growing steadily every year as a result of the expansion of our industrial plants and the friendly attitude shown to visitors by the citizens of our city."
22. I will ask him by telephone assuming he has a telephone.
23. How dare he do such a thing
24. I just cannot believe it
25. These unlawful acts for that is what they are should be forbidden

Name: _____ **Date:** _____

" - : ; , ' Please insert only the following in the sentences below: **quotation marks, hyphen, colon, semicolon, comma,** and **apostrophe.** One sentence requires no additional punctuation.

1. Supervisors make decisions on an hour to hour basis.

2. A good supervisor is a people oriented person as well as a job oriented person for he or she must get the job done through others.

3. If you can't take the heat get out of the kitchen said Harry S. Truman.

4. After eating the elephants yawned and then dozed.

5. As you know nothing was done about the shortage.

6. He liked to eat in first class restaurants in far flung places.

7. It is a small scale operation for public spirited citizens.

8. He needs a 12 inch ruler and a two ton truck.

9. On any floor where we did manufacturing such as the second floor the rental was $5 a square foot.

10. We are operating a railroad not a brokers office. (one broker)

11. Did you read the book PEOPLE ARE FUNNY?

12. I read the article entitled People Are Funny.

13. At first said Ms. Dees the capacity of our Orange Coast plant was small the efficiency low and the performance of equipment uncertain.

14. The wholesale salesperson serves a limited and select class of buyers the retail salesperson meets a large number of people every day.

15. All my products have a money back guarantee.

16. The attorneys office is in that building but she's on a weeks vacation right now.

17. An advertising agency provides a client with
    Research and marketing strategy
    Market forecasts
    Analysis of media possibilities
    Execution of media contracts

18. Insurance companies are divided into two major classifications those that deal with property and liability and those that deal primarily with life insurance.

19. Shirley could remember only three dates 1492 the year Columbus discovered America 1948 the year of her birth and 1963 the year President Kennedy was assassinated.

20. Did Nancy say that she hoped never to set foot in Idahos fields again?

21. That book is out of date for example it contains nothing about laser printers.

22. Felixs job is in the mens department.

Use a diagonal (/) to show where these words may be divided at the end of a line. If there is no approved division, place the line at the end. Use your dictionary if necessary.

23. preferred   obliged   25. permitting   selling

24. stopped   capital

Name: _____   **Date:** _____

Pop Quiz for Units 65–66 (Section Eleven)

A. Underline the correct answer.

1. A form made out by a transportation company listing the goods shipped is called a/an
   (a) by-product (b) bid (c) bill of lading (d) annuity (e) appraisal

2. A statement in writing sworn to before a person authorized by law to administer oaths is
   a/an (a) affidavit (b) beneficiary (c) agenda (d) appraisal (e) audit

3. A statement of assets, liabilities, and net worth as of a certain date is a/an (a) amalgamation
   (b) audit (c) balance sheet (d) bid (e) attachment

4. An offer to buy or sell goods at a certain price is a/an (a) capital (b) audit (c) attachment
   (d) bid (e) arbitration

5. A merger, or joining of two or more businesses into a single body, is also called a/an
   (a) adjuster (b) affidavit (c) amalgamation (d) consignment (e) collateral

6. The decline in value of property because of wear and age is called (a) dividend (b) down time
   (c) capitalism (d) data processing (e) depreciation

7. All the property owned by a business or an individual is its (a) assets (b) disbursements
   (c) dividend (d) collateral (e) bill of lading

8. An itemized statement of the allowance given a buyer for goods that have been returned to
   the seller is called a/an (a) cashier's check (b) certified check (c) deficit (d) credit memorandum (e) annual report

9. The opposite of surplus is called (a) deficit (b) disbursements (c) cash discount (d) assets
   (e) attachment

10. A collection of information stored in the computer's memory bank is called (a) a clone
    (b) disbursements (c) down time (d) capitalism (e) a database

B. Write a sentence using each of these words, or combine them all into one or two sentences.

11. annual report
12. amalgamation
13. assets
14. employee profit-sharing
15. corporations

_____

_____

_____

_____

_____

Name: _____ **Date:** _____

420

Pop Quiz for Units 65–67 (Section Eleven)

A. Underline the correct answer.

1. The year between one annual balancing of accounts and another is called what kind of a year? (a) equity (b) exemption (c) fiscal (d) dividend (e) corporation

2. A wholesale dealer who buys from manufacturers or importers and sells relatively small quantities to retail merchants is called a/an (a) franchise (b) jobber (c) employee profit-sharing plan (d) auditor (e) adjuster

3. A company that is unable to pay its debts is (a) gross (b) insolvent (c) escrow (d) lien (e) collateral

4. A rise and fall, as of prices, is known as (a) foreclosure (b) endorsement (c) itinerary (d) fluctuation (e) deficit

5. A check that has been guaranteed by the bank to be worth the amount for which it is written is called a/an (a) deficit (b) cashier's check (c) certified check (d) endorsement (e) arrears

6. A specified amount of money that is not subject to taxation is called a/an (a) franchise (b) exemption (c) invoice (d) journal (e) depreciation

7. The obligations or debts of a business or a person are called (a) liabilities (b) assets (c) bankruptcy (d) exemptions (e) equity

8. Written evidence of property ownership that is held by a third party until certain conditions are fulfilled is called (a) escrow (b) equity (c) insolvent (d) bill of lading (e) distribution

9. Information or ideas in raw form fed into data processing or word processing systems is called (a) fluctuation (b) lapsed policy (c) equity (d) input (e) distribution

10. Insurance that has expired because payments have not been kept up-to-date is called what kind of policy? (a) lapsed (b) franchise (c) amalgamation (d) bankrupt (e) consignment

B. Insert in the blank the words from Units 65–67 that make sense in the blanks. The first letter of each missing word is shown.

Because there has been considerable d_____ [11], it will be necessary to l_____ [12] during the current f_____ [13] y_____ [14]. While we are not yet i_____ [15], we must sell everything below l_____ p_____ [16]. Otherwise f_____ [17] of our property will be inevitable. The b_____ s_____ [18] shows that our l_____ [19] are greater than our a_____ [20].

Name: _____ **Date:** _____

421

Pop Quiz for Units 65–68 (Section Eleven)

Underline the correct answer.

1. A word processing and data processing term to describe the information after it has been processed is called (a) litigation (b) output (c) per diem (d) gross (e) overhead

2. A written plan of travel showing arrival and departure dates as well as hotels where reservations have been made is called a/an (a) endorsement (b) itinerary (c) plaintiff (d) lien (e) beneficiary

3. A determination of the value of the property by an expert is called a/an (a) affidavit (b) appraisal (c) depreciation (d) inventory (e) option

4. Exclusive control of the supply of a commodity or service is called a/an (a) monopoly (b) lien (c) list price (d) agenda (e) escrow

5. A public officer who administers oaths and witnesses signatures is called a/an (a) middleman (b) jobber (c) adjuster (d) notary public (e) defendant

6. A small sum of money kept on the premises of a business to pay for minor purchases is called (a) petty cash (b) per annum (c) overhead (d) good will (e) fluctuation

7. The amount remaining after all deductions are made is (a) net (b) markup (c) list price (d) cash discount (e) overhead

8. The person against whom a legal action is brought is called the (a) plaintiff (b) adjuster (c) debtor (d) creditor (e) defendant

9. An examination of the records of a business to determine their correctness is called a/an (a) appraisal (b) annual report (c) audit (d) per annum (e) negotiable

10. A person who plans the steps necessary to produce the information to be obtained from a computer is called a/an (a) notary public (b) middleman (c) beneficiary (d) auditor (e) programmer

Write a sentence using each of these words or combine them all into one or two sentences.

11. programmer
12. modem
13. desktop publishing
14. ergonomic
15. software

_____

_____

_____

_____

_____

Name: _____ **Date:** _____

422

Pop Quiz for Units 65–69 (Section Eleven)

A. Fill in the blanks.

1. The number of members required to be present in order to constitute a formal meeting is called a q _____.

2. Something stated in exactly the same form as the original—that is, word for word—is v _____.

3. Property offered as security for the repayment of a loan is called c _____.

4. A statement in writing sworn to before a notary public is called an a _____.

5. The person designated to receive the benefits from an insurance policy or will is called the b _____.

6. When somebody buys a check from a bank, the check is called a c _____ c _____.

7. The opposite of surplus of money is called a d _____.

8. A duty on imported goods is a t _____.

9. Comparing the bank's statement with the depositor's own records is called a r _____.

10. Several business letters ready to be signed and mailed could be an example of the o _____ from a word processing center.

B. Based on Units 65–69, write in the blanks the words that are the opposites of the listed words.

11. input _____

12. assets _____

13. bull market _____

14. insolvent _____

15. plaintiff _____

16. depreciation _____

17. deficit _____

From Units 65–69, write in each blank a word that is preceded by *per*.

18. _____

19. _____

20. _____

Name: _____ **Date:** _____

Pop Quiz for Units 70–74 (Section Twelve)

Circle the correct answer.

1. No one is here but (I, me).
2. The law was (past/passed) at the last session of Congress.
3. He went (past/passed) the school.
4. The (effects/affects) of the strike were evident.
5. The Student (Council/Counsel) voted to spend $1,000 for the entertainment.
6. Can you reduce the expenditures without (affecting/effecting) the company's sales?
7. The plane leaves for the (capital/capitol) of Tanzania in 15 minutes.
8. The surface of the race (course/coarse) was not smooth enough.
9. His actions could (affect/effect) a shutdown of the entire industry.
10. Will you (accept/except) the responsibility for having costumes made?
11. Will the 22-below weather (affect/effect) your cold?
12. I hope my credit rating will not be (affected/effected) by that error.
13. The (principal/principle) and interest total $45,000.
14. They are trying to teach the children the (principals/principles) of good citizenship.
15. Do you know all the mathematics (principles, principals) involved in that kind of problem?
16. (Whose/Who's) book is torn?
17. I'll be glad to (cite/site) an example.
18. She will (advise/advice) anyone on anything.
19. (You're/Your) going to need a new assistant soon.
20. The drought is likely to (affect/effect) the peach crop.
21. Only (minor/miner) changes will be made in the plans.
22. Her idea seems more logical (then/than) his.
23. What is the result of (they're/their/there) vote?
24. All prices will remain (stationery/stationary) for a while.
25. Jane said that she might (accept/except) the nomination.
26. I (could of/could have) gone, but I preferred to remain.
27. They borrowed some books (off of/from/off) us.
28. Please hire a secretary with top skills for the president and (me/I).
29. How many cabinet members (besides/beside) Mr. Berglund voted?
30. "Please (proceed/precede) to your seat," said Elvis.

Name: _____ **Date:** _____

Pop Quiz for Units 76–78 (Section Thirteen)

Three sentences below are correctly written, but the others have one of these faults:

(a) comma splice   (d) nonparallel parts
(b) fragment   (e) dangler
(c) run-on   (f) misplaced part

Write OK or the letter of the sentence fault in the blank.

_____ 1. Our bank approves loans to reliable people of any size.

_____ 2. The plan for Tuesday's session includes:
    a. introduce new officers.
    b. reviewing current budget.
    c. to go over agenda for annual meeting.

_____ 3. Your decision will not be easy several experienced, capable applicants want the job.

_____ 4. Enclosed are several carpeting samples. Each of which will be on sale starting next week.

_____ 5. The class did not begin on time, however, it ended at 3 p.m.

_____ 6. To master grammar, you must give attention to the rules.

_____ 7. To keep your files in order, the alphabet must be learned.

_____ 8. Our newest catalog is in the mail, it should reach you by the end of the week.

_____ 9. In the parade will be several hundred children carrying flags and many important people.

_____ 10. Replying to your letter of May 7.

_____ 11. Thanking you for your attention to this problem.

_____ 12. Jordan Lawrence is attending the annual convention for the purpose of presenting a paper and to listen to the keynote address.

_____ 13. The cook fried the eggs in a large frying pan.

_____ 14. Enjoying the magnificence of Maui, the second largest island of Hawaii, the few raindrops didn't bother him.

_____ 15. While cruising through the inside passage of Alaska, I shot 25 rolls of film.

_____ 16. To be well baked, you should leave the potatoes in the oven for one hour.

_____ 17. The letter, which required Michael to settle a debt or forfeit his farm.

_____ 18. Michael thought for two days about the debt, then he decided what his family had to do.

_____ 19. Professor Givens had the choice of giving up her ideals and principles or to remain faithful to them.

_____ 20. Contestants were required to dance to both rock and country rhythms and explaining why they liked their jobs.

Name: _____ **Date:** _____

Pop Quiz for Units 79 and 80 (Section Thirteen)

Change these sentences to the direct style. Add any missing facts.

1. More than 1,000 calculators have already been sold by one of our salesmen.

   _____

   _____

2. The element typewriter was developed during the 1960s.

   _____

   _____

3. The emerald necklace was finally purchased for $100,000.

   _____

   _____

Change these sentences to the indirect style.

4. Several managers expressed approval of the new software.

   _____

   _____

5. J. Dolan predicted a daily attendance of 300 at the Palomar meeting.

   _____

   _____

6. S. Fechtman visited our Anaheim branch last year.

   _____

Improve item 7 so that it doesn't sound choppy.

7. Ms. Jensen is a teacher. She teaches office occupation classes. She teaches at Long Beach City College.

   _____

   _____

Correct the pronoun usage in this sentence.

8. Roberta Simon orders directly from Emerson, which prevents shipping delays.

   _____

   _____

For items 9–12, indicate whether the sentence construction is better in (a) or (b). Circle the letter of your choice.

9. (a) Badminton was devised in the 1860s at a home called Badminton Hall. It was located in Gloucestershire, England.
   (b) Badminton was devised in the 1860s in Gloucestershire, England, at a home called Badminton Hall.

10. (a) Baseball, a totally American derivative of the English game of cricket, evolved about the end of the 18th century.
    (b) Baseball is a totally American derivative of the English game of cricket, and the game evolved about the end of the 18th century.

11. (a) In the early 17th century, the ancient European game of ninepins was first played in the United States; and when the legislatures of Connecticut and other states prohibited the game, a tenth pin was added to evade the ban.
    (b) In the early 17th century, the ancient European game of ninepins was first played in the United States. When the legislatures of Connecticut and other states prohibited the game, a tenth pin was added to evade the ban.

12. (a) A purchasing agent buys raw materials, supplies, and equipment, and any other items a company might need to conduct its business.
    (b) A purchasing agent is a person who purchases raw materials that the company needs to conduct its business, and a purchasing agent also buys supplies and equipment. He or she also buys any other items the company might need.

Name: _____ **Date:** _____

427

Pop Quiz for Units 81–84 (Section Fourteen)

A. Answer the following questions.

1. What are two advantages of writing a business letter rather than phoning?

    (a) _____

    (b) _____

    _____

2. After a properly folded letter is removed from a small business envelope, how many folds does it have? _____

3. Write today's date in the international or government style. _____

4. A suitable nonsexist salutation to use when the first line of the inside address is an organization name is _____ or _____.

5. The company name may be typed a double space below the _____.

6. The letters *bc* mean _____.

7. Two letter styles that have all lines beginning at the left margin are:

    (a) _____

    (b) _____

8. Paragraphs may be indented if desired in what style letter? _____

9. Which word of the complimentary close should be capitalized? _____

10. The two shortest paragraphs of a well-written business letter are often the _____ and _____.

B. Please redo the following letter: Correct format errors, modernize out-of-date wording, change needlessly negative wording to positive wording, and eliminate redundancies.

June 8th, '9—

Teresa McGlennon

Niagara County Technologies Company

3111 Saunders Rd.

Sanborn, N.Y., 14132

Dear Ms. Teresa,

This is to inform you so that you will know that we received your letter of June 6th about opening your account for you and in reply to same must advise that we cannot give you credit in our company unless you fill out the enclosed application and forward it to us with your credit references.

Respectfully yours,

Mr. Jim Dandy

xzq

enc.

C. XZQ are the initials of the new employee who composed and typed the letter for Mr. Dandy's signature. As the office manager, send a short, but tactful, interoffice memo to XZQ suggesting the *English for Careers* course.

Name: _____ **Date:** _____

Spelling for Careers

Spelling checkers in computers and in electronic typewriters decrease the number of spelling errors. They are not, however, always available. For example, an applicant's opportunity for a good job may be ruined by a single spelling error on an application blank. Surveys and interviews with office managers reveal that competent spelling skill is essential to success on the job and chances for promotion.

Not only are electronic spelling checkers often unavailable, but these devices don't catch spelling errors that form a new word such as *a line* for *align* or *affect* for *effect*. In business, spelling is one of the few skills that requires perfection. With a methodical step-by-step plan and a positive attitude, everyone can be a good speller.

The **1-3-2-1 Plan** is an efficient way to master the spelling of an entire list of words. Here's how it works:

1 Have someone dictate the words in a list to you. Check them carefully and note any you misspelled or were not sure of.

3 Write each misspelled word *three* times, saying the word aloud and spelling it aloud. Use the dictionary when in doubt about pronunciation.

2 Next, write each misspelled word *twice*.

1 Finally, dictate the words on a cassette and then play it back, or ask someone to dictate them to you. Write each originally misspelled word *once* from the tape or live dictation. After checking for correct spelling, list the words you misspelled or felt unsure about and practice these few using the 1-3-2-1 Plan again.

Here are 14 groups of 25 words each. Perhaps you'd like to master one list along with each section of the text. Use the lists also for vocabulary development by verifying definitions in the dictionary when in doubt.

ONE	TWO	THREE	FOUR	FIVE
abbreviate	analyze	carriage	confidently	deductible
absence	announcement	category	conjecture	default
absolutely	annually	cautious	Connecticut	deferred
absurd	annuity	census	connoisseur	deficient
abundance	anticipate	certain	conscientious	definitely
accelerate	anxiety	certificate	conscious	deluge
accessible	apologize	challenge	consensus	dependent
accompanying	apparatus	changeable	consistent	description
accountant	apparent	changing	continually	desirable
acknowledgment	appreciable	chargeable	controversy	desperate
acquaintance	approximately	chauffeur	convertible	determine
acquitted	architect	chronicle	cooperation	deterrent
adequacy	argument	colloquial	correspondence	develop
adjournment	ascertain	column	corroborate	development
advantageous	assessment	combustion	counselor	different
aggressive	bulletin	commencement	courageous	diligent
align	buoyancy	compelled	courteous	dimension
allotment	bureau	compensate	crisis	disappearance
allotted	bureaucracy	competent	criticism	disapprove
altogether	bylaw	competition	criticize	disastrous
amateur	calendar	concede	currency	discrepancy
ambassador	campaign	conceive	customary	discretion
ambiguous	canceling	concession	debatable	disguise
amendment	cancellation	concurred	deceive	dissatisfied
amortize	candidacy	confidentially	decision	distributor

SIX	SEVEN	EIGHT	NINE	TEN
divided	erroneous	fiscal	immediately	manageable
dual (double)	especially	fluorescent	impromptu	management
duplicate	etiquette	forcible	improvement	maneuver
economical	Europe	foreign	incidentally	marketable
edition	exaggerate	forfeit	indispensable	Massachusetts
effervescent	excel	forth (forward)	initiative	measurement
efficiency	excellent	forty	insistence	media (plural)
eighth	excusable	fourth (4th)	intangible	mediator
electronic	execute	fragile	interpretation	mediocre
elementary	exercise	fraudulent	intolerable	memorize
eligible	exhibit	freight	irrelevant	messenger
eliminate	exorbitant	fulfill	itemize	miniature
emergency	expedient	fundamentally	itinerary	minimize
emphasize	expenditure	generalize	jeopardize	miscellaneous
encouragement	experience	government	jewelry	necessarily
encouraging	extension	grandeur	judgment	necessitate
endorsement	extraordinary	grateful	justifiable	negotiate
enforceable	extravagant	grievance	knowledge	nineteen
enormous	facilities	guarantee	laboratory	notarize
en route	fallacy	handful	launch	numerous
enthusiastically	familiarize	harass	league	observant
entirely	fascinate	hazardous	legible	occasionally
enumerate	feasible	hesitant	legitimate	occurred
environment	fictitious	hindrance	lucrative	occurrence
equipped	financier	hypocrite	maintenance	omission

ELEVEN	TWELVE	THIRTEEN	FOURTEEN
outrageous	referred	specialize	transferred
pamphlet	regrettable	specifically	treacherous
participant	reiterate	sphere	triplicate
patronize	relevant	spontaneous	ultimately
per annum	remittance	statistical	unanimous
perceive	repetition	statistician	unavoidable
perceptible	representative	subsidize	undeniable
perennial	rescind	substantial	undoubtedly
permitted	residual	substantiate	unduly
petroleum	respectability	suburb	unprecedented
plausible	restaurant	succeed	usable
politics	ridiculous	summarize	vacillate
possession	salable	supersede	vacuum
precede	satellite	supplement	validate
precedent	satisfactorily	surmise	vengeance
precision	scarcity	surplus	verbatim
preferable	scheme	survey	vice versa
preferred	scrutinize	synthetic	visible
prominent	seize	systematically	whereas
questionnaire	sensible	taxable	wholly
quota	serviceable	tedious	withhold
receipt	similar	temperament	workable
reconciliation	solemn	tourist	writing
recurrence	sophisticated	tournament	yield
reference	souvenir	tragedy	zealous

Memo from the Wordsmith

Shanty Hogan, who was the football coach at Phoenix Junior College, claims this is a true story.

He asked his freshman players to fill out a card to be used in case of serious injury. The card lists whom to notify and such information. One blank is for religion. One player wrote "Bhaptizz."

Hogan chuckled and then asked, "Now, son, what religion are you?" The young man answered, "Presbyterian."

"But you wrote Baptist," the coach said.

"I know," said the player, "but I can't spell Presbyterian."

Spelling Tips

The tips that follow govern the spelling of many frequently misspelled words. However, use these tips with care because of the many exceptions.

ie or ei?

The old verse you may have learned in elementary school is still true:

> I before E
> Except after C
> Or when sounded like A
> As in neighbor and weigh

Apply this tip only to words with the long *e* or long *a* sound.

I BEFORE *E*:

achieve	believe	chief	field	fierce	grievance
piece	relieve	siege	wield	yield	

E BEFORE *I* AFTER *C*:

ceiling   conceit   deceive   perceive   receipt   receive

E BEFORE *I* FOR A LONG *A* SOUND:

eight   freight   neighbor   reign   surveillance   vein   weigh

EXCEPTIONS   **Leisure**ly eating **protein**, the **weird sheik seize**d the **financier**.—Plus **either/neither** (which I couldn't fit into the sentence).

Adding Prefixes to Root Words

Perhaps the most useful spelling tip concerns adding prefixes (word beginnings) to root words:

> When the root word begins with the last letter of the prefix, a double letter results.

mis + spell = misspell	dis + satisfaction = dissatisfaction
im + movable = immovable	il + legal = illegal
un + noticed = unnoticed	ir + responsible = irresponsible

BUT

in + comparable = incomparable	in + animate = inanimate
dis + appear = disappear	re + commend = recommend
dis + appoint = disappoint	un + able = unable

Final Silent *e* + Suffix

Here's a tip for deciding whether to drop silent *e* before a suffix (word ending):

Drop the silent *e* before a suffix that begins with a vowel.

enclose	enclosure	advise	advisable
guide	guidance	use	usable
argue	arguing	desire	desirous
arrive	arrival	sale	salable

EXCEPTIONS   mileage
dyeing   [changing a color]

BUT

If the word ends with *ce* or *ge*, keep the *e* before suffixes beginning with *a* or *o*.

notice/noticeable   advantage/advantageous
enforce/enforceable   service/serviceable

Keep the final *e* before an ending that begins with a consonant.

encourage/encouragement   manage/management
false/falsehood   sincere/sincerely
hope/hopeful   sure/surely

EXCEPTIONS
acknowledgment	ninth
argument	truly
duly	wholly
judgment	

Final Consonant + Suffix

These tips determine whether to double a final consonant before adding a suffix:

If the suffix begins with a vowel, double the final consonant of a one-syllable word ending in a single consonant (except *y*, *w*, or *x*) preceded by a single vowel.

plan/planned	run/runner	sad/sadden
ship/shipping	slip/slippage	wrap/wrapping

EXCEPTION   bus [*buses* or *busses, busing* or *bussing, bused* or *bussed*]

Apply the preceding rule to *two*-syllable words if the second syllable is accented.

admit/admitted	occur/occurrence	refer/referring
confer/conferred	prefer/preferred	transfer/transferring

EXCEPTION   transferable

If the accent shifts to the first syllable when you add the suffix beginning with a vowel, don't double the final consonant.

confer/conference   refer/reference   prefer/preferable, preference

When a word of more than one syllable is not accented on the last syllable, keep the consonant single before adding a suffix.

benefit/benefited   cancel/canceled   credit/crediting
differ/difference   happen/happened   profit/profiting
retail/retailing   total/totaled   travel/traveler

EXCEPTIONS   cancellation
programmed, programming, programmer

Regardless of syllables, don't double a final consonant if the ending begins with a consonant.

commit/commitment   equip/equipment   glad/gladness
hand/handful   sad/sadly   ship/shipment

If a word doesn't end with a single consonant preceded by a single vowel, keep the final consonant single.

confirm/confirming   exist/existence   look/looking
prevail/prevailing   return/returned   treat/treated

Changing Final *y* to *i*

If a consonant precedes the final *y*, change the *y* to *i* before adding an ending.

defy/defiant   happy/happiness   heavy/heaviest
hurry/hurried   likely/likelihood   plenty/plentiful

BUT

If the ending begins with *i*, keep the *y*.

try/trying   forty/fortyish   accompany/accompanying

If a vowel precedes the *y*, keep the *y* before any ending.

annoy/annoyance   delay/delayed   employ/employable

EXCEPTIONS   day/daily
pay/paid
slay/slain
lay/laid

Unpredictable Suffixes

Look up words ending in *able/ible, ant/ent, ance/ence, ize/ise/yse*. Because these suffixes aren't governed by clear rules, consult your dictionary.

-Sede, -Ceed, or -Cede?

It's easy to spell correctly the syllable pronounced "seed."

Supersede is the only word that ends in *sede*.

Exceed, proceed, and *succeed* are the only three words spelled with *ceed*. Memory aid: To suc**ceed**, you must pro**ceed** to ex**ceed**. The spelling remains when adding *-ed, -ing,* or *-s.* However, drop one of the *e*'s when spelling *procedure.*

All other words with the syllable pronounced "seed" are spelled *cede: intercede, precede, recede, secede,* and others.

APPENDIX

D

Proofreaders' Marks

Proofreader's Mark	What it Means	How to Use It	Corrected Version
ℒ	Delete or omit	beginn	begin
∧	Insert	occurence	occurrence
∽	Transpose	revelant, decied	relevant, decide
STET · · · ·	Retain crossed-out characters with a dot underneath	STET if you, Harry, and I go	if you and I go
#	Insert space	fountain#pen	fountain pen
⌢	Close up space	stock⌢holder	stockholder
¶	Start a new paragraph	days. ¶ We are ready	days. We are ready
⌊	Move left	⌊ Dear Ms. Adams:	Dear Ms. Adams:
⌐	Move right	Sincerely, ⌐	Sincerely,
/	Change capital letter to lower case	the /Advertising /Budget	the advertising budget
≡	Change lower case letter to capital	new year's eve	New Year's Eve
SP	Spell out	⑤ days in NYC	five days in New York City
SS	Single space	This plan is under SS consideration now.	This plan is under consideration now.
DS	Double space	This plan is under DS consideration now.	This plan is under consideration now.
⌒	Run in; no new line	four years. ⌒ We'll be	four years. We'll be

APPENDIX

E Final Rehearsal

Correct the errors and write *C* next to the correct sentences. Please don't make a change because you think some other words would "sound" better. Correct specific errors only. Some sentences have more than one error; careful proofreading is a must.

1. The passerby throw coins to the musicians who especially pleases them.

2. The sidewalks are an art display in theirselves.

3. Noone is bored when they stroll along the Seine.

4. One of the most spectacular sights are the light demonstration at Notre Dame.

5. This up to the minute information is invaluable to our company.

6. The architect, as well as the drafters, will give their advice on the details.

7. Neither Walter nor he wished to give the report to the controller.

8. The secretaries' desks were crowded with yesterdays' work.

9. We've recently learned that Toombs & Irwin, Inc., have been invited to move into the new building.

10. On what criterias did you base your findings?

11. Neither Benedict nor him wished to give the report to the secretary.

12. What is the name of the witness whom we subpoenaed yesterday?

13. I saw the man today whom they say is supposed to be the leader.

14. The principal point in favor of this transaction is the absolute safety of the principal.

15. Our stationary department carries several kind of three-ring binders.

16. The ability to write shorthand is just one of the skills needed for your success.

17. If anyone calls while I'm out, please ask them to leave a message.

18. There will be a few week's delay in filling your order.

19. The report shows that we are loosing money on this product.

20. The purpose of this regulation is to affect economies in our organization.

21. "A adverb describes a adjective, a verb or another adverb, said the instructor."

22. Neither Ms. Reid nor Lisa are hear today.

23. In the file was a chart and a photograph.

24. The news today are nothing but politics.

25. Each one of us have succeeded.

438

26. The congregation were quiet.

27. One memoranda was in his box.

28. Either one boy or two girls are going to sing.

29. There's six letters on the desk.

30. Mathematics are an important part of your education.

31. Each committee must make their own rules.

32. The typewriter key was broke when the machine fell to the floor.

33. We hung our coats on the hooks.

34. His sweater had shrank.

35. She give him a book yesterday.

36. The bird has flew away.

37. As soon as the alarm sounded, he sprang into action.

38. He don't intend to visit the showroom today.

39. If I was you, I'd go.

40. The moral in our school is high.

41. You do not have excess to your textbook during tests.

42. Most people would prefer to have a business that is insolvent.

43. I told your manager that you done the work well.

44. He has came to work every day this month.

45. I think he works good under pressure.

46. She cannot afford to buy the mink coat but she might buy a rabbit jacket next week.

47. The defendant has no assets, consequently, there are no prospects of recovering anything.

48. He is lazy, insolent and dishonest.

49. Where is his home at?

50. Give the book to John and he.

51. The Crestwood Agency has just completed Marketing Research in the east.

52. The Department of Health, Education, and Welfare are making plans to transfer their headquarters to a larger Building.

53. One of the fundamental principals of our democracy is rule by the majority.

54. Two ton trucks are to be driven in the right lane only.

55. Going over her work carefully, the error was soon found.

56. Having failed to punch the time card, the manager reprimanded me.

57. Many languages, not only english, is used in the United Nations.

58. We have beat all previous sales records for this territory.

59. No body takes we amateurs seriously.

60. The new manager hired Kathy and I last week.

61. Everyone of the trainees went home.

62. Have you took notes of what the consultant recommended?

63. If you had went with Uriah, you could of helped him.

64. The studio has already chose the actors for the new film.

65. How often has this error occur in the past?

66. Most of the ideas were offered by three people; Rachel, Sean, and Jordan.

67. These three items the bookcase, the cash register, and the display rack, are not for sale.

68. The owner is real pleased with how you manage the store.

69. The communication technician refused my advise.

70. The business failed because we did'nt have enough capitol.

71. The Floreses are all sopranoes.

72. About one hundred alumnus attended the football game and dance.

73. Please don't buy no more typewriter ribbons until we take inventory.

74. You couldn't hardly expect him to except such a low paying job.

75. If you dont understand the work, you'll get a F on the test.

76. Of the two applicant's we are considering the first seems best qualified.

77. Jesse has done real good in his new position.

78. The book, that is on the shelf, has lose pages.

79. Our new TV, which works very well, was purchased before the sale.

80. Dame Fortune may smile very sweet today, but tomorrow she may frown real severely.

81. Once Chance has went by there are no future opportunities.

82. Dr. Banta will be their before dinner.

83. Their planning to expand the New Jersey plant.

84. She will have arrive before the tornado strikes.

85. I be working on this job for a long time.

86. We don't know nothing about those kind of distribution systems.

87. The new policy effected some of we girls in the drafting department.

88. If anyone here wants to object, let them do so now.

89. As she preceded with her speech, her words flowed more and more easy.

90. He was tall, blond, and had blue eyes.

91. While opening a can of juice, his hand was cut bad.

92. While driving to the conference, my brakes stopped working.

93. They needed to raise the money quick.

94. After adjusting the carburetor, the car ran smooth.

95. We stopped at the service station for gas and to put water in the radiator.

96. Yes you may believe me.

97. "Good morning Red Riding Hood", said the big bad wolf.

98. He dug, and hoed his little field, and planted sweet potatoes.

99. Innsbruck which is in Austria, is one of the most beautiful citie's in the world.

100. His answers were alright, but his math skill was deplorable.

101. A 16 foot pole will not be long enough.

102. When you take a cruise, you'll find a upper berth is less comfortable than a lower.

103. She is more unhappier than ever.

104. Do you know who's in charge of the barracks

105. Please remember to destroy them letters.

106. Landing on the southern coast and driving the original inhabitants north and west into the wilder parts of England.

107. Scotland and Ireland were occupied by Celts, they were known, however, as Gaels.

108. The Romans organized Britain as a province, Christian missionaries converted it.

109. The Celts were known as people who used bronze weapons, but they later learned the use of iron.

110. The native food tasted strangely to the American tourists.

111. A certified check is a check drawn on a bank by its cashier.

112. A signature on the back of a check is called an equity.

113. Per capita means by the day.

114. A request for supplies is called a requisition.

115. The general costs of running a business—such as taxes, rent, and heating—are called markup.

116. A person designated to receive the benefits from an insurance policy, annuity, will, or trust fund is called an adjuster.

117. The letters PS are required before typing a postscript.

118. When typing a letter in the modified block style, type the date at the left margin.

119. Use a 70-space line when typing a long letter.

120. The inside address should be typed 4 to 10 lines above the date.

121. June 2nd, 1995, is the correct way to type the date in a letter.

122. The second syllable of PREFACE is pronounced with a "long *a*" sound.

123. MISCHIEVOUS is correctly pronounced with four syllables.

124. A word used to join two words or two groups of words is called a preposition.

125. The derivation or history of a word is known as the usage label.

126. *We, us,* and *ourselves* are usually used as adjectives.

127. Antonyms are words with similar meanings.

128. If you don't no where your going you'll probably end up somewheres else.

129. It's true that this company's policy provides a discount for payment in 30 days, but your account is eight months over-due.

130. Are all employees' required to use the employee's cafeteria?

131. Milk that has been standing in the hot sun a long time is unfit to drink.

132. The quotations in our price list see page 4 apply to jobbers not consumers.

133. Marks of punctuation act like road signs they tell us when to slow down and when to stop.

134. The YWCA's campaign has illicited the support of women's organizations.

135. Mr. Wheeler's 2 daughter-in-laws majored in english literature.

136. Doing things right is not enough, you must do the right things.

137. Just to stand up in the face of lifes problems. That takes courage.

138. Although Philadelphia has been compared with Boston, the resemblance is superficial.

139. A good college or desk dictionary has about a half million entrys.

140. Any insurance man can give you information about rates.

141. Scientists know that mathematics are essential.

142. She told her that she had made a mistake.

143. The letters *bc* at the end of a letter mean "Be Careful."

144. Seattle is the nearest of the two cities'.

145. She was a granddaughter of J. P. Morgan, a man who controled a large part of Tex. and a Vassar graduate.

146. I have a friend. Her mother is an engineer.

147. We visited a factory, it makes computer parts.

148. You can effect these reductions without affecting the company's sales.

149. "Why did the peanut cross the road"? asked Ms. Hechanova

150. "To get to the Shell Station"! replied the student.

Read and Replay Reference Manual

READ ABOUT NUMBERS IN BUSINESS

Numbers are an important part of business and technical writing. Write them in figures on invoices, orders, requisitions, and so on, as well as in statistical documents.

Refer to the following information to determine whether to spell out a number or write it in figures in letters and reports. The rules given below are a consensus of the style used by better business writers today.

1. General

a. Spell out numbers up to ten; use figures for specific numbers over ten. If numbers under ten and over ten are used in a related way in the same category, use figures for all. (The second example sentence illustrates this guideline.)

We need **five** electronic engineers in our Dallas plant.

We need **5** electronic engineers, **25** typists, and **30** assemblers in our Dallas plant.

b. Spell out approximate numbers that can be written in one or two words.

Nearly **five thousand** employees were laid off last year.

We have developed about **a hundred** new by-products during the past year.

c. When a number begins a sentence, spell it out unless it requires more than two words. In that case, rephrase the sentence.

Six hundred crates were shipped to you yesterday.

Yesterday **642** crates were shipped to you.

d. When expressing millions or billions, make the reading easier by combining figures with words.

We produced **1½ million** electric fans during the past fiscal year. [or *1.5 million*]

Our company's gross sales during that same period were **66 million** dollars.   [or *$66 million*]

e. When two numbers appear together, spell out the number that can be written with fewer letters.

This architect has already designed **twenty 16-unit** apartment buildings.

This architect has already designed **25 sixteen-unit** apartment buildings.

2. Time

a. Use figures with *a.m.* and *p.m.* Type *a.m.* and *p.m.* in lowercase letters with no space after the first period. Notice that the colon and zeros are not used for "on the hour" time.

The conference will be held from **9 a.m.** through **5:30 p.m.**

b. When not using *a.m.* or *p.m.*, either spell out the time or use figures.

The conference will begin at nine.   [or *nine o'clock, nine in the morning, 9 o'clock,* etc.]

c. Use just one way to express the time. Avoid redundancy.

DON'T 9 a.m. in the morning
DO   9 a.m. *or* 9:30 a.m.
OR   nine in the morning
OR   9 o'clock
OR   nine o'clock

3. Dates

a. Use figures when the date follows the name of the month; with the date in this position, never use *-th, -d, -st, -rd,* or *-nd* after the figure.

The American Bankers Association will meet on **May 7** this year.

b. In military, foreign, and some government correspondence, the date usually appears before the month or month and year.

The American Bankers Association will meet on **7 May** this year. [or *7 May 199–*]

c. In ordinary business correspondence, *of* may be placed between date and name of month if desired. In that case, use *-th, -nd, -rd,* or *-st* after the figure, or else spell out the number.

The American Bankers Association will meet on the **7th of May**.

The American Bankers Association will meet on the **seventh of May.**

d. When the date is given without the name of the month, follow rule (c).

The American Bankers Association will meet on the **7th**.

e. Spell out or use figures for centuries and decades.

This book is about **nineteenth**-century poets.   [or *19th-century*]
He was a college student during the **sixties**.   [or *1960s*]
During the early **1900s** many immigrants who had been victims of cruel persecution in their native lands arrived in the United States.

4. Money

a. Use figures for amounts of money. The decimal point is unnecessary with even dollar amounts (no cents).

A **$5** registration fee is required for membership.
Members pay a **$5** registration fee and **$5.50** a month thereafter.
We'll need about **$50,000** for remodeling.

b. Use the dollar sign and decimal point style for *cents* to be consistent with other amounts used in the same context.

The project requires 1,000 wheat chiz at **$.15** each, 42 sedus at **$7.80,** and one large ramir at **$82**.

c. Spell out the word *cents,* but use figures for the number.

The plugs cost **8 cents** each.

d. In legal documents the amounts are often spelled (notice capital letters) and then written in figures enclosed in parentheses. In ordinary correspondence, do not repeat numbers in this legal style.

The fee for use of said property is to be **Two Hundred and Fifty Dollars ($250.00)** a month.

5. Addresses

a. Spell out names of streets under 11th.

The store is on **Sixth Street**.
Professor Maxey of Oroville moved to **11th Avenue** in Newport.

b. Use figures for all house numbers except One.

Their new suite is at **One Abercrombie Street**.
The Atlanta factory is at **8 Leland Avenue**.

6. Percentages and Fractions

a. Spell out *percent,* but use figures for the number (use the % sign in statistical reports).

Unemployment was at the **5 percent** level that year.

b. Spell out a common fraction when there is just one in the sentence.

We have received only **one-fourth** of our order.

c. Use figures for less common fractions.

The new specifications require **⅜** of an inch.

d. Use figures for a mixed number (fraction and whole number).

Our profits are **4½** times those of last year.

7. Measurements

Spell out measuring words, such as feet, pounds, and inches but use figures for the numbers.

The boards are **5 by 6 by 2 inches**. [Use *by* instead of x.]
Each one weighs **6 pounds 4 ounces**.
The mine is **8 miles** away.

8. Age

Usually spell out an age expressed in years only, unless it immediately follows the person's name. Notice that no commas are used in the third example, which illustrates age expressed in years as well as months and days.

Mr. Weber will be **sixty-three** on the day of the presentation.
Carl Weber, 63, is the new chairman.
The birth records show that she is **24 years 5 months 6 days** as of this date.

9. Books

Use figures for numbers of pages, chapters, volumes, and the like.

The information you need is on **page 46**.

REPLAY NUMBERS IN BUSINESS

Change the number style where necessary to make the following sentences correct in the paragraphs of a business letter or a formal business report.

1. At 9 a.m. in the morning on June 4th we will have completed forty-two jobs.

2. There are about 50 different ways to make 50 million dollars.

3. 210 boxes were shipped to your London office by Acme Air Freight on 6 June 1989.

4. Please send $5.00 for the book and fifty cents for postage.

5. On page six his age is given as 40.

6. Almost 5,000 attended the Alliance for Survival rally.

7. Our new office is at 62 4th Street.

8. The prime interest rate went to eleven % today.

9. We need 12 8X10 offices in the new building for the members of the sales staff.

10. This store opened its doors at eight a.m. on the 31st of June.

READ ABOUT CAPITALIZATION*

Capitalization is the process of giving a word special importance or emphasis. That's why the first word of a sentence is capitalized to give it the emphasis a word in this important position deserves. Many specific things have two names: the classification name, such as *girl,* and the official name, such as *Mary.* Some conventions of capitalization in business writing are explained in Section Four. Use the following as an easy reference for capitalization questions.

1. General

a. Capitalize the official names of specific people, animals, places, days, months, holidays, gods, documents, and historical events.

Joseph	United Airlines	Uganda
Veteran's Day	Declaration of Independence	Fabulous Forties
Atomic Age	Wednesday	March

b. Do not capitalize seasons

fall spring winter summer

c. Capitalize titles, headings, and the first word of each item in an outline. Use lowercase for short prepositions, articles, *to* in infinitives, and the conjunctions *and* or *or* unless one of these words begins the line.

TITLES OR HEADINGS

How to Cook with Electricity

OUTLINES

I. How to cook with electricity

2. Titles of People

a. Capitalize a title that directly precedes a person's name.

Professor Washington
Reverend Juan Perez
Madame Curie

* See Read and Replay Unit 22 for capitalization instruction.

b. Use lowercase for the title when the name of the person or the title are parenthetical and require commas.

One English **professor**, Janice Stern, . . .

The **captain**, Patrick O'Connor, was . . .

c. Do not capitalize the title when it appears *after* the name of the person, unless it is a title of very high government or church rank.

Capitalize the following U.S. government titles even when used after or instead of the name: President, Vice President, cabinet member, Senator, Representative, Chief Justice, head of a federal agency, Governor, and Lieutenant Governor. Also capitalize these titles when they refer to specific people: ambassador, queen, king, prime minister.

Elizabeth, **Queen of England**

The **Senator** from Florida is the president of Elks Club International.

d. Do not capitalize occupations, such as typist, lawyer, accountant, engineer, and the like.

3. Titles of Publications and Art Works

Capitalize the first word and all principal words of books, movies, plays, songs, and so on. Do not capitalize articles (*a, an, the*) or prepositions of three or fewer letters unless they begin the title. Titles of full-length published works should be either underlined or typed in all capital letters (not both).

I read GONE WITH THE WIND (or Gone With the Wind)*

Titles of portions of full-length works (newspaper or magazine articles, chapters of books, for example), as well as movies, plays, poems, songs, and so on, should be in quotation marks.

Section Eight is entitled "The Taming of the Apostrophe."

4. Names of Organizations

a. Capitalize names of organizations and of specific government groups.

Supreme Court	Sheimer College
Royal Inn	Department of Internal Revenue
United States Army	Greenland Paper Company

b. Unless you are preparing a legal document or a very formal communication, do not capitalize words such as *company, department, college,* and so on when they are used without the name.

---

* In typeset published materials, titles are in italics.

Dawn works in **a Washington hospital.**
Our company will not issue any more common stock this year.
Give the papers to **the chairman of the committee.**

c. Capitalize names of departments within your own organization but not in other organizations.

Our Shipping Department has packed your order.
Does **your purchasing department** have our latest catalog?

5. Names of Places

a. Capitalize complete names of specific places.

Atlantic Ocean   Victory Boulevard
Yosemite National Park   Mississippi River

b. When two or more specific places are named, do not capitalize the plural noun that completes the meaning.

the Atlantic and Pacific oceans
the Missouri and Mississippi rivers

6. Compass Points

a. Capitalize compass points that name areas thought of as geographical, cultural, or political units.

Far East   West Coast   Midwest

b. Do not capitalize compass points that indicate direction or name general areas.

The sun sets in the west.
Drive north along Main Street.
He would like to settle in northern Massachusetts.

c. Do capitalize derivatives of compass points that refer to people.

I believe Northerners usually appreciate Southern hospitality.

7. Trade Names

Capitalize the trade name of a product but not the product word itself unless you work for the company.

Chef Boyardee Pizza [if you work for the producer]
Nescafe coffee [if you don't work for the producer]

8. Business Letters

a. Capitalize all titles used in the inside address or signature. (Do not use Mr. or any other courtesy title in a signature. Do use a courtesy title in an address except as shown in Unit 82, No. 3.)

FIRST LINE OR TWO OF INSIDE ADDRESS

Mr. Morris Garber, Assistant Manager

Mr. Morris Garber
Assistant Manager

b. Capitalize the first word of complimentary close.

Sincerely yours,

c. Capitalize the first word of salutation and any noun or title in salutation.

Dear Friends:
My dear Mr. President:

9. Family Relationships

a. Capitalize a family relationship title when used as part of the name or instead of the name.

Do you think **Uncle George** will retire soon?
Do you think **Uncle** will retire soon?

b. Do not capitalize a family relationship title when a possessive noun or pronoun comes before it.

Steve and **Sue's uncle** was the principal of Saturn Street School.
I believe **my cousin** should apply for the job.

10. School Subjects and Degrees

a. Capitalize official names of courses. Do not capitalize the name of a subject or course when it is not the official name—except for languages, which are always capitalized.

Mr. Ivener will teach **Business 38.**
Mr. Sandell has taught **business law** for the past three years.
Are you planning to take **Spanish** or **business English** this year?

b. Capitalize the name of a degree directly after the person's name. Do not capitalize degrees used in any other way unless they are abbreviated. Notice the comma before and after the degree when the degree follows a name.

Margie Sorenson, **Ed.D.,** teaches at Golden West College.
Clara Chung is about to receive **a bachelor of science** degree.

11. Government Terms

Do not capitalize governmental terms that are used instead of the full official name.

This state has the highest income tax rate in the nation.
We don't wish to violate **the city ordinance.**

12. Ethnic Terms

a. Nationalities and religions are capitalized.

Dutch   Korean   British
Catholic   Hindu   Jewish

b. Races are not capitalized when named by color, but the scientific names for racial groups are capitalized.

black   white   yellow   red

BUT

Negroid   Caucasoid   Mongoloid

REPLAY CAPITALIZATION

Correct the capitalization so that the following sentences will be correct in a business letter or a formal report.

1. The atomic age may be said to have begun on August 5, 1945, when the atomic bomb was dropped on Hiroshima.
2. I flew on American airlines last Summer with the prime minister of Israel and the senator from south Dakota.
3. Eric A. Smith is an independent Auditor who conducts audits for various Department Stores.
4. Winston Churchill wrote <u>Triumph And Tragedy</u>, an important book about world war II.
5. The supreme court decision was favorable to my Company.
6. By september I will know how to speak spanish well enough to take a College course called spanish 2.
7. The Atlantic and Pacific Oceans are natural borders of the United States.
8. I prefer Hunt's tomato sauce for Spaghetti, but Aunt Mimi says that it contains too much salt.
9. Lalitha, a Hindu woman from the South of India, has a bachelor's degree in education.
10. The salutation of a letter: Dear customer:
    The complimentary close: Sincerely Yours,

READ ABOUT WORD DIVISION*

The picture-frame effect results in an attractive-looking business letter. Left and right margins should be approximately equal. In order to maintain a neat right margin, it is sometimes necessary to divide a word at the end of a line. Because a divided word tends to distract the reader, certain word-division customs have been established for keyboarded documents to promote greater readability.

1. A careful writer never divides:
   a. the last word on a page.
   b. a word containing an apostrophe.

* Review pages 275–276.

c. a number expressed in figures.
d. an abbreviation.
e. on more than two consecutive lines.
f. a word with fewer than five letters.
g. a word with just one syllable.
h. a proper noun.
i. between the number and *a.m., p.m., noon, midnight,* or *percent.*
j. unless at least three letters can be carried to the next line.

2. A careful writer may divide:
   a. between syllables. When consulting the dictionary, refer to the syllables in the entry word, not in the pronunciation. Dots, spaces, or accent marks indicate the syllables, depending on the dictionary.

fol · low · ing   [may be divided between the *l*'s or after the *w*]
stopped   [may not be divided because it is all one syllable]

   b. when at least two letters (preferably three) of the word can be typed on the line before the hyphen

OK   re-veal
NO   a-gainst

   c. when at least three letters of the word can be typed on the next line.

OK   compil-ing
NO   compa-ny

If the syllables do not permit the minimums of rules b and c, do not divide the word at all.

   d. after a one-letter syllable unless the vowel is part of a word ending, such as *ible* or *able.*

OK   cata-log
OK   credit-able, incred-ible
NO   credita-ble, incredi-ble

   e. between double consonants unless the division breaks the spelling of a root word.

OK   begin-ning
OK   spell-ing

If the second of the double consonants is needed to form a suffix, place the hyphen between the double letters.

OK   posses-sion
NO   possess-ion

f. at the hyphen when that mark is part of the spelling of the word.

OK   self-confidence
NO   self-confi-dence

g. nonhyphenated compound words between the main parts of the word.

OK   under-developed

3. A careful writer may separate:
a. a date between the day and the year.

Harold and Esther were married on March 8, 1976, in Albany.

b. the first name or middle initial from the last name.

The most capable auditor we have ever had is Mr. Martin L. Simon.

The most talented dancer in the troupe is Abby Asher.

c. a spelled-out title, but not an abbreviated or short title, from the name

YES   The most outstanding teacher in our English Department is **Professor Janice Stern**.
NO   The signature on the receipt was **Ms. Jeanne Dey**.
YES   The signature on the receipt was **Ms. Jeanne Dey**.
YES   The signature on the receipt was **Ms. Jeanne Dey**.
YES   The signature on the receipt was **Ms. Jeanne Dey.**

d. an address between the street name and the city or between the city and the state.

We have moved our office to **990 Kennedy Street, Minneapolis, Minnesota**.
We have moved our office to **990 Kennedy Street, Minneapolis, Minnesota.**

REPLAY WORD DIVISION

Write *T* (true) or *F* (false) in the blank.

_____   **1.** It's okay to divide a four-letter word if it has two syllables.

_____   **2.** Never divide the last word on a page.

_____   **3.** It's OK to divide a one-syllable word as long as it has more than five letters.

_____ 4. Never divide a number expressed in figures; for example, *1,500, −463.*

_____ 5. Never divide a word containing an apostrophe; for example *have-n't.*

_____ 6. If you can't carry at least three letters to the next line, don't divide the word.

_____ 7. If it's necessary to divide a date, type the month on one line and the day on the next; for example, *April* on one line and *18* on the next line.

_____ 8. If an address must be divided, separate the house number from the name of the street; for example, *2166* on one line and *Clinton Avenue, Bronx,* on the next line.

_____ 9. A hyphenated word may be divided only at the hyphen; for example, *self-propelled.*

_____ 10. Divide between double consonants unless the division breaks the spelling of a root word; for example, *spell-ing* but *win-ning.*

READ ABOUT ABBREVIATIONS

Spelling words out instead of abbreviating them has a favorable psychological effect on the reader. It helps to create an image for the company of thoroughness, carefulness, and accuracy. Also, it does not take much more time to spell out a word than to abbreviate it. In letters and reports, therefore, avoid most abbreviations except for technical or statistical ones. Abbreviations are common in many other kinds of business communications, however, including interoffice memos, informal notes, invoices, receipts, and all kinds of business forms.

1. Abbreviations That *Are* Acceptable in Business Correspondence

a. Always abbreviate the following: *Mr., Mrs., Dr., Jr., Sr., Esq.,** *Ph.D., CPA,* and similar academic degrees following names. Also see 1g, below. (*Ms.* is correctly typed with a period, even though it isn't an abbreviation. Do not use a period after *Miss.*)

Ronald Rosenberg, **Esq**.

b. Military and professional titles before a name may be abbreviated if used with the full name of the person. When in doubt, spell it out, except for *doctor. Dr.* is preferred with either full name or last name only.

The Rev. Jonathan Flaherty

The Reverend Jonathan Flaherty

The Reverend Flaherty

* In the United States, *Esq.* is used only after an attorney's name—either male or female. In Great Britain, however, *Esq.* (for *Esquire*) is a general courtesy title equivalent to *Mr.* but used after a man's name.

Dr. Marvin Belzer

Dr. Belzer

c. Names of well-known organizations are okay to abbreviate if you are certain the reader will recognize the abbreviation. Periods are often omitted in these familiar capital-letter abbreviations.

CIA   FBI   AFL-CIO   CBS

d. Time words may be abbreviated: for example, *a.m., p.m., EST* (Eastern Standard Time), *B.C., A.D.*

e. Abbreviate parts of names and addresses, such as *Inc., Co.,* or *Ltd.* (Limited) when they appear that way in the company letterhead, or *St.* (Saint) or *Mt.* (Mount) when this is how the place name is spelled in your dictionary. Spell out words such as *Street, Avenue,* or *Boulevard,* and names of cities. (See 1h, below, for state abbreviations.)

f. It's okay to use common business abbreviations and acronyms when you're sure the reader will understand them.

ASAP—as soon as possible; for use in memos
AT&T—American Telephone and Telegraph
CEO—chief executive officer (of a large corporation)
c.o.d. or COD—collect on delivery
CPA—certified public accountant
EEO—Equal employment opportunity
e.o.m. or EOM—end of month
etc.—and so on
Ext.—when followed by a number for a telephone extension (Ext. 302)
FDIC—Federal Deposit Insurance Corporation
FIFO—first in, first out
f.o.b. or FOB—free on board (the point from which the customer pays shipping charges)
FYI—for your information; for use in memos; implies no reply is required
GM—General Motors
GNP—gross national product
HRD—human resources department
IBM—International Business Machines
Inc., Corp., or Ltd.—when part of a company's name; Incorporated, Corporation, Limited.
IRS—Internal Revenue Service
LIFO—last in, first out
Memo—memorandum
Messrs.—plural of Mister (abbreviation of the French "Messieurs")
MIS—management information systems
NASA—National Aeronautics and Space Administration
No.—before a serial number (Style No. 2348)
OPEC—Organization of Petroleum Exporting Countries
OSHA—Occupational Safety and Health Administration

PC—personal computer
P.O. Box—Post Office Box No. 0000
PR—public relations
PS or P.S.—postscript
RE—regarding or concerning
R&D—research and development
RSVP—please respond (translated from French)
SEC—Securities and Exchange Commission
SOP—standard operating procedures (the way things are done)
TV—television
VIP—very important person

g. An academic degree is abbreviated after a person's name. When it doesn't follow a name, abbreviate only if you're sure the reader can interpret the abbreviation. Most of these abbreviations are used with or without the periods.

A.A.—Associate in Arts
A.A.S.—Associate in Applied Science
B.A. or A.B.—Bachelor of Arts
B.B.A.—Bachelor of Business Administration
B.S.—Bachelor of Science
D.A.—Doctor of Arts
D.B.A.—Doctor of Business Administration
D.D.—Doctor of Divinity
D.D.S.—Doctor of Dental Surgery or of Dental Science
Ed.D.—Doctor of Education
Ed.M.—Master of Education
J.D.—Doctor of Jurisprudence
J.M.—Master of Jurisprudence
J.S.D.—Doctor of the Science of Laws
LL.B.—Bachelor of Laws
M.A. or A.M.—Master of Arts
M.B.A.—Master of Business Administration
M.D.—Doctor of Medicine
M.S.—Master of Science
Ph.D.—Doctor of Philosophy
Th.D.—Doctor of Theology

h. State and territory names appearing in the address may be abbreviated if the official Post Office Abbreviation is used. The ZIP follows the abbreviation.

Alabama	AL	Montana	MT
Alaska	AK	Nebraska	NE
Arizona	AZ	Nevada	NV
Arkansas	AR	New Hampshire	NH
California	CA	New Jersey	NJ
Colorado	CO	New Mexico	NM
Connecticut	CT	New York	NY
Delaware	DE	North Carolina	NC
District of Columbia	DC	North Dakota	ND
Florida	FL	Ohio	OH
Georgia	GA	Oklahoma	OK
Hawaii	HI	Oregon	OR

Idaho	ID	Pennsylvania	PA
Illinois	IL	Rhode Island	RI
Indiana	IN	South Carolina	SC
Iowa	IA	South Dakota	SD
Kansas	KS	Tennessee	TN
Kentucky	KY	Texas	TX
Louisiana	LA	Utah	UT
Maine	ME	Vermont	VT
Maryland	MD	Virginia	VA
Massachusetts	MA	Washington	WA
Michigan	MI	West Virginia	WV
Minnesota	MN	Wisconsin	WI
Mississippi	MS	Wyoming	WY
Missouri	MO		

Territories:

Canal Zone	CZ	Guam	GU
Puerto Rico	PR	Virgin Islands	VI

For business and professional writing, spell out the name of the state if you don't use the official abbreviation as shown above. Two-letter Post Office abbreviation should be used *only* when followed by a ZIP code.

2. Other Abbreviations Often Used in Business Communications

The following abbreviations would usually be spelled out in the body of a business letter or in a formal report but are often abbreviated in less formal business communications

acct.	account
amt.	amount
assn. *or* assoc.	association
bal.	balance
b.l., b/l, *or* B/L	bill of lading
c/o	care of
ctn.	carton
cwt.	hundredweight
e.g.	for example
et. al. (used after names of people)	and others
frt.	freight
ft.	foot, feet
g.	gram
gal.	gallon
h.p.	horsepower
i.e.	that is
lb.	pound
LCL	less than carload lot
mdse.	merchandise
mfr.	manufacturer
mgr.	manager
misc.	miscellaneous
mo.	month
p.	page
pp.	pages

pd.	paid
rec'd *or* recd.	received
retd. *or* ret'd	returned
sec. *or* sec'y	secretary
supt.	superintendent
viz	namely
vs.	versus
yd.	yard
yr.	year

REPLAY ABBREVIATIONS

True/False

_____ 1. To save time in business communications, abbreviate as much as possible.

_____ 2. A good writer will not abbreviate in statistical and technical material.

_____ 3. It's important to include the periods in abbreviations of names of well-known organizations.

_____ 4. It's correct to abbreviate an academic degree when it appears after the person's name.

_____ 5. When typing an address in a business letter, spell out the word "Boulevard."

_____ 6. When "Saint" is part of the name of a city, always spell it out.

_____ 7. Miss., Okla., Calif., and Mass. are examples of correct abbreviations to use in the address of a letter.

_____ 8. A military title may be abbreviated when it precedes the full name of the person.

_____ 9. When writing a business letter, it's correct to abbreviate business terms such as account (acct.) and amount (amt.).

10. What do the following abbreviations stand for?

LIFO _____ SEC _____

MBA _____ EOM _____

Grammar Supplement for the Expert

Grammar Supplement for the Expert provides traditional grammar terminology and rules excluded from various sections. If you learned traditional grammar in the past, you will find this supplement a helpful review. Most of the main section information is not repeated here.

Section 1

PARTS OF SPEECH

Traditional grammar recognizes eight parts of speech, seven of which are defined in Section One. The eighth is the interjection, a single exclamatory word such as *Oh* or *Gosh.* The part of speech of a word, phrase, or clause is determined by its function in the sentence.

Nouns, Pronouns, and Verbs

Nouns and pronouns function as subjects, objects, or subject complements; any word that functions in one of those roles is a noun or a pronoun. Verbs along with their objects and complements are called predicates.

Sentence Subjects and Objects

Subjects The subject names who or what is doing or being. Although subjects are usually at the beginning of sentences, they may be elsewhere.

Although never a mother, she loved children.   [subject = *she*]

Direct Object of a Verb A direct object directly receives the action of the verb. Many, but not all, action verbs may have direct objects. Existence verbs do not have objects.

To find out whether an action verb has a direct object, say the subject and the verb; then add the question *Whom?* or *What?* If a word or group of words answers the question, that answer is the direct object. A verb that may be used with a direct object is **transitive**.

The secretary is typing a letter.   [*Letter* is the direct object of the verb *typing,* which is therefore transitive.]

459

When *Whom?* or *What?* doesn't get answered, the verb is **intransitive**:

The secretary is typing quickly.   [*Quickly* doesn't answer either *whom* or *what*. The verb *is typing* does not have a direct object and is intransitive.]

Indirect Object of a Verb   An indirect object answers the questions To whom? or For whom? Only a verb that has a direct object may also have an indirect object.

To locate an indirect object, say the subject, verb, and direct object; then ask To whom? or For whom? If a word or group of words answers the question, that answer is the indirect object:

We gave the president a gift.   [*President* is the indirect object. You can tell that *president* isn't the direct object because we can't give the president—but we can give something *to* the president. *Gift* is the direct object.]

Object of a Preposition   A noun or pronoun that follows a preposition is the *object* of that preposition. Each object (like all other words) serves just one function in a sentence. Therefore, if a word is an object of a preposition, it cannot be an object of a verb, nor can it be a subject.

The elephant in the zoo ate two bags of peanuts.
sub.   obj. of prep.   dir. obj.   obj. of prep.

Complements

A complement completes or makes whole. A subject complement completes the meaning of the subject by renaming it in some way (noun or pronoun) or by modifying it (adjective). It isn't necessary to ask Whom? or What? questions. A noun or pronoun that follows an existence verb is a **subject complement**, also known as a **predicate nominative**. An adjective that follows an existence verb is a **predicate adjective**, also known as a **predicate complement**.

Susan's mother was the president.   [predicate nominative]
    sub.   comple.

Susan's mother is attractive.   [predicate adjective]
    sub.   comple.

When an existence verb links the subject to its complement, as in the two sentences above, the verb is known as a **linking verb**.

If the subject complement is a noun or pronoun, it is usually possible to reverse the positions of subject and subject complement.

He is my father.
subj.

My father is he.   [A pronoun subject complement is in the nominative
subj.   case, the same as the subject.]

Conjunctions

Conjunctions are joining words.

Coordinate Conjunctions   Coordinate conjunctions join parts of sentences that are grammatically equal.

A well-organized "good news" letter starts with the good news, **and** the details follow.   [coordinating conjunction *and* joins independent clauses]

Subordinate Conjunctions   Subordinate conjunctions introduce clauses that function as adverbs, adjectives, or nouns. These clauses are always dependent. A subordinate clause can come *before* or *after* the main, or independent, clause. Some words often used as subordinate conjunctions are *although, when, if, after, unless, even though, as, since, because, so that.*

Chaya and Eric will take their vacations together *if* they can.

If they can, Chaya and Eric will take their vacations together.

In both sentences, the subordinate conjunction *if* preceding a subject and verb results in a subordinate (dependent) clause.

Prepositions

A preposition begins a phrase that ends with a noun or pronoun. The preposition shows how that noun or pronoun (which is the object of the preposition) relates to another word elsewhere in the sentence.

Some of the words shown above as subordinate conjunctions can also function as prepositions, in which case they will begin a *phrase*, not a clause:

PREPOSITIONAL PHRASES

after midnight

since five o'clock

until Christmas

A number of these words may also function as adverbs, in which case they will neither have an object nor introduce a clause:

We have seen these paintings **before**.

She went out for a loaf of bread and hasn't been seen **since**.

Correlative Conjunctions   Correlative conjunctions come in pairs:

either . . . or   not only . . . but also

neither . . . nor   both . . . and

Not only did she call in the order, **but** she **also** sent a follow-up memo to Purchasing.   [independent clauses introduced and joined by a correlative conjunction]

Conjunctive Adverbs   Conjunctive adverbs are transition words that bridge ideas from one *independent* clause to another. They're called conjunctive adverbs because they combine the conjunction and adverb functions. They include *however, nevertheless, moreover, thus, then, otherwise, accordingly, consequently, therefore, furthermore, yet, additionally.*

Generally speaking, a contract is valid whether it is written or oral; **however**, certain cases require specific forms.

When the words listed above do *not* join independent clauses, they are usually adverbs:

The courts have ruled, **however**, that an advertisement to sell a car is not a genuine offer.

Phrases and Clauses

Phrases and clauses may function as nouns, adjectives, and adverbs. Noun, adjective, and adverb clauses are always dependent.

NOUN CLAUSE

He said **that you would go**. [*He said* is an independent clause; *that you would go* is a noun clause functioning as the direct object of the verb *said*.]

ADJECTIVE CLAUSE

She is the manager **who makes the most scheduling changes**. [*Who makes the most scheduling changes* is an adjective clause modifying the noun *manager*.]

ADVERB CLAUSE

We'll ship the five dozen sweaters today if they're in stock. [*If they're in stock* is an adverb clause that modifies the verb *ship*.]

NOUN PHRASE

To know me is to love me. [*To know me* is a noun phrase because it is the subject of the verb *is*; *to love me* is also a noun phrase, the subject complement following the linking verb *is*.]

ADJECTIVE PHRASE

The girl in the blue dress is my sister. [*In the blue dress* is a prepositional adjective phrase because it modifies the noun *girl*.]

ADVERB PHRASE

We'll ship the five dozen sweaters by UPS. [*By UPS* is a prepositional adverb phrase that modifies the verb *ship*.]

Section 2

SENTENCES

A sentence is a related group of words that has a subject, a predicate, and at least one independent clause.

Sentence Parts

Subjects A **simple subject** is a noun or pronoun that tells who or what the sentence is about.

A **complete subject** is the simple subject plus any words or phrases that modify it:

Business English instructor *Kay Killen* is at Louisiana Business College.　[*Kay Killen* = simple subject; *Business English instructor Kay Killen* = complete subject]

A **compound subject** consists of two or more subjects (simple or complete) joined together to make one subject.

Larry and Kasey produced a new film.　[*Larry and Kasey* = compound subject]

Predicates　A **simple predicate** is the sentence's verb.
A **complete predicate** is the verb plus any modifiers or complements (completing expressions).

Larry and Kasey ***produced a new film***.　[*Produced* = verb; *produced a new film* = complete predicate]

A **compound predicate** consists of two or more predicates (simple or complete) joined together.

Larry and Kasey **produced and directed a new film**.　[*produced and directed a new film* = compound predicate]

Clauses　A clause is a related group of words containing a subject and a predicate.
An **independent clause** is grammatically complete in itself. It can be used as a sentence.

The manager received a raise.

A **dependent clause** (also called a subordinate clause) begins with a subordinating word. It cannot be used as a sentence.

When the manager received a raise　[subordinating word = *when*]

Whoever transcribed these tapes　[subordinating word = *whoever*]

Phrases　A phrase is a related group of words that does not have a subject and predicate.

in the office　　wearing a navy suit　　to go home

The Whole Sentence

The parts may be assembled according to English syntax principles to form simple, compound, or complex sentences.

Simple Sentence　A simple sentence has one independent clause, which may consist of words and phrases.

I love you.
Wearing a navy suit, he went to the office.

Compound Sentence　A compound sentence has two or more independent clauses joined with a coordinating conjunction or a semicolon.

I love you and I always will.

He was wearing a navy suit, and he looked quite businesslike.

Complex Sentence A complex sentence has one independent clause plus one or more dependent clauses.

I love you more than words can tell.

When he wears the navy suit, he wears black socks.

Compound-Complex Sentence A compound-complex sentence has two or more independent clauses joined with a coordinating conjunction plus one or more dependent clauses. It is a compound sentence and complex sentence combined.

I love you and I hope that you love me. [*I love you* and *I hope* are independent clauses; *that you love me* is a dependent clause]

Fragments, Run-ons, Comma Splices
How to Correct Them

Fragments, run-ons, and comma splices are sentence construction errors in business writing.

Fragment A fragment is a related group of words that is not a sentence. A fragment may be a dependent clause.

FRAGMENT When you submit a report to the president. [dependent clause] To correct the fragment, either remove the dependent conjunction or add an independent clause.

CORRECT Submit a report to the president.

CORRECT When you submit a report to the president, sign it.

A fragment may be a word group without a subject or predicate.

FRAGMENT Hope to hear from you soon. [no subject]

To correct the fragment, add a subject:

CORRECT We hope to hear from you soon.

Run-on A run-on is two or more independent clauses joined without a conjunction or punctuation:

RUN-ON The president comes from Kenya he's now an American citizen.

Comma Splice A comma splice is a run-on with a comma but no conjunction between the independent clauses:

COMMA SPLICE The president comes from Kenya, he's now an American citizen. To correct the run-on or comma splice, do one of the following:

COMPOUND SENTENCE

The president comes from Kenya, but he's now an American citizen. or The president comes from Kenya; he's now an American citizen.

TWO SENTENCES

The president comes from Kenya. He's now an American citizen.

COMPLEX SENTENCE

Although the president comes from Kenya, he's now an American citizen.

SIMPLE SENTENCE REPLACING A CLAUSE WITH A PHRASE

The president, a native of Kenya, is now an American citizen.

Section

5

PRONOUNS

Case

The case of a noun or pronoun defines how it functions in a sentence. A nominative case pronoun is used as a subject or a subject complement (predicate nominative). An objective case pronoun functions as a direct object of a verb, a verbal, or a preposition; as an indirect object of a verb or verbal; or as a subject of a verbal. A possessive case pronoun functions as an adjective and hence is often referred to as a possessive adjective.

Although both nouns and pronouns may be classified by "case," identification of case is unimportant with nouns as they do not change in form.

Nominative Case Pronouns   Nominative case pronouns are used as subjects and as subject complements.

1st person	I, we
2nd person	you
3rd person	he, she, it, they, who

SUBJECTS

Terri and **he** plan to go to the conference.

Who may I tell her called?   [*who* = subject of *called*]

SUBJECT COMPLEMENTS (AFTER LINKING VERB)

It was probably **she** who asked for the new keyboard.

It might have been **they**.

Objective Case Pronouns   Objective case pronouns are used as objects or as subjects of infinitives.

1st person	me, us
2nd person	you
3rd person	him, her, it, them
	whom

DIRECT OBJECT OF VERB

Please try to motivate Debbie and **him**.

Whom shall I take to the concert?

INDIRECT OBJECT OF VERB

Please give the president and **me** the papers on the Dickinson case.   [*papers* = direct object; *president* and *me* = indirect objects]

OBJECT OF PREPOSITION

Please give all the papers on the Dickinson case to the president and **me**.   [*to* = preposition]

SUBJECT OF AN INFINITIVE

I want **him** to go.

Possessive Case Pronouns—or Adjectives

In addition to uses explained in Section 5, use a possessive case pronoun (possessive adjective) to modify a verbal noun (also known as a *gerund*).

1st person	my, mine, our, ours
2nd person	your, yours
3rd person	him, her, hers, its, their, theirs, whose

YES   I don't approve of **his** working overtime.   [Possessive before verbal noun is correct.]

NO   I don't approve of **him** working overtime.   [Objective pronoun before verbal noun is disapproved of in formal writing or speech.]

Antecedents and Agreement

An antecedent is a noun or pronoun that means the same as the pronoun. Every pronoun needs a clear antecedent. The pronoun must agree with the antecedent in number (singular or plural) and gender (masculine, feminine, or neuter).

John ate **his** sandwich.   [*John* is the noun antecedent for *his*.]

Everyone did **her** own work.   [*Everyone* is the pronoun antecedent for *her*.]

If *nor* or *or* joins the elements of the antecedent, the pronoun should agree in gender and number with the antecedent that follows the joining word.

Either the president or the *vice president* will do *her* best to help you.   [The vice president is female.]

When a singular and a plural noun are joined by *or* or *nor*, use the plural one after the joining word:

Either the president or the **managers** will do **their** best to help you.

Section

6

VERBS

Tense

Tense states the time of the verb; that is, when the action or state of being takes place.

Simple Tenses   The simple tenses are past, present, and future, as identified in Section Six.

Perfect Tenses   The perfect tenses are past perfect, present perfect, and future perfect. The perfect tenses are formed by combining *have, has,* or *had* with a past participle.

The past perfect tense shows that the action was completed at a specific time in the past.

PAST PERFECT

had + past participle

I **had planned** to visit the Ford plant while I was in Detroit.

The present perfect tense shows that the action began in the past but was completed just before the present, is being completed in the present, or is continuing.

PRESENT PERFECT

has or *have* + past participle

He **has worked** on that report for six hours.

I **have known** Marie Mueller for a long time.

The future perfect tense shows that the action will have been completed before some specific future time.

FUTURE PERFECT

will have or *shall have* + past participle

When you get married next June, you **will have known** each other for five years.

Progressive Tenses   The progressive tense combines a form of *to be* with the present participle of a verb to show that action is or was in progress. Each of the simple and perfect tenses is shown below in the progressive form.

PAST PROGRESSIVE

was or *were* + present participle

He **was working** all day.

PAST PERFECT PROGRESSIVE

had been + present participle

He **had been working** all day.

PRESENT PROGRESSIVE

is, am, or *are* + present participle.

Dan McGavin **is working** today.

PRESENT PERFECT PROGRESSIVE

have been or *has been* + present participle

They **have been working** all week.

FUTURE PROGRESSIVE

will be or *shall be* + present participle.

They **will be working** next week.

FUTURE PERFECT PROGRESSIVE

will have been or *shall have been* + present participle

They **will have been working** for two weeks before their vacation begins.

Emphatic "Tenses"   The emphatic tenses—or forms—are used to show emphasis; that is, to add special importance to the verb. The emphatic form is the combination of *do, does,* or *did* with the basic form of the verb. Only the past and present tenses have special forms for expressing emphasis.

PAST EMPHATIC

did + basic form.

Despite the problems, we **did leave** here on time.

PRESENT EMPHATIC

do or *does* + basic form.

Evelyn and Stan **do live** in Solano Beach.

Emerson Milligram **does live** in Pittsburgh.

Shall/Will and Should/Would

Traditional or Formal Use of Shall/Will and Should/Would   In U.S., Canadian, and British communication, the distinction between *shall/will* and *should/would* related to person* is mostly ignored, except in legal documents. In fact these *shall/should* rules have never reflected usage accurately in most American or British English. In southern England, however, these person-related *shall/will* and *should/would* distinctions are used traditionally by a small percentage of the population, principally those with university educations. In most of the English-speaking world, however, *will* and *would* predominate for these usages.

The principles for traditional or formal person-related use of *shall/will* and *should/would* are shown below as a reference in case you require this information.

To express **simple future**, use *shall* or *should* with first person singular or plural pronoun subjects. Use *will* or *would* with all other subjects.

---

* *Shall* and *should* for first person; *will* and *would* for second and third person.

I shall prepare a report for your advertising department. [1st person singular]

We should like to assist you. [1st person plural]

The **auditors will examine** the records next month. [3rd person plural]

You **would be arriving** about 7:00 a.m. [2nd person]

To express strong determination, a firm promise, or a command, use *will* with first person singular or plural pronoun subjects and *shall* for all others.

I will finish college no matter what happens.
The **enemy shall** not succeed.

Colloquial and Ordinary Use of Shall/Will and Should/Would When asking a question about the future, use *shall* or *should* if the subject is a first person pronoun.

Shall (**Should**) I prepare a report for your advertising department?
Shall (**Should**) we fly to Atlanta with you?

Would or *Will* (or contractions such as I'll or you'll) is used with all noun or pronoun subjects for statements about the future.

I **will** prepare a report for your marketing department.
We**'ll** obtain the information for you.
"You **will** go to school today whether you like it or not," said the principal's mother.
We would* like to see you soon.

Use *should* with all subjects to mean "ought to."

She should get to work on time.
I should eat the fruit instead of the chocolate.

Use *would* with all subjects to mean something that habitually occurs.

She would get to work late every morning.

Subjunctive Mood

The **subjunctive mood**, or **mode**, of a verb shows something is not true, not yet true, unlikely, or impossible to ever be true. The use of *were* to express this aspect of the subjunctive mood is explained in Unit 38.

Additionally, the subjunctive is used to express necessity, strong request, demand, or a resolution at a meeting. For this purpose, use *be* after such verbs as *order, insist, ask, request, demand*, and *move* (for motions at meetings).

* *We'd, I'd, You'd*, etc., are appropriate in conversation, in personal letters, and in brief, informal memos to coworkers—but not in business letters or other documents.

I *move* that the meeting *be* adjourned.

Mr. Alston *demands* that she *be* fired.

We *ask* that the work *be* done by noon.

Verbals

Verbals are forms of verbs that are not being used as verbs. They function instead as nouns, adjectives, or adverbs. The three kinds of verbals are gerunds (also called verbal nouns), participles (verbal adjectives), and infinitives (which may be nouns, adjectives, or adverbs).

Gerunds or Verbal Nouns   As the alternate name implies, a gerund is a word that looks like a verb and may even have an object—but always functions as a noun. Gerunds always end in *ing*. You can distinguish them from verbs because a verb ending in *ing* is always preceded by an auxiliary (helping) verb.

He is majoring in **marketing**.   [*Marketing*, a gerund, is the object of the preposition *in*.]

Marketing ice to Eskimos would be rather difficult.   [Because *Marketing* is the subject of the verb *would be*, it is a gerund; *ice* is the object of the gerund.]

Participles   A participle looks like a verb, has tenses, and may have an object. Participles that are verbals function as adjectives. Below are the three tenses of participles

The **present participle** always ends in *ing* and can be readily distinguished from a verb; a verb ending with *ing* is always preceded by an auxiliary verb.

The woman **wearing** the red dress saw the reporter.   [*Wearing* is a participle used to introduce the participial phrase *wearing the red dress*. This phrase modifies the noun *woman*. The verb is *saw*.]

The **past participle** may end with *ed* or may be irregular.

The merchandise **ordered** last month will be shipped tomorrow. [*Ordered,* the participle, begins the participial phrase *ordered last month*. This phrase modifies the noun *merchandise*, which is the subject of the verb *will be shipped*.]

Ground up, the meat tastes much like beef hamburger.   [*Ground* is an irregular past participle]

The **perfect participle** also indicates action that took place in the past but has a helping verb.

Having ordered the merchandise last month, they are eager to receive it.   [*Having ordered* is the participle modifying the pronoun *they; merchandise* is the object of the participle *having ordered.*]

Infinitives   Infinitives are verbals that function as adjectives, adverbs, or nouns. They consist of *to* plus the basic verb form or the past participle. Sometimes *to* is omitted from an infinitive but understood.

'Tis better to have loved and lost than never to have loved at all. [*Lost* is an infinitive with *to have* understood.]

You can see it move. [*Move* is an infinitive with *to* understood.]

The present *tense of an infinitive* uses the basic verb form and signifies that the action of the infinitive and of the sentence's verb take place at the same time.

We plan **to dictate** the reports now. [present infinitive]

The **perfect infinitive** is used when the action took place before the action of the verb.

We expected **to have dictated** them yesterday. [perfect infinitive]

In the two example sentences above, the infinitives are nouns because they function as the object of the verbs *expected* and *plan*. *Reports* and *them* are the objects of the infinitives.

Split Infinitives Infinitives are "split" by inserting an adverb between *to* and the verb, as in *to finally succeed*. Grammar traditionalists recommend that infinitives not be split:

AVOID He wants **to *quickly* do** the work. [Adverb *quickly* splits the infinitive.]

USE He wants **to do** the work **quickly**. [Move the modifier to a logical place in the sentence.]

The "don't split infinitives" rule, however, may result in awkward writing:

He hopes to finish finally this project. [awkward]

He hopes finally to finish this project. [awkward]

He finally hopes to finish this project. [meaning changes]

He hopes to finally finish this project. [split infinitive improves sentence]

Transitive and Intransitive Verbs

Transitive Verbs A transitive verb is an action verb that has a direct object. A direct object answers the questions Whom? or What?

        tr. v.   ⌐—— dir. obj. ——⌐
Steve **teaches industrial arts** in Saratoga Springs.

A transitive verb may also have an indirect object. After saying the verb and direct object, ask To whom? or For whom? If there is an answer, that answer is the indirect object.

      tr. v. indir. obj.   dir. obj.
Fran **gave Jenny** a new **toy** .

A prepositional phrase may replace an indirect object.

obj. of prep.
Fran gave a new toy **to Jenny**.   [prepositional phrase]

Intransitive Verbs   An intransitive verb either is a state-of-being (or linking) verb, which never has an object, or is an action verb that does not require an object to complete its meaning.

Sue and Steve **drove** to Laurelton.   [*Drove* is an action verb with no object.]

Fran and Fred **are** happy about it.   [*Are* is a linking verb, which never has an object.]

Section

7

ADJECTIVES AND ADVERBS

Comparison of Absolute Adjectives

According to traditional grammar rules, careful communicators do not compare adjectives that represent an "absolute" idea. For example, either a room is *square* or it isn't. How can one room be "squarer" than another? Since *unique* means "one of a kind," how can one restaurant be the "most unique" one? Here are other adjectives to avoid in comparative or superlative forms:

complete	genuine	stationary
correct	parallel	unanimous
dead	perfect	wrong
empty	round	right

Substitutes for comparative and superlative forms are available for the types of words shown above; *more nearly* or *most nearly* used with some absolute adjectives results in a logical kind of comparison. In other cases, choose another adjective:

His work is **more nearly correct** [or **more accurate**] than yours. [instead of *more correct*]

These lines are **closer to being parallel** than are the others. [instead of *more parallel*]

Else/Other   When using the comparative form to compare one noun or pronoun with all the others in its classification, exclude the original person or object from the classification. Use *other* or *else* to "exclude" and thus achieve a logical comparison.

ILLOGICAL   He types **better than anyone** in the office.

LOGICAL   He types **better than anyone *else*** in the office.

ILLOGICAL   The Denova method is **less expensive than any** that I've tried.

LOGICAL   The Denova method is **less expensive than any** *other* that I've tried.

Adjectives with Linking Verbs

When a linking verb joins a subject to a modifier, that modifier is an adjective, which is called either a **predicate adjective** or **subject complement**. A subject complement is a noun, a nominative case pronoun, or an adjective.

The solutions **seem correct**.   [*seem* = linking verb; *correct* = predicate adjective]

The tenor was hoarse.   [*was* = linking verb; *hoarse* = predicate adjective]

Possessive Adjectives

Possessive nouns and pronouns are considered to be adjectives or possessive adjectives because they function as such. A possessive modifies the noun or pronoun that it possesses in the same way as an adjective:

green pencil   **my** pencil   **boy's** pencil

The adjective *green*, the possessive pronoun *my*, and the possessive noun *boy's* all modify the noun *pencil*.

It is simpler, however, to think of possessives as nouns or pronouns; this terminology does not affect the correctness of the resulting possessive expression.

Section 8

APOSTROPHES

The most important apostrophe principles are listed in Section Eight of the text. Here are additional principles for guidance in the use of possessives.

Joint Ownership or Separate Ownership

To show that something is possessed by more than one—joint ownership—make the final noun or pronoun possessive. To show separate ownership, make each noun or pronoun possessive.

JOINT OWNERSHIP

Rozini and Marino's factories are now in seven cities.

If they dissolve their partnership and divide the factories between them:

SEPARATE OWNERSHIP

Rosini's and Marino's factories are in competition with each other.

Title Following Possessor

If a title follows the name of the "possessor," it is better to use a prepositional phrase instead of a possessive form.

DON'T Sidney Berger, Ph.D.'s, report on Chaucer and Keats won all the literary awards.

DO The report on Chaucer and Keats, written by Sidney Berger, Ph.D., won all the literary awards.

Verbal Noun Modified by Possessor

Traditional grammar calls for a possessive to modify a gerund (verbal noun).

The doctor appreciated **Ann Blank's training** the new assistant. [possessive *Ann Blank's* modifies verbal noun *training*]

The manager was greatly impressed by **Mr. Powell's working** overtime to finish the accounts. [possessive *Mr. Powell's* modifies verbal noun *working*]

USE We'll appreciate **your sending** it to us.

AVOID We'll appreciate **you sending** it to us.

Abbreviations Made Possessive

To make an abbreviation of a singular noun possessive, add *'s.*

Nancy Cohen & Co.'s catalog arrived today.

To make an abbreviation of a plural noun possessive, add an apostrophe only, or rephrase to avoid using a possessive.

Two M.D.s' offices are on this floor.
The offices of two M.D.s are on this floor.

Possessives of Inanimate Objects

The traditional grammar rule states that inanimate objects should not be made possessive. A statement that better agrees with good usage, however, is:
Avoid using the possessive form for inanimate objects when doing so results in an awkward-sounding construction.

DON'T That chair's leg is broken. [awkward]

DO The leg of that chair is broken

BUT

DO Old Man Winter's coat is covered with ashes. [Possessive personification is good usage.]

DO The critic tried to explain the portrait's appeal. [This possessive inanimate object is good usage.]

Possessive Followed by Appositive

When an appositive follows the name of the possessor, avoid using the possessive form; instead, rephrase the sentence:

DON'T   Gary Goetz, our chief engineer's, new office is in Hartford.

DON'T   Gary Goetz's, our chief engineer, new office is in Hartford.

DO   The new office of Gary Goetz, our chief engineer, is in Hartford.

Section

COMMAS

Below are traditional grammar terms for some of the punctuation principles given in Units 50–53.

Unit 50

Use a comma between **coordinate adjectives** when *and* is omitted.

A manager needs an open-minded, adaptable attitude for making sound decisions.

Unit 51

Use a comma before a **coordinating conjunction** that joins the independent clauses of a compound sentence.

Chain stores have regional and district offices, and individual store units are supervised by these offices.

Unit 52

Use a comma after an **introductory verbal phrase** unless the verbal phrase is the subject of the sentence.

To be a buyer, you need a good sense of fashion.

NO COMMA   **To talk with the president** is an honor.   [Introductory verbal phrase is the subject of the verb *is*.]

Use a comma after an **introductory adverbial clause**.

Although the buyers are not responsible for the general training of salespeople, they instruct the salespeople on the merchandise they are to sell.

Use a comma after a long **introductory prepositional phrase**.

In addition to supervision of salespeople, buyers select merchandise for sale.

Use a comma after a short introductory prepositional phrase when the comma is needed for clarity.

After all, these men have been invited.   [Omission of the comma results in a sentence that seems like an adverbial clause.]

Unit 53

Set off with commas **parenthetical expressions**.

Last week, for example, five people were absent because of illness.

Set off with commas **nonrestrictive phrases or clauses**.

In the small enterprise, such as a dry-cleaning business or a shoe store, all employees may report directly to the owner or manager.

Local managers of chain stores are permitted to buy goods needed in the store from local dealers, particularly when immediate delivery is desired.

Do **not** set off with commas **restrictive phrases or clauses**.

Ryerson Polytechnic Institute is the school that was chosen.   [*that was chosen* = restrictive clause]

Set off with commas **nonrestrictive appositives**.

At the head of the merchandising division is Ellen D. Alderman, the general merchandise manager.

Ellen D. Alderman, the general merchandise manager, is at the head of the merchandising division.

Do **not** set off with commas **restrictive appositives**.

The song "Tie a Yellow Ribbon" became popular around the time of the Korean War.

Section

10

MISCELLANEOUS PUNCTUATION

Units 58 and 62

Ellipses show that words have been left out of quoted material. Three periods (. . .), with spaces before and after each, show that words have been omitted. Four periods (. . . .) show that the omitted words end the sentence.

According to the newsletter *Printout*, ". . . Continental Group, the largest U. S. can manufacturer, saved over $60,000 on type costs during 1989 . . . ."

Unit 63

If the first word of a compound modifier is an adverb ending in *ly*, do not use a hyphen.

The **newly developed** procedure is not yet available for general use.

When a compound adjective includes an interrupting word, space before the interrupting word:

Organizing the fall merchandise is usually a **one- to two-day** job.
Several **two- and three-ton** trucks are usually parked outside the diner.

Punctuation Rarely Occurring in Business Writing

Brackets [] enclose a parenthetical expression within material already in parentheses. Also use brackets to enclose extra words inserted in quoted material.

Dow said that this event (which is mentioned in Chapter 15 [1971 edition only]) isn't included in the film.
The student wrote, "The personal [sic] division does not actually supervise store workers."

In British English the term "brackets" usually refers to what Americans call "parentheses," while the latter are called "round brackets."
Single quotes, also known as inside quotes, enclose a quotation within another quotation.

Fana Spielberg, the keynote speaker, said, "Nineteenth-century writer William Wallace alluded to the power of women when he wrote, 'The hand that rocks the cradle is the hand that rules the world.'"

In British English, single quotes are often used instead of the standard double mark seen in American writing.

Section

12

LIE/LAY

Lay is a transitive verb meaning to place or to set.

Simple past—*laid*
Past participle—*laid*
Present participle—*laying*

The hen is **laying** eggs. The farmer **laid** the eggs in the carton. He had **laid** them there yesterday also.

Lie is an intransitive verb meaning to recline or to rest.

Simple past—*lay*
Past participle—*lain*
Present participle—*lying*

He is **lying** on the beach.
They **lie** on the beach every day.
He **lay** there last month also.
He has **lain** there for two hours.

Section

13

SENTENCES

Unit 77

Danglers are verbals—phrases or single words—that modify the subject of the independent clause even though that subject cannot logically be modified by this verbal phrase. To fix, make the phrase into a clause that expresses the appropriate subject, or change the subject in the independent clause.

DANGLER   To complete the job early, efficient work habits are required.   [infinitive phrase is dangling because it modifies *habits*]

CORRECT   To complete the job early, the staff must have efficient work habits.

CORRECT   If we are to complete the job early, efficient work habits are required.

Unit 79

A verb in the passive voice is always a past participle preceded by a form of *be* as an auxiliary verb (*am, are, is, was, were, be, been, being*).

PASSIVE VOICE

The financial division **is directed** by a controller.

ACTIVE VOICE

A controller **directs** the financial division.

Recap and Replay Answers

PRETEST

1.	b	**5.**	c	**9.**	a	**13.**	c	**17.**	a
2.	d	**6.**	b	**10.**	b	**14.**	b	**18.**	b
3.	d	**7.**	b	**11.**	a	**15.**	d	**19.**	a
4.	b	**8.**	b	**12.**	c	**16.**	b	**20.**	a

REPLAY—THE FRESH START

1.	Standard English	**3.**	F	**5.**	F	**7.**	T	**9.**	F
2.	F			**4.**	F	**6.**	T	**8.**	F	**10.**	T

SECTION 1 TOOLS OF THE TRADE

RECAP UNIT 1

1. school
2. child
3. day
4. People jobseekers intelligence integrity adaptability
5. Scarsdale
6. rug window lamp flower chair
7. Sean boy student pianist

REPLAY UNIT 1

A.

1.	need have	**3.**	asking	**5.**	mail make
2.	spend	**4.**	typed had		

B.

	Nouns	Verbs		Nouns	Verbs
1.	secretaries	type	**6.**	clerks	were typing
2.	Students	think		answers	
	careers			blanks	
3.	manager	have	**7.**	salesperson	will have completed
	accountant			work	
	reports			Tuesday	
	subject		**8.**	Martha	should go
4.	Fred	is		conference	
	president			Milford	
	company		**9.**	wife	had arrived
5.	Sheela Danielle	was		manager	
	winner			Nebraska	
	scholarship				

	Nouns	Verbs		Nouns	Verbs
10.	Joan Sterns letter	will ask	**16.**	bookkeeper invoice	will mail
11.	instructions Southeast Community College	have been sent	**17.**	Aldrich Company check	received
12.	Nina lawyer building	knows	**18.**	auditor books accuracy	checked
13.	Reuben Singer actor concert	will present	**19.**	Frankenstein factory city moon	built
14.	Joe tickets	should mail	**20.**	office managers terminals	have
15.	paper box window	is			

REPLAY UNIT 2

A.

1. It **3.** Who **5.** They her him
2. Everyone **4.** She her

B.

1. I me my mine myself
2. we us our ours ourselves
3. you your yours yourself yourselves
4. she her hers herself
5. he him his himself
6. it its itself
7. they them their theirs themselves

C.

1. you whose
2. He it she she hers
3. I myself these them
4. They Anyone who anybody your
5. We our we everything

REPLAY UNIT 3

A.

	Nouns	Adjectives
1.	offices carpeting	These any
2.	windows	many
3.	office	This
4.	floors departments	Some five
5.	managers year	Several this

B.

1. an exclusive resort **6.** Spanish
2. the beautiful **7.** gourmet
3. the crystal blue **8.** a heated
4. the white sandy **9.** The serene smogless sunny
6. exquisite guest **10.** this

C. **Possible Answers**

handsome modern high-tech dirty drab huge

D. Possible Answers

1. SOME people in THIS room have A GOOD attitude.
2. THIS morning I found TWO quarters near AN ORANGE phone.
3. He has SEVERAL OLD typewriters in THAT room, but he can't find A typist.
4. In A FEW years he opened THOSE CHICKEN restaurants.
5. She went to A NEW post office to buy SOME stamps for THESE letters.

RECAP UNIT 4

1. too 3. Marjorie 5. Marjorie
2. intelligent 4. intelligent

RECAP UNIT 4

1. manufactures 2. cheaply

REPLAY UNIT 4

A. Here are some possible answers.

1. today, immediately
2. well, poorly
3. carefully, fast
4. correctly, accurately
5. never, always
6. home, there
7. less, more
8. finally, eventually
9. frequently, not, never
10. sometimes, usually, often
11. exceptionally, especially
12. somewhat, rather, very
13. most, exceedingly
14. beautifully, tastefully
15. usually, very, often
16. not
17. very, extremely, so
18. rather, very, especially
19. too
20. even, much, somewhat

B.

1. verbs 2. adjectives 3. other adverbs

RECAP UNIT 5

1. if 3. so 5. but
2. because or 4. Since

RECAP UNIT 5

Hid is a verb; *newly* is an adverb. A prepositional phrase doesn't have a verb and begins with a preposition.

REPLAY UNIT 5

A.

1. nor 6. and
2. but 7. until
3. when 8. If
4. and 9. so that
5. Although 10. or

B. Possible Answers

above	behind	into	on	toward
across	below	near	through	under
along	beneath	off	to	up
around	inside			

C.

1. IN touch WITH you DURING the first part OF next week
2. ON the behavior OF people ON their lifestyles
3. BETWEEN a wish and a goal

4. FOR advertising   IN several ways
5. AT producing spot announcements   FOR their customers

REPLAY UNIT 6

A.

1. verb
2. adjective
3. noun

B.

1. noun
2. verb
3. adjective

C. **Possible Answers**

1. He is typing a report for the president.
2. Typing is an important function in any office.
3. Have you ever tried using typing paper for that job?

D. **Possible Answers**

1. I plant pansies every spring.
2. In our Las Vegas plant the power has been out.

E. **Possible Answers**

1. adjectives
2. I moved from the city to the country.

REPLAY UNIT 7

A.

1. pronoun   **3.** verb   **5.** adjective   **7.** verb
2. noun   **4.** preposition   **6.** adverb

B.

1. believe   **2.** conduct

C.

1. We   **2.** we   **3.** that   **4.** we   **5.** us

D.

of the warranty

E.

1. adjective   **5.** pronoun
2. noun   **6.** conjunction
3. noun   **7.** noun
4. verb   **8.** preposition

SECTION 2   SECRET LIFE OF A SENTENCE REVEALED

RECAP UNIT 8

1. Ms. Ramirez   **7.** Embezzlement
2. She   **8.** coat
3. horse   **9.** horse
4. he   **10.** I
5. treasurer   president   **11.** money   jewelry
6. He   **12.** You (understood)

REPLAY UNIT 8

A.

1. around the race course
2. at the stockholders' meeting
3. to South America
4. in the closet
5. at the computer
6. under your mattress

B.

	Subject	Verb
1.	Joanna Warner	was
2.	You	introduced
3.	winner	sees
4.	loser	sees
5.	books	were
6.	He	wanted
7.	members	have
8.	visitors	arrived
9.	You (understood)	give
10.	supervisor	found

C.

1. V	**3.** S	**5.** V	**7.** V	**9.** V
2. S	**4.** S	**6.** S	**8.** S	**10.** V

D.   Possible Answers

1. The former treasurer of this company runs for exercise every day.
2. The big black race horse in my stable is a very good typist.
3. The experienced and competent accountant usually eats hay every morning.
4. The little old lady in tennis shoes was caught stealing the sugar.
5. A new factory equipped with the latest in robotics costs a great deal of money.

REPLAY UNIT 9

A.

1. F	**3.** F	**5.** C	**7.** F	**9.** C
2. C	**4.** C	**6.** F	**8.** C	**10.** F

B.   Possible Answers

1. If you do a good job on the Mendocino project, you will get a raise in salary after the first of the month.
2. Although most corporations use the services of an auditor to examine the books, some errors may never be found.
3. Now that Ms. Berg has completed the training, she will start to work for the new treasurer.
4. The company stopped paying its bills so that it would have enough cash to keep its shelves stocked through the holiday season.
5. Caye resigned because this policy is illegal and immoral.

REPLAY UNIT 10

A.

1. F	**3.** F	**5.** S	**7.** S	**9.** S
2. F	**4.** S	**6.** F	**8.** F	**10.** S

B.   Possible Answers

2. The Personnel Department, which is on the third floor, is closed today.
3. Mr. Shade, feeling that he was right, went on ahead to Tucson.

6. The staff, having been on vacation last week, had to pack all the widgets in one day.
8. Are you on the team that won all the games last year?

REPLAY UNIT 11

1.	program. The	**6.**	inaccurate. He	**11.**	C	**16.**	C
2.	C	**7.**	C	**12.**	C	**17.**	C
3.	symptoms. They	**8.**	career. They	**13.**	C	**18.**	C
4.	C	**9.**	C	**14.**	IBM. It	**19.**	C
5.	aged. It	**10.**	C	**15.**	C	**20.**	C

RECAP UNIT 12

1. Don't fill a letter with very long sentences or with words of many syllables, for it doesn't impress anyone.
2. Don't fill a letter with very long sentences or with words of many syllables; it doesn't impress anyone.
3. Don't fill a letter with very long sentences or with words of many syllables. It doesn't impress anyone.

REPLAY UNIT 12

A.

1. CS	word; that is,	**3.** CS	symptoms; therefore,	**5.** C		**7.** R	job; also
2. CS	conscious; however,	**4.** R	distinctive; they	**6.** C			

B.

1. C	**3.** R	floor, but	**5.** R	conference, or	**7.** C
2. C	**4.** CS	once, and	**6.** CS	bones, but	**8.** C

C.

1. also, for example, hence, however, in addition, in fact, moreover, nevertheless, otherwise, then, therefore, thus, yet
2. True
3. True
4. True
5. False
6. False
7. to insert a period before the transition or to insert a semicolon before the transition
8. True
9. True
10. True

REPLAY UNIT 13

A.

1. CS
2. C   Because Ms. Hicks buys a new car every year,
3. R
4. C
5. C   Even though you have broken one of our important rules,
6. R
7. C   After Susan Dennis succeeded in closing the difficult sale,
8. C
9. R
10. CS
11. C   that cannot be answered by a simple "yes" or "no."
12. C
13. C   Since he was a native of the place,
14. C   because he was a native of the place.
15. C

B.

1. When I exceeded last year's sales by 150 percent, I was extremely proud of myself.
2. Ari Optical companies place big orders with us because the manager gives them a special discount.
3. Even though the plant was operating on a 24-hour basis, top management refused to adopt a three-shift schedule.
4. Professor Sumner explained that studying English is fun although the new student wouldn't believe it.
5. Although the method of shipment was not vital, we gave it careful consideration.

REPLAY UNIT 14

1st paragraph:	month. She . . . you.
2nd paragraph:	BUSINESS. This . . . now. We . . . carefully.
3rd paragraph:	APPLICATIONS. A . . . month.
4th paragraph:	available. If . . . know. Best . . . season.
PS:	splices. They

SECTION 3 *AIN'T* IS IN THE DICTIONARY

REPLAY UNIT 15

1. Answers will vary.
2. Answers will vary.
3. guide words
4. Answers will vary.
5. They show the alphabetic range of the page.
6. spelling, syllables, pronunciation, definitions, parts of speech
7. etymology, usage, illustrations, synonyms, derivatives, plurals, capitalization
8. unabridged
9. desk or college, pocket
10. desk or college
11. pocket
12. pronunciation key
13. Answers will vary.
14. front matter
15. Answers will vary depending on the dictionary you are using. For example, the appendix of *Random House Webster's College Dictionary* contains Guide for Writers, Avoiding Sexist Language, From Sounds to Spelling, and Index.

RECAP UNIT 16

1. Know how to pronounce these words.

2. banana collect easily gallop circus

REPLAY UNIT 16

1. 3
2. 1st
3. 3rd
4. 2nd
5. Jules Leotard, French arial gymnast (Wording will vary, depending on dictionary.)
6. 1st
7. WNCD bet; AHD pet
8. AHD false; WNCD maybe (see usage notes at DISINTERESTED entry)   Random House maybe
9. ticker tape
10. cooperate
11. yes
12. antitrust
13. 1st
14. ONTRApraNUR   one who organizes, manages, and assumes the risk of a business (wording will vary)
15. WNCD abut; AHD about, item, edible, gallop, circus; Webster's New World ago, agent, sanity, comply, focus (inside front cover)

RECAP UNIT 17

1. Webster's New World: Colloquial.   WNCD: Substandard.   AHD: Nonstandard
2. Slang (be sure you've looked up the *verb*)

REPLAY UNIT 17

1. loquacious   adjective
   apparent   adjective
   waver   verb
2. diacritical and accent marks vary, depending on dictionary
3. Janus
4. a social blunder, be sure you can pronounce it, accent on 2nd syllable—fō pä′
5. Victoria, Texas 77901
6. space, transpose, leave it in
7. Frankfort
8. CXXXVII
9. 35
10. shilling
11. Organization of Petroleum Exporting Countries
12. Answers will vary depending on dictionary consulted.
13. False
14. irregardless: nonstandard
    anyways: AHD nonstandard; WNCD archaic & chiefly dial.
    critter: AHD regional; WNCD dial.
    nerd: slang
15. informal/conversational

REPLAY UNIT 18

A.

1. F	**3.** F	**5.** T	**7.** T	**9.** T
2. T	**4.** T	**6.** F	**8.** T	**10.** T

B.

1. separate	**6.** bachelor	**11.** conscious
2. weird	**7.** superintendent	**12.** pursue
3. recommend	**8.** persistent	**13.** congratulate
4. accommodate	**9.** dilemma	**14.** pronunciation
5. privilege	**10.** villain	**15.** embarrassed

C.

1. accidentally	**3.** deductible	**5.** height	**7.** occasion	**9.** personnel
2. existence	**4.** fulfilled	**6.** irrelevant	**8.** occurred	**10.** ridiculous

SECTION 4   APPLES, TIGERS, AND SWAHILI

RECAP UNIT 19

nutritionists turkeys knives turkeys days years chefs potatoes kitchens loaves burgers

REPLAY UNIT 19

A.

1. allies	**3.** itineraries	**5.** facilities	**7.** journeys	**9.** accessories
2. alleys	**4.** proxies	**6.** copies	**8.** authorities	**10.** surveys

B.

1. sopranos	**3.** embargoes	**5.** heroes	**7.** potatoes	**9.** portfolios
2. dynamos	**4.** pianos	**6.** egos	**8.** cargoes, cargos	**10.** mementos, mementoes

C.

1. thieves	**3.** knives	**5.** calves	**7.** safes	**9.** plaintiffs
2. handkerchiefs	**4.** tariffs	**6.** halves	**8.** wolves	**10.** selves

D.

Line 1: Globetrotters   Line 4: audiences
Line 2: States   Line 5: routines
Line 3: fans, games

REPLAY UNIT 20

A.

1. formulas, formulae	**6.** bureaus, bureaux	**11.** mediums, media
2. addenda	**7.** censuses	**12.** geese, gooses
3. alumni	**8.** AHD: criteria, criterions WNCD: criteria	**13.** AHD: oxen WNCD: oxen also oxes
4. appendixes, appendices	**9.** data, datums	**14.** parentheses
5. bases	**10.** indexes, indices	**15.** diagnoses

B.

1. S	**3.** P	**5.** P	**7.** P	**9.** P
2. S	**4.** S	**6.** S	**8.** P	**10.** S

C.

1. media   **2.** vertebrae   **3.** criteria   **4.** parenthesis   **5.** alumni

REPLAY UNIT 21

A.

1. corps	**4.** Marys	**7.** Fifes	**10.** DeSotos
2. politics	**5.** series	**8.** aircraft	**11.** statistics
3. AHD: deer WNCD: deer also deers	**6.** Japanese	**9.** fish, fishes	**12.** Ramirezes

B.

1. P   **2.** S   **3.** S   **4.** P   **5.** S

C.

1. have	**3.** are	**5.** are	**7.** is	**9.** has
2. is	**4.** were	**6.** are	**8.** was	**10.** were

REPLAY UNIT 22

A.

	Singular	**Plural**
1.	spoonful	AHD: spoonfuls WNCD: spoonfuls also spoonsful
2.	textbook	textbooks
3.	WNCD: postcard AHD: post card also postcard	postcards post cards postcards
4.	editor in chief	editors in chief
5.	stockholder	stockholders
6.	AHD: passer-by also passerby WNCD: passerby	passers-by passersby passersby
7.	businesswoman	businesswomen
8.	brother-in-law	brothers-in-law

9. AHD: out-of-towner   out-of-towners
   WNCD doesn't show this compound; therefore, WNCD
   considers it three separate words with no hyphens
10. bill of lading   bills of lading

B.   See Answers On Page 504

C.

1.	general manager	6.	Catholic	11.	uncle, business, English, colleges
2.	C	7.	Office Manager	12.	black, company
3.	manager, shipping department	8.	north, spring, City	13.	C
4.	C	9.	city, state	14.	C
5.	Secretary of State	10.	English, Spanish	15.	Academy Award, Nobel Prize

REPLAY UNIT 23

These are possible answers; yours may vary somewhat.

1. The women in my office go to lunch at 12.
2. He promised to send his secretary over with the contracts.
3. Harry does the job well.
4. The president invited the managers and their spouses or guests to a dinner at his club.
5. Our hotel offers special rates for businesspeople.
6. We have several police officers guarding against intruders.
7. He is studying to be a nurse.
8. A programmer is installing the new software, and an assistant from Data Processing is helping him.
9. The author of the book you ordered is going on a book tour next month.
10. The director of the organization is doing an excellent job.

REPLAY UNIT 24

1. sisters-in-law	6.	software	11.	portfolio	16.	chassis
2. alumni	7.	allies	12.	write-off	17.	chassis
3. plaintiff	8.	alley	13.	proceeds	18.	proxy
4. criterion	9.	cargo	14.	itinerary	19.	hypothesis
5. criteria or criterions	10.	bill of lading	15.	memento	20.	embargo

SECTION 5   BE KIND TO THE SUBSTITUTE WEEK

REPLAY UNIT 25

1.	me	7.	me	13.	They	19.	me	25.	they
2.	me	8.	him	14.	him	20.	me	26.	he
3.	he	9.	we	15.	He and I	21.	me	27.	she
4.	us	10.	she	16.	me	22.	he	28.	I
5.	I	11.	me	17.	her	23.	him	29.	they
6.	We	12.	us	18.	We	24.	me	30.	I

RECAP UNIT 26

1. do   (2.) he likes me

REPLAY UNIT 26

A.

1.	C	5.	me	9.	himself	13.	C	17.	themselves
2.	themselves	6.	he (is)	10.	I (do)	14.	C	18.	himself
3.	he	7.	I (do)	11.	I	15.	C	19.	C
4.	C	8.	C	12.	ourselves	16.	ourselves	20.	he

B.

1. (does)   2. (he loves)   3. (does)   4. (I know)   5. (can)

REPLAY UNIT 27

1. who's	**5.** ours	**9.** You're	**13.** C	**17.** It's
2. C	**6.** Yours	**10.** yours	**14.** Who's	**18.** C
3. its, it's	**7.** C	**11.** They're	**15.** anyone's, theirs	**19.** Something's
4. C	**8.** theirs	**12.** one's	**16.** It's	**20.** Anything's

REPLAY UNIT 28

A.

1. class, company	**3.** union, family	**5.** name of any organization
2. committee, team	**4.** staff, group	**6.** club, jury, herd

B.

1. (a) singular	**8.** their
2. (b) plural	**9.** its
3. (a) singular	**10.** its
4. its	**11.** its
5. it	**12.** its
6. its	**13.** its
7. its	**14.** their, their

RECAP UNIT 29

1. whoever   **2.** Who

REPLAY UNIT 29

1. whom (I met <u>him</u>)
2. Whom (you do prefer <u>him</u>)
3. Whom (you would like <u>him</u> to)
4. who (<u>he</u> needs it most)
5. who (<u>he</u> are [is] needed)
6. whom (I took <u>him</u> to be)
7. (support <u>him</u>) whomever (the convention chooses <u>him</u>)
8. who (<u>he</u> will do)
9. Whoever (<u>he</u> is willing)
10. whom (you will want <u>him</u>)
11. who (<u>he</u> must make)
12. whoever (<u>he</u> gets there)
13. who (<u>he</u> was chosen)
14. whoever (<u>he</u> needs it)
15. whom (you sent for <u>him</u>)
16. who (<u>he</u> would be best able)
17. whom (we met <u>him</u>)
18. who (<u>he</u> helped me)
19. whom (I told you about <u>him</u>)
20. who (<u>he</u> has been active)
21. Who (<u>he</u> will get)
22. Whom (we should get <u>him</u>)
23. who (<u>he</u> should handle)
24. whoever (<u>he</u> can identify it)
25. who (<u>he</u> has courage)

REPLAY UNIT 30

A.

Students should use singular pronouns with singular nouns in their writing. OR In written language, students should use singular pronouns with singular nouns. OR Every student should use singular pronouns with singular nouns in his or her writing.

B.

1.	No one	**9.**	her
2.	anyone	**10.**	someone, he
3.	Everybody	**11.**	somebody, his, he
4.	someone	**12.**	Every one
5.	Any one	**13.**	Everyone, his or her
6.	no body	**14.**	his
7.	his	**15.**	Everybody, his or her
8.	his		

C.

	Best	**Wrong**
1.	c	b
2.	a	d
3.	c	b
4.	b	c
5.	c	b

SECTION 6   LOOKING FOR THE ACTION? THEN STUDY VERBS!

RECAP UNIT 31

1. wrote   **2.** told   **3.** were

REPLAY UNIT 31

A.

1.	types	**14.**	offered
2.	needs	**15.**	will select or should select
3.	arrived	**16.**	looks
4.	are sailing	**17.**	looked
5.	waxed	**18.**	will consider or should consider
6.	paints	**19.**	is considering
7.	looks	**20.**	wanted
8.	climbed	**21.**	stay
9.	gained	**22.**	are staying
10.	want	**23.**	watched
11.	wants	**24.**	need
12.	wanted	**25.**	talked
13.	will want		

B.

1. is	**3.**	are	**5.**	is	**7.**	flow	**9.**	are
2. is	**4.**	are	**6.**	are	**8.**	knows	**10.**	is

REPLAY UNIT 32

1.	broken	**6.**	C	**11.**	gone	**16.**	saw	**21.**	doesn't
2.	begun	**7.**	eats	**12.**	risen	**17.**	C	**22.**	rang
3.	chooses	**8.**	did	**13.**	run	**18.**	wear	**23.**	C
4.	chosen	**9.**	fly	**14.**	worn	**19.**	seen	**24.**	C
5.	does	**10.**	gave	**15.**	stayed	**20.**	C	**25.**	give

REPLAY UNIT 33

A.

1. being, was, been
2. biting, bit, bitten
3. blowing, blew, blown
4. coming, came, come

5. costing, cost, cost
6. drawing, drew, drawn
7. falling, fell, fallen
8. forecasting, forecast or forecasted, forecast or forecasted
9. forgetting, forgot, forgotten
10. freezing, froze, frozen
11. grinding, ground, ground
12. hiding, hid, hidden
13. leading, led, led
14. paying, paid, paid
15. shaking, shook, shaken
16. sinking, sank, sunk or sunken
17. singing, sang, sung
18. throwing, threw, thrown
19. winning, won, won
20. writing, wrote, written

B.

1. beaten   **2.** did   **3.** broken   **4.** hung   **5.** stayed

(A few of these answers may vary, depending on the dictionary you're using.)

REPLAY UNIT 34

1. were	**6.** will	**11.** Were	**16.** were	**21.** were
2. are or will be	**7.** are	**12.** was	**17.** are	**22.** was, is, or will be
3. are	**8.** C	**13.** is	**18.** has	**23.** C
4. have been	**9.** C	**14.** C	**19.** C	**24.** was, is, or will be
5. are	**10.** are	**15.** were	**20.** Were	**25.** is

RECAP UNIT 35

1. (bird) is
2. (Everyone) was laid
3. (Lewis, Martin) told, sang

REPLAY UNIT 35

	Subject	**Verb**
1.	I	enjoy
2.	salespeople	are doing
3.	you	do read
4.	He, I	did, could find
5.	We, he	voted, was elected
6.	we	won't issue
7.	manner	is
8.	Advancement, who	comes, do
9.	work	turns
10.	Playing	is
11.	sales	have risen
12.	students	study
13.	Brian, who	is, presented
14.	typewriters	are
15.	Rachel	will receive
16.	Everyone	is working
17.	Xerox	manufactures
18.	assistant, who	is, will help
19.	you	would like
20.	turnover	is
21.	poverty and riches	are
22.	The English Shoe Company	distributes
23.	We, you	are returning, hope, will take

24. Mr. J. C. Penney, who   started, built
25. mind   functions

RECAP UNIT 36

1. works   **2.** was   **3.** is   **4.** votes

RECAP UNIT 36

1. have   **2.** are   **3.** goes   **4.** serve

REPLAY UNIT 36

	Subject	Verb	Number
1.	groups	were invited	P
2.	stores	were called	P
3.	family	took	P
4.	family	Piled, left	S
5.	Wong & Lopez, Inc.	has	S
6.	Everyone	was waiting	S
7.	Neither	seems	S
8.	report and the letter	were	P
9.	letter	was	S
10.	engineer, drafters	are	P
11.	story, story	sound	P
12.	story, story	sounds	S
13.	battery, the radio, and the antenna	are	P
14.	everything	is	S
15.	Mr. O'Day, Ms. Goldberg	will work	S
16.	person	rides	S
17.	staff	took	P
18.	jury	arrived	S
19.	one	can do	S
20.	lawyer and a layman	should be	P
21.	Half	is	S
22.	pie	is	S
23.	All	are	P
24.	All	is	S
25.	workers	are	P

RECAP UNIT 37

Ouch! One in three accidents **is** caused by falls.

REPLAY UNIT 37

	Subject	Verb
1.	groups	were
2.	She	doesn't
3.	people	were
4.	Warren & Chilson, Inc.	has
5.	figures	are
6.	report and the letter	C
7.	report	has
8.	he, they	C
9.	he, assistant	wraps
10.	machines	C
11.	Ms. Svendsen	arrives
12.	dean and his assistant	drive
13.	He	does
14.	copier	doesn't
15.	cousin	works
16.	attorney, director	C

17.	I	meet
18.	models	C
19.	which (typewriters)	have
20.	class	C
21.	Roberta Simon	deserves
22.	carton	C
23.	man and woman	wants
24.	calendars	were
25.	One-third	have

REPLAY UNIT 38

1.	C	3.	C	5.	were	7.	were	9.	C
2.	were	4.	were	6.	C	8.	was, was	10.	were

SECTION 7   LOVE LINES

REPLAY UNIT 39

1. those kinds of PCs OR that kind of PC
2. Those or These instead of Them
3. these types of errors OR that type of error
4. Those sorts of books are OR That sort of book is
5. those types of people OR that type of person
6. Delete here
7. Delete there
8. tell those people
9. Delete there
10. These kinds of advertisements don't OR That kind of advertisement doesn't

REPLAY UNIT 40

1.	an	7.	a	13.	a	19.	an
2.	a	8.	an	14.	a	20.	a
3.	an	9.	a	15.	an	21.	an
4.	an	10.	an	16.	an	22.	an
5.	a	11.	a	17.	an	23.	an
6.	an	12.	an	18.	a	24.	an

REPLAY UNIT 41

1.	a, an	6.	An, an	11.	An, a
2.	A, an, an	7.	A, a, a	12.	an, an
3.	an, a, an	8.	a, an	13.	An, an
4.	a, an	9.	a, a, an	14.	an, a
5.	A, an	10.	a, a, an	15.	A, a, an

RECAP UNIT 42

wiser

RECAP UNIT 42

wisest

REPLAY UNIT 42

A.

	Comparative	**Superlative**
1.	worse	worst
2.	littler, less, lesser	littlest, least
3.	more	most
4.	better	best
5.	farther, further	farthest, furthest

B.

1.	bigger	**6.**	oldest	**11.**	most beautiful
2.	farther	**7.**	better	**12.**	worse
3.	delete most	**8.**	delete more	**13.**	less
4.	worse (delete the)	**9.**	more recent	**14.**	brighter
5.	C	**10.**	wider	**15.**	delete more

RECAP UNIT 43

bad

RECAP UNIT 43

smoothly

RECAP UNIT 43

Possible Answers

1. especially   **2.** extremely

REPLAY UNIT 43

A.

	Underlined Adjective	**Circled Word**	**Answer**
1.	rapid	walked—verb	rapidly
2.	bad	fumes—noun	C
3.	clear, correct	should write—verb	clearly, correctly
4.	beautiful	Dr. Linville—noun	C
5.	bad	sister—noun	C
6.	careful	do—verb	carefully
7.	legible	wrote—verb	legibly
8.	delicious	pie—noun	C
9.	deep	should think—verb	deeply
10.	fair	will treat—verb	fairly
11.	good	works—verb	well
12.	sure	wish—verb	surely, really, etc.
13.	good	know—verb	well
14.	logical	speaks—verb	logically
15.	sweet	rose—noun	C

B.

1. again   **2.** back to you   **3.** together   **4.** s   **5.** s

RECAP UNIT 44

more speedily

RECAP UNIT 44

1.	well	**4.**	well
2.	well	**5.**	bad, worse
3.	either good or well		

REPLAY UNIT 44

1.	logically	**6.**	better	**11.**	worse	**16.**	worse
2.	satisfactorily	**7.**	more widely	**12.**	distinctly	**17.**	best
3.	calmer *or* more calm	**8.**	C	**13.**	more smoothly	**18.**	gracefully
4.	worst	**9.**	really well	**14.**	C	**19.**	C
5.	surely *or* really	**10.**	beautiful	**15.**	more clearly	**20.**	satisfactorily

REPLAY UNIT 45

1. rarely or hardly ever
2. a instead of no
3. any instead of none
4. any instead of no
5. C
6. doesn't know anything
7. won't go anywhere
8. would never or wouldn't ever
9. anymore
10. doesn't need a secretary
11. is
12. hardly ever saw
13. could hardly
14. hardly any
15. Everybody likes

SECTION 8   THE TAMING OF THE APOSTROPHE

RECAP UNIT 46

1. minutes' planning, hour's work, New Year's day, Jose's mother
2. Seward's Folly, critics' (foolishness), William H. Seward's (foolishness)

REPLAY UNIT 46

	Circled Noun	Underlined Noun
1.	C	
2.	editors	stories
3.	C	
4.	brother-in-laws	manager
5.	C	
6.	attorneys	offices
7.	South Dakotas	resources
8.	Mens, womens	clothes
9.	Lopezs	orders
10.	industrys	directors
11.	crews	strength
12.	C	
13.	Californias	vineyards
	nations	wine
14.	Sashas	invention
15.	Mens	College
16.	C	
17.	Claudes	book
18.	weeks	work
19.	Penneys	success
20.	Sandys	visit

RECAP UNIT 47

1. Mr. Smith's, Ms. Perkins'   2. sons-in-law's

RECAP UNIT 47

1. brothers', Lopezes   2. Women's, women's, men's   3. sons-in-law's

REPLAY UNIT 47

A.

	Singular Possessive	Plural	Plural Possessive
1.	freshman's	freshmen	freshmen's
2.	week's	weeks	weeks'
3.	witness's	witnesses	witnesses'
4.	James's	Jameses	Jameses'

5. country's	countries	countries'
6. employee's	employees	employees'
7. clerk's	clerks	clerks'
8. goose's	geese	geese's
9. wife's	wives	wives'
10. father-in-law's	fathers-in-law	fathers-in-law's
11. congresswoman's	congresswomen	congresswomen's
12. minute's	minutes	minutes'
13. fox's	foxes	foxes'
14. hour's	hours	hours'
15. Wolf's	Wolfs	Wolfs'
16. wolf's	wolves	wolves'
17. principal's	principals	principals'
18. boss's	bosses	bosses'
19. lady's	ladies	ladies'
20. child's	children	children's

B.

1. boy's	**11.**	ladies' coats
2. members	**12.**	Goldsteins, days
3. communities	**13.**	San Diego's, years
4. years'	**14.**	Mr. Jones's
5. person's	**15.**	chairman's, details, workers'
6. men's fashions, women's	**16.**	Keats's
7. company's assets	**17.**	Knox's
8. editors in chief's remarks	**18.**	Fritz's
9. minute's	**19.**	Hendrix' or Hendrix's
10. Perkins', days	**20.**	guests' names

C.   Possible Answer

Both editors in chief made helpful remarks.

REPLAY UNIT 48

1. couldn't, o'clock	**11.**	C
2. i's	**12.**	'90s
3. C	**13.**	l's, they'll, t's
4. 1922	**14.**	Won't
5. It's, '90s	**15.**	A's
6. Don't, R.N.s'	**16.**	C
7. C	**17.**	What's
8. C	**18.**	You've
9. 1989, '75	**19.**	Aren't
10. '29	**20.**	Couldn't

SECTION 9   THE PAUSE THAT REFRESHES

REPLAY UNIT 49

1. 12, 6,
2. C
3. Chevrolets, Fords, Plymouths, Chryslers, Cadillacs,
4. desk, trash,
5. report, accuracy,
6. Motors, Corporation
7. in, at,
8. objectives, them,
9. first, second,
10. Machines, Motors, Telegraph,

REPLAY UNIT 50

1. pleasant,
2. C
3. came, wanted,
4. small,
5. ethical,
6. Paris, Brussels,
7. profitable,
8. bonus, salary,
9. C
10. settled,

REPLAY UNIT 51

1. carefully,
2. today,
3. C
4. division,
5. payment,
6. C
7. Rochester,
8. creative,
9. Miami, Dade,
10. C

RECAP UNIT 52

1. discreet,
2. C
3. car,
4. Twileen,
5. note,

REPLAY UNIT 52

1. now,
2. attractive, Street,
3. know,
4. report,
5. C
6. salesperson,
7. No,
8. Lee, washer, dryer, toaster,
9. C
10. be,
11. C
12. quickly,
13. time,
14. factory,
15. C

RECAP UNIT 53

1. Home, talk,
2. parts, Environment,
3. want, however,
4. system, Association,
5. Davidson, Turtles,
6. courthouse,

RECAP UNIT 53

1. C
2. manager, office,
3. C
4. C
5. C

REPLAY UNIT 53

1. office, however,
2. costs, you,
3. employees, Washington,
4. office, 103,
5. Department, floor,
6. Simon, auditor,
7. C
8. C
9. work, therefore,
10. proposal,
11. today,
12. equipment, yet,
13. tomorrow,
14. C
15. will, believe,
16. George,
17. C
18. C
19. C
20. worth,
21. C
22. booklet, information,
23. language,
24. idea, said,
25. C

REPLAY UNIT 54

1. 9, 1992,
2. C
3. Smith, Ph.D.,
4. Beach, York,
5. Friday, 4, 1989,
6. C
7. Rock, Arkansas,
8. Inc., Plains, York,
9. Edinburgh, Scotland,
10. C
11. boss, store,
12. C
13. C
14. market, recently,
15. Intel, IBM, semiconductors, microprocessors,

REPLAY UNIT 55

1. See samples in Note 2, Read Unit 55.
2. See sample in Note 4, Read Unit 55.
3. no

REPLAY UNIT 56

1.	p.m.,	3.	you, however,	5.	years,	7.	very, very	9.	run, run
2.	Yes, quiet,	4.	7, 1964,	6.	know," said,	8.	morning,	10.	excellent,

REPLAY UNIT 57

1. Use a comma after an introductory dependent expression with a verb or a verbal.
2. Use commas to separate parts of addresses.
3. Use a comma before BUT when it joins two independent clauses.
4. Counting from right to left, use a comma after each group of three numbers.
5. Use a comma before each item in a series.
6. Use a comma in place of an important word that is omitted—usually a verb.
7. If the date is within a sentence, use a comma before and after the year. Do not use a comma within identification numbers.
8. Use a comma after an introductory expression that includes a verb or a verbal.
9. Do not use commas to set off an essential (i.e. not parenthetical) expression.
10. Use a comma after Yes, No, Well, or Oh when it's used as an introductory expression.

SECTION 10   PUNCTUATION POTPOURRI

REPLAY UNIT 58

1.	conference.	6.	convention.	11.	mail.
2.	pepperoni?	7.	you?	12.	come?
3.	express.	8.	now!	13.	come.
4.	convention?	9.	letters.	14.	fire!
5.	decisions. out.	10.	Wonderful!	15.	fell. A . . . him.

RECAP UNIT 59

1.	high;	1.	criticism;
2.	high;	2.	here;
3.	money;	3.	out;
4.	C	4.	C

REPLAY UNIT 59

A.

1.	C	6.	ambition;	11.	C	16.	C
2.	C	7.	of;	12.	low;	17.	C
3.	year;	8.	Illinois;	13.	dividend;	18.	C
4.	C	9.	C	14.	1902; 1913;	19.	kills;
5.	properly;	10.	understand;	15.	C	20.	late;

B.

Charles the First walked and talked; half an hour after, his head was cut off.

REPLAY UNIT 60

1.	following:	3.	C	5.	cities:	7.	Valley:	9.	duty:
2.	life:	4.	life:	6.	shoplifting:	8.	about:	10.	C

B.

1.	yesterday:	3.	qualifications:
	secretary.	4.	qualifications?
2.	well;	5.	Office!

REPLAY UNIT 61

1. (I'll check the address)
2. (a treasury of synonyms, antonyms, parallel words, and related words)
   (Look up the pronunciation of Roget.)
3. machines—they are the best money can buy—
4. charm—
5. C
6. attributes:
7. once—
8. skills:
9. (not $156)
10. live: or —
11. ($100,000)
12. 3—
13. (where fewer than one hundred persons are employed).
14. (not now at least)
15. government—the executive, the legislative, and the judicial— or ( )

REPLAY UNIT 62

1. He shouted, "Your house is on fire!"
2. "Your house is on fire!" he shouted.
3. She whispered, "Are you sure you love me?"
4. "Are you sure you love me?" she whispered.
5. Do you know whether he said, "I love you"?
6. "Since many people are price-conscious, we must look at more cost-efficient methods," said Dave Young, the spokesperson for Chevron.
7. Do you know what the phrase "negotiable instrument" means?
8. The following information is quoted from the letter: "The train departs Chicago at two p.m. and arrives in Springfield at 5 p.m."
9. Was it Mr. Higgins who said, "Results are what count"?
10. It's important that Craig doesn't think you are too pushy.
11. C
12. I believe that Elaine and Michelle will be considered for the management positions; Rosemary will receive the diplomatic post.
13. Alexander Smith, who lives in Toronto, will write the screenplay for us.
14. Please tell the chef how many tacos you need for the company party.
15. "This shipment of stationery," the manager clearly stated, "will arrive in time for the January sale."
16. I have this to say regarding his "abject poverty": It is fictitious.
17. "Are you all right?" asked Ann.
18. "Yes," groaned Len, as he lifted the box of posters that had fallen.
19. "Bach Suite No. 2 in B Minor" is first on the program at the Laredo Junior College Music Festival.
20. Ms. Sumner whispered, "Did you know that the item marked 'fragile' was broken on arrival in Sacramento?"

RECAP UNIT 63

1. brother-in-law
2. vice president
3. inasmuch as
4. double boiler
5. up-to-date
6. off-the-record (AHD, WNCD)

REPLAY UNIT 63

B.

1. I work in a ten-story building.
2. I need a 10-foot ladder.
3. My father is a hard-working man.
4. She made an off-the-record comment.
5. The case against the Dallas-based company was handled in Seattle.

C.

1. re-creation
2. C
3. C
4. overpayments
5. father-in-law, commander in chief

6. off-the-record, self-made
7. self-sufficient
8. twenty-one
9. Johny-come-lately
10. anti-intellectual

D.

func/tion	be/lieve	hori/zontal	wouldn't/
thou/sands	punctu/ation	aligned/	impos/sible
inter/rupt	syl/lables	stopped/	guess/work

REPLAY UNIT 64

A.

1. agent's clerk's
2. Hill's
3. women's girls'

4. Here's Beth's money's salesperson's
5. Perkins' year's

B.

Answers will vary.

SECTION 11   A BUSINESS DICTIONARY

REPLAY UNIT 65

a. 17	**c.** 21	**e.** 1	**g.** 6	**i.** 2	**k.** 3	**m.** 10	**o.** 12	**q.** 4	**s.** 5	**u.** 19
b. 20	**d.** 14	**f.** 11	**h.** 7	**j.** 9	**l.** 18	**n.** 15	**p.** 13	**r.** 16	**t.** 8	**v.** 22

REPLAY UNIT 66

a. 43	**d.** 32	**g.** 41	**j.** 44	**m.** 27	**p.** 31	**s.** 35	**v.** 33
b. 25	**e.** 26	**h.** 34	**k.** 39	**n.** 38	**q.** 29	**t.** 40
c. 24	**f.** 42	**i.** 36	**l.** 23	**o.** 30	**r.** 28	**u.** 37

REPLAY UNIT 67

a. 58	**d.** 57	**g.** 45	**j.** 50	**m.** 63	**p.** 46	**s.** 55	**v.** 51
b. 66	**e.** 49	**h.** 47	**k.** 53	**n.** 59	**q.** 54	**t.** 61
c. 48	**f.** 62	**i.** 56	**l.** 65	**o.** 64	**r.** 52	**u.** 60

REPLAY UNIT 68

a. 82	**d.** 81	**g.** 86	**j.** 80	**m.** 74	**p.** 84	**s.** 77	**v.** 88
b. 68	**e.** 78	**h.** 87	**k.** 79	**n.** 71	**q.** 85	**t.** 76
c. 72	**f.** 67	**i.** 83	**l.** 70	**o.** 69	**r.** 73	**u.** 75

REPLAY UNIT 69

A.

a. 104	**d.** 110	**g.** 92	**j.** 105	**m.** 107	**p.** 106	**s.** 100	**v.** 94
b. 101	**e.** 90	**h.** 109	**k.** 108	**n.** 96	**q.** 103	**t.** 98
c. 91	**f.** 89	**i.** 95	**l.** 93	**o.** 99	**r.** 97	**u.** 102

SECTION 12   WORD POWER

REPLAY UNIT 70

1.	accept	**10.**	affect	**19.**	site	**28.**	descent
2.	except	**11.**	alter	**20.**	coarse	**29.**	hear
3.	access	**12.**	altar	**21.**	course	**30.**	here
4.	excess	**13.**	bizarre	**22.**	course	**31.**	heir
5.	add	**14.**	bazaar	**23.**	counsel	**32.**	elicit
6.	ad	**15.**	Capitol	**24.**	Council	**33.**	illicit
7.	effect	**16.**	capital	**25.**	die	**34.**	physical
8.	effect	**17.**	capital	**26.**	dye	**35.**	fiscal
9.	effect	**18.**	cite	**27.**	dissent		

REPLAY UNIT 71

1.	It's	**11.**	passed	**21.**	principal	**31.**	Their
2.	its	**12.**	peace	**22.**	raze	**32.**	there
3.	led	**13.**	piece	**23.**	raise	**33.**	They're
4.	lead	**14.**	pare	**24.**	residents	**34.**	waste
5.	lead	**15.**	pairs	**25.**	residence	**35.**	waist
6.	miner	**16.**	pear	**26.**	role	**36.**	wave
7.	minor	**17.**	peddle	**27.**	role	**37.**	waive
8.	Naval	**18.**	pedal	**28.**	rolling	**38.**	You're
9.	navel	**19.**	principal	**29.**	stationery	**39.**	your
10.	passed	**20.**	principles	**30.**	stationary	**40.**	you're, your

REPLAY UNIT 72

1.	adopt	**11.**	bibliography	**21.**	differ
2.	adapt	**12.**	conscience	**22.**	illegible
3.	adept	**13.**	conscious	**23.**	eligible
4.	advise	**14.**	chose	**24.**	imminent
5.	advice	**15.**	choose	**25.**	eminent
6.	advise advice	**16.**	dessert	**26.**	envelop
7.	besides	**17.**	desert	**27.**	envelope
8.	beside	**18.**	devise	**28.**	Humane
9.	Besides	**19.**	device	**29.**	human
10.	biographical	**20.**	defer	**30.**	regardless

REPLAY UNIT 73

1.	lose	**11.**	persecuted	**21.**	Reality	**31.**	than
2.	loose	**12.**	perspective	**22.**	resent	**32.**	than
3.	lose	**13.**	prospective	**23.**	resentment	**33.**	thought
4.	Morale	**14.**	perspective	**24.**	recent	**34.**	thorough
5.	moral	**15.**	proceed	**25.**	respectfully	**35.**	through
6.	Personal	**16.**	precede	**26.**	Respectfully	**36.**	whether
7.	personnel	**17.**	proceed	**27.**	respectively	**37.**	weather
8.	prerequisite	**18.**	quite	**28.**	suit	**38.**	We're
9.	perquisites (or perks)	**19.**	quiet	**29.**	suite	**39.**	were
10.	prosecute	**20.**	realty	**30.**	then	**40.**	where

REPLAY UNIT 74

1.	omit of	**11.**	change off of to from
2.	change I to me	**12.**	should have
3.	change of to have	**13.**	omit to
4.	omit at	**14.**	change off of to from
5.	change I to me	**15.**	change between to among
6.	omit to	**16.**	change between to among
7.	change he to him	**17.**	change on to for
8.	change she to her	**18.**	change among to between
	and I to me	**19.**	change of to have;
9.	omit to		change off of to from
10.	C	**20.**	C

REPLAY UNIT 75

A.

1. 3 **2.** 3 **3.** 3 **4.** 3 **5.** 2

B.

1. s, s **2.** s **3.** b **4.** s **5.** e

C.

1.	T	**4.**	F	**7.**	F	**10.**	T	**13.**	F
2.	F	**5.**	F	**8.**	F	**11.**	T	**14.**	F
3.	T	**6.**	F	**9.**	T	**12.**	F	**15.**	F

SECTION 13   SENTENCE POWER

REPLAY UNIT 76

A.

1. again.   **5.** happened.   **6.** it. Ask   **9.** home.

B.

1.	downtown; therefore,	**6.**	forms, but
2.	it, but	**7.**	stable; that is,
3.	working: economists	**8.**	Many, perhaps most, feel, however,
4.	process, and	**9.**	perfect; most
5.	agree, however,	**10.**	employees, stockholders,

C.

1.	C	**3.**	F	**5.**	F	**7.**	S	**9.**	R
2.	C	**4.**	F	**6.**	C	**8.**	C	**10.**	S

RECAP UNIT 77

While strolling along the beach, you can find unusual shells and pebbles.

RECAP UNIT 77

As you are one of our most discriminating customers, we invite you to attend this private showing.

REPLAY UNIT 77

1.	D	**6.**	D	**11.**	C	**16.**	C	**21.**	C
2.	C	**7.**	D	**12.**	D	**17.**	D	**22.**	D
3.	C	**8.**	D	**13.**	D	**18.**	D	**23.**	D
4.	D	**9.**	D	**14.**	D	**19.**	C	**24.**	C
5.	C	**10.**	D	**15.**	C	**20.**	C	**25.**	D

RECAP UNIT 78

1. At the age of 96, Genevive Astor died in the home in which she had been born.
2. The fire was brought under control by the fire department before much damage was done.

RECAP UNIT 78

1. Linda is a full-time securities analyst, and her husband Tom is a part-time insurance agent.
2. We are particularly interested in learning your views on how to introduce change, control quality, and motivate employees.

REPLAY UNIT 78

1. M	**5.** P	**9.** P	**13.** P	**17.** M
2. C	**6.** M	**10.** C	**14.** C	**18.** C
3. M	**7.** P	**11.** M	**15.** P	**19.** P
4. M	**8.** P	**12.** C	**16.** P	**20.** P

REPLAY UNIT 79

1. I	**4.** D	**7.** I	**10.** I	**13.** I
2. I	**5.** D	**8.** D	**11.** D	**14.** D
3. I	**6.** D	**9.** I	**12.** I	**15.** I

REPLAY UNIT 80

A.

These are possible answers; yours will probably be different.

1. I like biscuits, especially when they're served hot with plenty of butter and honey.
2. While Ella was repairing a table, she mashed her left index finger with a hammer.
3. On the wall of that side of the room are a college pennant, a Millet painting, and a medical diploma.
4. Claude and Alex spent all afternoon walking to the offices of the telephone, gas, and electric companies to pay their bills.
5. An animal that appeared to be a hyena paced restlessly back and forth in the cage.

B.

1. A house that needs painting sits far back among the trees.
2. From the rear door of the house, a stairway leads to the housekeeper's room.
3. A tall man, who was the owner of the garage, came forward.
4. Well-cured hams hung in the smokehouse.
5. When Shari and Peter saw the coat belonging to their father, they knew the man was a thief.
6. Respectable lady seeks comfortable room where she can cook on an electric stove.
7. FOR SALE: Discarded clothing collected by the ladies of the First Presbyterian Church. The clothing may be seen in the church basement any day after six o'clock.
8. We have a nursery downstairs for small children.
9. This is Ms. Mosson's friend from La Jolla.
10. We can't allow the children to visit the neighbors, for the Joneses are mean and intolerant.

SECTION 14   SINCERELY YOURS

REPLAY UNIT 81

1. $8\frac{1}{2}''$ by $11''$	**3.** 9 or a 10	**5.** signature	**7.** 3	**9.** Proofread
2. $6\frac{3}{4}$	**4.** copy	**6.** 2	**8.** False	**10.** 443–458

REPLAY UNIT 82

A.

1. F	**3.** F	**5.** F	**7.** T	**9.** T
2. F	**4.** T	**6.** T	**8.** T	**10.** F

B.

1. letterhead
2. date
3. inside address
4. salutation
5. body
6. complimentary close
7. letter writer's name and title
8. typist's initials
9. enclosure notation
10. copy notation

REPLAY UNIT 83

1. F	3. F	5. F	7. T	9. T	11. T	13. T	15. F	17. F	19. T
2. F	4. F	6. F	8. F	10. F	12. F	14. T	16. T	18. T	20. F

RECAP UNIT 84

1. b   2. b

RECAP UNIT 84

1. We hope you will be pleased.
2. You can shop at Frederick's from 9 a.m. until 8 p.m. on weekdays and until 5 p.m. on weekends.

RECAP UNIT 84

1. First you should pack the essentials.
2. The investigation revealed a small triangular purple UFO.

REPLAY UNIT 84

1. F	3. F	5. F	7. F	9. F	11. T	13. F	15. F	17. F	19. F
2. F	4. F	6. F	8. F	10. F	12. T	14. F	16. T	18. T	20. T

ANSWERS TO REFERENCE MANUAL REPLAYS

NUMBERS IN BUSINESS

1. At 9 a.m. on June 4, we will have completed 42 jobs.
2. There are about fifty different ways to make 50 million dollars. (or $50 million.)
3. On 6 June 1989 Acme Air Freight shipped 21 boxes to your London office.
4. Please send $5 for the book and $.50 for postage.
5. On page 6 his age is given as 40.
6. Almost five thousand attended the Alliance for Survival rally.
7. Our new office is at 62 Fourth Street.
8. The prime interest rate went to 11 percent today.
9. We need twelve 8 by 10 offices in the new building for the members of the sales staff.
10. This store opened its doors at 8 a.m. on the 31st of June.

CAPITALIZATION

1. Atomic Age
2. Airlines   summer   Prime Minister   Senator   South
3. auditor   department stores
4. *Triumph and Tragedy* or TRIUMPH AND TRAGEDY   World War
5. Supreme Court   company
6. September   Spanish   college   Spanish
7. oceans
8. spaghetti
9. south
10. Customer   yours

WORD DIVISION

1. F	2. T	3. F	4. T	5. T	6. T	7. F	8. F	9. T	10. T

ABBREVIATIONS

1. F	2. F	3. F	4. T	5. T	6. F	7. F	8. T	9. F

10. last in; first out   Securities and Exchange Commission   Master of Business Administration   end of month.

NOTES

NOTES

NOTES

NOTES

NOTES

NOTES

NOTES

NOTES

NOTES

NOTES

NOTES

C. 9/1994 存